Ultimate Enterprise Data Analysis and Forecasting using Python

Leverage Cloud platforms with Azure Time Series Insights and AWS Forecast Components for Time Series Analysis and Forecasting with Deep learning Modeling using Python

Shanthababu Pandian

www.orangeava.com

First published: December 2023

Published by: Orange Education Pvt Ltd, AVA™

Address: 9, Daryaganj, Delhi, 110002

ISBN: 978-81-19416-44-8

www.orangeava.com

Dedicated To

My beloved Parents:

Shri Pandian Marimuthu Subbiah

Smt Muthulekshmi Pandian

About the Author

Shanthababu Pandian holds a Bachelor's degree in engineering in Electronics and Communication, followed by three Master's degrees - MTech, MBA, and M.S. - from a prestigious university in India. Additionally, he completed a Post Graduate Program in Artificial Intelligence and Machine Learning from the University of Texas, along with a Post Graduate Certification in Data Science from the Indian Institute of Technology, Guwahati. With over 21 years of extensive experience in information technology (IT), Shanthababu specializes in data engineering and analytics solutions, development and implementation using agile methodologies, and building complex data models for Business Intelligence (BI) and data science products for various customers located across the UK and US regions. As part of his responsibilities, Shanthababu is accustomed to liaising with key stakeholders and business teams, gathering and eliciting requirements, and architecting cost-effective data modeling solutions as per delivery frameworks. He is efficient at mitigating project delivery risks while managing stakeholders and leading project team members across different locations.

- Technical Author at:
  - Analytics Vidhya:
    - https://www.analyticsvidhya.com/blog/author/shanthababu/
  - Data Science Central
    - https://www.datasciencecentral.com/author/shanthababup/
- Technical author engagement with the following Data Industries:
  - Octopus Data Inc. Shenzhen, Guangdong, China
  - dezyre.com (https://www.projectpro.io/)
  - neptune.ai
  - StrictlyByTheNumbers.com
  - Shanthababu's AI Views: https://shanthababu.com/blog-2/
- Technical Book Reviewer for Packt Publications – BIRMINGHAM, UK. Reviewed more than 30 books from international authors on various technical aspects
- National and International Technical Speaker in the AIML domain, with more than 40 webinars presented
- Technical Mentor for various Engineering and Technical institutions across Tamil Nadu, India

About the Technical Reviewers

S.Ponmalar is an Academician with over 25 years of field and domain experience in Information and Communication Engineering including optical communication, Networks, Machine Learning, and Computer vision. She has obtained her Doctoral degree in Information and Communcation Engineering from Anna University. She is a recognized supervisor and guides many PG and PhD scholars. She has published over 30 research papers in many reputed Journals and Conferences. Her interest in upgrading with recent trends and technology has obligated her to read and review articles and books from different publishers.

Vidhya Veerabahu is a Professor and Head of IT at Sri Venkateswara College of Engineering, Sriperumbudur. With over 23 years of experience in the fields of data science and Natural Language Processing (NLP), she is an expert in these domains. She has used statistical, semantical, and contextual methods to automate various specific processes in the education sector. Additionally, she has developed several smart mobile-based applications to provide solutions to societal challenges and has helped the organization analyze trends for better decision-making. She has published and presented over 40 papers in international journals and conferences.

Preface

This book covers various aspects of Time Series Analysis and Forecasting using the Python language, emphasizing the importance of time series analysis from an industry perspective for in-depth analysis and forecasting, with real-time use cases and required examples. The primary objective of this book is to provide a detailed pack of time series analysis and forecasting methods, essential in the current digital market, and grow business opportunities using various techniques from an AIML perspective. This book aims to connect the Time Series and Forecasting problem statements across multiple industries and demonstrate how to provide solutions using currently available tools, technology, and evidence of success stories. This book promises that by the end of the reading, the readers will understand time series and forecasting techniques, and also learn how to analyze, design, and maintain the solutions. In this manner, readers can follow the correct path to take the time series components, work on them with Python packages, and understand the data for analysis and productive solutions, such as predicting or forecasting.

This book covers the expectations of Data Analysts, Data Scientists, and Machine Learning Engineers who will be involved in time series analysis and forecasting-related projects. This book helps those interested in time series analysis. The book begins with an introduction to Python and its essential packages. It then delves into various aspects of time series data analysis and models from both traditional and ML methods, followed by their implementation in the cloud environment.

This book is divided into four parts and 11 chapters. It will cover everything, starting with an introduction to Python and its essential packages for data science and machine learning. The book will explore various time series analysis and forecasting techniques, along with the implementation of time series analysis in Azure and AWS environments. The chapter-wise details are listed as follows.

Chapter 1. Introduction to Python and its key packages for DS and ML Projects: This chapter will discuss the basics of Python and its libraries. It will begin with Python's IDEs and Jupyter Notebook installation, utilization, and benefits to build Time Series Analysis and Forecasting solutions for the readers before delving into the rest of the chapters of this book. A quick overview of packages supporting Data Science and Machine Learning implementation and their significance, along with sample code snippets will be provided including Data Structure, File Operations,

Packages such as Pandas, NumPy, Matplotlib, SciKit-Learn, and Statsmodel. This chapter would give confidence in Python and its features.

Chapter 2. Python for Time Series Data Analysis: This chapter will discuss Data Analysis and its benefits. It will delve into why Python is the best choice for Data Analysis. Also, it will cover Time Series Data Management. Further discussion will focus on various aspects surrounding Data Cleansing, Preparation, and Wrangling with Time Series Analysis. This section will cover Data preparation for Time Series Analysis, converting String data into DataTime format, Resampling and Frequency conversion techniques, Generating Date ranges, Time Zone handling, and Period Arithmetic techniques. This chapter will highlight the importance of Data Visualization in Time Series Analysis. It will help discovering the scope of data mining in Time Series Analysis and understanding the Statistics Essentials for Analytics in relation to time series and forecasting. Exploratory Data Analysis (EDA) for the time series, along with sample code snippets to understand all the concepts mentioned will be covered.

Chapter 3. Time Series Analysis and its components: This chapter will help readers understand the background of time series analysis. This chapter will cover the importance of time series analysis and its significance. Also, a detailed walk-through of Time Series components – Trend, Seasonality, Cyclic patterns and Irregularity - with classic examples and distinctions between them will be provided. The nature of the data in Time Series Analysis is specific to their component's classification. This chapter focusses on realizing the WHITE NOISE in Time Series dataset. The acid test for data stationarity – ADF, KPSS test is also covered. Handing non-stationary data in Time Series Analysis and techniques to make a time series stationary are also discussed. What are ACF and PACF in time series, and how do they assist in determining the order of AR, MA, and ARMA models are discussed along with sample code snippets to better understand all the concepts mentioned.

Chapter 4. Time Series Analysis and Forecasting Opportunities in Various Industries: This chapter will assist the reader in understanding the opportunity and scope of time series analysis and forecasting and learning how to implement it. Gaining clarity on time series analysis is helpful in business and industry. This chapter will cover the advantages of Time Series Analysis in Forecasting. Demand forecasting and Price prediction in Retail, and Forecasting in Healthcare for diagnosis and medication planning are also covered. Anomaly detection, predictive maintenance, time series analysis, and sales forecasting in the automotive industry are discussed. This chapter will also address the challenges and major drawbacks of time series forecasting-

Chapter 5. Exploring various aspects of Time Series Analysis and Forecasting: This chapter will help the readers understand the detailed study of Time Series Analysis starting from statistical inference. The statistical properties of the time series are covered. The shapes in Time Series are discussed. Power, Log, and Box-Cox Transformation for Time Series are discussed. The chapter will explore forecasting metrics, providing an overview of Naive Forecasting and various Forecasting Metrics. We will also learn about univariate and multivariate models, generic types of Forecasting Methods and Time Series Analysis for both traditional and Machine learning approaches. It will also include sample code snippets to better understand all the concepts mentioned.

Chapter 6. Exploring Time Series Models - AR, MA, ARMA, and ARIMA: This chapter will help readers in exploring various Time Series models and their implementation. It will provide detailed discussions on a variety of models Autoregressive Models - AR(p), Moving Average Models - MA(q), ARMA (AR +MA). The chapter will guide on how to calculate AR and MA step by step, including training model and forecasting and validation. It will also explain about why ARIMA came into picture and do a detailed studies. The chapter will also cover Residual Analysis, Plotting, and Scaling Techniques. Use cases for the above-mentioned methods and sample code snippets are included to understand all the concepts mentioned.

Chapter 7. Understanding Exponential Smoothing and ETS Methods in TSA: This chapter will help the readers in understanding exponential smoothing and ETS methods in time series analysis, their characteristics and various types. It will explain what exponential smoothing is and how to calculate it. It will also cover how exponential smoothing is used for forecasting purposes. The chapter will also delve into ETS (Error, Trend, Seasonal), selecting the best ETS and why ETS models are implemented. The chapter will discuss a few more models, including Simple Moving Average (SMA), Exponentially Weighted Moving Averages (EWMA), Single Exponential Smoothing (SES), Holt's Linear Trend Model, and Winters along with sample code snippets to understand all the concepts mentioned.

Chapter 8. Exploring Vector Autoregression and its Subsets (VAR, VMA, and VARMA): This chapter will help the readers in understanding various Vector Autoregression methods and the essential requirements for using the VAR model in Time Series problems. It will cover the distinctions between VAR and AR. It will also discuss sub-types such as VA-VAR, VMA, VARMA and VARMAX for multivariate time series. The chapter will cover the characteristics of Vector Autoregression and its implementation. This chapter will also discuss Extension of ARIMA - Seasonal Auto-Regressive Integrated Moving Average (SARIMA) with Exogenous Variables and Fractional Auto-Regressive Integrated Moving Average (FARIMA). Sample code snippets are provided to understand all the concepts mentioned.

Chapter 9. Deep Learning for Time Series Analysis and Forecasting: This chapter will assist readers in understanding whether deep learning is good for time series forecasting. It will discuss the interpretability and promises by Deep Learning for Time Series Forecasting. The chapter will cover basic concepts such as the Activation Function and explain how a Neural Network learns. It will delve into various types of deep learning models such as ANNs, CNNs, RNNs, and LSTMs for time series forecasting. The chapter will focus on understanding the Multilayer Perceptrons, CNNs, Long Short-Term Memory Networks (LSTMs) and their use cases and will include sample code snippets for better understanding of all the concepts mentioned.

Chapter 10. Azure Time Series Insights: This chapter will help the readers in understanding Azure Time Series insights and its significance. It explores how this is a fully managed analytics, storage and visualization service for managing IoT-scale time-series data in the cloud. The chapter will further discuss Azure Time Series Insights Gen2 for industrial IoT concerning various industries. Also, the chapter will cover topics such as data exploration and visual anomaly detection using Azure Time Series Insights. The chapter will also provide insights into the best practices for planning and preparing the Azure Time Series Insights Gen2 environment. It will include a comparison between Gen1 and Gen2 exploring their capabilities, key benefits, and critical jobs.

Chapter 11. AWS Forecast: This chapter will assist readers in understanding Amazon Forecast and its significance. It will cover the working of Amazon Forecast, delve into its features in detail, and explore the time series forecasting principles. The chapter will also guide the readers to set up permissions for Amazon Forecast. It will walk through the process of importing, building, evaluating, and cleaning for Amazon Forecast's future. It will discuss the algorithms followed by the steps for preparing and cleaning data for Amazon Forecast. The chapter will highlight the best practices of Amazon Forecast.

Downloading the code bundles and colored images

Please follow the links or scan the QR codes to download the **_Code Bundles and Images_** of the book:

https://github.com/ava-orange-education/Ultimate-Enterprise-Data-Analysis-and-Forecasting-using-Python

The code bundles and images of the book are also hosted on **_https://rebrand.ly/5e9b56_**

In case there's an update to the code, it will be updated on the existing GitHub repository.

Errata

We take immense pride in our work at **Orange Education Pvt Ltd,** and follow best practices to ensure the accuracy of our content to provide an indulging reading experience to our subscribers. Our readers are our mirrors, and we use their inputs to reflect and improve upon human errors, if any, that may have occurred during the publishing processes involved. To let us maintain the quality and help us reach out to any readers who might be having difficulties due to any unforeseen errors, please write to us at :

errata@orangeava.com

Your support, suggestions, and feedback are highly appreciated.

DID YOU KNOW

Did you know that Orange Education Pvt Ltd offers eBook versions of every book published, with PDF and ePub files available? You can upgrade to the eBook version at **www.orangeava.com** and as a print book customer, you are entitled to a discount on the eBook copy. Get in touch with us at: **info@orangeava.com** for more details.

At **www.orangeava.com**, you can also read a collection of free technical articles, sign up for a range of free newsletters, and receive exclusive discounts and offers on AVA™ Books and eBooks.

PIRACY

If you come across any illegal copies of our works in any form on the internet, we would be grateful if you would provide us with the location address or website name. Please contact us at **info@orangeava.com** with a link to the material.

ARE YOU INTERESTED IN AUTHORING WITH US?

If there is a topic that you have expertise in, and you are interested in either writing or contributing to a book, please write to us at **business@orangeava.com**. We are on a journey to help developers and tech professionals to gain insights on the present technological advancements and innovations happening across the globe and build a community that believes Knowledge is best acquired by sharing and learning with others. Please reach out to us to learn what our audience demands and how you can be part of this educational reform. We also welcome ideas from tech experts and help them build learning and development content for their domains.

REVIEWS

Please leave a review. Once you have read and used this book, why not leave a review on the site that you purchased it from? Potential readers can then see and use your unbiased opinion to make purchase decisions. We at Orange Education would love to know what you think about our products, and our authors can learn from your feedback. Thank you!

For more information about Orange Education, please visit **www.orangeava.com**.

Table of Contents

CHAPTER 1

Introduction to Python and its key packages for DS and ML Projects

Introduction

Hello, my friends! I hope you are all aware that the focus of this book is on various Time Series Analysis and Forecasting techniques and their implementation using the Python Language. Python language is highly-demanded and powerful in recent scenarios, not only for building web applications but also for implementing AIML analytics and advanced analytics products. Before we dive into the objective of this book, let me take you through some of the basics of Python programming language skill sets that are required to build the TS&F model and analyze the same. Please note that throughout this book, we will refer to "Time Series Analysis and Forecasting" as TS&F for a quick reference to the content.

The major objective of this chapter is to discuss the basics of Python and its libraries, specifically targeting those who are new to programming.

Structure

In this chapter, we will discuss the following topics:

- Introduction to Python programming language
- Key features of Python
- Python programming IDEs and comparisons
- Installing Jupyter notebook
- Python libraries
    - Pandas
    - Date and time data
    - NumPy
- Python statistics libraries
- Working with various files in Python

Introduction to Python programming language

There are multiple answers that you can find on Google, but my straightforward answer is "*Python is a very simple, English, general-purpose programming language*".

It has been designed with the base idea of emphasizing code readability in mind by using significant indentation for programmers at any level to read. Similar to Java programming language, Python is a dynamically typed, garbage-collected language that supports multiple programming patterns, including structured, object-oriented, functional programming and many more. That's fine for all purposes, specifically, this is an interpreter language which means that the code can be executed as soon as it is written.

You may have a lot of questions, such as "*What can Python do and Why use Python?*" Let's quickly explore these points.

Python was created by Guido van Rossum and released in 1991. It has been used like other programming languages for web development, software development, mathematical modeling and frequently for system scripting.

Key features of Python

The following are the key features of Python:

- It can support and work on multiple platforms
  - Windows, Linux, Mac – Web application, ML programming
  - Raspberry Pi – IoT programming
- It has very simple syntax, similar to the English language so that the developers can write code that is straightforward and easy to understand.
- It requires fewer lines of code to accomplish the requirements compared to other programming languages such as C, C++, and Java.
- It provides robust and standard libraries such as Pandas, NumPy, Scikit-learn and many more.
- It comes under the Interpreted category, which makes it easy to debug and execute.
- It supports both object-oriented and programming-oriented making it portable and extensible.

From an AIML perspective, Python is simple, powerful, easy to write and read, well-structured and extendable.

While there are many programming languages in the market to support ML programming, Python provides the following modules which strengthen the ML model and easily manage the code in any environment (Development to Production).

- NumPy
- Pandas
- SciPy
- Matplotlib
- Scikit-learn
- TensorFlow and Keras
- PyTorch

To develop programming scripts, we need an IDE (Integrated Development Environment). Let's start with a very familiar environment in the current scenario for developers and practitioners to demonstrate their Python code using Jupyter notebook. It provides a very simple and understandable way of executing the code cell by cell and getting the output. This allows developers to confirm their objectives and goals for the modules and products.

Let's focus on the installation and utilization aspects shortly which is very simple and easy.

The following topics will help you learn how to install Anaconda which installs Python and a bunch of auxiliary packages useful for Data Science, Machine learning, and Deep Learning.

Python programming IDEs and comparisons

In the software industry, we use specific environments to build software, which are generally called IDEs(Integrated Development Environments). Here, we code, debug, compile, test, and so on. Python is no exception to this. There are multiple tools available in the market.

Let me share the steps to install Jupyter Notebook, This notcbook is available in the Azure environment in the name of Azure Data Brick,

In the AWS environment, this notebook is available in the name Sage Maker IDE so this Jupyter Notebook would help you all to understand how to write and execute the code during the real-time scenario.

Although we have other options based on availability, the following are some popular Python IDEs:

- Jupyter Notebook
- PyCharm
- Spyder
- Microsoft Visual Studio
- PyDev

Jupyter Notebook

As mentioned earlier, the Jupyter Notebook is everyone's favorite and is one of the most widely used editor in the AIML industry. It is browser-based and allows you to create, manipulate and play around with a notebook as a document with .ipynb as an extension. It is best suited for interpreted language environments. Specific to AIML and Data Science product development, Jupyter Notebook is a perfect fit and all cloud environments (Azure, AWS, and GCP) utilize it in their own environment. If we develop anything on-premises using the Jupyter Notebook, it will be easier to implement projects on the cloud.

The features are as follows:

- Supports markdowns - which is helpful for various documentation purposes.
- Easy creation and editing of code - a simple way to load the data once and play around.
- Ideal for beginners/practitioners to build Data Science/Machine Learning solutions.

PyCharm

PyCharm is another renowned IDE used for Python programming. It is easy to code, analyze and debug, provides excellent graphical visualization, and is an integrated unit tester and debugger. It provides integration with version control systems, which is a plus, and supports web development along with Django.

The features are as follows:

- Smart code navigation and auto code completion
- Excellent error detection and correction as part of "*Errors Highlighting*"
- Powerful debugger
- Distributed development support

Spyder

Spyder stands for Scientific Python Development Environment. This is another open source and is an excellent IDE in laboratory development and is most suitable for a Python environment to build Scientific programs, Data Science and ML solutions. It supports multiple platforms including Windows, Linux, and MacOS X.

The features are as follows:

- Customizable syntax highlighting capabilities
- Excellent interactive and execution environment
- Highly integrated and strong with the IPython console
- The auto code completion feature helps developers significantly
- Performs well in a multi-language editor and auto code completion mode

Installing Jupyter notebook

For Windows

1. Link: https://www.anaconda.com/products/distribution.

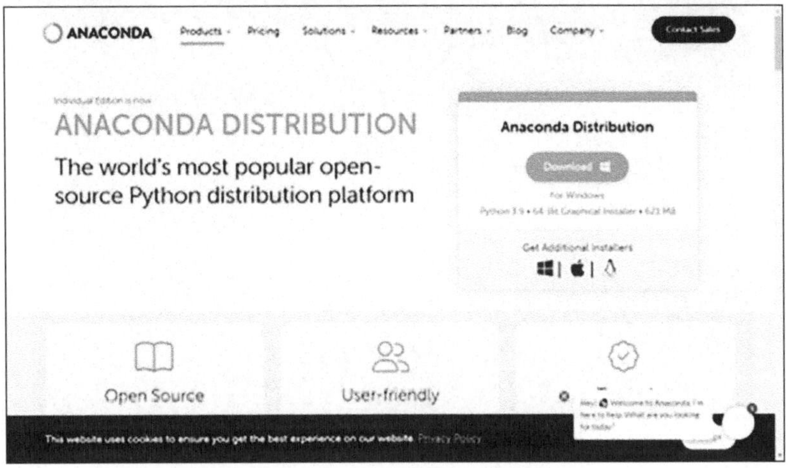

***Figure 1.1**: URL for Anaconda download*

2. Click on the **`Download`** button.
3. Anaconda will start downloading and will be available for installation.

***Figure 1.2**: Installable Anaconda*

4. Double-click the installable Anaconda. After a few simple clicks, Anaconda will be successfully installed on your desktop.

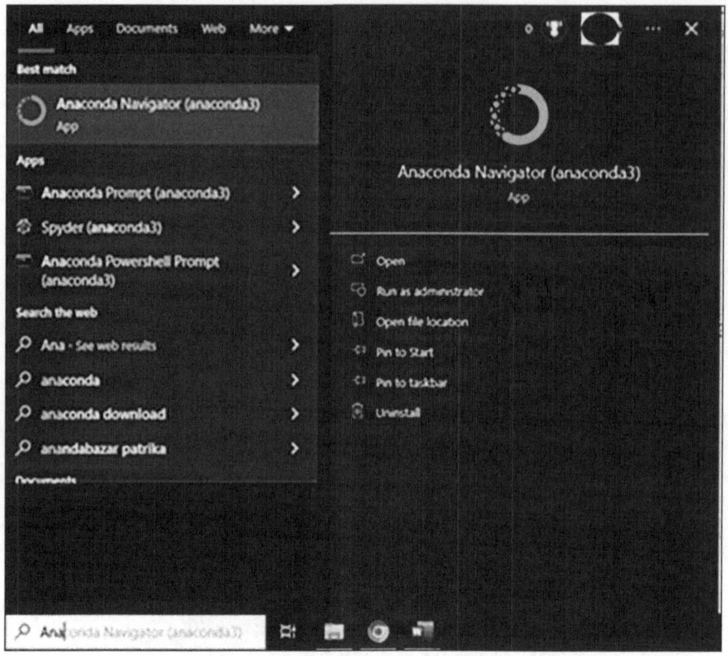

Figure 1.3: *Anaconda on the desktop*

5. Click on the Anaconda icon.

Figure 1.4: *Anaconda loading on the desktop*

***Figure 1.5**: Anaconda Navigator launching*

6. Click **Ok**. This will take you to **ANACONDA NAVIGATOR**.

***Figure 1.6**: Anaconda Navigator*

7. Here you can find multiple IDE options such as:
    - Jupyter Lab
    - Jupyter Notebook
    - Spyder

    Jupyter Notebook IDE is a popular choice.

8. Click on the Launch button below **`Jupyter Notebook`** and wait until the browser opens.

9. You will see three tabs - **`Files`**, **`Running`**, and **`Cluster`**. Let's focus on the **`File`** tab. Click on **`New`**.

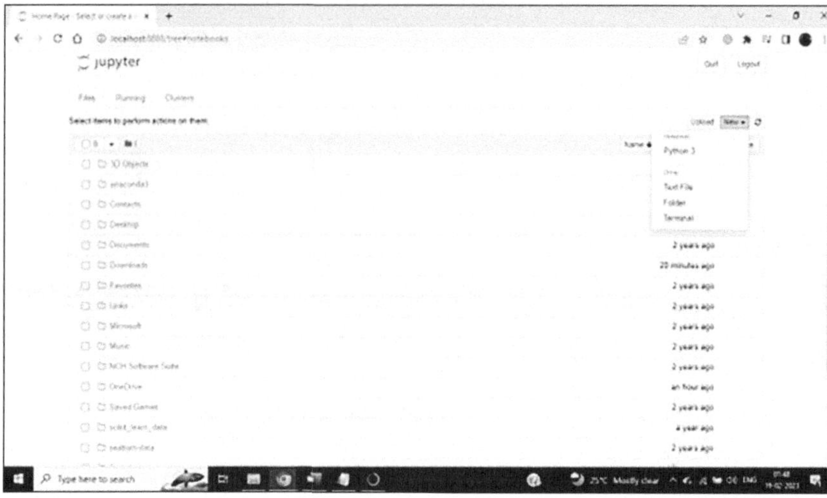

Figure 1.7: *Jupyter environment (folders/structure) – Notebook options*

10. You can see the options : **`Text File`**, **`Folder`**, and **`Terminal`**. Click on **`Folder`**.

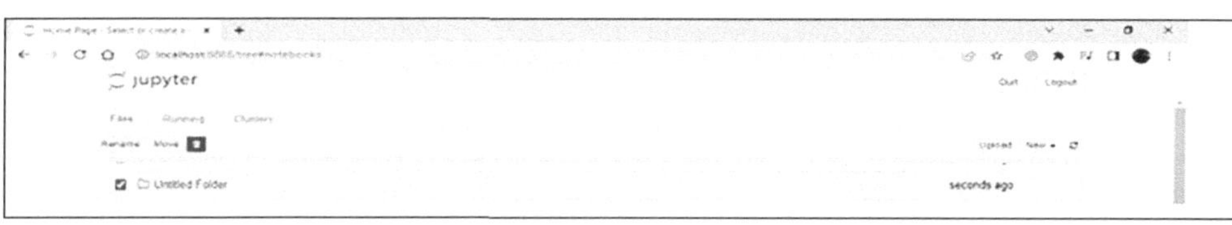

Figure 1.8: *Jupyter notebook environment*

11. Click on **`Rename`** and give the desired name.

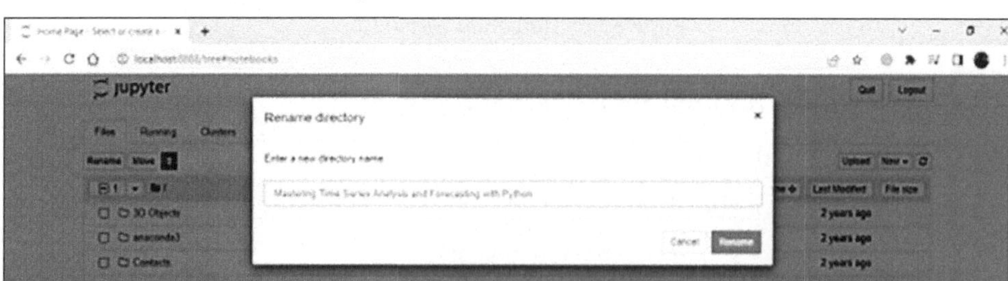

Figure 1.9: *Jupyter notebook environment (Naming the folder)*

12. Your folder is ready to use.

Figure 1.10: *Jupyter notebook environment (the folder is ready to use)*

13. Click on **`New`**. From the following menu, click on **`Python 3`**.

Figure 1.11: *Jupyter notebook environment (creating a new file)*

14. A new window for your programming is ready.

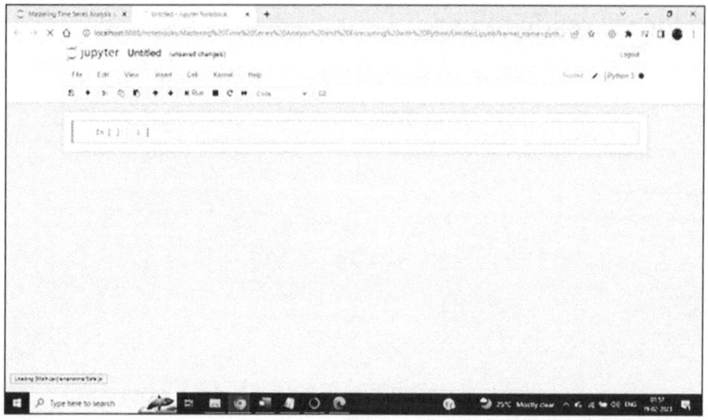

Figure 1.12: *Jupyter notebook environment (new file is ready to use)*

Python libraries

Now it's time to explore various libraries in Python. Every Data Scientist/ML engineer should know the Pandas and NumPy features and their capabilities, which support the building of ML solutions.

Before we start any AIML projects, it's important to master these libraries to handle data as it comes from multiple sources in different formats.

You are expected to bring all the necessary data into one place and arrange them for data analysis and visualization purposes.

Pandas

We can define Pandas as follows:

Panel + Data = Pandas

Figure 1.13: Pandas Logo ()

Pandas has the following features:

- It offers well-defined data structures for data analysis and their functions are robust.
- It transforms very complex operations by using plain commands that are similar to SQL.
- Concatenating, filtering, and grouping data require minimal effort.
- It provides a way to organize and perform time-series functionality.
- Indexing and re-indexing are simple commands.
- It allows reshaping, sorting, aggregation, and iteration of the data and its structure.
- It is easy to slice and dice data based on our requirements.
- The commands execute quickly and efficiently.
- It provides extensive support from a data handling perspective including data manipulation, missing data, and cleaning data with simple lines of code.
- Highly capable of handling tabular data, ordered, unordered and time series data and is ideal for unlabeled data.

The following figure displays the outstanding features of Pandas.

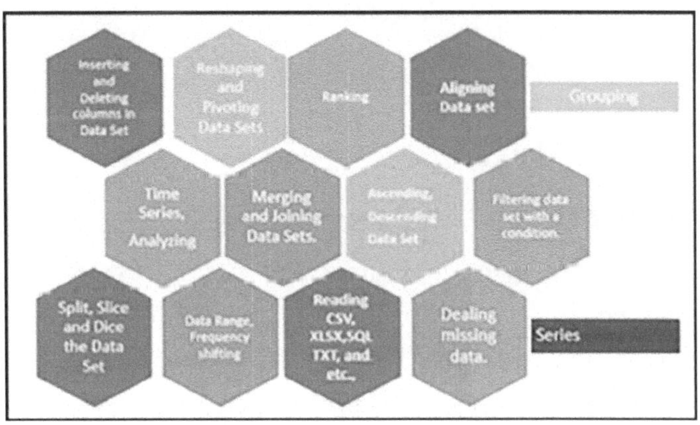

Figure 1.14: *Pandas - outstanding features (Source: DataScienceCentral.com - Big Data News and Analysis)*

Series and DataFrame

First, let's understand **Series** and **DataFrame** in Pandas. These are the primary components in the data structures of Pandas. In simple terms, a Series is similar to a dictionary, while merging collections of series results in a dataframe. The resulting dataframe is a structured dataset that can be used for further analysis.

Series: It contains just one column and row, in the form of one-dimensional array with a fixed length and the same data type. We can simply say that it is homogenous in nature.

DataFrame: This is a collection of series with multiple columns and respective rows, two-dimensional arrays with fixed-length and different data types, We can say this to be heterogeneous in nature,

Both are rectangular-tabular tables of data.

Building Series

```
import pandas as pd
series_dict={1:"C",2:"C++",3:"Java",4:"Python"}
series_obj=pd.Series(series_dict)
series_obj
```

Output

```
1         C
2       C++
3      Java
4    Python
dtype: object
```

Building a Dataframe

```
import pandas as pd
Eno=[100, 101,102, 103, 104,105]
Empname=["John","Peter","Julia","Bell","Andrew","Shantha"]
Eno_Series = pd.Series(Eno)
Empname_Series = pd.Series(Empname)
df = {"Eno": Eno_Series, "Empname": Empname_Series }
employee = pd.DataFrame(df)
employee
```

Output

	Eno	Empname
0	100	John
1	101	Peter
2	102	Julia
3	103	Bell
4	104	Andrew
5	105	Shantha

Figure 1.15: *Pandas – series+ series=dataframe*

Let's quickly discuss some advanced features of Pandas. As mentioned earlier, Pandas is a very powerful library that accelerates data pre-processing during the lifecycle of machine learning. We can execute the following features (refer to *Figure* 1.16) in the data frame and perform various data analytics by applying simple code.

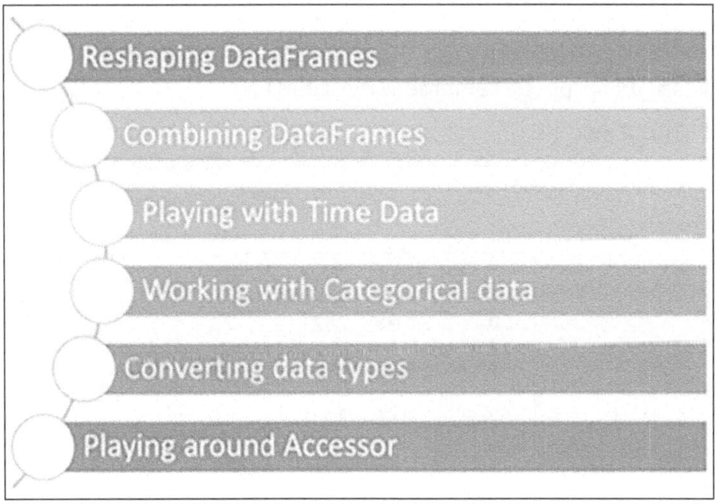

Figure 1.16: *Advanced features of Pandas (Source: DataScienceCentral.com - Big Data News and Analysis)*

Reshaping DataFrame

Reshaping is a necessary action when dealing with data during data analytics. There are multiple ways to reshape the data frame. We will cover them one by one with examples.

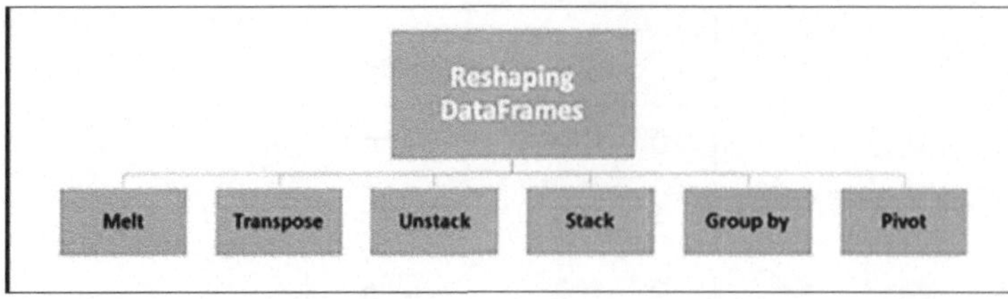

Figure 1.17: *Pandas - Reshaping DataFrame Options (Source: DataScienceCentral.com - Big Data News and Analysis)*

```
import pandas as pd
import numpy as np
#building the Dataframe
IPL_Team = {“IPL Team”: [“CSK”, “RCB”, “KKR”, “MI”, “SRH”,
“PK”, “RR”, “DC”, “CSK”, “RCB”, “KKR”, “MIS”, “SRH”,”PK”, “RR”,
“DC”],
“Year”:[2021,2021,2021,2021,2021,2021,2021,2021,2022,2022,2022,20
22,2022,2022,2022,2022],
“Points”:[23,43,45,65,76,34,23,78,89,76,92,87,50,45,67,89]}
IPL_Team_df = pd.DataFrame(IPL_Team)
print(IPL_Team_df)
```

Output

	IPL Team	Year	Points
0	CSK	2021	23
1	RCB	2021	43
2	KKR	2021	45
3	MI	2021	65
4	SRH	2021	76
5	PK	2021	34
6	RR	2021	23
7	DC	2021	78
8	CSK	2022	89
9	RCB	2022	76

Figure 1.18: *Pandas - Reshaping DataFrame Output*

- **Groupby**

The groupby feature is used to split the dataframe into multiple groups based on a column.

```
groups_df = IPL_Team_df.groupby("IPL Team")
for Team, group in groups_df:
    print("--{}--".format(Team))
    print(group)
print("")
```

```
--CSK--
  IPL Team  Year  Points
0      CSK  2021      23
8      CSK  2022      89
--DC--
  IPL Team  Year  Points
7       DC  2021      78
15      DC  2022      89
--KKR--
  IPL Team  Year  Points
2      KKR  2021      45
10     KKR  2022      92
--MI--
  IPL Team  Year  Points
3       MI  2021      65
--MIS--
  IPL Team  Year  Points
11     MIS  2022      87
--PK--
  IPL Team  Year  Points
5       PK  2021      34
13      PK  2022      45
--RCB--
  IPL Team  Year  Points
1      RCB  2021      43
9      RCB  2022      76
```

Figure 1.19: *Pandas - Reshaping DataFrame Output (Grouping) (Source: DataScienceCentral.com - Big Data News and Analysis)*

- **Transpose**

This feature swaps the given dataframe rows with its columns.

```
IPL_Team__Tran_df=IPL_Team_df.T
IPL_Team__Tran_df.head(3)
```

	0	1	2	3	4	5	6	7	8	9	10	11	12	13	14	15
IPL Team	CSK	RCB	KKR	MI	SRH	PK	RR	DC	CSK	RCB	KKR	MIS	SRH	PK	RR	DC
Year	2021	2021	2021	2021	2021	2021	2021	2021	2022	2022	2022	2022	2022	2022	2022	2022
Points	23	43	45	65	76	34	23	78	89	76	92	87	50	45	67	89

Figure 1.20: *Transpose output (Source: DataScienceCentral.com - Big Data News and Analysis)*

- **Stack**

This feature transforms the dataframe by compressing the columns into multi-index rows.

```
IPL_Team_stack_df = IPL_Team_df.stack()
IPL_Team_stack_df.head(5)
```

```
0  IPL Team      CSK
   Year         2021
   Points         23
1  IPL Team      RCB
   Year         2021
dtype: object
```

Figure 1.21: *Pandas - Reshaping DataFrame output (Stack)*

- **Unstack**

This feature is similar to stack, and it transforms the dataframe by compressing the row into a column.

```
IPL_Team_stack_df = IPL_Team_df.unstack()
IPL_Team_stack_df.head(5)
```

```
IPL Team  0     CSK
          1     RCB
          2     KKR
          3      MI
          4     SRH
dtype: object
```

Figure 1.22: *Pandas - Reshaping DataFrame output (Unstacking)*

Both functions are the most popular transposing functions from row to column and vice versa.

- **Pivot** The pivot function is used to reshape the dataframe based on specific columns in the index,

```
IPL_Team_pivot_df=pd.pivot_table(IPL_Team_df,index =['IPL Team',
'Points'])
IPL_Team_pivot_df.head(5)
```

		Year
IPL Team	Points	
CSK	23	2021
	89	2022
DC	78	2021
	89	2022
KKR	45	2021

Figure 1.23: *Pandas - Reshaping DataFrame output (Pivot)*

- **iMELT**

It transforms the dataframe into a long format. It provides flexibility in how transformations should occur. This allows selecting the column(s) and transforming them into rows while leaving the other columns unchanged.

```
IPL_Team_df_melt = IPL_Team_df.melt(id_vars =["IPL Team", "Points"])
print(IPL_Team_df_melt.head(5))
```

	IPL Team	Points	variable	value
0	CSK	23	Year	2021
1	RCB	43	Year	2021
2	KKR	45	Year	2021
3	MI	65	Year	2021
4	SRH	76	Year	2021

Figure 1.24: *Pandas - Reshaping DataFrame O/P (MELT)*

Now that you are familiar with all these pivot table operations, let's move ahead.

Combining DataFrame

Combining DataFrame is one of the significant features used to combine dataframes for different facets, which are listed in the following figure.

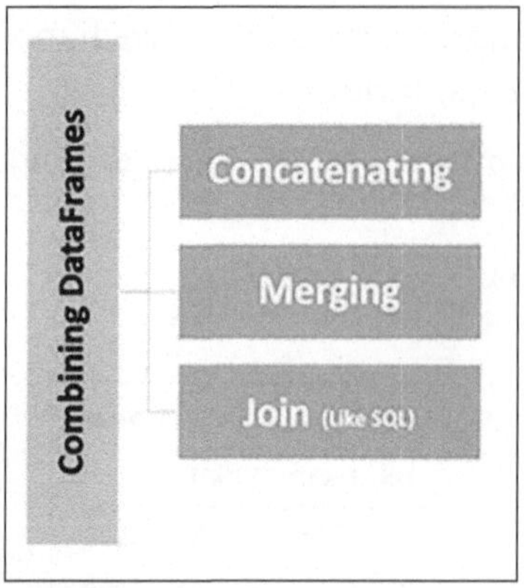

Figure 1.25: *Pandas - Combining DataFrame (Source: DataScienceCentral.com - Big Data News and Analysis)*

- **Concatenation**

This is a very simple and direct operation of Dataframes. Using this function and along with the parameter, just say `ignore_index` as True.

```
#Dataframe -1
import pandas as pd
Eno=[100, 101,102, 103, 104,105]
Empname= ["John","Peter","Julia","Bell","Andrew","Shantha"]
Eno_Series = pd.Series(Eno)
Empname_Series = pd.Series(Empname)
df = { "Eno": Eno_Series, "Empname": Empname_Series }
employee1 = pd.DataFrame(df)
employee1

#Dataframe -2
Eno1=[106, 107,108, 109, 110]
Empname1= ["James", "John", "Philp","David","Donald"]
Eno_Series1 = pd.Series(Eno1)
Empname_Series1 = pd.Series(Empname1)
df = { "Eno": Eno_Series1, "Empname": Empname_Series1 }
employee2 = pd.DataFrame(df)
employee2
```

	Eno	Empname
0	100	John
1	101	Peter
2	102	Julia
3	103	Bell
4	104	Andrew
5	105	Shantha

	Eno	Empname
0	106	James
1	107	John
2	108	Philp
3	109	David
4	110	Donald

Figure 1.26: *Pandas - Combining DataFrame (DF1 and DF2)*

- **Concatenation Operation**

```
df_concat = pd.concat([employee1, employee2], ignore_index=True)
df_concat
```

	Eno	Empname
0	100	John
1	101	Peter
2	102	Julia
3	103	Bell
4	104	Andrew
5	105	Shantha
6	106	James
7	107	John
8	108	Philp
9	109	David
10	110	Donald

Figure 1.27: *Pandas - Combining DataFrame (Concatenated dataframe)*
(Source: DataScienceCentral.com - Big Data News and Analysis)

- **Concatenation Operations with Key Options**

```
frames_collection = [employee1,employee2]
df_concat_keys = pd.concat(frames_collection, keys=["Section-A",
"Section-B"])
df_concat_keys
```

		Eno	Empname
Section-A	0	100	John
	1	101	Peter
	2	102	Julia
	3	103	Bell
	4	104	Andrew
	5	105	Shantha
Section-B	0	106	James
	1	107	John
	2	108	Philp
	3	109	David
	4	110	Donald

Figure 1.28: Pandas *- Combining DataFrame - Concatenated dataframe with keys*

- **Merging**

We can merge two different Dataframes by linking them with a common feature/ column. To implement this, we must pass the names of the dataframes with the common column as an "on" parameter.

```
#Dataframe -1
Eno1=[106, 107,108, 109, 110]
Empname1= ["James", "John", "Philp","David","Donald"]
Eno_Series1 = pd.Series(Eno1)
Empname_Series1 = pd.Series(Empname1)
df = { "Eno": Eno_Series1, "Empname": Empname_Series1 }
employee2 = pd.DataFrame(df)
employee2


#Dataframe -2
Eno1=[106, 107,108, 109, 110]
Designation= ["UX Programmer", "Data Architect", "Project
Lead","Data Analyst","Business Data Analyst"]
Eno_Series1 = pd.Series(Eno1)
Designation_Series1 = pd.Series(Designation)
df = { "Eno": Eno_Series1, "Designation": Designation_Series1 }
```

```
Designation_df = pd.DataFrame(df)
Designation_df
```

	Eno	Empname
0	106	James
1	107	John
2	108	Philp
3	109	David
4	110	Donald

	Eno	Designation
0	106	UX Programmer
1	107	Data Architect
2	108	Project Lead
3	109	Data Analyst
4	110	Business Data Analyst

Figure 1.29: *Pandas - Combining DataFrame (Before merging the dataframe)*

```
df_merge_columns = pd.merge(employee2, Designation_df, on="Eno")
df_merge_columns
```

	Eno	Empname
0	106	James
1	107	John
2	108	Philp
3	109	David
4	110	Donald

	Eno	Designation
0	106	UX Programmer
1	107	Data Architect
2	108	Project Lead
3	109	Data Analyst
4	110	Business Data Analyst

⇨

	Eno	Empname	Designation
0	106	James	UX Programmer
1	107	John	Data Architect
2	108	Philp	Project Lead
3	109	David	Data Analyst
4	110	Donald	Business Data Analyst

Figure 1.30: *Pandas - Combining DataFrame (Merging dataframe)*

This is very similar to SQL. It comes with different options such as Left Join, Right Join and Outer Join with the additional parameter how="join type". [join-type `outer,inner,left,right`]. Let's try it now.

Defining two dataframes

```
df1 = pd.DataFrame({"Eno": [100,101,102,103,104],"Ename": ["James",
"John", "Philp","David","Donald"]})
df2 = pd.DataFrame({"Eno": [100,101,102,103,105],"Salary": [1000, 1200,
1500, 1750,2000],"Designation": ["UI Developer", "Sr.Business Analyst",
"Program Head", "Project Lead","System Manager"]})
print(df1,"\n############################")
print(df2)
```

```
   Eno   Ename
0  100   James
1  101    John
2  102   Philp
3  103   David
4  104  Donald
############################
   Eno  Salary          Designation
0  100    1000         UI Developer
1  101    1200  Sr.Business Analyst
2  102    1500         Program Head
3  103    1750         Project Lead
4  105    2000       System Manager
```

Figure 1.31: *Pandas Sample DataFrame to join.*

- **Simple Join**

This is used to join two dataframes using a common column which is available in both dataframes.

```
df_join = pd.merge(df1, df2, left_on=”Eno”, right_on=”Eno”)
df_join
```

- **Full Outer Join**

```
df_outer = pd.merge(df1, df2, on=”Eno”, how=”outer”)
df_outer
```

- **Left Outer Join**

```
df_left = pd.merge(df1, df2, on=”Eno”, how=”left”)
df_left
```

- **Right-Outer Join**

```
df_right = pd.merge(df1, df2, on=”Eno”, how=”right”)
df_right
```

- **Inner Join**

```
df_inner = pd.merge(df1, df2, on="Eno", how="inner")
df_inner
```

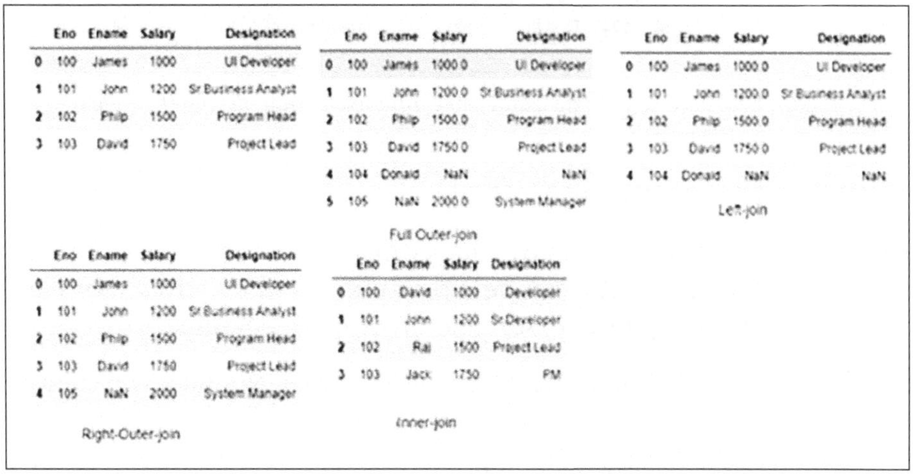

	Eno	Ename	Salary	Designation
0	100	James	1000	UI Developer
1	101	John	1200	Sr Business Analyst
2	102	Philp	1500	Program Head
3	103	David	1750	Project Lead

	Eno	Ename	Salary	Designation
0	100	James	1000.0	UI Developer
1	101	John	1200.0	Sr Business Analyst
2	102	Philp	1500.0	Program Head
3	103	David	1750.0	Project Lead
4	104	Donald	NaN	NaN
5	105	NaN	2000.0	System Manager

Full Outer-join

	Eno	Ename	Salary	Designation
0	100	James	1000.0	UI Developer
1	101	John	1200.0	Sr Business Analyst
2	102	Philp	1500.0	Program Head
3	103	David	1750.0	Project Lead
4	104	Donald	NaN	NaN

Left-join

	Eno	Ename	Salary	Designation
0	100	James	1000	UI Developer
1	101	John	1200	Sr Business Analyst
2	102	Philp	1500	Program Head
3	103	David	1750	Project Lead
4	105	NaN	2000	System Manager

Right-Outer-join

	Eno	Ename	Salary	Designation
0	100	David	1000	Developer
1	101	John	1200	Sr Developer
2	102	Raj	1500	Project Lead
3	103	Jack	1750	PM

Inner-join

Figure 1.32: *Pandas Sample DataFrame using different Joins*

Note: We can also merge dataframes by specifying keywords right_on or left_on columns.

JOIN

We have other simple options to join the dataframes. **`join()`** will perform left join the indices.

```
df1 = pd.DataFrame({"Eno": [100,101,102,103,104],"Ename": ["James", "John", "Philp","David","Donald"]},
index = ["0", "1", "2", "3","4"])
df2 = pd.DataFrame({"Salary": [1000, 1200, 1500, 1750,5000],"Designation": ["UI Developer", "Sr.Business Analyst", "Program Head", "Project Lead","Data Architect"]},
index = ["0", "1", "2", "3","4"])
df1.join(df2)
```

	Eno	Ename	Salary	Designation
0	100	James	1000	UI Developer
1	101	John	1200	Sr.Business Analyst
2	102	Philp	1500	Program Head
3	103	David	1750	Project Lead
4	104	Donald	5000	Data Architect

Figure 1.33: *Pandas Sample DataFrame different joining (Using the index)*

Working with categorical data

Categorical variables are a group of values which can be easily labelled and have a set of possible values. They can be either numerical or string. For example, location, designation, grade, age, sex, and many more columns.

We could further divide Categorical Data into Ordinal, Nominal and Continuous Data.

- **Ordinal Data**: It has proper inherent order such as Grade and Designation.
- **Nominal Data**: There is no inherent order here.
- **Continuous Data**: It consists of an infinite number of values with certain boundaries and can be numeric, date, or time data type.

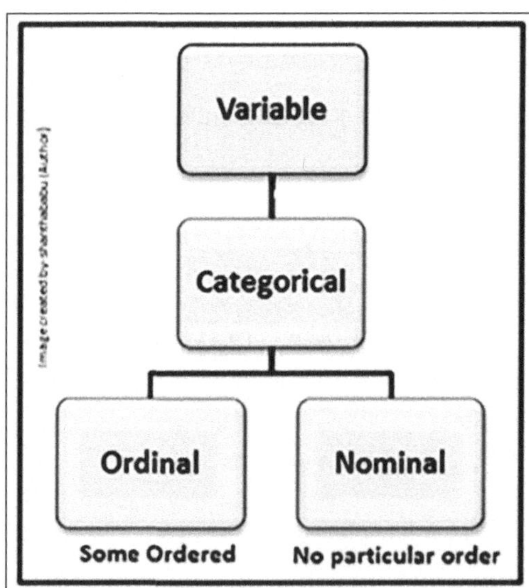

Figure 1.34: *Categorical data types. (Source: DataScienceCentral.com - Big Data News and Analysis)*

Encoding

The process of converting categorical data into numerical data is an inevitable and essential activity while dealing with categorical data.

We have the following encoding techniques:

- One-Hot encoding
- Ordinal encoding
- Dummy encoding
- Label encoding
- Target encoding
- Mean encoding

- **One-Hot encoding:** In Feature Engineering, transforming the given data into a sensible form is essential to interpret and make data more transparent. This involves creating a new variable for each level of the categorical feature. Here, the categories can be mapped with a binary variable of 0 or 1 based on the presence or absence of the expected value.

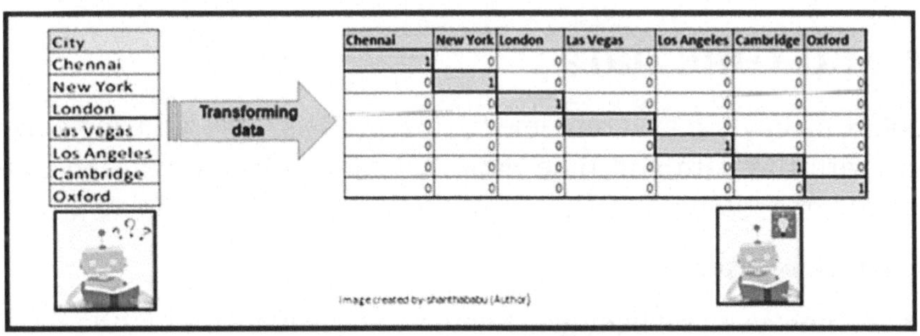

***Figure 1.35**: Categorical Data Encoding (One-Hot Encoding) (Source: DataScienceCentral.com - Big Data News and Analysis)*

```
data=pd.DataFrame({"City":["Chennai","Bangalore","Delhi","Mumbai",
"Bangalore","Delhi","Chennai","Mumbai","Kolkata","Cochin"]})
data

#Create object for one-hot encoding
import category_encoders as ce
encoder=ce.OneHotEncoder(cols="City",handle_unknown="return_nan",
return_df=True,use_cat_names=True)
data_encoded = encoder.fit_transform(data)
data_encoded
```

	City
0	Chennai
1	Bangalore
2	Delhi
3	Mumbai
4	Bangalore
5	Delhi
6	Chennai
7	Mumbai
8	Kolkata
9	Cochin

	City_Chennai	City_Bangalore	City_Delhi	City_Mumbai	City_Kolkata	City_Cochin
0	1.0	0.0	0.0	0.0	0.0	0.0
1	0.0	1.0	0.0	0.0	0.0	0.0
2	0.0	0.0	1.0	0.0	0.0	0.0
3	0.0	0.0	0.0	1.0	0.0	0.0
4	0.0	1.0	0.0	0.0	0.0	0.0
5	0.0	0.0	1.0	0.0	0.0	0.0
6	1.0	0.0	0.0	0.0	0.0	0.0
7	0.0	0.0	0.0	1.0	0.0	0.0
8	0.0	0.0	0.0	0.0	1.0	0.0
9	0.0	0.0	0.0	0.0	0.0	1.0

Figure 1.36: *Categorical Data Encoding (One-Hot Encoding) - O/P*

- **Dummy encoding**: This is very similar to the one-hot encoding. As discussed above, the categorical variables are converted into equivalent binary values as separate columns also known as dummy variables. It is an improved version of over one-hot-encoding technique. In simple terms, it uses N-1 features to represent N categories from the dataset.

Date and time data

This book is mainly focused on Time Series Analysis. Before diving deeper, let's first deal with the date and time data. We can use the dedicated Date Time library that comes along with the Pandas packages as Datetime objects.

Python datetime classes

- **datetime**: used to manipulate date and time in terms of year, month, day, hour, second, and microsecond
- **date**: used to manipulate date (y, m, and d)
- **time**: used to manipulate time – (h, m, s, and ms)
- **Timedelta**: measures date and time
- **tzinfo**: time zones dealing

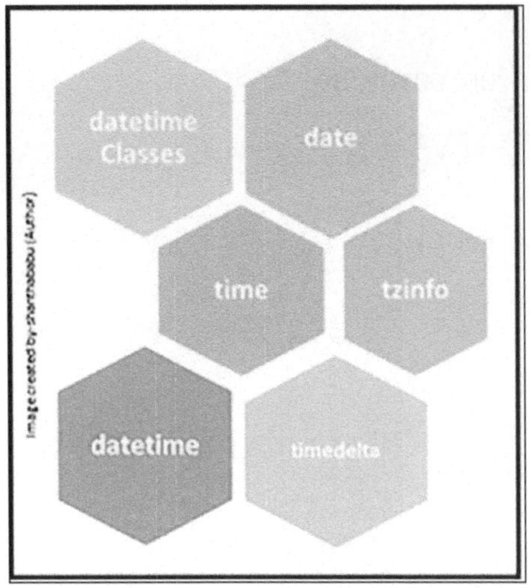

***Figure 1.37**: Pandas - Date and Time Capabilities (Source: DataScienceCentral.com - Big Data News and Analysis)*

Date and time format

%a	Short version of weekday	Mon, Tue, Wed, Thu, Fri
%A	Full version of weekday	Monday and Tuesday
%d	Day of the month	01-31
%b	Short version of the month	Feb
%B	Full version of the month	February
%y	Short version of the year	23
%Y	Full version of the year	2023
%H	Hour	00-23
%M	Minutes	0-59
%S	Second	0-59
%Z	Time zone	CST

***Table 1.1**: Pandas - Date and Time Capabilities*

```
import pandas as pd
date=pd.to_datetime("16th December,2004")
date
```

Output

```
Timestamp('2004-12-16 00:00:00')
```

```
import datetime
x = datetime.datetime.now()
print(x)
```

Output

```
2023-03-05 21:09:34.896421
```

```
import datetime
x = datetime.datetime.now()
print(x.year)
print(x.strftime("%a"))
print(x.strftime("%A"))
print(x.strftime("%d"))
print(x.strftime("%b"))
print(x.strftime("%B"))
print(x.strftime("%y"))
print(x.strftime("%Y"))
print(x.strftime("%H"))
print(x.strftime("%M"))
print(x.strftime("%S"))
print(x.strftime("%Z"))
```

Output

```
2023
Sun
Sunday
05
Mar
March
23
```

```
2023
22
08
37
```

Converting data types

Data conversion is a common practice in any programming language and Python is no exception. It provides various conversion functions to convert one data type to another.

Type conversion in Python

The following are the type conversions in Python:

- **Explicit type conversion**: The developer must write the code to change the data type as per their requirement during development.
- **Implicit type conversion**: Python can convert data types automatically without any manual intervention.

Explicit Type conversion

```
# Type conversion in Python
strA = "2022" #Sting type
# printing string value converting to int
intA = int(strA,10)
print ("Into integer : ", intA)
# printing string converting to float
floatA = float(strA)
print ("into float : ", floatA)
```

Output

```
Into integer :  2022
into float :  2022.0
```

 # Type conversion in Python

initializing string

```
strA = "Python"
ListA = list(strA)
print ("Converting string to list :",(ListA))
tupleA = tuple(strA)
print ("Converting string to list :",(tupleA))
```

Output

```
Converting string to list : ['P', 'y', 't', 'h', 'o', 'n']
Converting string to list : ('P', 'y', 't', 'h', 'o', 'n')
```

A few other functions are:

`dict()` : Used to convert a tuple into a dictionary.

`str()` : Used to convert an integer into a string.

Implicit Type conversion

```
a = 100
print("a is of type:",type(a))
b = 100.6
print("b is of type:",type(b))
c = a + b
print(c)
print("c is of type:",type(c))
```

Output

```
a is of type: <class 'int'>
b is of type: <class 'float'>
200.6
c is of type: <class 'float'>
```

NumPy

Numerical Python □ NumPy

Figure 1.38: *NumPy Logo (Source: DataScienceCentral.com - Big Data News and Analysis)*

Next to Pandas, NumPy is a powerful package for fast manipulation, which is required to handle data structures and various algorithms for scientific applications involving large numerical data.

The following are the features of NumPy:

- NumPy's array is simply an object called ndarray, which supports multi-dimensional array manipulations.
- NumPy allows us to reshape, slice, and dice arrays of any size with fast processing capabilities.
- It performs various numerical functions, trigonometry functions such as sin, cos, tan, mean, median, and so on, and complex mathematical implementations.
- It provides outstanding support for Linear Algebra, Statistics, Probability, Fourier Transform, Laplace Transform, and more.
- NumPy works closely with other packages in Python environments such as SciPy and Matplotlib.

NumPy Cando

The capabilities of NumPy are illustrated in the following figure. Let's discuss them one by one.

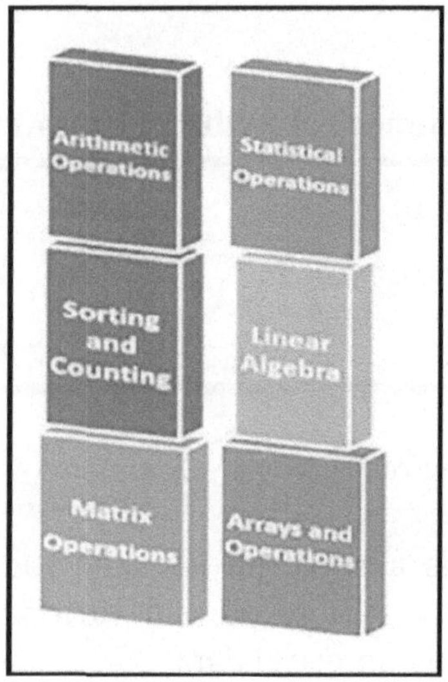

Figure 1.39: *Pandas - Date and Time Capabilities*
(Source: DataScienceCentral.com - Big Data News and Analysis)

Dimensions in the array

One-dimension

```
import numpy as np
print("1-D")
a = np.array([200,400,600,800,1000])
print (a)
```

Output

```
1-D


1-D
[ 200  400  600  800 1000]
```

```
print("n-D")
a = np.array([[500, 1000], [2000, 4000]])
print (a)
```

Output

```
n-D
[[ 500 1000]
 [2000 4000]]
```

Number of dimensions

Finding dimensions of the given array

```
x = np.array(1)
y = np.array([5, 10, 15, 20, 25])
z = np.array([[2, 4, 6], [8, 16, 32]])
print("No of Dimension(s):",x.ndim)
print("No of Dimension(s):",y.ndim)
print("No of Dimension(s):",z.ndim)
```

Output

```
No of Dimension(s): 0
No of Dimension(s): 1
No of Dimension(s): 2
```

Finding the type of array

```
arr = np.array([10, 20, 30, 40, 50])
print(arr)
print(type(arr))
```

Output

```
[10 20 30 40 50]
<class 'numpy.ndarray'>
```

Accessing array elements by specifying the index value

```
arr = np.array([10, 20, 30, 40, 50])
print(arr[0])
```

Output

```
10
```

Output

```
print(arr[3])
40
```

Slicing array element, by specifying the index range

```
import numpy as np
arr = np.array([101, 201, 301, 401, 501, 601, 701])
print(arr[1:4])
```

Output

```
[201 301 401]
```

Data type objects specific to NumPy

NumPy has its own built-in data types.

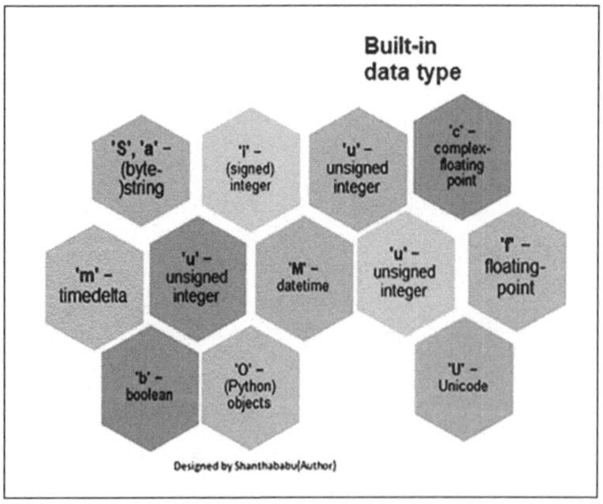

Figure 1.40: *NumPy Capabilities (Built-in data types) (Source)*

Finding shape and re-shape of the ndarray

a. Shape of the array

Array has an attribute that returns array dimensions.

```
import numpy as np
a = np.array([[4,8,12],[5,10,15],[20,25,30],[30,35,40]])
print ("Shape of the array:",a.shape)
a = np.array([[10,20,30,40],[30,40,50,60],[40,45,50,50]])
print ("Shape of the array:",a.shape)
```

OUTPUT

```
Shape of the array: (4, 3)
Shape of the array: (3, 4)
```

b. Re-shape the array

You can easily resize the array with simple steps.

```
import numpy as np
a = np.array([[5,10,15],[40,50,60]])
b = a.reshape(3,2)
print ("Array a(Actual shape):\n",a)
print ("Shape of the array:\n",a.shape)
print ("Array b(After reshape):\n",b)
print ("After Re-shape of the array:\n",b.shape)
```

OUTPUT

```
Array a(Actual shape):
 [[ 5 10 15]
 [40 50 60]]
```

```
Shape of the array:
 (2, 3)
Array b(After reshape):
 [[ 5 10]
 [15 40]
 [50 60]]
After Re-shape of the array:
 (3, 2)
```

Converting List and Tuple into ndarray

(a) List into Array

```
import numpy as np
x = [5,10,15]
print("As-List:",x)
a = np.asarray(x)
print("As-Array:",a)
```

OUTPUT

```
As-List: [5, 10, 15]
As-Array: [ 5 10 15]
```

(b) Tuple into Array

```
import numpy as np
x = (2,4,6)
print("Tuple:",x)
a = np.asarray(x)
print("As Array:",a)
```

OUTPUT

```
Tuple: (2, 4, 6)
As Array: [2 4 6]
```

Array Join and Split

(a) Join Array

Using the concatenate function, we can join two or more arrays into a single array.

```
import numpy as np
arr1 = np.array([100, 200, 300])
arr2 = np.array([400, 500, 600])
print(arr1)
print(arr2)
arr = np.concatenate((arr1, arr2))
print("Concatenated Array :",arr)
```

OUTPUT

```
[100 200 300]
[400 500 600]
Concatenated Array : [100 200 300 400 500 600]
```

(b) Splitting Array

We can split the arrays into small arrays with the **`split()`** function.

```
import numpy as np
arr = np.array([20, 25, 30, 35, 40, 45,50,55])
print("Actual Array:",arr)
newarr = np.array_split(arr, 4)
print("Splitting into 4")
print("Split:",newarr)
```

OUTPUT

```
Actual Array: [20 25 30 35 40 45 50 55]
Splitting into 4
Split: [array([20, 25]), array([30, 35]), array([40, 45]), array([50,
55])]
```

Create an array with ranges

- Start-value, Stop-value, Step-value

```
import numpy as np
x = np.arrange(1000,2000,100)
print (x)
```

OUTPUT

```
[1000 1100 1200 1300 1400 1500 1600 1700 1800 1900]
```

Array multiplication

We can perform simple multiplication with row and column counts that are equal. This is called broadcasting.

- Same shape of arrays
- Same number of dimensions and length of arrays

```
a = np.array([1,2,3,4])
b = np.array([2,2,2,2])
print (a)
print (b)
c = a * b
print("Array Multiplication\n")
print (c)
```

OUTPUT

```
[1 2 3 4]
```

```
[2 2 2 2]
Array Multiplication
[2 4 6 8]
```

NumPy – Mathematical functions

NumPy supports most mathematical operations, making it easier for us to handle numbers. They include:

- Arithmetic operations
- Statistical functions
- Trigonometric functions
- Linear algebra

Arithmetic operations

During these operations, the arrays should have the same shape/size and conform to array broadcasting rules.

```
a = np.array([4,8,12])
b = np.array([5,5,5])
print ("Array-A:",a)
print ("Array-B:" ,b)
print ("A+B of arrays:",np.add(a,b))
print ("A-B of arrays:",np.subtract(a,b))
print ("A*B of arrays:" ,np.multiply(a,b))
print ("A/B of arrays:" ,np.divide(a,b))
```

OUTPUT

```
Array-A: [ 4  8 12]
Array-B: [5 5 5]
A+B of arrays: [ 9 13 17]
A-B of arrays: [-1  3  7]
A*B of arrays: [20 40 60]
A/B of arrays: [0.8 1.6 2.4]
```

Statistical functions

NumPy supports the following statistical functions:

- **`Minimum`**
- **`Maximum`**
- **`Percentile`**
- **`Standard Deviation`**
- **`Variance`**

```
import numpy as np
a = np.array([[10,15,20],[4,8,12],[5,15,20]])
print ("Given array is:")
print("---------------------")
print (a)
print ("Maximum :",np.amax(a))
print ("Minimum :",np.amin(a))
print ("Standard Deviation :",np.std(a))
print ("Variance :",np.var(a))
print("Percentile :",np.percentile(a, 4))
print("---------------------")
```

OUTPUT

```
Given array is:
---------------------
[[10 15 20]
 [ 4  8 12]
 [ 5 15 20]]
Maximum : 20
Minimum : 4
Standard Deviation : 5.566655577722377
Variance : 30.98765432098765Percentile : 4.32
```

Linear algebra

NumPy package provides linear algebra functions through the **`numpy.linalg`** libraries, such as matrix and vector products, matrix eigenvalues, solving equations and inverting matrices. Let's see a few samples.

```
import numpy.matlib
import numpy as np
import numpy.linalg as npla
a = np.array([[5,10],[15,20]])
b = np.array([[3,6],[9,12]])
print("Matrix and vector products")
print("****************************")
print ("Dot Operation:", np.dot(a,b))
print("*****************************************")
print ("vdot :",np.vdot(a,b))
print("**************************")
print("Matrix eigenvalues")
print(npla.linalg.eig(a))
print("*****************************************")
print(npla.linalg.eigvals(a))
print("*****************************************")
print("Solving equations and inverting matrices")
print(npla.linalg.solve(a, b))
print("*****************************************")
print(npla.linalg.inv(a))
```

OUTPUT

```
Matrix and vector products
****************************
Dot Operation: [[105 150]
 [225 330]]
*****************************************
vdot : 450
```

```
*************************
Matrix eigenvalues
(array([-1.86140662, 26.86140662]), array([[-0.82456484, -0.41597356],
       [ 0.56576746, -0.90937671]]))
****************************************
[-1.86140662 26.86140662]
****************************************
Solving equations and inverting matrices
[[6.00000000e-01 1.77635684e-16]
 [4.99600361e-17 6.00000000e-01]]
****************************************
[[-0.4  0.2]
 [ 0.3 -0.1]]
```

NumPy with Matplotlib

To create various charts, Numpy works along with the Matplotlib library allowing us to create interesting pieces of work.

Plotting – Line

```
import numpy as np
from matplotlib import pyplot as plt
x = np.arrange(1,11)
#simple linear equation
y = 5 * x + 2
plt.title("Matplotlib demo")
plt.xlabel("height")
plt.ylabel("weight")
plt.plot(x,y)
plt.show()
```

OUTPUT

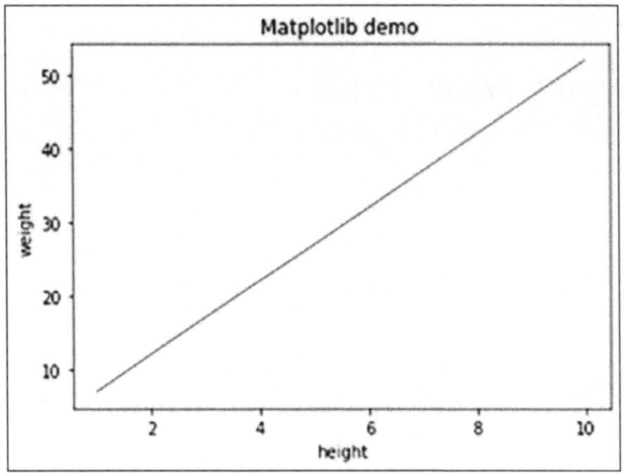

***Figure 1.41**: NumPy Capabilities (Line chart)*

Plotting - Sine Wave Form

```
import numpy as np
import matplotlib.pyplot as plt
x = np.arrange(0, 6 * np.pi, 0.5)
y = np.sin(x)
plt.title("Sine Wave Form")
plt.plot(x, y)
plt.show()
```

OUTPUT

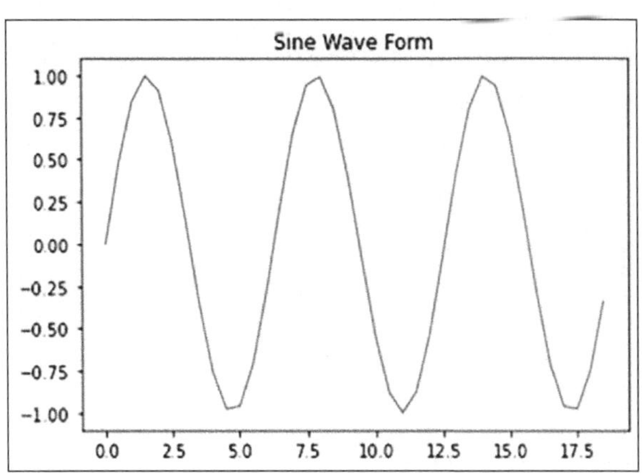

***Figure 1.42**: NumPy Capabilities (Sine waveform)*

Plotting Bar chart

```
from matplotlib import pyplot as plt
x = [15,25,30]
y = [20,25,35]
x2 = [9,5,16]
y2 = [5,10,6]
plt.bar(x, y, align = "center")
plt.bar(x2, y2, align = "center")
plt.ylabel("Performance")
plt.xlabel("Slots")
plt.show()
```

OUTPUT

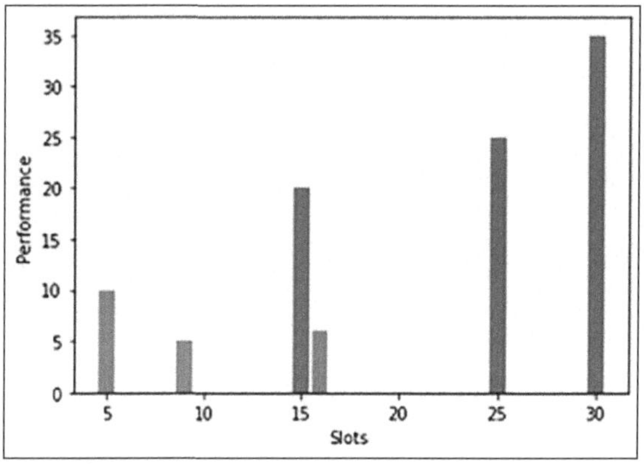

Figure 1.43: *NumPy Capabilities (Bar chart)*

Working with a string array: NumPy library provides various string functions to play around with string values.

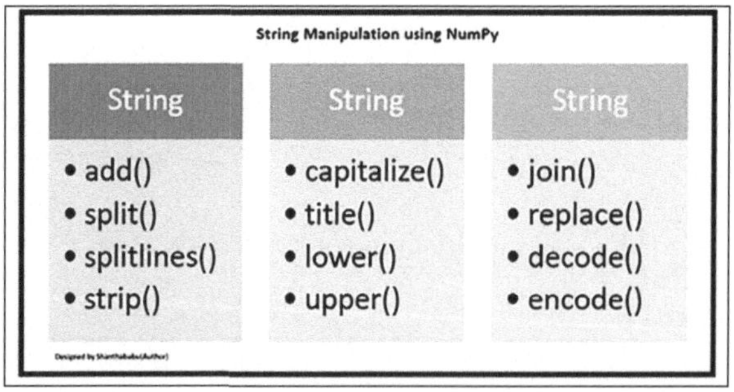

Figure 1.44: *NumPy Capabilities (String functions)*
(Source: DataScienceCentral.com - Big Data News and Analysis)

```
import numpy as np
print("Capitalize (Welcome to Python):",np.char.capitalize("Welcome to Python"))
print("Title (Welcome to Python):",np.char.title("Welcome to Python"))
print("Lower (PYTHON):",np.char.lower(["PYTHON"]))
print("Upper (python):",np.char.upper("python"))
print("Split (hello how are you?):",np.char.split ("hello how are you?"))
print("Split (Python,Pandas,NumPy):",np.char.split ("Python,Pandas,NumPy", sep = ","))
print("Strip (welcome watts):",np.char.strip("welcome watts","w"))
print("Join (dmy):",np.char.join(":","dmy"))
print("Join (dmy):",np.char.join([":","-"],["dmy","ymd"]))
print("Replace Python is a programming language:", np.char.replace
("Python is a programming language","programming","powerful is
programming"))
print("Concatenate two strings Hello,Mr.Babu:",np.char.add
(["Hello"],["Mr.Babu"]))
print("Concatenation example [Hello, Hi],[ Shantha , Babu]:",np.char.
add(["Hello", "Hi"],[" Shantha ", " Babu"]))
```

OUTPUT

```
Capitalize (Welcome to Python): Welcome to python
Title (Welcome to Python): Welcome To Python
Lower (PYTHON): ['python']
Upper (python): PYTHON
Split (hello how are you?): ['hello', 'how', 'are', 'you?']
Split (Python,Pandas,NumPy): ['Python', 'Pandas', 'NumPy']
Strip (welcome watts): elcome watts
Join (dmy): d:m:y
Join (dmy): ['d:m:y' 'y-m-d']
Replace Python is a programming language: Python is a powerful programming language
Concatenate two strings Hello,Mr.Babu: ['HelloMr.Babu']
```

```
Concatenation example [Hello, Hi],[ Shantha , Babu]: ['Hello Shantha '
'Hi Babu']
```

There are many more capabilities in NumPy. We have learned the most important ones used during DS and ML project-specific implementation while dealing with datasets.

Python statistics libraries

Python programming language provides extensive support for statistics through specific statistics libraries that will support you in working with data. Since DS and ML products require more mathematical support to prove various problem statements, this specific library supports extensively solving statistical problems.

Let us go through some high-level requirements with respect to statistics.

- **Population**: In statistical terms, population refers to the process of choosing and examining the accountable subset of that population which are interested in analysis.
- **Samples**: In simple terms, this is a subset of population.
- **Outliers**: It is the data point that stands out from the majority of the data population, in simple terms, an "*odd man out*".

The above-mentioned are quantitative approaches to statistics, which means this can be represented by numerically-summarized data and sometimes represented by charts, distribution curves, plots, and other graphs.

- Coming to Measures of Central Tendency, we are all familiar with the following basic statistical calculations:
- Mean
    - Weighted mean
    - Geometric mean
    - Harmonic mean
- Median
- Mode

Let's try a few of them here.

```
_list = [15,20,50,16,10,25,60,70,20,60,35,51,50]

#mean

x = statistics.mean(_list)

print("mean :",x)
```

```
print("****************************************")
#median
y = statistics.median(example_list)
print("median :",y)
print("****************************************")
#mode
z = statistics.mode(example_list)
print("mode :",z)
print("****************************************")
#stdev
a = statistics.stdev(example_list)
print("stdev :",a)
print("****************************************")
#variance
b = statistics.variance(example_list)
print("variance :",b)
```

Output

```
mean : 37.07692307692308
****************************************
median : 35
****************************************
mode : 20
****************************************
stdev : 20.536396707884023
****************************************
variance : 421.7435897435897
```

There are more advanced concepts which we will discuss in the following chapters.

Working with various files in Python

Python has excellent file-handling techniques compared to other languages such as C, C++, and Java. The process is very straightforward. Will discuss a few of them here.

File handling in Python consists of three steps: **`Open, Write/Read`**, and **`Close`**.

- **`open()` function**: If you're familiar with file operations in other programming languages, this is pretty simple. For those who are new, it should not be difficult to understand. Before performing file operation(s), we have to open the specific file by passing the path of the file location. With the help of **`open()`**, you can open the file and it will be available for further action.

Syntax

```
fp = open(filename, mode)
f.write(<<content>>)
f.read()
f.close()
```

`filename`□ file path along with the file extension

Mode of operations of the files in Python file operation mode:

- **`r`** - For read operation
- **`w`** - For a write operation
- If the file is not present, then it creates a new file
- If the file is already present and contains some data, then it will be overridden
- **`a`** - For appending an existing file and will not override the existing data
- **`r+`** and **`w+`** - To perform both read and write operations in the file and previous data, if any, will be overridden
- **`a+`** For an existing file to append and read data from the file

Open, Write, Read, and Append

```
import pandas as pd
f= open("sample.txt","w+")
f.write("Welcome to Python\n")
```

```
f.write("****************Pandas****************\n")
f.write("Provides data structures of high-level and a wide variety of tools for analysis\n")
f.write("Ability to translate complex operations with data using one or two commands.\n")
f.write("Methods for grouping, combining data, and filtering, as well as time-series functionality.\n")
f.write("Re-indexing, Iteration, Sorting, Aggregations, Concatenations and Visualizations")
f.close()


f=open("sample.txt", "r")
contents =f.read()
print(contents)
```

Output

```
Welcome to Python
****************Pandas****************
Provides data structures of high-level and a wide variety of tools for analysis
Ability to translate complex operations with data using one or two commands.
Methods for grouping, combining data, and filtering, as well as time-series functionality.
Re-indexing, Iteration, Sorting, Aggregations, Concatenations and Visualizations
```

```
f.close()

f=open("sample.txt", "a+")
f.write("\n****************Pandas - Append  ****************\n")
f.close()
f=open("sample.txt", "r")
contents =f.read()
```

```
print(contents)
```

Output

```
Welcome to Python
****************Pandas****************
Provides data structures of high-level and a wide variety of tools for
analysis
Ability to translate complex operations with data using one or two
commands.
Methods for grouping, combining data, and filtering, as well as
time-series functionality.
Re-indexing, Iteration, Sorting, Aggregation, Concatenation and
Visualizations
****************Pandas - Append  ****************

f.close()
```

Other methods for handling the files

with **open(…)** option makes reading and writing data into files using Python language straightforward.

```
with open("sample.txt", 'a+') as f:
    data = '\n some data to be written on the file.'
    f.write(data)
    f.close()


with open('sample.txt', 'r') as f:
    data = f.read()
data
```

Output

```
'Welcome to Python\n****************Pandas****************\nProvides
data structures of high-level and a wide variety of tools for
analysis\nAbility to translate complex operations with data using one
```

```
or two commands.\nMethods for grouping, combining data, and filtering,
as well as time-series functionality.\nRe-indexing, Iteration, Sorting,
Aggregation, Concatenation and Visualizations\n*****************Pandas -
Append  *****************\n\n some data to be written to the file’
```

Read the different file formats in Python:

- CSV (Comma-separated values)

  ```
  df = pd.read_csv("/Project/Product_details.csv")
  ```

- XLSX

  ```
  df = pd.read_excel("/Project/train.xlsx", sheetname =
  "Product_details")
  ```

- Plain Text (txt)

  ```
  f = open("test.txt", "r")
  ```

- JSON

  ```
  df = pd.read_json("/Project/Product_details.json")
  ```

- XML

  ```
  import xml.etree.ElementTree as xmlFile
  tree = xmlFile.parse("/Project/Product_details.xml')
  ```

- HTML
- Images and many more

Conclusion

In this chapter, we have discussed various aspects of Python programming from scratch, including the Python programming language and its significant features. We also learned about the various IDEs available in the market and their features and benefits. We provided detailed installation steps for Anaconda and learnt about the exploration of the environment.

Then we moved on to major Python libraries such as Pandas, NumPy and Statsmodel with extensive and exclusive examples with coding and output to understand each sub-topic better. We have covered file handling as well.

This chapter will serve as a solid foundation for beginners and practitioners to understand Python programming. In the next chapter, we will discuss data analytics and advanced data analytics using Python. We will also touch on time series and data preparation and provide a detailed study of **EDA** (Exploratory Data Analysis).

Points to remember

In this chapter, it is important to keep a few things in mind that would be handy and useful throughout this book.

As mentioned earlier, "*Python is a very simple, general-purpose programming language*". So writing and understanding the code should not be a big deal for a good programmer. Additionally, fewer lines of code would be required to accomplish the complex requirements. , which we saw during the detailed study of TS&F. It provides robust and standard libraries such as Pandas, NumPy, and Scikit-learn.

Pandas

- It offers well-defined data structures for Data Analysis.
- It transforms very complex operations by using plain commands such as SQL.
- It provides indexing, re-indexing, reshaping, sorting, aggregation, and iteration of the data and its structure.
- This allows for slicing and dicing data based on our requirements.

NumPy

- It supports multi-dimensional array manipulation.
- We can reshape, slice, and dice arrays of any size with fast processing capability.
- We can perform various numerical functions, trigonometric functions, linear algebra, statistics, probability, Fourier transforms, Laplace transforms, and many more.

CHAPTER 2

Python for Time Series Data Analysis

Introduction

In the previous chapter, we discussed various aspects of Python programming and its significant features. We covered major Python libraries, including Pandas, NumPy and Statsmodel, with extensive and exclusive examples. This chapter will discuss **Data Analysis** in detail along with Python programming. We will then move on to **Time Series Data Preparation, management and its Characteristics**. The focus will be specifically on data remediation in terms of data cleansing, preparation, wrangling, and data visualization in Time Series Analysis. We will discover the scope of data mining in Time Series Analysis. Understanding statistics is essential for analytics and connecting with time series and forecasting analysis. Additionally, we will explore the scope of Exploratory Data Analysis (EDA) in time series, along with classical examples.

Structure

In this chapter, we will discuss the following topics:

- Data analysis and its benefits
- Python - the best choice for data analytics
- Data preparation and management
- Data remediation techniques

  - o Cleaning/Cleansing
  - o Wrangling
- Data visualization in time series analysis
- Exploratory data analysis

Data analysis and its benefits

Data analysis is a set of process analysis that enable businesses to obtain real-time insights from the data extracted from various upstream applications in their business sectors. During data analysis, data analysts work on the data and transform it into meaningful ways by applying business rules. The outcome of the data analysis would be in the following formats based on the customer's demands and requirements, by extracting insights from the data:

- Tabular format with/without custom calculations
- Rich visualization with/without custom calculations

This process is not a straightforward representation of data from any given data source. Will look into the detailed process and steps involved later in this chapter.

Generally, the outcome would be about the nature of the business, its performance, and solutions for upcoming challenges. The outcome would differ based on the type of business and its processes. Some examples of domains include **Manufacturing, Retail, Consumer Goods, Insurance, Banking, Finance**, and more.

Note: Data Analysis helps businesses work together to achieve better solutions. The major objective is to analyze business performance from historical data and improve future business processes and new opportunities.

Benefits

The following are the main benefits of data analysis:

- Helps in overall business performance and understanding of past success and failure paths from historical data.
- Provides valuable suggestions and guidance for organizations to make better decisions and improve strategy plans.
- Helps product-based organizations to improve the quality and services of their personalized products in the market.
- Improves customer behavior and increases work efficiency

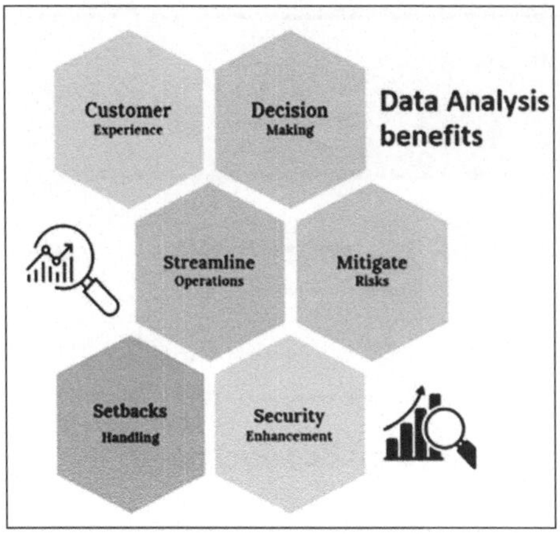

Figure 2.1: *Benefits of Data Analysis*

Note: Difference between Data Analysis and Data Analytics

The straightforward answer is that both are quite similar, with little difference between them.

- **Data Analysis** is a process that involves the collection, manipulation, and validation of data to find insights.
- **Data Analytics** takes forward the analyzed outcomes of the data to make valuable business decisions **using business intelligence tools (Power BI, Tableau, and so on)**

Advanced Analytics

Advanced analytics is also involved in a set of processes right from the collection of data, application of data analysis techniques, and algorithms (s) to build predictive, classification, and clustering models based on problem statements. Businesses use these strategies to improve their decision-making processes and prepare future strategies. We shall discuss this in terms of **TS&F** from *Chapter* 5, *Exploring various aspects Time Series Analysis and Forecasting* onwards.

Python - the best choice for data analytics

In *Chapter* 1, *Introduction to Python and its key packages for DS and ML Projects*, we discussed various Python packages and classical examples. Let's discuss now why Python is the best choice for data analytics, with the help of specific data-oriented libraries available in the Python ecosystem.

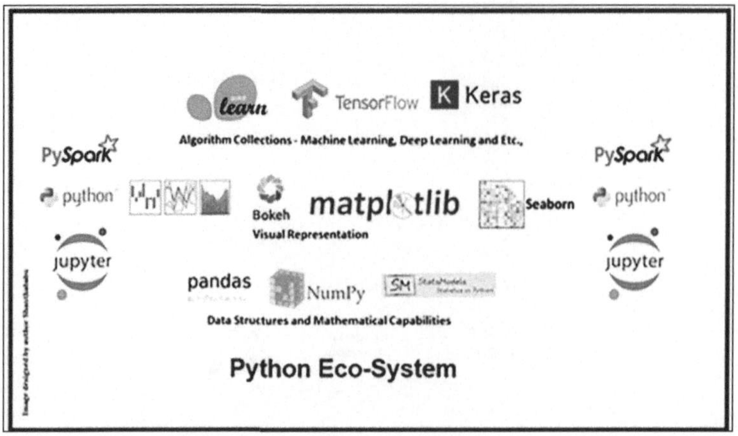

Figure 2.2: *Python ecosystem*

Python is one of the most popular interpreted programming languages used predominantly for web development and scripting purposes. So, it is also called **scripting language**. Over the past decade, the Python community has built numerous libraries in newer versions of Python, with larger mathematical and scientific computational aspects. In particular, there are powerful algorithms built in Python to support data science, machine learning, deep learning, and AI subsets.

Python completely supports all broader groups in the AIML lifecycle as follows:

- Source data identification (provider)
- Data preparation
- Data transformation
- Modeling and computation
- Presentation (consumer)

Time series data

Before we start exploring time series and data management, let's understand data types in Python. Python offers a range of built-in data types called **Scalar Types**, which include **int, float, str, bytes, bool, date-time,** and **none.** Since the scope of this book is precisely on **Date and Time,** will focus on understanding date and time data types first and then delve into time series data and its management.

Python's datetime built-in type provides the following data types:

- Datetime

- Date
- Time

Dealing with dates and times in Python:

```
from datetime import datetime, date, time
my_dt=datetime(2023,3,30,10,10,10)
print(my_dt)

print("Date components")
print("**********************")
print("Day:",my_dt.day)
print("Month:",my_dt.month)
print("Year:",my_dt.year)
print("Time components")
print("**********************")
print("Hour:",my_dt.hour)
print("Minutes:",my_dt.minute)
print("Seconds:",my_dt.second)
print("**********************")
print("Date:",my_dt.date())
print("Day:",my_dt.strftime("%d/%m/%Y"))
print("Day:",datetime.strptime("20230330","%Y%m%d"))
```

Output

```
Date components
**********************
Day: 30
Month: 3
Year: 2023
Time components
**********************
Hour: 10
```

```
Minutes: 10
Seconds: 10
**********************
Date: 2023-03-30
Day: 30/03/2023
Day: 2023-03-30 00:00:00
```

Time series data management

Let's gain an understanding of time series data and its management from an industry perspective. Time series data is the process of collecting the time-stamped data that is queried and indexed based on period.

These data points are sequential quantities obtained from sources over a fixed interval period and are used to track changes over a period. You can represent this by plotting the points on a graph with one of the axes representing time constantly.

Time series data is observable across all domains and increases drastically with each passing nanosecond. Numerous web applications across industries generate data either manually or through manufacturing instruments, sensor devices (IoT), and signaling systems. These constantly transfer or transmit data along with time stamps in the form of time series data to the landing layer of PaaS architecture.

Examples of time series analysis include the following:

- Weather and forecasting
  - Rainfall measurements
  - Temperature readings
  - Air pollution levels
  - Wind speed
- Healthcare
  - Heart rate monitoring
  - Brain monitoring
  - Blood pressure tracking
  - Weight tracking
  - Cholesterol measurements

- Stocks, sales, and marketing
  - Annual retail sales
  - Quarterly sales
  - Stock prices
  - Automated stock trading
- Manufacturing
  - Anomaly detection
  - Industry forecasts
  - Rate of production
  - Efficiency of the equipment
- Media and entertainment
  - Monthly subscribers
  - Mostly watched movies
  - Rating on web series
- Banking and financial services
  - Interest rates
  - Gross domestic product rates
  - Anomaly detection for fraud detection

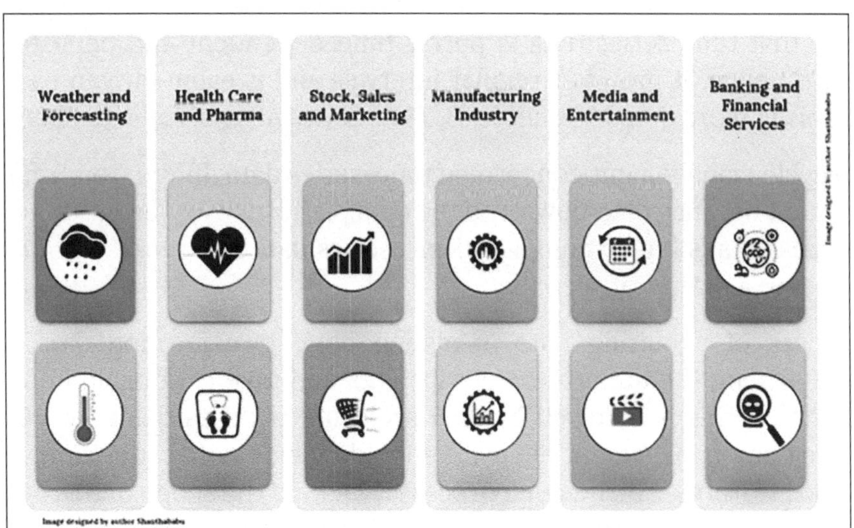

Figure 2.3: *Examples of time series analysis*

Time series data can be measured in different time stamps, ranging from seconds and minutes to annual. Data can be at regular intervals or irregular.

The following table shows some of the time series - time stamp examples.

Data measured in terms of period	Source of Data
Seconds and minutes	Sensor-based devices
Hourly based	Shit timing register – in the manufacturing unit
Daily	Gold/Fuel prices
Weekly based	Employee timesheet
Monthly	Consumption of water and electricity
Quarterly	Organization/Students performance
Half-yearly	Organization/Students performance
Yearly	Organization-level profits and revenue

Table 2.1: *Time series samples*

Data lifecycle management (DLM)

Let's understand the data lifecycle management specific to regular intervals or irregular datasets.

We know that time series data is purely time-dependent and persistent on a different timeline. It grows at regular intervals and is event-driven based. Will discuss this in more detail in *Chapter 3, Time Series Analysis and its Components.*

Data lifecycle management concerning time-series data differs from application management because data flows into the data platform with various timeframes. Time-series data is highly complex. Time-series data has generated millions of data points in a matter of seconds.

The process of acquiring data, ingesting data, transforming data, storing data, and serving the data to extract insights and take actionable information is continuous. This is followed by data archiving and data deletion. Without a doubt, the data management life cycle should include data protection and data governance features. The detailed process is beyond the scope of this book, let's get an understanding of the overview of this lifecycle.

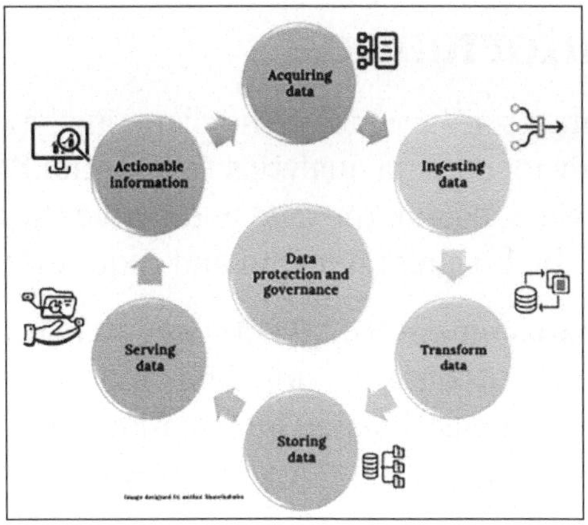

Figure 2.4: *Data lifecycle management*

Data acquisition or collection

Data acquisition is the first stage of the data management lifecycle and is decided by the subsequence stages. The data originates from various data sources such as application databases, data warehouses and data produced from devices (IoT), and so on.

Ingesting data

Ingesting is a major part of the data management lifecycle followed by the collection stages. The ingestion process into the data platform can be straightforward, it would be either pulling or pushing methods to bring them into the staging area. Depending on the cloud technology choices (Azure, AWS and GCP), the components would be configured to bring the data into the database, data warehouse, or data lake depending on the requirements.

Transforming data

The transformation process is a significant task followed by data ingestion. Based on the business rules, data engineers will apply ETL or ELT tasks on ingested data along with data cleaning, wrangling, and preparing the gold data set to be stored in the storing layer.

Storing data

After the transformation process, the golden data set has to be stored in storing data layer which would be the database, data warehouse or data lake.

Actionable information

Once the golden dataset is available, the data analytics team (BI-Business Intelligence) or the advanced data analytics team (Data Scientists and Machine Learning Engineers) will consume the data and derive the actionable items from the dataset, based on the business demand and requirements.

Note: Data lifecycle management (DLM) is a sequential process of acquiring data, ingesting data, transforming data, storing data, and serving the data to extract insights and constantly take actionable information. This can be demonstrated by cloud environments such as Azure, AWS and GCP.

Data remediation

Data remediation is a major and mandatory process by enforcing certain rules and procedures on the raw data collected from different sources. It involves a set of processes, including **data cleansing, data wrangling, preparing a well-organized dataset** and **adapting data quality, policies, governance requirements** and **recommended guidelines.**

In simple terms, we can say that data remediation is **correcting mistakes from the raw data source for business benefits**. With the help of this processed data, we can enable data analytics and advanced analytics and extract insight from the data. Following this, we can demonstrate prediction, classification, clustering, and forecasting.

A data remediation process is necessary for any organization to ensure the best sanitization and legal fulfilment concerning data and building data platform solutions.

There are certain conditions where data remediation is necessary. They are:

- Human errors
- Device-generated errors
- Business change
- Finding new opportunities
- Identifying risks and mitigations

If an organization plans to consolidate its data and identify business challenges, opportunities, risks, and strategy roadmaps, it may adopt data remediation techniques to bring the new cleansed data to a new storage environment and implement data analytics and advanced data analytics, as we discussed earlier.

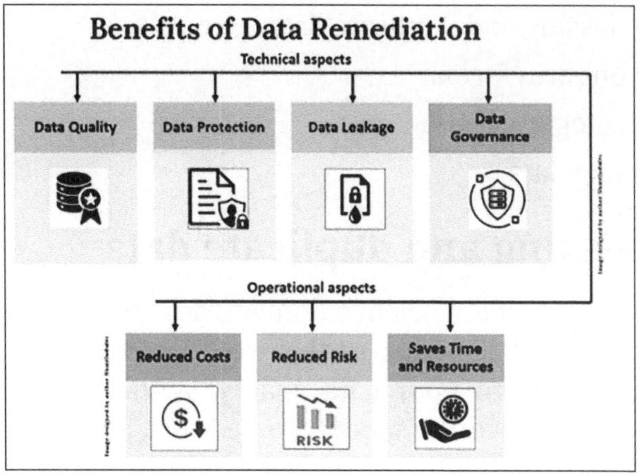

Figure 2.5: *Benefits of data remediation*

So far, we have discussed data remediation, let's focus on the process and techniques involved in it along with examples.

Note: Data remediation is a well-defined process aimed at improving the quality of data. The process involves **data cleansing, data wrangling, and preparing a well-organized dataset**. The major goal of data remediation is to help the organization in making better decisions with the data, either in the form of cold or hot storage.

Data cleansing and preparation

Data cleaning and cleansing is an architectural approach for data analysts and data scientists involved in critical processes to eliminate data redundancy, missing values, irregular formatting, outliers, abnormal records, and other factors that can cause issues during visualization or model building. Ultimately, this process improves the overall results.

Especially in the Data Science and Machine Learning lifecycle, almost 40% to 45% of that timeline will be required for data cleaning (or) cleansing, transforming, and reshaping, rearranging the data for further processing.

We will certainly leverage the powerful Pandas and NumPy libraries from Python as we discussed in *Chapter 1,Introduction to Python and its key packages for DS and ML Projects* to clean and prepare the data.

When we start inspecting the cleaning and preparation process, we can utilize the following list of methods (or) techniques provided by Python's library:

- Handling missing and duplicate data
- Handling uniform format
- Handling categorical column
- Transforming data

Handling missing and duplicate data

In the data analytics and data science domain, dealing with missing data from data sources is always challenging as this would impact outcome results and model accuracy, leading to poor data quality. With the help of appropriate techniques, we can improve the models to be more accurate and valid. While handling missing data, certain exercises have to be implemented to handle the situation.

- **Find null values**

In Python, it is easier to detect the missing values across the dataframe object for any column or data type. The Pandas library provides the following functions to find null or missing values: **`isnull()`** and **`notnull()`**. These can also be used for a series.

```
import pandas as pd
import numpy as np
my_series=pd.Series(['C','C++','Python',np.nan,'Golang'])
print(my_series)

output
0         C
1       C++
2    Python
3       NaN
4    Golang
dtype: object

Upon checking, is there any NaN

my_series.isnull()
```

```
Output
0    False
1    False
2    False
3     True
4    False
dtype: bool
```

The fourth value in this series is the Null value.

Since the fourth value in the series is a null value, we can either remove it or fill it with appropriate values. Let's try to remove it first.

```
my_series.dropna()
```

```
0          C
1        C++
2     Python
4     Golang
dtype: object
```

Let's do this with the defined dataset **Advertising.csv**, finding the Null across the dataset.

```
import numpy as np
import pandas as pd
import matplotlib.pyplot as plt
import seaborn as sns
%matplotlib inline
df_Advertising = pd.read_csv("Advertising.csv")
df_Advertising.head(5)
```

output

Out[2]:

	Sno	TV	Radio	Newspaper	Sales
0	1	230.1	37.8	69.2	22.1
1	2	44.5	39.3	45.1	10.4
2	3	17.2	45.9	69.3	9.3
3	4	151.5	41.3	58.5	18.5
4	5	180.8	10.8	58.4	12.9

Figure 2.6: *Advertising-dataset (Head of 5)*

Find out if there is any Null in the dataset.

```
df_Advertising.isnull().any()
```

```
output
Sno          False
TV            True
Radio         True
Newspaper     True
Sales         True
dtype: bool
```

We observed that the **TV**, **Radio**, and **Newspaper** columns have null values. Let's count the null values.

```
print("Null Count(TV) :",df_Advertising['TV'].isnull().sum())
print("Null Count(Radio) :",df_Advertising['Radio'].isnull().sum())
print("Null Count(Newspaper) :",df_Advertising['Newspaper'].isnull().
sum())
```

```
output
Null Count(TV) : 8
Null Count(Radio) : 5
```

```
Null Count(Newspaper) : 7
```

Try to see this null using a heatmap, you can observe the yellow lines as shown in the following figure.

```
sns.heatmap(df_Advertising.isnull(),yticklabels=False,cbar=True,
cmap='viridis')
```

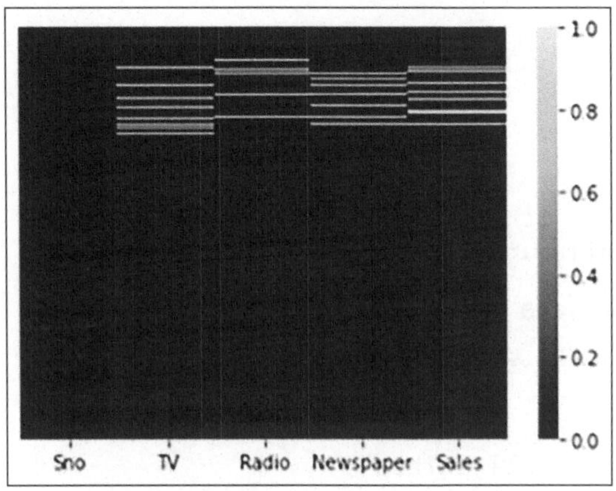

***Figure** 2.7: Finding Null using heatmap*

- **Filtering the missing data**

Missing values can be filtered either by using the dropna or non-null options provided by the Pandas library. Dropna and non-null methods help to remove the null row from the dataset.

```
import pandas as pd
import numpy as np
from numpy import nan as NA
data=pd.Series(["C","C++",NA,"Python",NA,"Ruby","Java",".Net"])
print("Actual data")
print("============")
print(data)
```

output

```
Actual data
=============
0          C
1        C++
2        NaN
3     Python
4        NaN
5       Ruby
6       Java
7       .Net
dtype: object
```

Applying dropna and non-null methods:

```
print("Impact of dropna method")
print("=======================")
print(data.dropna() )
print("Impact of  notnull method")
print("=========================")
print(data[data.notnull()])
```

output

```
Impact of dropna method
=======================
0          C
1        C++
3     Python
5       Ruby
6       Java
7       .Net
dtype: object
Impact of  notnull method
=========================
```

```
0          C
1        C++
3     Python
5       Ruby
6       Java
7       .Net
dtype: object
```

Try this with the Advertising dataset as follows:

```
import pandas as pd
import numpy as np
from numpy import nan as NA
df_Advertising_cleaned = df_Advertising.dropna()
print("Null Count(TV) :",df_Advertising_cleaned['TV'].isnull().sum())
print("Null Count(Radio) :",df_Advertising_cleaned['Radio'].isnull().
sum())
print("Null Count(Newspaper) :",df_Advertising_cleaned['Newspaper'].
isnull().sum())
```

Output

```
Null Count(TV) : 0
Null Count(Radio) : 0
Null Count(Newspaper) : 0
```

You can observe that all nulls have been removed and stored in the new dataframe **df_Advertising_cleaned**.

Try to see if null still exists in the dataset using a heatmap, you can observe that there are no yellow lines as shown in the following figure.

```
sns.heatmap(df_Advertising_cleaned.isnull(),yticklabels=False,
cbar=True,cmap='viridis')
```

Output

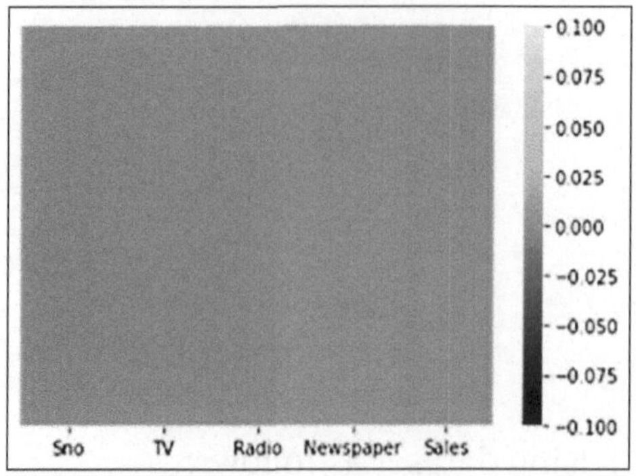

Figure 2.8: *Finds Null Existence After Data Cleanup Using Heatmap*

- Fill in the missing data

The solutions provided in the preceding examples are not exact solutions in the real-time scenarios. since we are losing data. Instead of removing the rows, we can fill the data to retain the volume of the data. Pandas provides the **fillna()** method to handle the situation.

```
import pandas as pd
import numpy as np
from numpy import nan as NA
data=pd.Series([“C”,”C++”,NA,”Python”,NA,”Ruby”,”Java”,”.Net”])
print(“Actual data”)
print(“=============”)
print(data)
```

Output

```
Actual data
=============
0        C
1      C++
2      NaN
3   Python
4      NaN
5     Ruby
6     Java
```

```
7        .NET
DTYPE: OBJECT
PRINT("IMPACT OF DROPNA METHOD")
PRINT("=======================")
PRINT(DATA.FILLNA("N/A"))
IMPACT OF DROPNA METHOD
=======================
0          C
1        C++
2        N/A
3     PYTHON
4        N/A
5       RUBY
6       JAVA
7       .NET
DTYPE: OBJECT
```

We will apply this approach to the `df_Advertising` dataset. Here, instead of N/A, let's fill with 0, with value and `mean()` options.

```
df_Advertising["TV"].fillna(int(df_Advertising["TV"].mean()),
inplace=True)
df_Advertising["Radio"].fillna(0, inplace=True)
df_Advertising["Newspaper"].fillna(4, inplace=True)
df_Advertising["Sales"].fillna(method="ffill",inplace=True)

print("Null Count(TV) :",df_Advertising['TV'].isnull().sum())
print("Null Count(Radio) :",df_Advertising['Radio'].isnull().sum())
print("Null Count(Newspaper) :",df_Advertising['Newspaper'].isnull().
sum())
print("Null Count(Sales) :",df_Advertising['Sales'].isnull().sum())
output
Null Count(TV) : 0
Null Count(Radio) : 0
Null Count(Newspaper) : 0
```

```
Null Count(Sales) : 0
```

```
sns.heatmap(df_Advertising.isnull(),yticklabels=False,cbar=True,c-
map='viridis')
```

Output

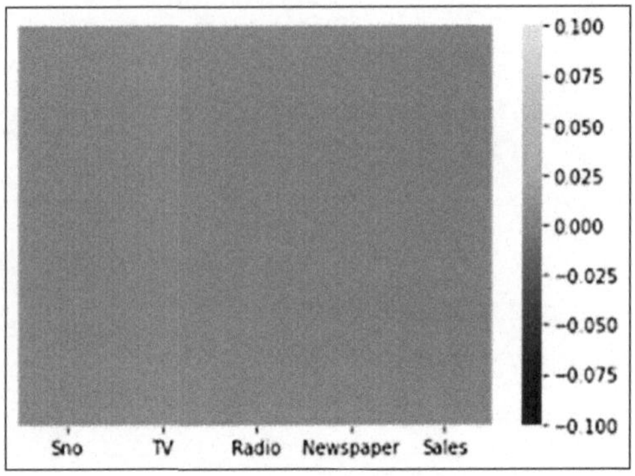

Figure 2.9: *Apply various options with fillna and visualise the dataset using the heatmap*

- **Removing duplicates**

This method is straightforward to rows from the dataframe, just using **drop_duplicates()**.

Let's take a look at the given dataset.

	A	B	C	D	E	F	G
1	Sno	TV	Radio	Newsp	Sales		
191	190	18.7	12.1	23.4	6.7		
192	191	39.5	41.1	5.8	10.8		
193	192	75.5	10.8	6	9.9		
194	193	17.2	4.1	31.6	5.9		
195	194	166.8	42	3.6	19.6		
196	195	149.7	35.6	6	17.3		
197	196	38.2	3.7	13.8	7.6		
198	197	94.2	4.9	8.1	9.7		
199	198	177	9.3	6.4	12.8		
200	199	283.6	42	66.2	25.5		
201	200	232.1	8.6	8.7	13.4		
202	197	94.2	4.9	8.1	9.7		
203	198	177	9.3	6.4	12.8		
204	199	283.6	42	66.2	25.5		
205	200	232.1	8.6	8.7	13.4		
206							
207							
208							
209							
210							
211							

Advertising

Figure 2.10: *Duplicate rows in Advertising dataset (from .csv file)*

```
df_Advertising.shape
output
(204, 5)
```

Please remove the duplicates.

```
df_Advertising.drop_duplicates()
```

	Sno	TV	Radio	Newspaper	Sales
0	1	230.1	37.8	69.2	22.1
1	2	44.5	39.3	45.1	10.4
2	3	17.2	45.9	69.3	9.3
3	4	151.5	41.3	58.5	18.5
4	5	180.8	10.8	58.4	12.9
...	...	...	...	...	...
195	196	38.2	3.7	13.8	7.6
196	197	94.2	4.9	8.1	9.7
197	198	177.0	9.3	6.4	12.8
198	199	283.6	42.0	66.2	25.5
199	200	232.1	8.6	8.7	13.4

200 rows × 5 columns

Figure 2.11: *After duplicates are removed from the Advertising dataset (from the dataframe)*

Handling uniform format

While dealing with data in data analytics, the format of the data plays a major role. Any issues with the format can make it difficult to analyze data. Therefore, we must always fix these issues before proceeding.

The best possible solution is to convert the impacted cells into a meaningful format or in the worst case we can remove that specific row. But remember this is not the best practice as data loss is not advisable in data analytics and machine learning.

- **Format conversion**

In most cases, format corrections are required for date-based columns. Let's see one classical example.

Loading **diesel_price.csv** and finding the datatype of the column:

```
import numpy as np
```

```
import pandas as pd
import matplotlib.pyplot as plt
import seaborn as sns
%matplotlib inline
df_Dateformat = pd.read_csv("diesel_price.csv")
df_Dateformat.head()
```

Output

	Sale_Date	Diesel price (in US$)
0	16-04-2022	5.00
1	17-04-2022	6.00
2	18-04-2022	5.60
3	18-04-2022	5.12
4	21-04-2022	5.10

Figure 2.12: *diesel_price.csv*

Find the datatype. We can observe that the **`Sale_Date`** is the Object type.

```
df_Dateformat.dtypes
```

Output

```
Sale_Date                 object
Diesel price (in US$)    float64
dtype: object
```

Change the data type to datetime using Pandas for further data analysis.

```
df_Dateformat['Sale_Date'] = pd.to_datetime(df_Dateformat.Sale_Date)
print (df_Dateformat)
```

Output

```
Sale_Date          Diesel price (in US$)
0  2022-04-16                5.00
1  2022-04-17                6.00
2  2022-04-18                5.60
```

```
3  2022-04-18                5.12
4  2022-04-21                5.10
5  2022-04-22                5.34
6  2022-04-24                5.45
7  2022-04-25                5.32
8  2022-04-26                6.17
9  2022-04-26                6.08
10 2022-04-29                5.95
11 2022-04-30                5.13
12 2022-02-05                4.99
```

Format changes for **Sale_Date** into **%m/%d/%Y** (We have discussed multiple options in *Chapter 1, Introduction to Python and its key packages for DS and ML Projects*).

```
df_Dateformat['Sale_Date']=df_Dateformat['Sale_Date'].dt.
strftime('%m/%d/%Y')
print (df_Dateformat)
```

Output

```
Sale_Date         Diesel price (in US$)
0   04/16/2022              5.00
1   04/17/2022              6.00
2   04/18/2022              5.60
3   04/18/2022              5.12
4   04/21/2022              5.10
5   04/22/2022              5.34
6   04/24/2022              5.45
7   04/25/2022              5.32
8   04/26/2022              6.17
9   04/26/2022              6.08
10  04/29/2022              5.95
11  04/30/2022              5.13
12  02/05/2022              4.99
```

Verify the Sale Date column data type after the format change:

```
df_Dateformat.dtypes
```

Output

```
Sale_Date                 datetime64[ns]
Diesel price (in US$)            float64
dtype: object
```

Handling categorical columns

In data analytics and data science, the categorical data type (Please refer to variable data types in *Chapter 1, Introduction to Python and its key packages for DS and ML Projects*) is a set of predefined values or groups of values. When capturing data from various sources, we find a variety of categorical data, for example, gender, educational qualifications, country names, city names, name of the manufacturer, and so on.

Let's explore here with **Manufacturers_products.csv**.

```
import numpy as np
import pandas as pd
import matplotlib.pyplot as plt
import seaborn as sns
%matplotlib inline
df_Manufacturers_products = pd.read_csv("Manufacturers_products.csv")
df_Manufacturers_products.head()
```

Output

	Product Name	Manufacturer_name
0	TV	Samsung
1	TV	Sony
2	TV	LG
3	TV	Videocon
4	TV	Thomson

Figure 2.13: *Manufacturers_products dataframe*

```
categoricalData = pd.get_dummies(df_Manufacturers_products,
columns=['Product Name'])
categoricalData.head()
```

Output

	Manufacturer_name	Product Name_Air Conditioners	Product Name_Computer monitors	Product Name_Digital Cameras	Product Name_Home theater systems	Product Name_Laptops	Product Name_Memory chips	Product Name_Mobile	Product Name_Refrigerators	Produ Name_Sm applianc
0	Samsung	0	0	0	0	0	0	0	0	
1	Sony	0	0	0	0	0	0	0	0	
2	LG	0	0	0	0	0	0	0	0	
3	Videocon	0	0	0	0	0	0	0	0	
4	Thomson	0	0	0	0	0	0	0	0	

Figure 2.14: *Manufacturers_products dataframe after converting them into dummy variables*

Transformation of data

Data transformation is a frequently used process in data analytics. Let's go through a few examples.

Column Header Transformation: When capturing data from different sources of datasets, we may encounter datasets that may not have either proper column names that are not easy to understand or negligible information in the first row of the file.

This could lead to errors and challenges when handling files for further analysis. We can handle such situations by giving a new name for the column header for easier file handling.

Let's load the **World_Test_cricket_points_table.csv** file.

```
import numpy as np
import pandas as pd
import matplotlib.pyplot as plt
import seaborn as sns
%matplotlib inline
df_World_Test_cricket_points = pd.read_csv("World_Test_cricket_points_
table.csv")
df_World_Test_cricket_points.head()
```

Output

	0	1	2	3	4	5	6
0	India	71.7	430	5.0	9	3	1
1	New Zealand	70.0	420	5.0	7	4	0
2	Australia	69.2	332	4.0	8	4	2
3	England	65.3	352	5.0	9	4	3
4	South Africa	40.0	144	3.0	3	6	0

Figure 2.15: *World_Test_cricket_points dataframe*

We can observe that there is no appropriate column name for the dataframe. Name each column after identifying the meaning of the row values.

```
new_names =  {'0': 'Country','1': 'PCT (%)','2': 'Points','3': 'Series','4': 'Won','5': 'Lost','6': 'Drawin'}

df_World_Test_cricket_points.rename(columns=new_names, inplace=True)

df_World_Test_cricket_points.head()
```

Now, we can observe the World_Test_cricket_points dataframe with appropriate column headers.

	Country	PCT (%)	Points	Series	Won	Lost	Drawin
0	India	71.7	430	5.0	9	3	1
1	New Zealand	70.0	420	5.0	7	4	0
2	Australia	69.2	332	4.0	8	4	2
3	England	65.3	352	5.0	9	4	3
4	South Africa	40.0	144	3.0	3	6	0

Figure 2.16: *World_Test_cricket_points dataframe after header fixes*

String Transforming: In some situations, we have to deal with string values in rows to maintain uniformity. This best practice will help data analysts and data scientists.

We are responsible for streamlining them for data analysis. Here is one classical sample that is most commonly faced.

In the given sample, the manufacturer's name should be consistent and spelt correctly.

The highlighted Manufacturer names are correctly spelt.

Thomsan	**Samsung**	**LG**
Thomson	Samsang	L-G
Thomsoon	Samsong	LG
	Shamsung	L G
		L@G

Table 2.2: *Manufacturer name in product.csv file*

```
import numpy as np
import pandas as pd
import matplotlib.pyplot as plt
import seaborn as sns
%matplotlib inline
df_products = pd.read_csv("products.csv")
df_products.head(10)
```

Output

	Product Name	Manufacturer_name
0	TV	Samsung
1	TV	Sony
2	TV	LG
3	TV	Thomsan
4	TV	Thomson
5	Mobile	L-G
6	Memory chips	Samsong
7	Digital Cameras	Shamsung
8	Laptops	Samsung
9	Home theater systems	L-G

Figure 2.17: *Manufacturer name in dataframe*

```
# Correcting  Manufacturer name
df_products['Manufacturer_name'] = df_products['Manufacturer_name'].
str.replace(
```

```
'Samsang|Samsong|Shamsung','Samsung')

df_products['Manufacturer_name'] = df_products['Manufacturer_name'].
str.replace(

'L-G|L@-G','LG')

df_products['Manufacturer_name'] = df_products['Manufacturer_name'].
str.replace(

'Thomsan|Thomsoon','Thomson')


df_products.head(10)
```

Output

	Product Name	Manufacturer_name
0	TV	Samsung
1	TV	Sony
2	TV	LG
3	TV	Thomson
4	TV	Thomson
5	Mobile	LG
6	Memory chips	Samsung
7	Digital Cameras	Samsung
8	Laptops	Samsung
9	Home theater systems	LG

Figure 2.18: *After correction Manufacturer name in dataframe*

Finding Outliers: The distribution of data plays a vital role in data analytics and machine learning because it can impact the outcome, specifically during the model evaluation process. The model would be either overfitting or underfitting, the root cause for this issue is the data from the source not managed properly keeping the abnormal data in the dataset. Python visualization library matplotlib. pyplot is used to find these outliers in visual form. Using Pandas will remove or scale them to fix the outliers. Let's try this with voters list.csv, where the voters' age appears to be abnormal and unrealistic.

```
import numpy as np

import pandas as pd
```

```
import matplotlib.pyplot as plt
import seaborn as sns
%matplotlib inline
df_voterslist = pd.read_csv("voters list.csv")
df_voterslist.head(10)
```

Output

	Name	Age	Gender
0	Raja	30	Male
1	Georgia	45	Male
2	Juliet	67	Female
3	Lily	89	Female
4	Olive	45	Male
5	Emmett	65	Male
6	Miles	76	Female
7	Oscar	12	Male
8	William	125	Male
9	Acharya	2	Male

Figure 2.19: *Voter's list dataframe*

```
import statsmodels as sm
from scipy import stats
sns.boxplot(x=df_voterslist["Age"])
```

Output

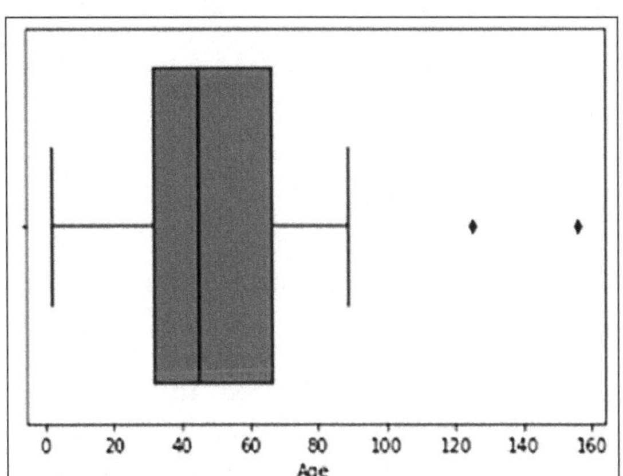

Figure 2.20: *Outliers in Voter's list data*

We can observe that in the preceding box plot, the age range is from 25 to 78 in the box and we can see that there were two black dots around 120 and 155; this is unrealistic data This is errored data, we should correct it as follows.

Let's set up a threshold.

```
z_scores = stats.zscore(df_voterslist["Age"])
age_z_scores = np.abs(z_scores)
filtered_entries = (age_z_scores < 1.5 )
new_df_voterslist = df_voterslist[filtered_entries]
```

Let's try now with both plots.

```
sns.boxplot(x=new_df_voterslist["Age"])
```

Output

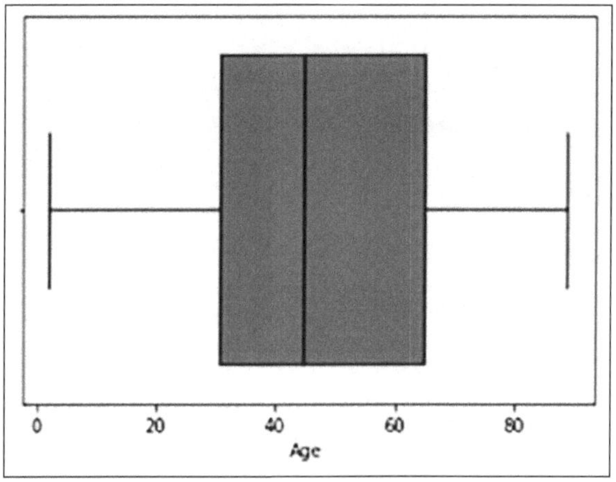

Figure 2.21: *After the outliers are fine-tuned in Voter's list data*

Handling time series data

The root cause for data missing values can be data corruption from the source application itself, human error, or failure to record correct data.

So far, we have discussed how to handle text, numerical, and categorical data types. The major objective of this book is to cover the time series data. So, let's explore how to handle time series data when we have a problem with missing or corrupted values.

The missing values in the time series dataset can be handled in a much simpler way compared to other datatypes, by either dropping the records with the missing values or imputing the missing information. We must remember that dropping or removing the data might lead to losing statistical references like correlations and distributions. We can adapt the method of imputing missing values which would help a lot.

```
import numpy as np
import pandas as pd
import matplotlib.pyplot as plt
import seaborn as sns
%matplotlib inline
df_products = pd.read_csv("diesel_price.csv")
df_products.head(10)
```

Output

	Sale_Date	Diesel price (in US$)
0	16-04-2022	5.00
1	17-04-2022	6.00
2	18-04-2022	5.60
3	18-04-2022	5.12
4	21-04-2022	5.10
5	22-04-2022	5.34
6	24-04-2022	5.45
7	25-04-2022	NaN
8	26-04-2022	6.17
9	26-04-2022	NaN

Figure 2.22: *diesel_price dataframe*

Let's find the missing values using the line plot.

```
df_products.plot.line()
```

Output

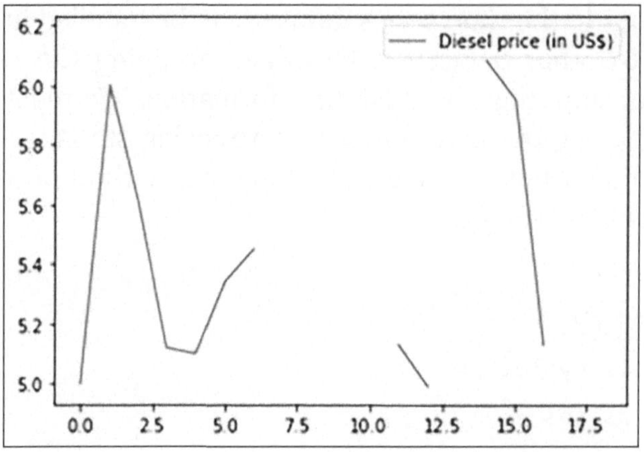

Figure 2.23: *diesel_price missing data visualisation*

In the time series, we can fill in the missing values using carried forward, backwards and rolling statistical methods as follows.

Last observation carried forward (LOCF): This is a simple method to fill in the previous valid values that are carried, copied forward and replaced with the following missing values.

```
df_products["Diesel price"] = df_products["Diesel price"].ffill()
df_products.plot.line()
```

Output

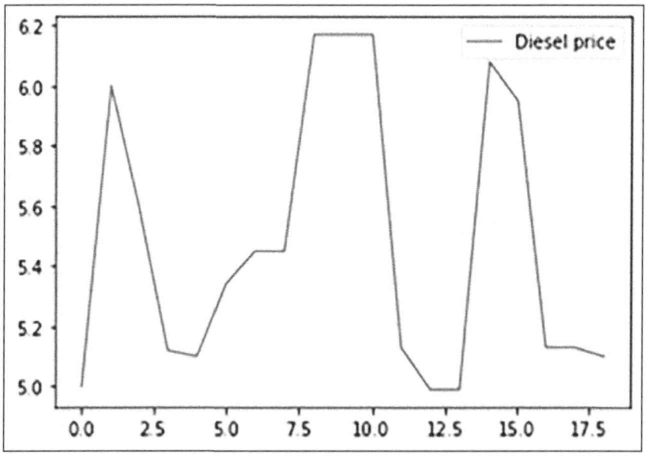

Figure 2.24: *diesel_price filled by LOCF*

Next observation carried backward (NOCB): This is a simple method for the following valid values to be copied and replaced with the previous missing values.

```
df_products["Diesel price"] = df_products["Diesel price"].bfill()
df_products.plot.line()
```

Output

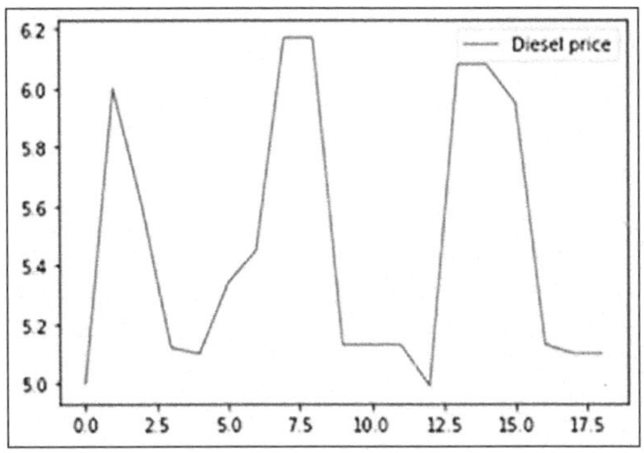

Figure 2.25: *diesel_price filled by* NOCB

Rolling statistical: This is a statistical method by aggregating the previous non-missing values to impute missing values. We have the Simple Moving Average and Weighted Moving Average (WA) techniques.

$$\mathbf{P_t = (P_1 + P_2 + P_3 + P_4 + P_5 + P_6 + \ldots\ldots\ldots P_{t-n})/n}$$

```
df_products["Diesel price"] = df_products["Diesel price"].
rolling(window=4).mean()
df_products.plot.line()
```

Output

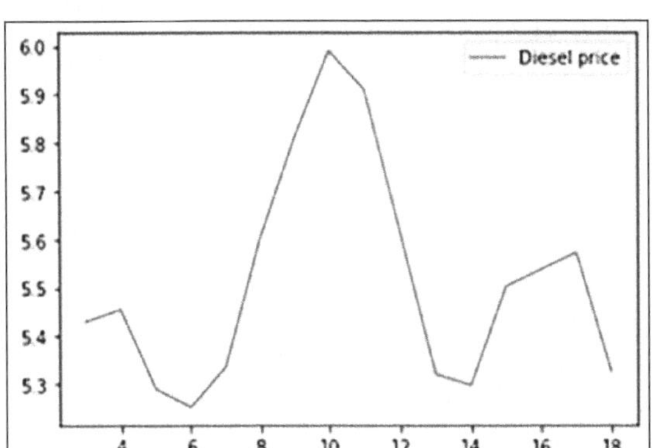

Figure 2.26: *diesel_price filled by Rolling Statistical*

Interpolation: This method assumes a relationship between the range of data points and involves finding and filling missing. This statistical method uses past and future data points with three different approaches: Linear, Spline, and Time.

- **Linear**: Based on the relationship and range of data points, estimate the values and fill data statistically.

```
df_products["Diesel price-linear"]= df_products["Diesel price"].interpolate(option="linear")
df_products.plot.line()
```

Output

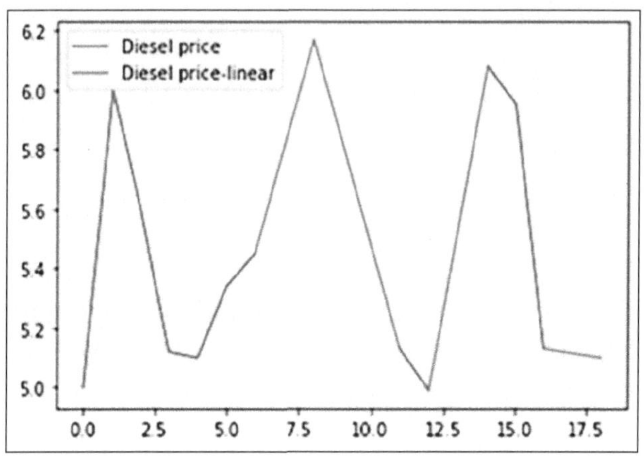

Figure 2.27: *diesel_price filled by Interpolation - linear*

- **Spline**: Minimize overall curvature, estimate the values, and fill data statistically.

```
df_products["Diesel price-spline"]= df_products["Diesel price"].interpolate(option="spline")
df_products.plot.line()
```

Output

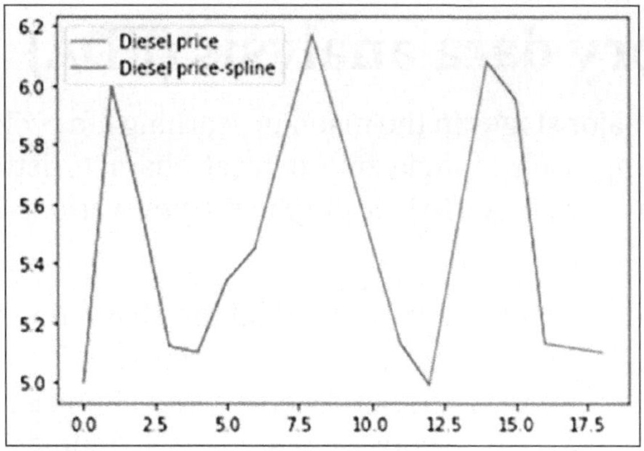

Figure 2.28: *diesel_price filled by Interpolation - spline*

- **Time**: Focus on nearby points and estimate the values and fill in data statistically.

```
df_products["Diesel price-time"]= df_products["Diesel price"].interpolate(option="time")
df_products.plot.line()
```

Output

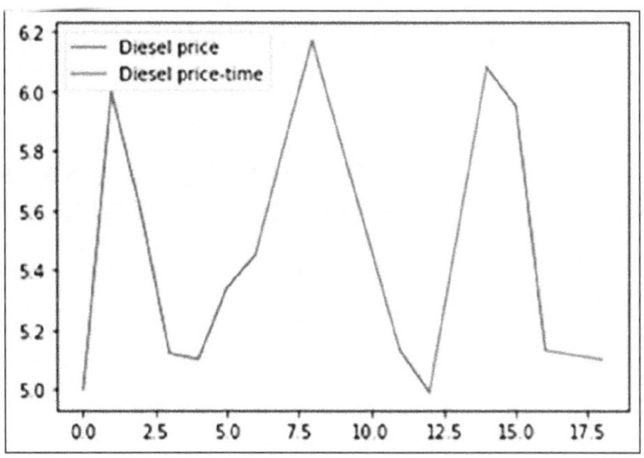

Figure 2.29: *diesel_price filled by Interpolation - time*

Note: Data cleansing and preparation is a major activity in data analytics and advanced data analytics. Since there are different data types available in the dataset, the cleaning process is very tedious. Python programming language provides an excellent feature to implement by handling missing and duplicated data, uniform format, categorical columns, data transformation and time series data.

Exploratory data analysis (EDA)

EDA is one of the major stages in the machine learning life cycle. In simple terms, it is a statistical approach of analyzing dataset characteristics and visualizing them in the form of rich statistical graphics using various data visualization methods.

EDA is mainly used to analyze and understand the characteristics of the dataset from each row and cell either individually or in combinational form by applying Pandas, NumPy, Statistical, and Data visualization libraries. These insights help us to discover patterns, trends, and statistical summaries of graphical or visualization representations.

The EDA process consumes major efforts and necessary steps in machine learning implementation during the data preparation stage.

In the EDA process, we have three different analyses as follows. Based on the nature of these analyses, we can extract the insights using specific visualization techniques.

- Univariate analysis
- Bivariate analysis
- Multi-variate analysis

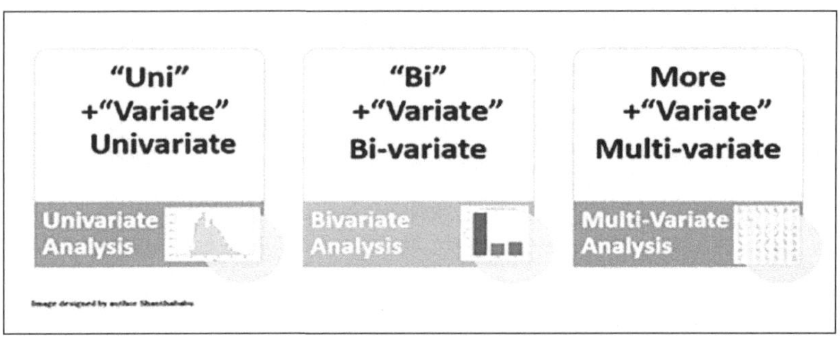

Figure 2.30: *Differnent analysis*

Univariate analysis: In simple terms, Univariate Analysis means dealing with one variable or column. The analysis exhibits the nature of the single column and tells us how data is distributed with the help of histogram, line plot, scatter plot, boxplot, violin plots, bar charts and pie charts.

We will explore various charts and patterns using the **diesel_price** from the **diesel_price.csv** file.

```
import numpy as np
import pandas as pd
import matplotlib.pyplot as plt
import seaborn as sns
%matplotlib inline
df_products = pd.read_csv("diesel_price.csv")
```

Histogram: We can find the **diesel_price** distribution clearly in the following figure.

X-axis: are intervals of values in the Y-axis.

Y-axis: shows the number of times the values are shown in X intervals.

```
plt.hist(df_products["Diesel price"])
```

output

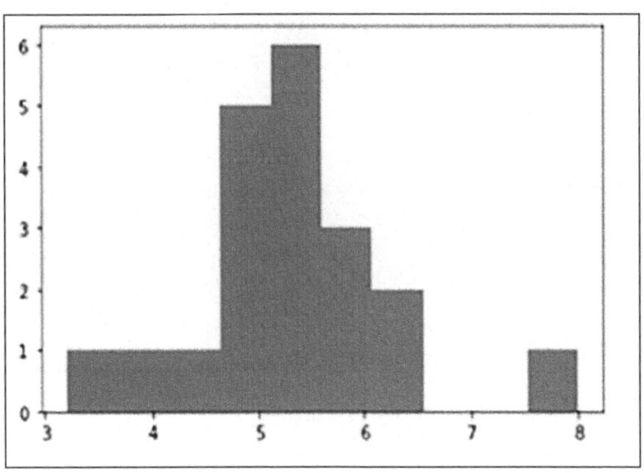

Figure 2.31: *diesel_price in histogram form*

Line plot: We can find the diesel_price variations up and down clearly in the following figure.

```
plt.plot(df_products["Diesel price"])
```

Output

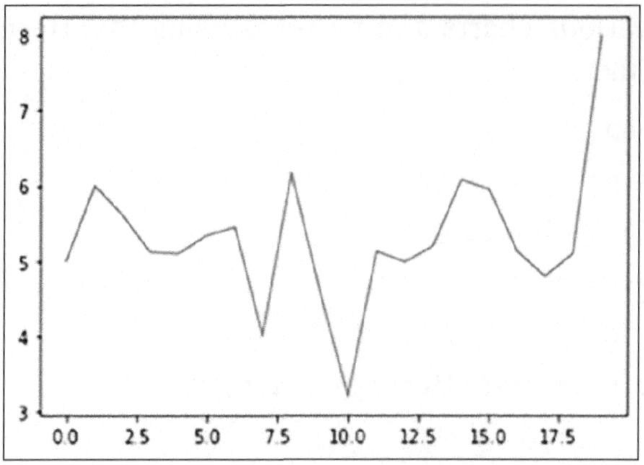

***Figure 2.32:** diesel_price in line chart*

Scatter plot: The plot graphically depicts the distribution of the data concerning Y axis and shows the spread of individual interpretation for a given column.

```
plt.scatter(df_products.index, df_products["Diesel price"])
```

Output

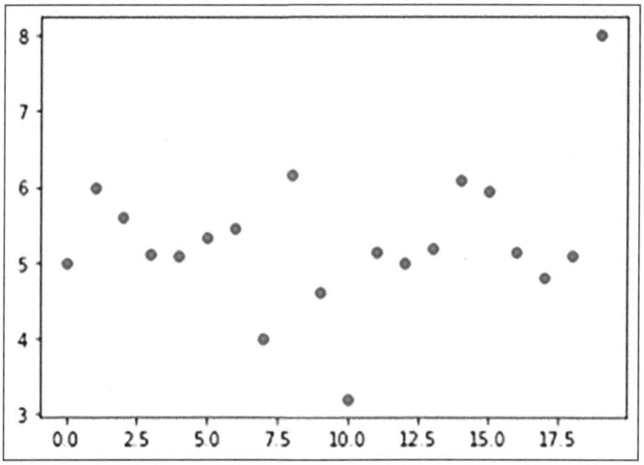

***Figure 2.33:** diesel_price in scatter plot*

Boxplot: This plot graphically depicts the groups of numerical values through their quartiles. The box plot is a summary of the five data in sequential form – minimum, first quartile(Q1), median(Q2), third quartile(Q3), and maximum.

The box spreads from Q1 to Q3, with a line at the median (Q2). In our case, this Q2 will be above 5.0. The whiskers extend from the box edges to show the range of the values from the column.

```
plt.boxplot(df_products["Diesel price"])
```

Output

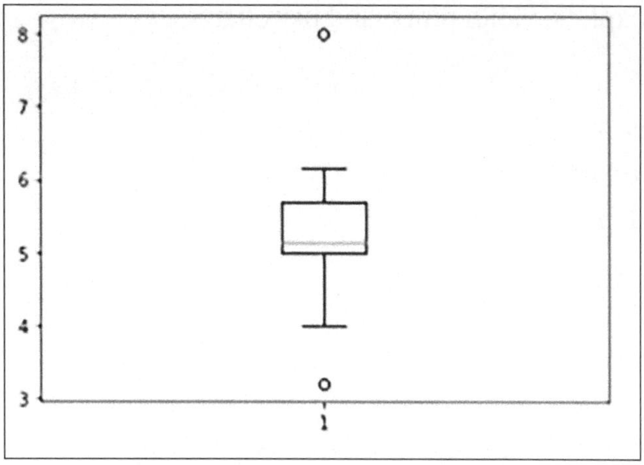

Figure 2.34: *diesel_price in box plot*

Violin plot: It helps to understand the density of the variable and we could observe this in *Figure* 2.35 between 5 and 5.5 on the Y-axis.

```
plt.violinplot(df_products["Diesel price"])
```

Output

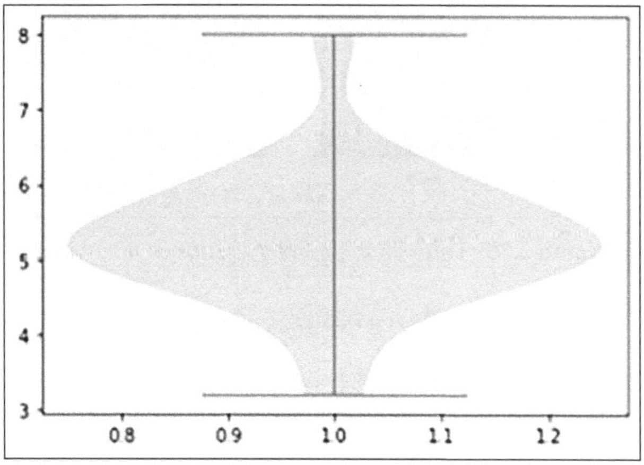

Figure 2.35: *diesel_price in violin plot*

Bi-variate analysis: Like univariate analysis, the bi-variate analysis deals with two variables or columns. This analysis exhibits the correlation between the two columns. We should say this as features or attributes. In data science and machine learning, this technique is used to identify the relationship between dependent and independent variables during feature selection for model building.

We will explore with the help of voter list.csv and plot the following charts: scatter plots, boxplots, violin plots, and bar charts.

Bar plot

```
import numpy as np
import pandas as pd
import matplotlib.pyplot as plt
import seaborn as sns
%matplotlib inline
df_voterslist = pd.read_csv("voters list.csv")

sns.barplot(x='Gender',y='Age',data=df_voterslist )
sns.countplot(x='Gender',data=df_voterslist)
```

Output

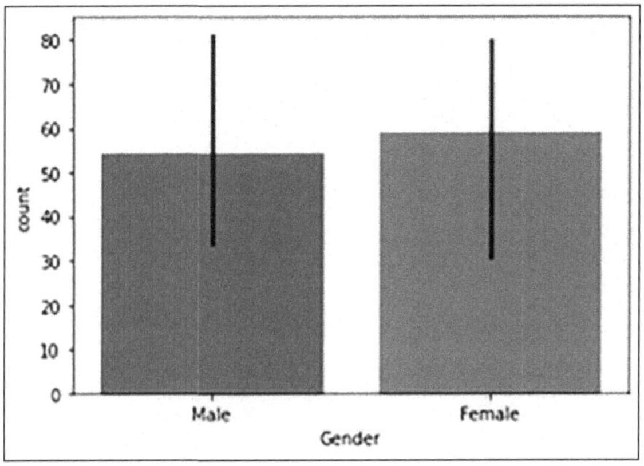

Figure 2.36: *voters list – gender vs. age in a bar plot*

Box plot

```
sns.boxplot( x=df_voterslist["Age"], y=df_voterslist["Gender"],
data=df_voterslist, )
plt.show()
```

Output

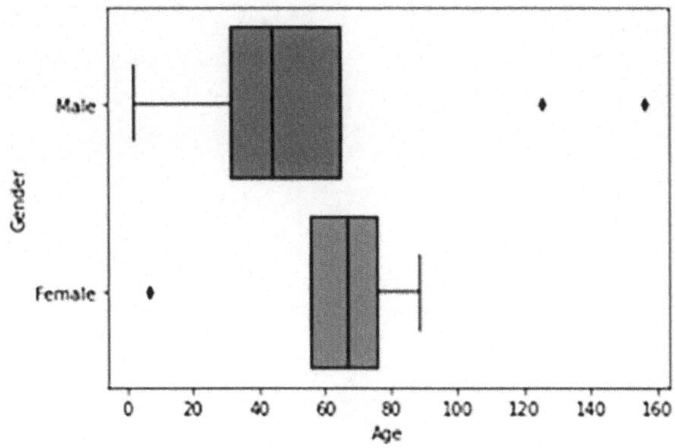

Figure 2.37: *voters list – gender vs. age in the box plot*

Violin plot

```
sns.violinplot(x="Gender", y="Age", data=df_voterslist,palette=
'rainbow')
```

Output

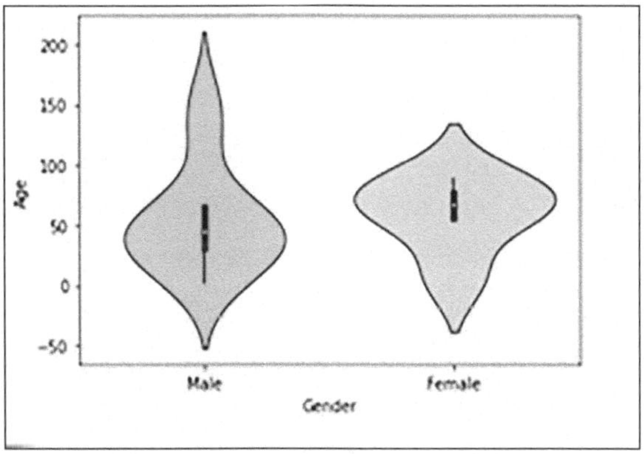

Figure 2.38: *voters list – gender vs. age in violin plot*

Scatter plot

```
plt.scatter(df_voterslist["Age"],df_voterslist["Gender"], c ="blue")
```

Output

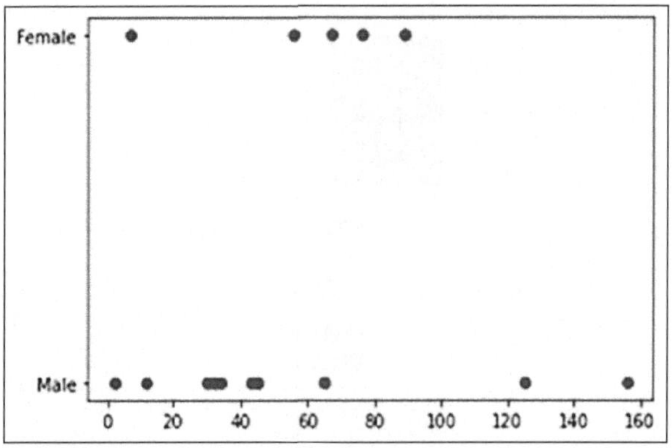

Figure 2.39: *Voters list – Gender Vs Age in violin plot*

EDA for time series

Performing EDA with time series data is a much-needed ability for data scientists and machine learning engineers.

```
import numpy as np
import pandas as pd
import matplotlib.pyplot as plt
import seaborn as sns
%matplotlib inline
df_products = pd.read_csv("diesel_price.csv")
df_products.head(10)
```

Output

	Sale_Date	Diesel price	City
0	16-04-2022	5.00	Chennai
1	17-04-2022	6.00	Bangalore
2	18-04-2022	5.60	Delhi
3	18-04-2022	5.12	Mumbai
4	21-04-2022	5.10	Mumbai
5	22-04-2022	5.34	Chennai
6	24-04-2022	5.45	Bangalore
7	25-04-2022	4.00	Bangalore
8	26-04-2022	6.17	Chennai
9	26-04-2022	4.60	Delhi

Figure 2.40: *Diesel price dataframe*

Box plot: Using a box plot, we can analyze the diesel price for different cities. Our observation is that Delhi has lower values than other cities.

```
sns.boxplot( x=df_products["City"], y=df_products["Diesel price"], data=df_products, )
plt.show()
```

Output

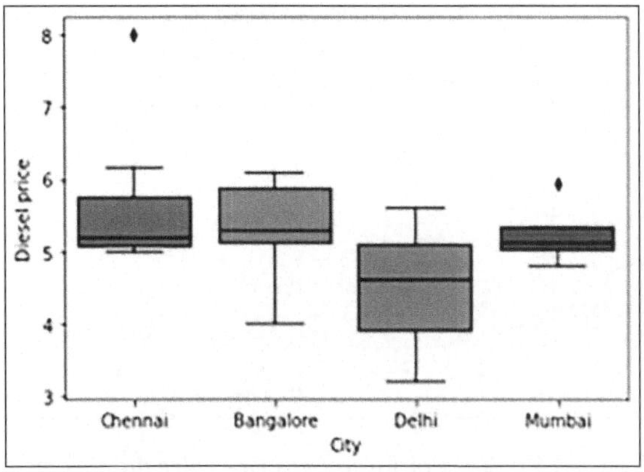

Figure 2.41: *Box plot for diesel price dataframe*

Scatter plot: Using a scatter plot, we can analyze the diesel price with different dates. Our observation is that on the 9th of May, diesel prices are high at $8 and Delhi has lower values on the 16th of April.

```
plt.scatter(df_products["Diesel price"],df_products["Sale_Date"], c
="blue")
```

Output

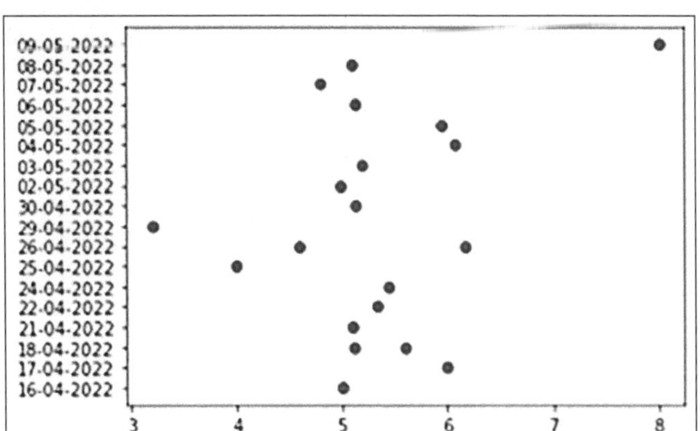

Figure 2.42: *Scatter plot for diesel price sales date vs. price*

Bar plot: Similar to the previous example, plot Diesel Price Sales Date vs. Price in the bar plot.

```
sns.barplot(x='Diesel price',y='Sale_Date',data=df_products)
```

Output

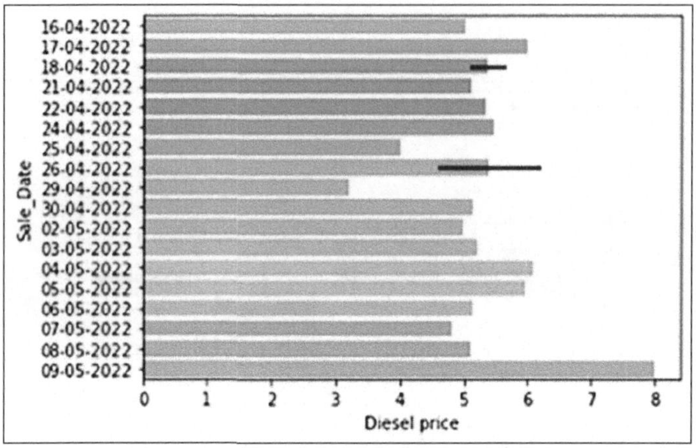

Figure 2.43: *Bar plot for diesel price sales date vs. price*

Violin plot: Using the violin plot, we can analyze the diesel price in different cities. Our observation is Chennai had $4 to $8.6 and Mumbai had $$ to $6.

```
sns.violinplot(x="Cour", y="Diesel price", data=df_products,
palette='rainbow')
```

Output

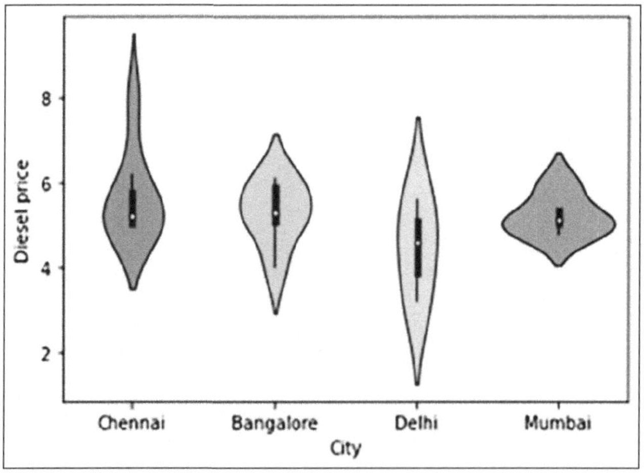

Figure 2.44: *Violin plot for diesel price sales date vs. price*

Note: We have discussed various techniques for handling data and representing them in a precise format to gain insights. Exploring the visualization approach always gives us more clarity. Under the EDA process, there are three different types of analyses -Univariate, Bivariate and Multivariate Analysis. Based on the nature of these techniques, we can extract insights using various visualization techniques.

Conclusion

In this chapter, we have discussed the very detailed objective of data analysis and its benefits, as well as why Python is the best choice for data analytics and data science aspects. We have introduced time series data and delved deep into time series data management and data lifecycle management (DLM) processes. We covered data remediation and also exclusive sections on data cleansing and preparation in terms of handling missing and duplicate data, uniform format, categorical columns and data transformation.

Detailed study of exploratory data analysis has been covered including univariate and bivariate analysis. In the upcoming chapter, we will delve into multivariate analysis focusing on EDA. We also went through various data including time-series data along with classical examples with outputs.

This chapter will provide a solid understanding of data analytics with Python for both beginners and practitioners. In the next chapter, we will discuss the background of time series analysis and its significance along with a detailed walkthrough of time series components and the basics of AR, MA, and ARMA

Points to remember

In this chapter, it is important to keep a few things in mind that will be handy and useful throughout this book

- Python is a powerful programming language that supports massive data analysis and data science projects. It's important to understand that Python is the best choice for data analytics, time series data, and data management.
- It is important to know the concept of Data Lifecycle Management (DLM), its different stages and their importance.
- Understanding the significance of data remediation and its importance.

- It is crucial to understand how to handle data and the various data cleansing processes and preparations for analytics and advanced analytics purposes.
- The topics of Exploratory data analysis (EDA) and various visualization techniques and how to apply them to the dataset are important. We should also learn to generate various plots and charts to gain insight into the data for further analysis.

CHAPTER 3
Time Series Analysis and its Components

Introduction

In the previous chapter, we discussed data analytics, data management, and its lifecycle, exploring the data remediation techniques and their significance. In terms of handling data and various data cleansing processes and preparations for data analytics and advanced analytics purposes, EDA, this chapter will help us understand the background of time series analysis and its importance. We will provide a detailed walk-through of time series component trends, seasonality, cyclic patterns, and irregularities with classical examples. We will learn about the acid test for data stationarity – ADF, and KPSS Test. We will also cover techniques for handling non-stationary data in time series analysis and methods to make time series stationary. We will delve into understanding ACF and PACF in time series and how it helps us understand the time series data and its stationarity.

Structure

In this chapter, we will discuss the following topics:

- Understanding time series analysis (TSA)
- Significance of time series data
- Time series components
    - Trends, seasonality, and cyclic patterns

- Data stationarity testing
  - ADF test
  - KPSS test
- Converting non-stationary data into stationary
  - Differencing, detrending, and transformation
  - ACF and PACF

Time series data analysis

We discussed Time Series Data Management and its classical examples in *Chapter 2: Python for Time Series Data Analysis*. Let's reiterate this chapter with some basic foundation and discuss details.

In TSA, data points are sequential in quantities prepared from various sources over fixed intervals (or) tracking the changes over a period of time. You can represent this by the different graphs on a time basis – the intervals could be minutes, hours, days, weeks, months, and years.

TSA is a well-defined step in extracting insightful and drill-down statistical information presented in meaningful ways.

The sources for TSA are across all domains and increase drastically every nanosecond. Numerous web applications are generating massive data by manual intervention, in manufacturing instruments. Data has been generated by various signaling systems and sensors devices. In recent years, IIoT devices (Industrial Internet of Things), have been constantly extracting the data from manufacturing equipment, and even the health care, pharmacy, banking, and financial service based applications are producing massive data and transferring them along with time stamps, will utilize all these data as time series data analysis. The most competent data from monitoring systems is captured and used for time series analysis to predict and forecast business solutions.

Sale_Date	Diesel price	City
16-04-2022	5	Chennai
17-04-2022	6	Bangalore
18-04-2022	5.6	Delhi
18-04-2022	5.12	Mumbai
21-04-2022	5.1	Mumbai
22-04-2022	5.34	Chennai
24-04-2022	5.45	Bangalore
25-04-2022	4	Bangalore
26-04-2022	6.17	Chennai
26-04-2022	4.6	Delhi
29-04-2022	3.2	Delhi
30-04-2022	5.13	Chennai
02-05-2022	4.99	Chennai
03-05-2022	5.2	Chennai
04-05-2022	6.08	Bangalore
05-05-2022	5.95	Mumbai
06-05-2022	5.13	Bangalore
07-05-2022	4.8	Mumbai
08-05-2022	5.1	Bangalore
09-05-2022	8	Chennai

Figure 3.1: *Sample time series data*

Significance of time series data

The main objective of time series analysis is to identify the time series variables, sequence of observations, and forecast by predicting the future values. Acting as the backbone for prediction and forecasting analysis for the data with time stamps. It would be historical data with patterns, influenced by the variables in different periods and how past data affect the future. We identify and demonstrate numerous time-based analyses and their outcomes, bringing out multiple phases and advantages to business past behavior, accomplishments, forecasting, and planning future operations.

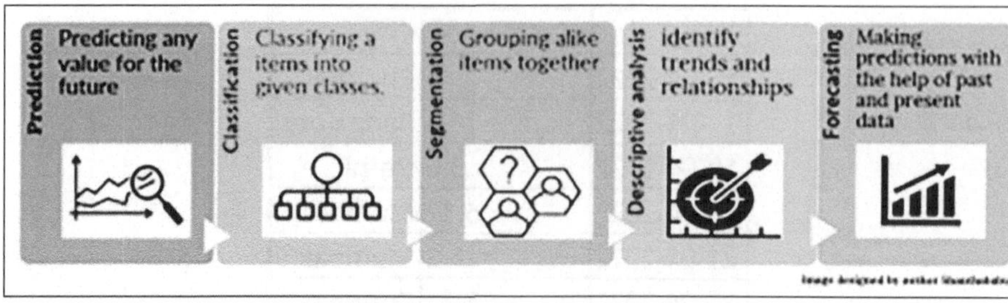

Figure 3.2: *Time-based analysis and results*

Note: Time series can be defined as a collection of well-defined data purely dependent on time, where time acts as an independent variable (or) attribute to estimate the dependent variable(s). It can be defined as follows X1,X2,X3 of variables at time t1,t2,t3 is written in the mathematical equation X=F(t).

Characteristics and components of time series data

So far, we have discussed the various aspects of the time series data, let's focus on the characteristics of time series data before we go and analyze and apply algorithms. When dealing with data in data science or machine learning, there are basic characteristics that we need to understand before diving into the scope of analysis, like prediction and forecasting.

We need to focus on the following three characteristics and understand the core:

- Stationarity
- Trend
- Seasonality

Stationarity

Stationarity is the base characteristic of time series; as the name implies, it is stable to analyze, in which the mean and variance of a time series data do not change over time. All basic and advanced time series data modeling referring to the time series should be **stationary**, which will be discussed in very detail in upcoming chapters.

Stationarity enables us to include the time base frequency effect of the series, as mentioned earlier, in terms of years, months, weeks, days, hours, and minutes.

There are two types of stationarity available: one is strictly stationarity (or) highly stationary, and another is weakly stationary.

- **Strict Stationarity**: In this process, the probability distribution is the same through time and the distribution does not change when shifted in time, it is also called highly stationary.
- **Weakly Stationary:** In this process, the mean and variance keep changing with time, not constant through time on the axis. It is also called wide-sense stationery (WSS) or weak-sense stationery.

From the characteristics of the data that the time series components are derived, let's discuss them as follows:

Trend

A trend depicting the linear behavior of an increase or decrease in the journey of the time series data ultimately allows us to capture the direction of the time series data, this characteristic leads to a better future forecast, and the trend is predictable. In simple terms, it represents a **continuous and long-term change** in time series form.

We can divide the Trend components into two different types based on the behavior of the data: **Secular Trend** and **Sessional Trend.**

- **Secular Trend**: This trend is wavering between upward and downward directions, recording endless data generated or created by nature (temperature, rainfall, and wind speed), human intervention (web application hits) or automated manufacturing devices (IoT). It can increase or decrease the order.
- **Sessional Trend:** This is typically a seasonality pattern; certain of this will occur at predetermined intervals every year. Let's discuss this type in detail.

Seasonality

Seasonality, the term itself, implies a pattern within an interval, mostly that it would be within the year or less than that. The graphical representation of this character is a bell curve or sawtooth form visualization. Seasonality helps us to forecast a good forecasting model that the seasonality occurs each calendar year like the festival sessions – **Christmas, New year, Thanksgiving Day, and Deepavali** are good examples of seasonality, where manufacturers and retailers have come to properly plan and work toward the higher manufacturing of the products and increasing the sales over these festive periods.

Components of time series data

When we talk about components of time series data, all the characteristics we have discussed earlier belong to this component as well, and additionally, there are two major components which are Cyclical and Irregularity, explained as follows:

- **Cyclical:** No fixed intervals and uncertainty in movement and its patterns.
- **Irregularity:** Unexpected situations, events, and spikes in a short span of time. It could be random residual fluctuations. The cost of mandatory things increases during a critical situation in the country.

	Trend	Seasonality	Cyclical	Irregularity
Time	Fixed Time Interval	Fixed Time Interval	Not Fixed Time Interval	Not Fixed Time Interval
Duration	Long and Short Term	Short Term	Long and Short Term	Regular/Irregularity
Prediction Capability	Predictable	Predictable	Challenging	Challenging
Visualisation	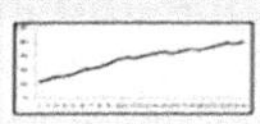	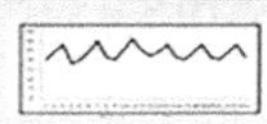	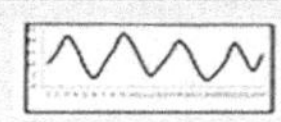	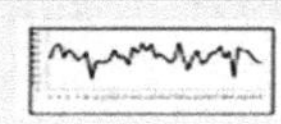

Image designed by author Shanthababu

***Figure 3.3**: Characteristics and Components of Time Series Data*

Note: Time series refers to continuous data points which are observed and recorded over a defined period. The most competent data from monitoring systems is captured and used for time series analysis to predict and forecast business solutions. The time series components are classified based on the nature of the data. Its major components are stationarity, trend, seasonality, cyclical and irregularity.

In time series forecasting, **WHITE NOISE** is an important concept. If the variables are independent of each other and identically distributed with zero meaning, then the time series is said to be white noise. It is a sequence of random numbers that cannot be predicted.

Stationarity versus non-stationarity

In time series analysis, data should be stationary, if not, we have to make them stationary. Three major statistical components are used to check stationarity - mean, variance and covariance. Various statistical tests are available to test the stationarity of the time series data. The root cause for non-stationarity is that the **mean** will not be constant, **variance** will vary with time intervals and **covariance** will be time-dependent.

We have the following options to check the stationarity:

- Visualization
- Statistics
  - Summary of time series data
  - Certain tests on time series data

Figure 3.4 shows the non-stationarity and stationarity time series data representation. We can explore their characteristics in both data models to understand them in detail.

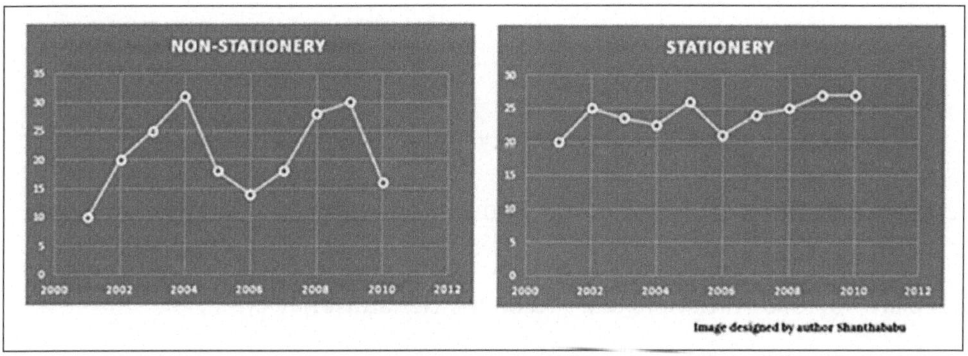

Figure 3.4: *Non-Stationarity and Stationarity Time Series Data*

The characteristics of non-stationarity and stationarity time series data are as follows:

- **Mean:** As per time series analysis, the mean value should be constant over the time.
  - Stationarity – Yes, it is constant.
  - Non-Stationarity – No, it is not a constant. It might increase or decrease.
- **Variance:** As per time series analysis, the spread of data should be constant with time.
  - Stationarity – Yes, it is constant with time.
  - Non- Stationarity – No, it is not a constant, varying with time.
- **Covariance:** As we know, covariance is the relationship between two variables, each dependent on the other.
  - Stationarity – spreads independent of time.
  - Non- Stationarity – spreads are getting closer as time increases.

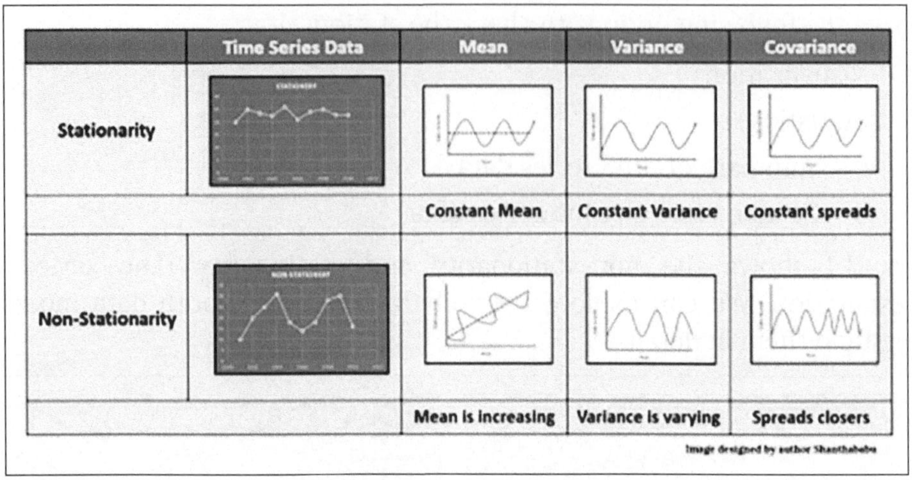

***Figure 3.5**: Characteristics of Non-Stationarity and Stationarity Time Series Data*

We must test the stationarity of the time series data before we take it forward for analysis.

There are various statistical tests to check the stationarity.

The following tests are widely used:

- Augmented Dickey-Fuller (ADF)
- Kwiatkowski-Phillips-Schmidt-Shin (KPSS)

Augmented Dickey-Fuller (ADF)

The ADF test is an extensively used test for checking the stationarity of time series data, and it checks for the null hypothesis presence of a unit root in the data with the following assumptions.

- Null Hypothesis (H0)
  - The series has a **unit root**, or else the series is non-stationary.
- Alternate Hypothesis (HA)
  - The series has **no unit root**, or else the series is stationary.

Here the p-value is the marginal significance for a hypothesis test and the probability of the event, there are two possibilities for this p-value concerning "α", in the stationarity of time series data analysis. α= 0.05 (well-defined level of significance).

- p-value >0.05 Fail to reject (**H0**)
- p-value <= 0.05 Accept (**H1**)

Let's try to find out the p-value using the diesel price dataset:

```
# Load the library - Numpy,Panda,Statsmodels and Matplotlib
import numpy as np
import pandas as pd
import statsmodels.api as sm
from statsmodels.tsa.stattools import adfuller
import matplotlib.pyplot as plt
%matplotlib inline

df_diesel_price = pd.read_csv("diesel_price.csv")
df_diesel_price.head()
```

Output

	Sale_Date	Diesel price
0	16-04-2022	5.00
1	17-04-2022	6.00
2	18-04-2022	5.60
3	18-04-2022	5.12
4	21-04-2022	5.10

Figure 3.6: *Diesel price dataset*

Converting the **Sale_Date** column into a date format (YYYY=MM-DD):

```
df_diesel_price["Sale_Date"]=pd.to_datetime(df_diesel_price["Sale_
Date"],infer_datetime_format=True)
index=df_diesel_price.set_index(["Sale_Date"])
from datetime import datetime
index.head()
```

Output

Sale_Date	Diesel price
2022-04-16	5.00
2022-04-17	6.00
2022-04-18	5.60
2022-04-18	5.12
2022-04-21	5.10

Figure 3.7: *Diesel price dataset (Date formatted)*

Visualization of **`Diesel Price`** versus Date:

```
print("\t\t\t\t*******************************************")
print("\t\t\t\t   Visualization of Diesel Price Vs Date    ")
print("\t\t\t\t*******************************************")
plt.figure(figsize=(12,5))
plt.xlabel("Sale_Date")
plt.ylabel("Diesel price")
plt.plot(index)
```

Output

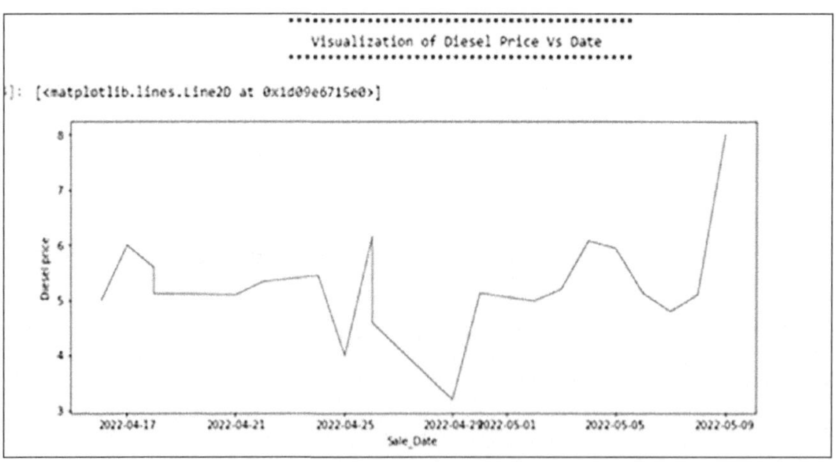

Figure 3.8: *Visualization Of Diesel price dataset*

Let's apply Dickey-Fuller Test to the dataset:

```
print("******************************")
print("Dickey-fuller Test - Result")
print("******************************")
#calling adfuller function for diesel price with autolag='AIC'
df_adftest = adfuller(df_diesel_price["Diesel price"],autolag='AIC')
#getting output from df_adftest
dfoutput=pd.Series(df_adftest[0:4],index=['Test Statistic','
p-value','#lags used','Observation numbers for test'])
for key,value in dftest[4].items():
    dfoutput['critical value (%s)'%key]= value
print(dfoutput)
```

Output

```
******************************
Dickey-Fuller Test - Result
******************************
Test Statistic                  -0.859970
p-value                          0.800869
#lags used                       8.000000
Observation numbers for test    11.000000
critical value (1%)             -4.223238
critical value (5%)             -3.189369
critical value (10%)            -2.729839
dtype: float64
```

Observation

Augmented Dickey-Fuller test: test statistic value -0.859970 is not less than the critical values at the different percentages (1% =>-4.22,5% =>-3.18,10% =>-2.72) In this case, we cannot reject the null hypothesis and we can conclude that data is not stationary.

Kwiatkowski-Phillips-Schmidt-Shin (KPSS) test

KPSS is one of the most common statistical tests used to test whether the time series is stationary or not. Similar to ADF, this test is also used for testing a NULL Hypothesis (H0)

This stationary check is mandatory before we apply the time series models, so this activity is to check if the given dataset is stationary, and if not, the model (AR, MA, ARMA, and ARIMA) cannot be forecasted on non-stationary time series data.

The KPSS test is reversed compared to the ADF test concerning the hypothesis:

- Null Hypothesis (H0)
  - The series has **no unit root**, or else the series is stationary.
- Alternate Hypothesis (HA)
  - The series has a **unit root**, or else the series is non-stationary.

Let's check the stationarity with KPSS:

```
from statsmodels.tsa.stattools import kpss
print("*****************************")
print("KPSS Test - Results          ")
print("*****************************")
kpsstest = kpss(df_diesel_price["Diesel price"], regression="c",
nlags="auto")
kpss_output = pd.Series(kpsstest[0:3], index=["Test Statistic","
p-value","#Lags Used"])
for key,value in kpsstest[3].items():
    kpss_output["Critical Value (%s)"%key] = value
print (kpss_output)
```

```
Output
*****************************
KPSS Test - Results
*****************************
Test Statistic            0.195304
p-value                   0.100000
```

```
#Lags Used                 0.000000
Critical Value (10%)       0.347000
Critical Value (5%)        0.463000
Critical Value (2.5%)      0.574000
Critical Value (1%)        0.739000
dtype: float64
```

Observation

Test statistics are 0.195304

Critical Value (10%) is 0.34700, (5%) is 0.463000, (2.5%) is 0.574000

p-value is 0.1

Test Statistic < Critical Value

p-value > 0.05.

Based on the results, the null hypothesis cannot be rejected. Hence, the series is stationary.

Note: TSA data should be stationarity, if not, we have to make them stationarity.

What is the root cause of non-stationarity? There are three major statistical components in the data itself which are mean, variance and covariance. There is a chance for mean will not be constant, variance will vary with time intervals and covariance will be time dependent.

How can we check this stationarity? The answer is straightforward, using statistical tests like ADF and KPSS to test whether the available data is stationarity or not. ADF test the null hypothesis presence of a unit root in the data and the KPSS test is reversed compared to the ADF test concerning the hypothesis apparently, we are checking Null Hypothesis (H0) and Alternate Hypothesis (HA) to define whether the data is stationarity or not stationarity.

Converting non-stationary data into stationary

So far, we have discussed how to perform the statistical tests to check the stationarity, along with examples using diesel prices and their visualizations to understand better. Let's discuss now how to convert non-stationary to stationary for a given dataset for further stages to apply time series modeling.

To convert non-stationary into stationary, we have three different methods for this conversion, as listed here:

- Differencing
- Detrending
- Transformation

Differencing

This is a method of transforming a time series dataset by computing the difference between consecutive terms in the series, and eliminating varying means from the series, and using to remove the series dependence on time. This method stabilizes the meaning of the time series, reducing the structure of trend and seasonality during this transformation process. We can write the first-order differencing as follows:

$$Y_t = Y_t - Y_{t-1}$$

As mentioned, where Y_t =Value with time.

In the same way, we can define **seasonal differencing**, which is calculated as the difference between a current observation and a previous observation

$$Y_t = Y_t - Y_{t-n}$$

Let's try to implement this with our diesel price dataset:

```
df_diesel_price = pd.read_csv("diesel_price.csv")

df_diesel_price.head()

df_diesel_price["Sale_Date"]=pd.to_datetime(df_diesel_price
["Sale_Date"],infer_datetime_format=True)

index=df_diesel_price.set_index(["Sale_Date"])


df_diesel_price["Sale_Date"].plot()
```

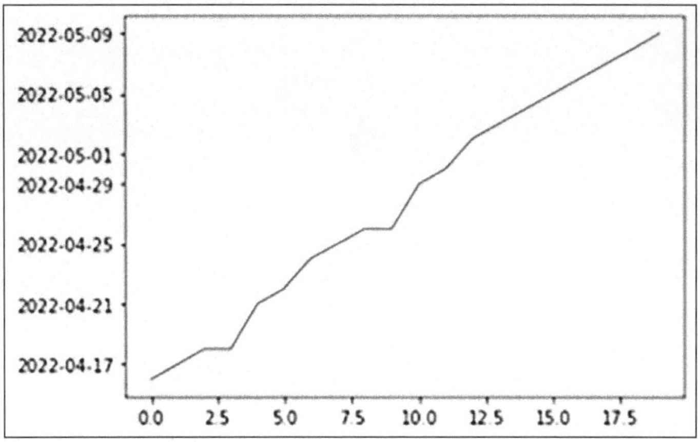

Figure 3.9: *Visualization Of Diesel price dataset before differencing*

```
df_diesel_price["Sale_Date"] = df_diesel_price["Sale_Date"] -
df_diesel_price["Sale_Date"].shift(1)

df_diesel_price["Sale_Date"].plot()
```

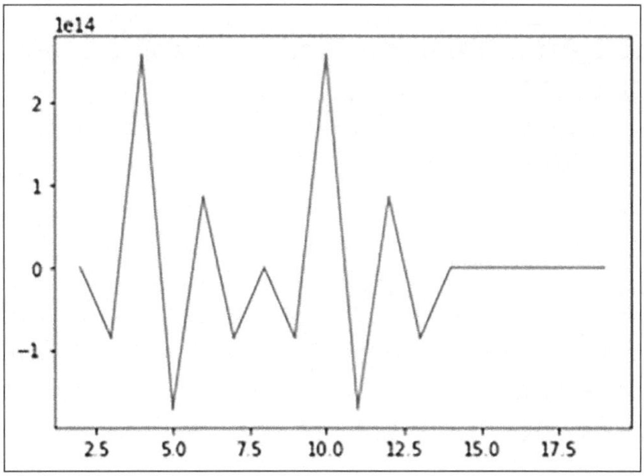

Figure 3.10: *Visualization Of Diesel price dataset after differencing*

Detrending

As the name implies, removing a causing trend in the data. The main reason behind this process is to see sub-trends more easily in the given time series data and identify if those subsets are seasonal or cyclical trends. In this detrending, we could detrend either by detrending or model fitting.

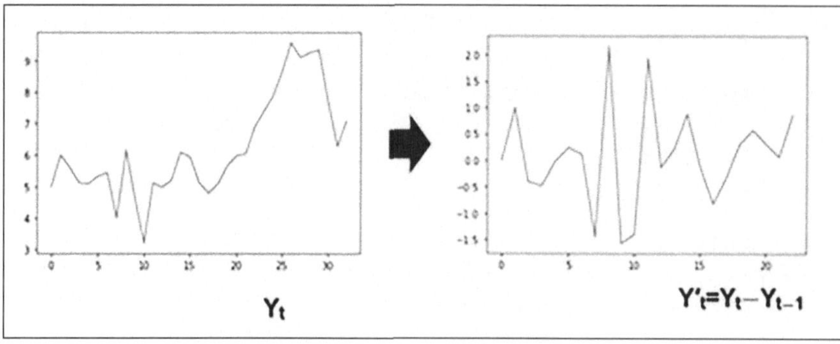

Figure 3.11: *Diesel price detrending*

Detrend by a differencing method

In this method, we are going to create a new dataset, simply getting the difference between the current and the previous observation.

$$Y'_t = Y_t - Y_{t-1}$$

Figure 3.12 shows how to use differencing to detrend the time data series.

Sale_Date	Diesel price	Detrend by a differencing
16-04-2022	5	0
17-04-2022	6	1
18-04-2022	5.6	-0.4
18-04-2022	5.12	-0.48
21-04-2022	5.1	-0.02
22-04-2022	5.34	0.24
24-04-2022	5.45	0.11
25-04-2022	4	-1.45
26-04-2022	6.17	2.17
26-04-2022	4.6	-1.57
29-04-2022	3.2	-1.4
30-04-2022	5.13	1.93
02-05-2022	4.99	-0.14
03-05-2022	5.2	0.21

Figure 3.12: *Diesel price dataset after being detrended by a differencing method*

```
df_diesel_price = pd.read_csv("diesel_price.csv")
df_diesel_price.head()
```

	Sale_Date	Diesel price	Detrend by a differencing
0	16-04-2022	5.00	0.00
1	17-04-2022	6.00	1.00
2	18-04-2022	5.60	-0.40
3	18-04-2022	5.12	-0.48
4	21-04-2022	5.10	-0.02

Figure 3.13: *Diesel price dataframe after being detrended by a differencing method*

Let's plot diesel price:

```
df_diesel_price["Diesel price"].plot()
```

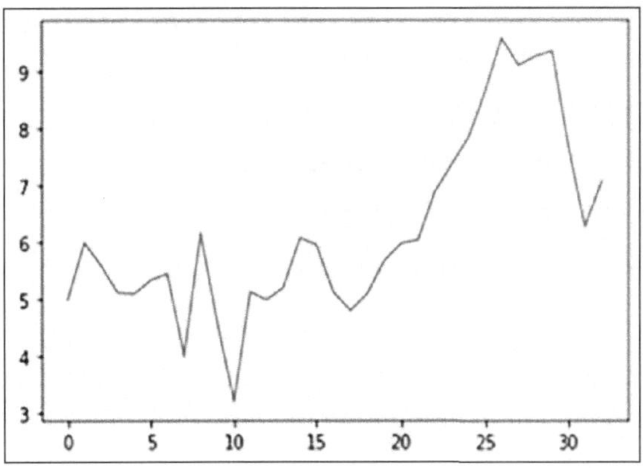

Figure 3.14: *Diesel price plot*

Let's plot diesel prices after they are detrended by a differencing method:

```
df_diesel_price["Detrend by a differencing"].plot()
```

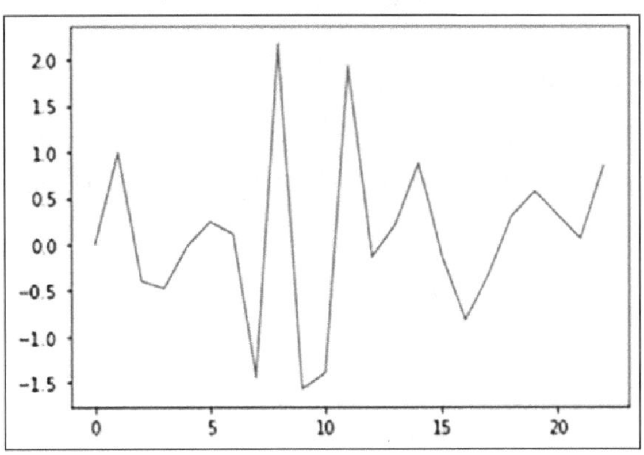

Figure 3.15: *Diesel price plot after being detrended by a differencing method*

Detrend with the model fitting method

In this method, we are going to create a new dataset, using a linear regression model for obtaining a predicted value for each observation in the dataset and calculating the difference between the observed values (original values) and the predicted values from the linear regression model as detrended data.

```
Import numpy as np
import pandas as pd
import seaborn as sns
import warnings
import matplotlib.pyplot as plt
import seaborn as sns
import statsmodels.api as sm
warnings.filterwarnings('ignore')
from klearn.linear_model import LinearRegression
df_diesel_price = pd.read_csv("diesel_price.csv")
```

Add 1 lag to the existing dataframe, create one column and apply a simple linear regression algorithm:

```
df_diesel_price['Lag_1'] = df_diesel_price['Diesel price'].shift(1)
X = df_diesel_price.loc[:, ['Lag_1']]
X.dropna(inplace=True)
y = df_diesel_price.loc[:, 'Diesel price']
y, X = y.align(X, join='inner')
model = LinearRegression()
model.fit(X, y)
y_pred = pd.Series(model.predict(X), index=X.index)
```

You can refer to *Figure 3.13: Diesel price dataframe after being detrended by a differencing method*, and after merging the new predicted column, the dataframe looks as follows:

Sale_Date	Diesel price	Detrend by a differencing	Predicted values
2022-04-16	5.00	0.00	5.26
2022-04-17	6.00	1.00	6.09
2022-04-18	5.60	-0.40	5.76
2022-04-18	5.12	-0.48	5.36
2022-04-21	5.10	-0.02	5.35

Figure 3.16: *Diesel price plot after being detrended by a model fitting method*

```
df_diesel_price["Detrend After  Predicted"].plot()
```

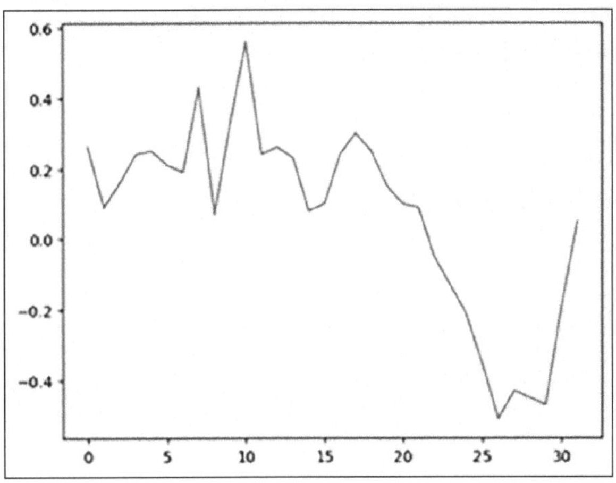

Figure 3.17: *Diesel price plot after being detrended by a model fitting method*

Figure 3.18 shows how non-stationary is converted to stationary:

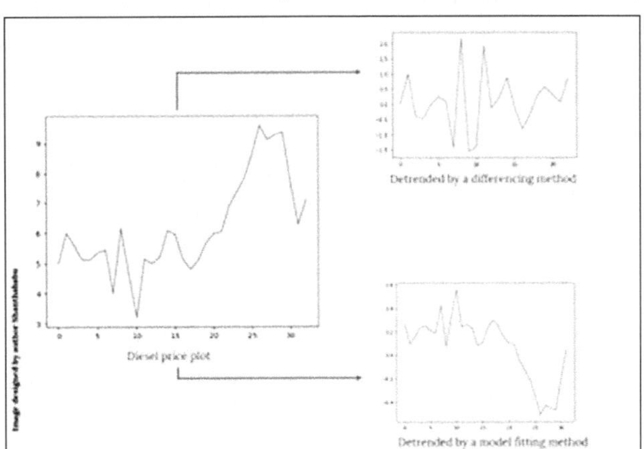

Figure 3.18: *Converting Non-Stationary into Stationary*

Transformation

In this technique, certain transformations are applied to the time series data, which are as follows:

- Power Transform
    - Log Transfer
    - Square Root
- Cube root

Power Transform: The square root transform and log transform belong to a class of transforms called power transforms.

Square Root: This is a straightforward method by applying the NumPy sqrt function on the diesel price column.

```
#Transformation - Square Root
df_log=np.sqrt(df_diesel_price["Diesel price"])
df_diff_diesel_price=df_log.diff().dropna()
```

New dataframe after applying to square root:

```
df_diff_diesel_price.head(5)
1     0.213422
2    -0.083058
3    -0.103690
4    -0.004424
5     0.052526
Name: Diesel price, dtype: float64
```

Note: 5 SQRT is 0.213422

Let's plot df_diff_diesel_price:

```
df_diff_diesel_price.plot()
```

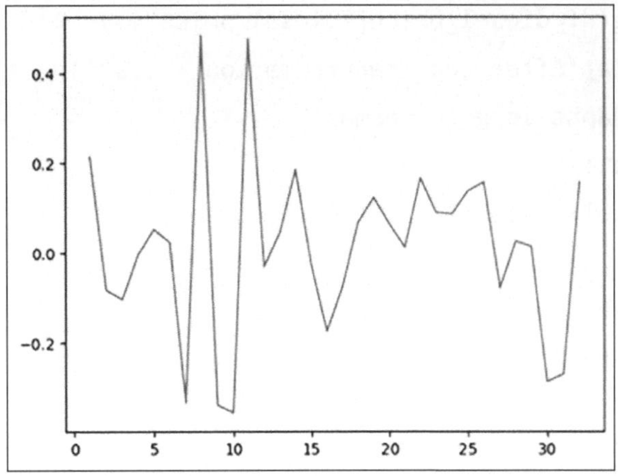

Figure 3.19: *Transformation - Square Root plot (Converting Non-Stationary into Stationary)*

Log Transfer: This is a straightforward method of applying the log function in the diesel price column. Here, each variable x is replaced with a log(x) with and line plot histogram.

```
from matplotlib import pyplot
from math import exp
from the numpy import log

print("\t\t\t*************************************************")
print("\t\t\t    Before and After Log - Transformation       ")
print("\t\t\t               Data Distribution                ")
print("\t\t\t*************************************************")
fig, ax = plt.subplots(2, 2)
# line plot
ax[0,0].plot(df_diesel_price["Diesel price"])
ax[0, 0].set_title('Before Transformation')
# histogram
ax[0,1].hist(df_diesel_price["Diesel price"])
ax[0,1].set_title('Before Transformation - Hist')

ax[1,0].plot(log(df_diesel_price["Diesel price"]))
ax[1,0].set_title('After Log Transformation')
# histogram
```

```
ax[1,1].hist(log(df_diesel_price["Diesel price"]))
ax[1,1].set_title('After Log Transformation - Hist')
#plotting the graphs in grid format
for axf in ax.flat:
    axf.set(xlabel='x-label', ylabel='y-label')

for axf in ax.flat:
    axf.label_outer()
```

The following figure shows the plot to view the original and the log-transformed distribution of the data.

```
************************************************
Before and After Log - Transformation
Data Distribution
***********************************************
```

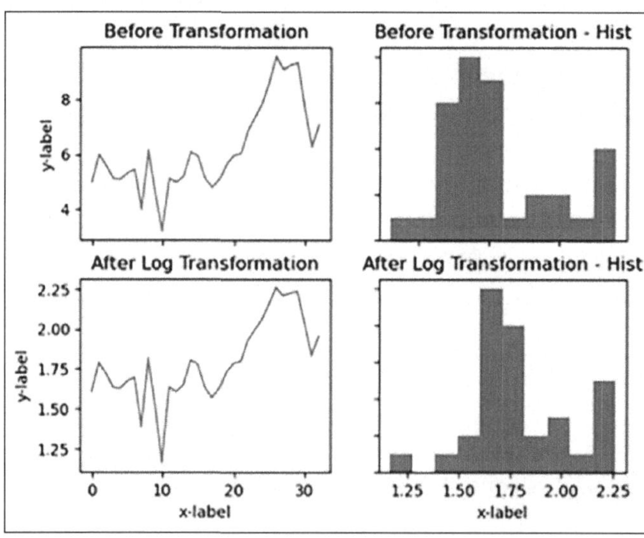

Figure 3.20: *Log Transformation - (Converting Non-Stationary into Stationary) and histogram*

Cube Root: This is also very similar to Log and Sqrt transformation in a variable.

```
print("\t\t\t************************************************")
print("\t\t\t    Before and After Cube root - Transformation ")
```

```
print("\t\t\t*************************************************")
fig, ax = plt.subplots(2, 2)
# line plot
ax[0,0].plot(df_diesel_price["Diesel price"])
ax[0,0].set_title('Before Transformation')

# histogram
ax[0,1].hist(df_diesel_price["Diesel price"])
ax[0,1].set_title('Before Transformation - Hist')

ax[1,0].plot(np.cbrt(df_diesel_price["Diesel price"]))
ax[1,0].set_title('After Log Transformation')



# histogram
ax[1,1].hist(np.cbrt(df_diesel_price["Diesel price"]))
ax[1,1].set_title('After Cube Root Transformation - Hist')

#plotting the graphs in grid format
for axf in ax.flat:
    axf.set(xlabel='x-label', ylabel='y-label')

for axf in ax.flat:
    axf.label_outer()
```

The following figure shows the plot to view the original and the cube root transformed the distribution of the data.

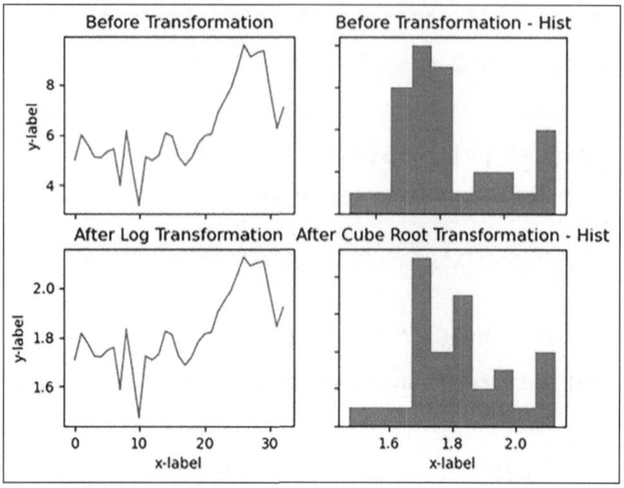

***Figure 3.21**: Cube Root Transformation - (Converting Non-Stationary into Stationary) and histogram*

Note: Converting non-stationary into stationary is a mandatory task in TSA, we have three different methods to convert data into stationary. Differencing and Detrending - with a differencing method, the model fitting method. The transformation method has power transform (log and square root) and cube root.

Before we explore AR, MA, and ARMA models, you should understand the correlation function.

- Auto-Correlation Function (ACF)
- Partial Auto-Correlation Function (PACF)

Auto-Correlation Function (ACF)

It measures the degree of relationship between a given time series data and the lagged version of the time series data at different intervals. In simple terms, the coefficient of correlation between two values in a time series data. Sample white noise value approximately 0 for all lags other than 0. This is symmetrical concerning positive and negative lags.

```
from statsmodels.graphics.tsaplots import plot_acf
plot_acf(df_diesel_price["Diesel price"])
plt.show()
plot_acf(df_diesel_price["Diesel price"], lags=30)
plt.show()
```

The following figure shows the plot for Auto-Correlation Function (ACF):

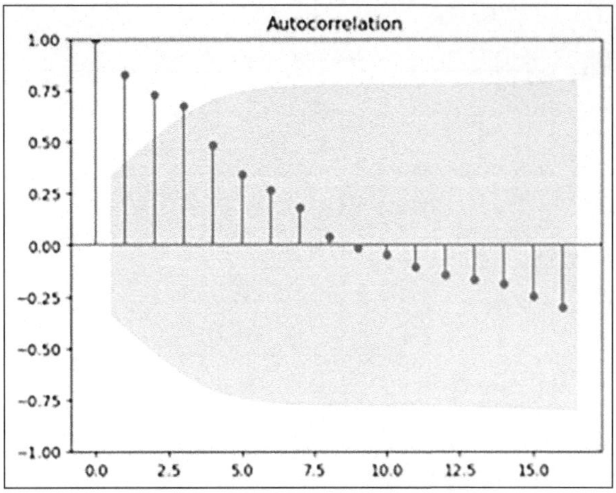

Figure 3.22: ACF *for diesel_price*

Figure 3.23 shows the plot for Auto-Correlation Function (ACF) for 30 lags:

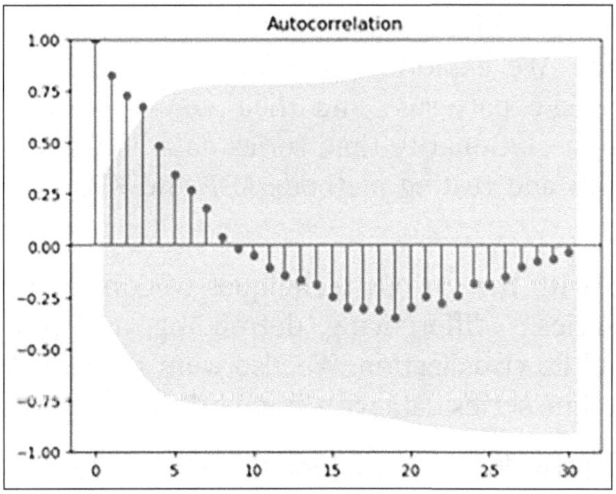

Figure 3.23: ACF *for diesel_price for 30 lags*

Partial Auto-Correlation Function (PACF)

PACF is a little more challenging to understand than the auto-correlation function and the partial correlation of a stationary time series with its own lagged values. The relationship between an observation in a time series with prior time steps and with the removed observations intervening relationships.

```
from statsmodels.graphics.tsaplots import plot_pacf
plt.rc("figure", figsize=(8,5))
```

```
plot_acf(df_diesel_price["Diesel price"])
pyplot.show()
```

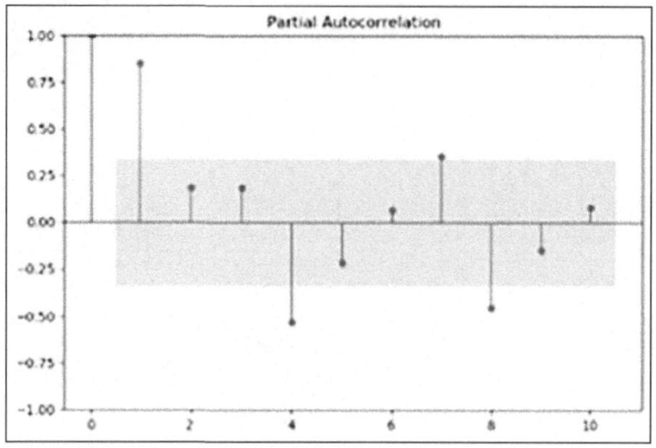

Figure 3.24: *PACF for diesel_price for 10 lags*

Conclusion

In this chapter, we have discussed the detailed studies of time series analysis and its significance. We explored various time series components - trends, seasonality, and cyclic patterns- and their comparisons. Detailed study of stationarity and non-stationarity time series data and the factors influencing their characteristics and testing methods ADF and KPSS, along with classical examples.

We experimented with the various techniques to convert non-stationary into stationary time series - differencing, detrending, and transformation- with sample dataset and its visualization. We also went through ACF and PACF and how to work with time series data with standard examples with outputs.

This chapter will provide a solid understanding of time series data and its components, characteristics, and various techniques to analyze the data and convert them into stationary form.

In the next chapter, we will discuss the opportunity and scope of time series analysis and forecasting and its benefits in business and industries in terms of price prediction in retail, forecasting in healthcare for diagnosis, and medication planning. We will also discuss about anomaly detection in cyber security and predictive maintenance in automotive. The chapter also covers the challenges and major drawbacks of time series forecasting.

Points to remember

In this chapter, it is important to keep a few things in mind that will be handy throughout this book:

- Understanding time series analysis and its significance with classical examples.
- The time series components are classified based on the nature of the data. Its major components are stationarity, trend, seasonality, cyclical, and irregularity.
- What are the root causes of non-stationarity, and what are the statistical components in the given data **mean, variance and covariance.**
- Check the stationarity techniques using statistical tests like **ADF** and **KPSS** to evaluate whether the given data is stationarity or not.
- ADF evaluates the null hypothesis presence of a unit root in the data, and the KPSS test is reversed compared to the ADF test concerning the hypothesis.
- We are checking the Null Hypothesis (H0) and Alternate Hypothesis (HA) to define whether the data is stationarity or not stationarity using ADF and KPSS.
- Converting non-stationary into stationary is a mandatory task in time series analyses. We have three different methods to convert data into stationary. Differencing and Detrending - with a differencing method, the model fitting method. The transformation method has Power Transform (Log and Square Root) and Cube Root.

CHAPTER 4
Time Series Analysis and Forecasting Opportunities in Various Industries

Introduction

In the previous chapter, we discussed in very detail the background of time series analysis and its significance. We dived deep into a clear understanding of time series component trends, seasonality, cyclic patterns, and irregularities with classical examples. We tested data stationarity using ADF and KPSS techniques, converting non-stationary into stationary processes and techniques, and understanding ACF and PACF in time series, and how it helps to understand the time series data and its stationarity perspectives. This chapter will help us understand the opportunity and scope of time series analysis and forecasting in business and industry, the benefits of time series analysis in forecasting, demand forecasting and price prediction in retail, forecasting in healthcare for diagnosis of diseases and medication planning, and also anomaly detection - cyber security, predictive maintenance, and the challenges and major drawbacks of time series forecasting.

Structure

In this chapter, we will discuss the following topics:

- Opportunity and scope of time series analysis and forecasting (TSA&F)
- Scope and benefits of time series analysis in forecasting
- Challenges and major drawbacks of time series forecasting
- Case studies on TSA&F
  - Price prediction in retail
  - Forecasting in healthcare for diagnosis
  - Predictive maintenance and anomaly detection

Opportunity and scope of TSA&F

Time series analysis and forecasting are the finest opportunities based on historical time-stamped data. It involves constructing time series analytics and models through historical time-based analysis to drive future decision-making strategies.

Opportunities are wider and limitless for TSA&F. The following domains are utilizing their historical data to get the benefits and enhance the business opportunities:

- Business development and its processes
- Healthcare and medical instruments
- Banking and financial services
- Weather forecasting and safety measurements
- Manufacturing processes and quality control
- Retail products, services, and forecasting
- Marketing and sales analysis and forecasting
- Budget and economic growth forecasting
- Order management and inventory forecasting
- Social media analysis and forecasting

Figure 4.1: *Opportunities Of TSA&F*

This chapter will explore some of the leading domains mentioned in the preceding list in terms of scope and use cases perspective, functional models and implementations of TSA&F.

Good forecasting works with clean, time-stamped data and can identify genuine trends and patterns in historical data. Analysts can tell the difference between random fluctuations and outliers and can separate genuine insights from seasonal variations. The major objective of time series analysis is to show the outcomes based on the data and how it changes over the period, and the data changing gives us the right direction and leads to suitable forecasting. There are many types of TSA&F techniques available which are as follows:

- Autoregression (AR)
- Moving Average (MA)
- Autoregressive Moving Average (ARMA)
- Autoregressive Integrated Moving Average (ARIMA)
- Seasonal Autoregressive Integrated Moving Average (SARIMA)

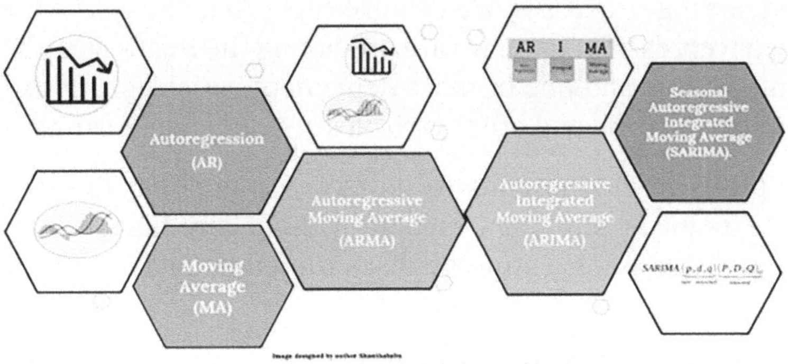

Figure 4.2: *TSA&F techniques*

Scope of price prediction

Let's understand how price prediction works.

We know that machine learning models use both data analysis and algorithms in the price forecasting process.

In data analysis, we look into the prices from historical data along with individual countries' economic growth rates and other closely related factors, and formulate an adjacent price value.

All these steps look at various internal and external factors, including the season and demands, and from there, will try to figure out what consumer is most likely to buy. It would be anything households, buying houses in a specific area, favorite car, bike, choice of dress, food, and movie tickets. Based on the consumer's choice, the price will be decided across all industries.

Figure 4.3: *Scope of price prediction*

In machine learning processes, we can use regression analysis either single or multiple linear regression. Here, we are predicting the relationship between one independent variable and one or more dependent variables. In this the price is the independent variable and other variables are dependent variables.

Automated price prediction aims to develop a model capable of finding the optimal price point at any point in time without any human input. If you're looking for a reliable pricing strategy that's rooted in data, this is the approach for you.

Benefits of forecasting in price prediction:

- A better understanding of the consumer base
- Increase company revenue and marginal profits
- Understand the competitor's strengths and weaknesses
- Predicting financial risk and mitigating processes
- Differing the price of the product and service-based consumer responses

Scope of forecasting in healthcare for diagnosis

In the healthcare industry, *Health Forecasting* is highly valuable, and the most demand is for predicting future health events or situations of the inpatients and outpatients for any clinic to provide value for health services and healthcare needs.

Process and implement health forecasting except for trustworthy and reliable data from genuine sources and the selection of the right analytical tools and techniques for the prediction of particular health conditions and consistency.

Opportunities for creating a *Machine Learning* model and providing remote healthcare processes and services through personalized treatment and medical advice from clinics and hospitals reduce risk and provide appropriate treatment to patients.

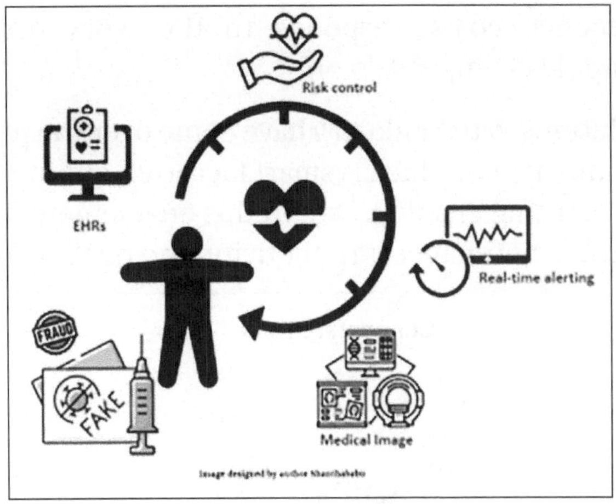

***Figure 4.4**: Scope of forecasting in healthcare for diagnosis*

Health forecasting describes the major issues that are essential for safeguarding health, based on the properties of health data along with classifications, and expectations which influence health forecasting methods and the choices of treatments. Remember, there is no single approach to derive the health forecasting methods since it depends on multiple factors, and so diverse methods have often been accepted and followed to forecast specific health conditions. There are no certain time frames for mapping the health forecasting methods and specific approaches that are often applied to health care issues and challenges.

Benefits of forecasting in healthcare:

- High-quality and continuous healthcare services for patient-centralized services
- Protective and risk-free care with a high rate of accuracy in diagnosis
- Mush improvement in diagnostics and services through an insights-driven approach
- Highly enhanced operational competence and cost-effectiveness
- Personalized and customized medical care for individual populations

Scope of predictive maintenance

In the manufacturing industry determining the conditions and performance of equipment is the major activity, this is so-called predictive maintenance; here the equipment is evaluated when maintenance should be performed. Thus, it minimizes unforeseen device downtime, extends the equipment lifecycle, decreases maintenance costs, responds to the work order pipelines and strengthens the supply chain, and so on.

We know the revolutions in the industry have come over the past many years and now we are all in industry 4.0, which is smart factories, autonomous systems, IoT, IIOT and machine learning enabled. Due to this enablement, the manufacturing industry's predictive maintenance, productivity, and quality are much improved.

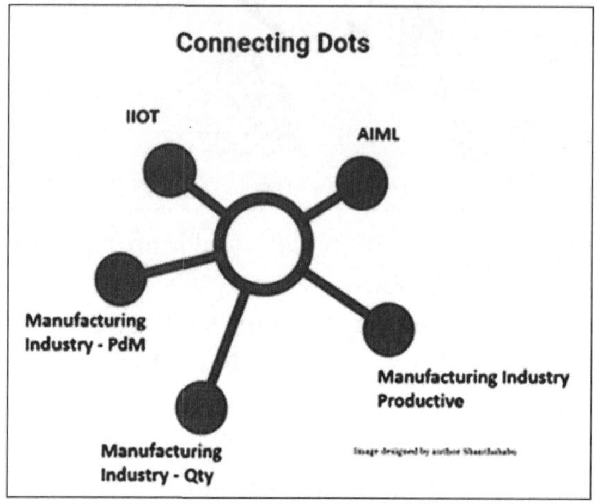

***Figure 4.5**: Connecting dots in manufacturing industry*

Using IoT or IIoT sensors in the equipment of machinery and sensing the outcome data collected from them was implemented with the help of a programmable interface controller and the data were collected and stored in a time series sequence. With the help of the data analytics lifecycle, the data has been pre-processed, cleaned, analyzed, and applied to the modeling techniques, then extracted the insights and the predictions which are used to provide necessary maintenance decisions.

The analysis decisively helps us to obtain more information, insights, and prediction about the equipment and its overall status. This would help the manufacturing floor-level operational team to determine the equipment's operational situation before unexpected anomalies occur in the manufacturing plant and prevent unexpected losses, thus improving the quality of services and equipment.

The major objective of preventive maintenance is to reduce asset degeneration, reduce downtime, and reduce maintenance costs.

Preventive maintenance is planned maintenance that increases the survival of company assets, equipment, and infrastructure. It is the process of maintaining equipment or a system in order to prevent failures. The process involves general maintenance like cleaning, lubrication, replacements, and repairs.

The most widely used sensors in the manufacturing industry are thermal sensors and vibration meters. These sensors are installed on equipment along with the server facilities to provide automated alerts when the equipment vents are in danger of overheating. Vibration meters are attached to centrifugal pump motors to identify unusual spikes in acceleration based on historical data.

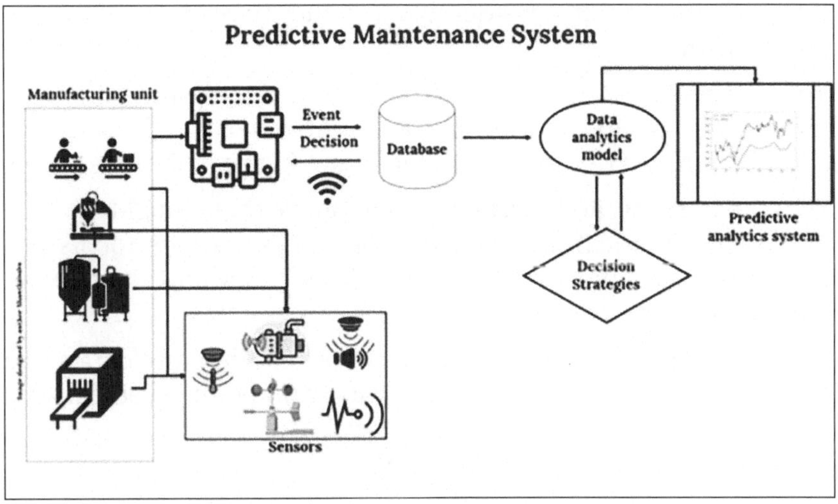

Figure 4.6: *Predictive Maintenance System*

Benefits of predictive maintenance:

- High-quality and service-oriented individual equipment with improved performance
- Protective and risk-free equipment(s) with a high rate of performance
- Prevent equipment failures and decrease maintenance downtime
- Reduced spare parts costs and improved supply chain management
- Enhanced operational and maintenance efficiency

Challenges with TSA&F

Any technology or technique that has its limitations and challenges in dealing with unpredictable and undetermined scenarios, with respect to time series forecasting techniques in machine learning, is not an exceptional case.

There are no defined rules for when you should or should not use time series analysis and forecasting; this is purely dependent on data and the models you can support. We must remember that not all machine learning models fit every dataset. Moreover, for the problem statement and capabilities to ask questions and get answers, they must clearly understand the data analytics and machine learning team and choose the time series analysis and forecasting.

The major challenges with TSA&F irrespective of any domains are as follows:

- **Data sufficiency and accuracy:** For TSA&F, we certainly need a huge volume of data to derive accuracy, so data collection is a tedious task. If the volume is not considerable at hand, then the accuracy might be questionable.
- **Assumptions:** Since we are considering the historical data for any forecasting method, this leads to assumptions or rough calculations. This approach makes our forecasts inaccurate in the worst-case scenario.
- **Data sensitivity and outliers:** Sometimes there might be a sensitive outlier in historical data and unavoidable situations for us to remove them from the dataset and go with that as it may impact our analysis and forecasting outcomes.
- **More testing and training:** TSA&F might require more data and effort to test and train the model than other data sources and problem statements.

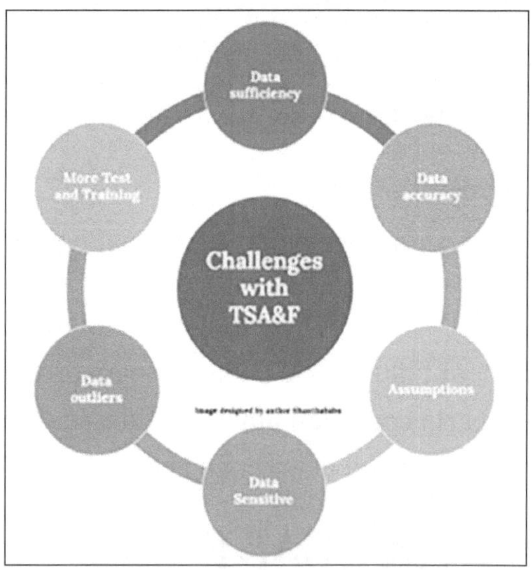

***Figure 4.7**: Challenges with TSA&F*

Case studies

Some case studies on TSA&F are explained here.

Price prediction in retail and use case

Every business domain must find a way to sustain itself in this large market demand and be highly competitive with other competitors. Customers try to stick to a specific product due to multiple benefits and choices to choose from the list of products and services available in the market. This would be because of the price coming down to their budget and they can acquire such products easily from the market either in shops or online with additional benefits and cashback options.

But retailers and sellers have to offer the best possible prices with required profit price prediction; this should be a competitive price for the company and set all market demands.

Price prediction is one of the major exercises in any industry, specifically in the retail industry. This key factor is directly proportional to increasing customer engagement in the product and faithfulness with manufacturers and producers in a highly competitive market.

The price of the product should reflect the prices of goods and services using exact data collected from in-house historical data related to earlier sales and used to predict expected sales. Customers are more likely to trust the product and company's business processes.

Data analytics and machine learning help us predict the price using various tools and techniques. Price prediction uses different algorithms to analyze a product and its service in the market based on its characteristics, demand, and trends. In the end, the machine learning models predict and recommend the price to attract customers and maximize sales at different levels. We will discuss the theoretical part of this chapter and deep-dive technical implementations in the upcoming chapters.

The three basic types of price predictions are as follows:

- Qualitative techniques
- Time series analysis and projection,
- Causal models.

We have a list of proven advanced techniques which are available to predict as follows, and most industries are using them. We will discuss all TSA&F techniques in great detail in the upcoming chapters.

Let's discuss how to create a workflow for price prediction:

This price prediction is also called **predictive pricing** or **pricing forecasting**. Generally, this would be skeptical for most of us. So, keep in mind that price prediction is an estimate of the number of expected products and services on demand from the customer side in the current situation, and sales or services provided over a period of time would be seasonal and regular. All these factors are to be considered during the price prediction of any high-demand product in the market.

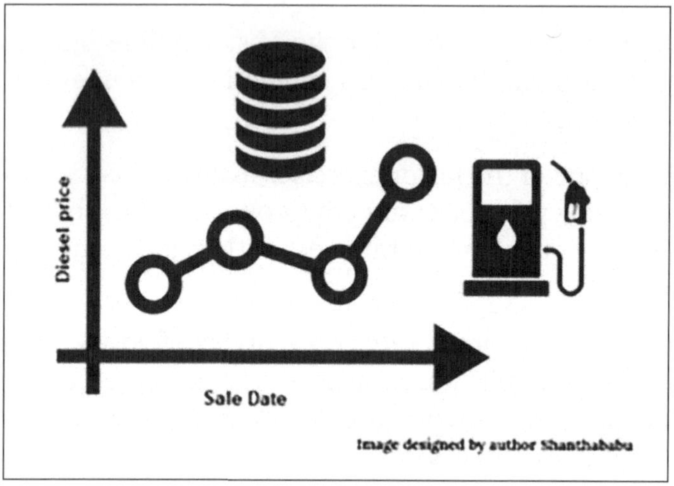

***Figure 4.8**: Price prediction in retail and use case*

This will also include the product cost, as well as the estimated profit which was derived by the company.

To build the workflow, here are the typical steps you'll need to take care of and create a price prediction:

- Collecting historical data demand and sales reports (Dataset)
    - List out the products and services
    - Approximate demand for products and services in the current market
    - Determine the cost of the product or services
- Set up the ML process with the required steps (this process is common across all use cases)

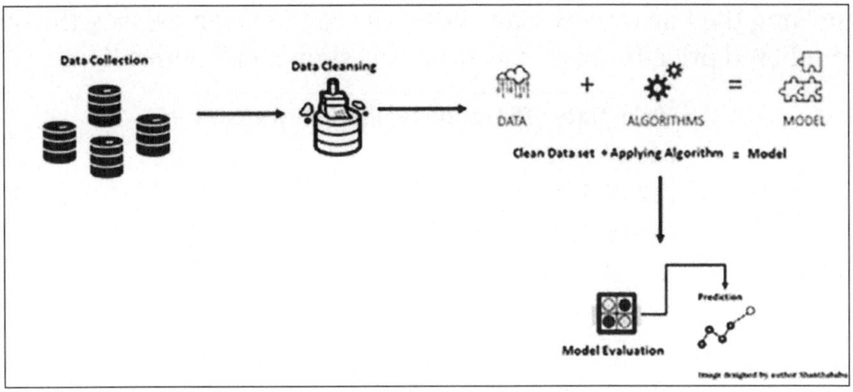

Figure 4.9: *Machine Learning life cycle process for prediction*

EDA and Stationarity Analysis

In *Chapter 2, Python for Time Series Data Analysis* and *Chapter 3, Time Series Analysis and its Components*, we have discussed various aspects of time series analysis and data stationarity testing methods, converting non-stationary into stationary processes in great detail, along with numerous sample codes and visualizations.

The given diesel price dataset is shown in *Figure 4.10*, and we are very familiar with this. The prediction would be decided by the historical data concerning the date.

Sale_Date	Diesel price
16-04-2022	5
17-04-2022	6
18-04-2022	5.6
18-04-2022	5.12
21-04-2022	5.1
22-04-2022	5.34
24-04-2022	5.45
25-04-2022	4
26-04-2022	6.17
26-04-2022	4.6
29-04-2022	3.2

Figure 4.10: *Diesel price dataset*

After applying the linear regression algorithm to the given dataset, the outcome of the predicted price for each row will be as shown in *Figure* 4.11.

Sale_Date	Diesel price	Predicted values
16-04-2022	5	5.26
17-04-2022	6	6.09
18-04-2022	5.6	5.76
18-04-2022	5.12	5.36
21-04-2022	5.1	5.35
22-04-2022	5.34	5.55
24-04-2022	5.45	5.64
25-04-2022	4	4.43
26-04-2022	6.17	6.24
26-04-2022	4.6	4.93
29-04-2022	3.2	3.76

***Figure* 4.11**: *Diesel price dataset with prediction column*

Benefits of price prediction systems:

- Data science techniques are used to analyze multiple data sources in a single place and extract insights and correlations
- Improved price predictions and profit margins with high accuracy
- Understand the price fluctuations of a product and service
- Machine learning algorithms help to observe price volatility at regular intervals and predict prices

Forecasting in healthcare for diagnosis and use case

In the previous session, we have discussed about the price prediction in the retail sector along with diesel price prediction. Now, forecasting in healthcare for diagnosis is another major benefit of TSA&F aspects. Let's bring the classic use case to healthcare.

In the healthcare industry, data analytics and machine learning techniques have been potentially transforming heavily as human lifespan increases in terms of individual and population levels. Essentially, it identifies insights in the form of trends and patterns and helps us to diagnose diseases and prevent them faster, and improve the quality of life and valuable care for patients.

In healthcare, there should be accurate forecasting with the help of a huge volume of periodicity and trend in the form of time series methods. Most likely, ARIMA is often used for short-term forecasting. Therefore, to further extend the predictions and improve the accuracy, the proposed hybrid model integrates the **ARIMA** and a **Self-Adaptive filtering** method. Here, the ARIMA model is first used to identify the trend of the given time series data and its model parameters. These parameters are then corrected by the adaptive filtering method to reduce the noise.

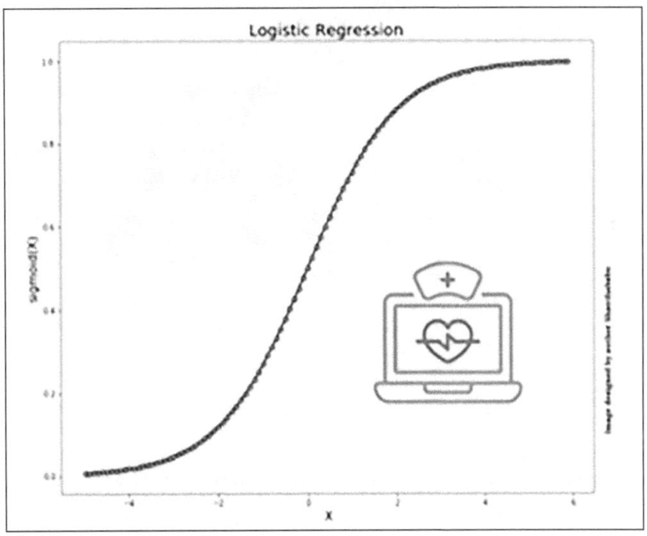

***Figure 4.12**: Healthcare diagnosis using logistic regression*

We know that the food we eat is broken down into multiple levels of glucose, and this will be released into your blood. When the level of this blood glucose goes up, it indicates your pancreas releases insulin, which can put a patient's life at the risk of dangerous problems, including stroke, eyesight, kidney, and heart disease.

For our use case, we will use the **`diabetes_analysis.csv`** files. In this analysis, let's consider only a few columns and forecast whether the patient is diabetic or not using logistic regression.

Pregnancies	BMI	SkinThickness	Insulin	Glucose	BloodPressure	Age	Glucose	Diabetes
6	33.6	35	0	148	72	50	148	1
1	26.6	29	0	85	66	31	85	0
8	23.3	0	0	183	64	32	183	1
1	28.1	23	94	89	66	21	89	0
0	43.1	35	168	137	40	33	137	1

***Figure 4.13**: diabetes_analysis.csv dataframe*

Before dropping the columns, let's understand the relationship between all columns, the following heatmap, and we can observe that there is a high relationship between Glucose and Diabetes (0.49):

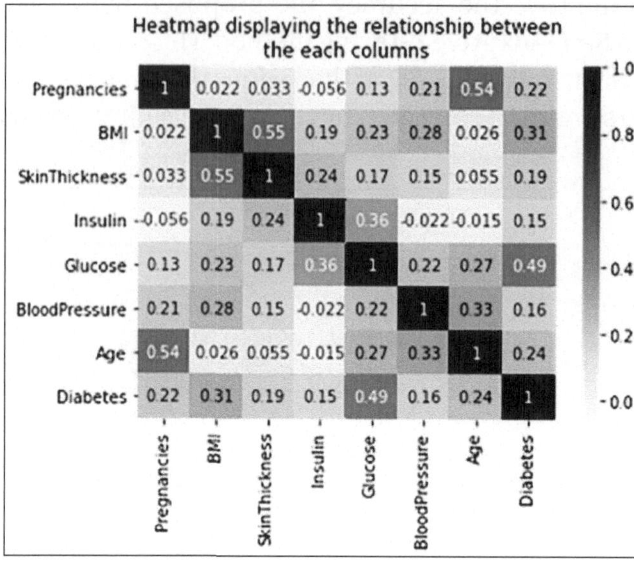

Figure 4.14: *diabetes_analysis.csv dataframe heatmap*

So, remove fewer correlation columns and keep the rest of the columns in the dataframe:

	Glucose	BloodPressure	Age	Diabetes
0	148.0	72.0	50	1
1	85.0	66.0	31	0
2	183.0	64.0	32	1
3	89.0	66.0	21	0
4	137.0	40.0	33	1
...	...	...	...	...
763	101.0	76.0	63	0
764	122.0	70.0	27	0
765	121.0	72.0	30	0
766	126.0	60.0	47	1
767	93.0	70.0	23	0

Figure 4.15: *diabetes_analysis dataframe after dropping the columns*

Analyze the columns and find the diagnosis of important features in the collection of columns using a random forest classifier.

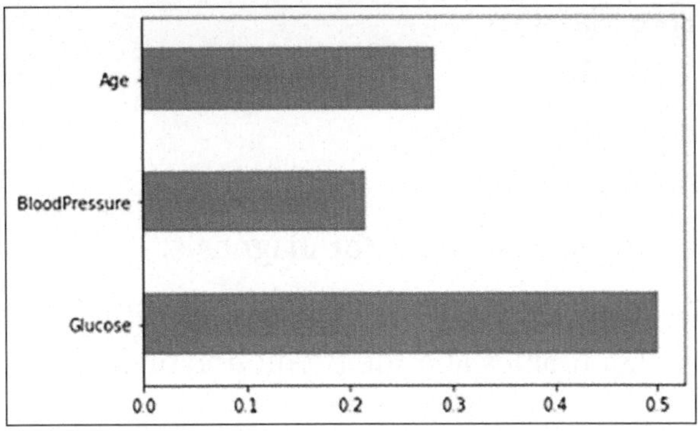

Figure 4.16: *Important features in diabetes_analysis*

After all these analyses, you will find the prediction as follows, which lets us understand the scatter plot visualization, you can coordinate to understand the actual and predicted in blue and orange, respectively.

```
array([0, 0, 1, 0, 1, 1, 1, 0, 1, 0, 0, 1, 0, 0, 1, 0, 0, 0, 1, 0, 0, 0,
       1, 1, 0, 1, 0, 0, 0, 1, 0, 1, 0, 1, 0, 0, 1, 0, 0, 0, 0, 1, 0, 0,
       0, 1, 0, 0, 1, 1, 0, 0, 0, 1, 1, 1, 0, 0, 1, 0, 0, 0, 0, 0, 0, 0,
       0, 0, 0, 0, 0, 1, 0, 0, 0, 0, 0, 1, 0, 0, 0, 0, 0, 0, 0, 1, 0, 1,
       1, 0, 0, 0, 1, 0, 0, 1, 0, 1, 0, 0, 1, 0, 1, 0, 0, 0, 1, 0, 0, 1,
       0, 0, 0, 0, 0, 0, 1, 0, 0, 0, 0, 1, 0, 0, 0, 0, 0, 0, 0, 0, 0, 1,
       1, 0, 0, 1, 0, 0, 0, 1, 1, 1, 0, 1, 0, 0, 0, 0, 0, 0, 0, 0, 0, 0,
       1, 0, 0, 0, 1, 0, 0, 0, 0, 0, 0, 0, 1, 0, 0, 0, 0, 1, 0, 0, 1, 1,
       1, 0, 1, 0, 1, 1, 0, 0, 1, 0, 0, 0, 0, 0, 1, 0], dtype=int64)
```

Figure 4.17: *diabetes_analysis prediction*

Figure 4.18 shows diabetes_analysis prediction:

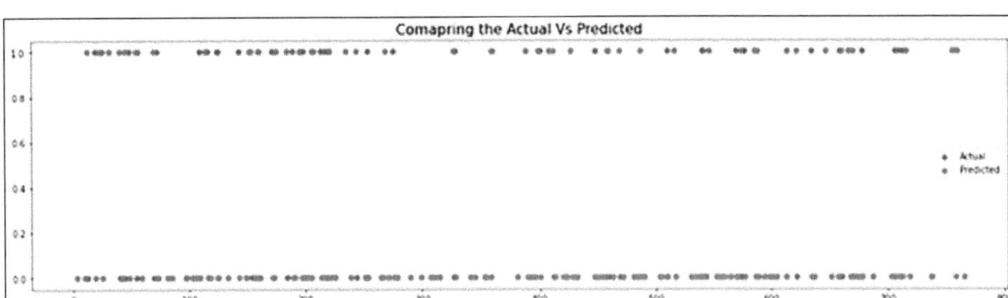

Figure 4.18: *diabetes_analysis prediction in a scatter plot*

Certainly, we can use the following machine learning models to predict whether the patient is diabetic or not:

- Decision Tree Classifier
- AdaBoost Classifier
- Gradient Boosting Classifier
- K-Neighbors Classifier

Benefits of forecasting in healthcare for diagnosis:

- Early-stage predictions of diabetes can help improve treatment
- Experimental outcomes and the prediction of diabetes show a high level of accuracy
- Prediction helps us to classify the type of diabetes and the appropriate treatment
- Researchers have a chance to compare and distinguish blood glucose levels in patients and monitor the functionality of the organ.

Predictive maintenance and anomaly detection use case

In the manufacturing industry, determining the conditions and performance of equipment is the major activity; this is so-called predictive maintenance. There are various components and parameters which help us to monitor the performance of each.

- Vibration sensor
- Sound sensor
- Current sensor
- Thermal sensor

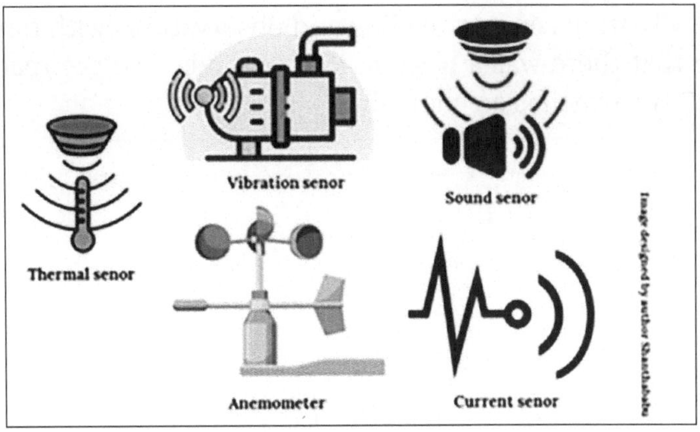

Figure 4.19: *Manufacturing industry's sensors*

Predictive maintenance and anomaly detection of ML process flow has been illustrated in the block diagram of *Figure* 4.20. This is very similar to other machine learning life cycle processes. Observing the sound of the sensors attached to the motor and finding the anomaly:

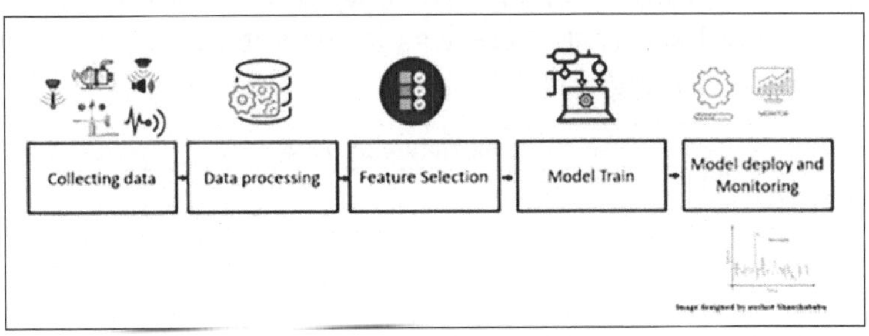

Figure 4.20: *Predictive maintenance and anomaly detection of ML process flow*

Figure 4.21 depicts the anomaly observed in the motor:

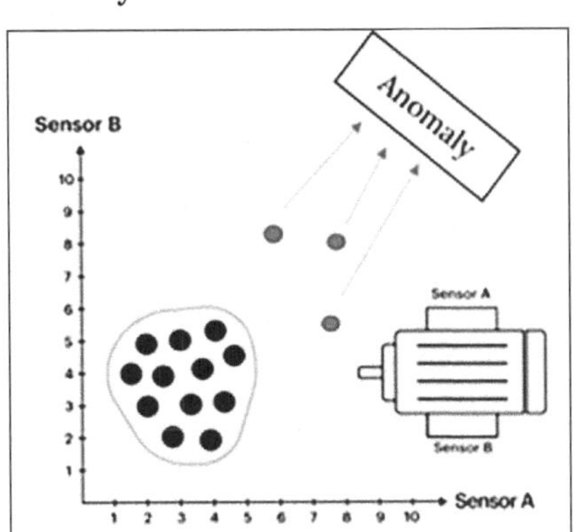

Figure 4.21: *Anomaly observation in motor*

Here we have vibration sensors reading and observations with time in seconds. We could see that there was a peak at 45th seconds, and the reading from the sensor was 2.5 Hz, which is an anomaly.

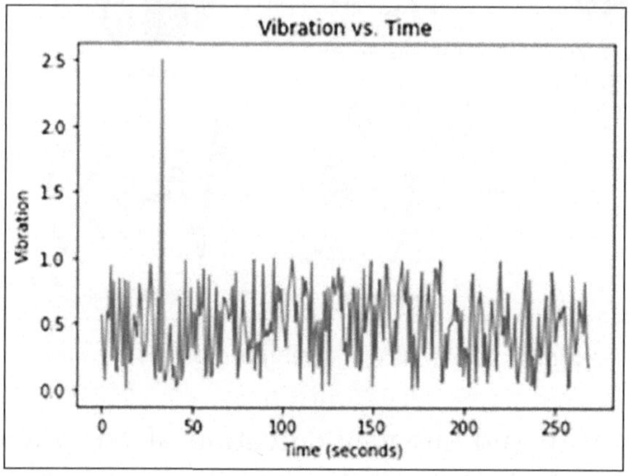

Figure 4.22: *Vibration versus time visualization*

Here we have temperature sensors reading and its observations with time in seconds. We could see that there was a peak at the 80th minute, and the temperature sensor reading was 35°C.

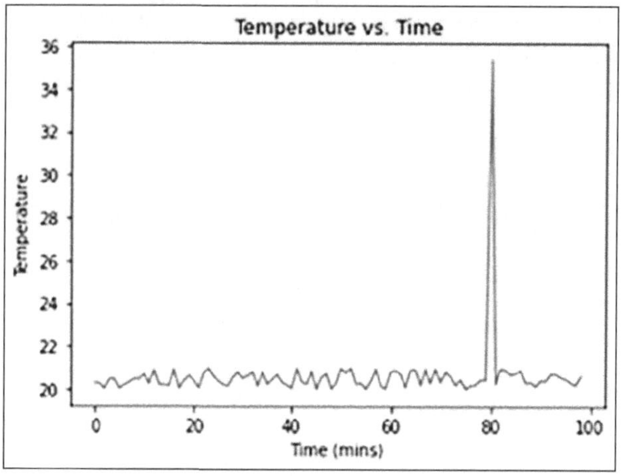

Figure 4.23: *Temperature versus time visualization*

Similarly, we could plot the other parameters and measure the performance of the equipment in the manufacturing plant.

Benefits of predictive maintenance and anomaly detection:

- Equipment performance and health have been monitored regularly
- Anomaly detection has been captured clearly from the visualization
- Reduces maintenance downtime and cost

Conclusion

In this chapter, we discussed time series analysis and forecasting opportunities in various industries. We understood the opportunity and scope of TSA&F. We performed a detailed scope study of price prediction using diesel sales and outcomes and benefits, forecasting in healthcare for diagnosis using diabetes and benefits of diagnosis in the healthcare industry, and predictive maintenance in the manufacturing industry, along with the challenges with TSA&F.

We have experimented with various case studies from different domains: price prediction, forecasting in healthcare diagnosis, predictive maintenance, and anomaly detection.

This chapter will provide a solid understanding of time series analysis and forecasting opportunities and their execution.

In the next chapter, we will understand statistical inference in time series and its properties, explore the shape of time series power, log, and box-cox transformations. We will also explore forecasting metrics and gain an understanding of naive forecasting, univariate models, and multivariate models.

Points to remember

In this chapter, it is important to keep a few things in mind that will be handy throughout this book:

- Time Series Analysis and Forecasting Opportunities in Various Industries
    - Healthcare and medical instruments
    - Manufacturing processes and quality control
    - Retail products, services, and forecasting
- Scope of
    - Price prediction and benefits
    - Forecasting in healthcare for diagnosis and benefits
    - Predictive maintenance

- Challenges with TSA&F
- Various case studies
  - Price prediction in retail
  - Forecasting in healthcare for diagnosis
  - Predictive maintenance and anomaly detection

CHAPTER 5

Exploring various aspects of Time Series Analysis and Forecasting

Introduction

In the previous chapter, we discussed the detailed studies of time series analysis and forecasting opportunities in various industries. Detailed scope studies and use cases for price prediction and forecasting in healthcare for diagnosis and predictive maintenance in the manufacturing industry. Challenges with TSA&F and benefits. This chapter will help us understand the time series analysis of statistical inference and the statistical properties of time series. Deep dive study of the shapes in time series and exploring forecasting metrics. Overview of Naive forecasting and forecasting metrics. Understanding the univariate and multivariate models. Quick wake through the various types of forecasting methods and time series analysis.

Structure

In this chapter, we will discuss the following topics:

- Understanding Time Series Analysis (TSA)
- Statistical inference in time series and its properties
- Study of the shapes in time series
  - Power
  - Log
  - Box-Cox
- Transformations
  - Box-Cox transforms for time series
- Exploring forecasting metrics and Naive forecasting
- Understanding the univariate and multivariate models

Understanding time series analysis (TSA)

We have been discussing the time series analysis from *Chapter 1, Introduction to Python and its key packages for DS and ML Projects* basically this is a sequential arrangement of data points in quantities and qualitative collected and pre-processed from various sources over a period or intervals. The intervals could be minutes, hours, days, weeks, months, and years. We can generate various visualization graphs using Python libraries. TSA takes well-defined steps to extract insights and derive statistical inference and its properties in significant methods.

Numerous web applications are generating massive amounts of data through manual intervention; they could be in commercial, social, and education-specific applications such as banking, stock, online trading, Facebook, Twitter, Gmail, auction websites, and university and school websites. The manufacturing industry equipment can capture data like temperature, sound, vibration, current, etc., and transmit it through respective sensor devices, nothing but IIoT devices (Industrial Internet of Things). These devices are constantly extracting the data from the equipment and in healthcare, devices as well help us to transmit the data to the data analytic server with time stamps. Will utilize all this data for time series data analysis purposes. Let's understand statistical analysis in general and explore statistical inference in time series and its properties.

Statistical inference is a mathematical approach that applies them to the data and analyses inferred properties underlying the dataset. Generally, it refers to the properties of a sample population considered for this exercise, for example, by testing mean, median, mode, interquartile range, standard deviation, variance, and hypothesis tests (Z, F, and T) and deriving estimations.

Statistical analysis

Statistics is the branch of mathematics and the backbone of data analytics, data science and machine learning (*Figure* 5.1). We did multiple statistical analyses using various datasets and plotted trends and patterns using numerical data. It can be categorized into two major divisions: **descriptive statistics** and **inferential statistics**. This is also known as quantitative analysis.

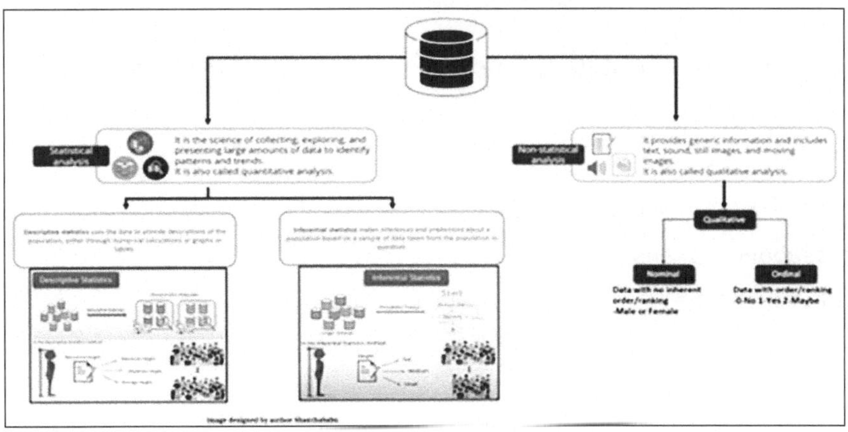

Figure 5.1: *How statistics transformed into Data Analytics and Data Science*

- **Descriptive Statistics**: It is a technique that describes the dataset characteristics and exhibits the meaning of the dataset in statistical ways. It describes each column in terms of the measure and description of the population in terms of numerical calculation, tables, and visualization charts. This technique is further divided into three types: distribution, a measure of central tendency and variability. We can describe both an individual sample and the entire population from the dataset with descriptive statistics.

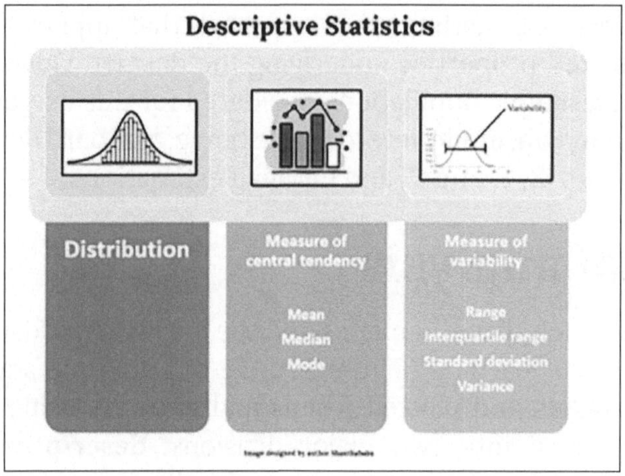

Figure 5.2: *Descriptive statistics*

Let's do the descriptive statistics using Pandas in the diesel dataset.

```
import numpy as np
import pandas as pd
import matplotlib.pyplot as plt
import seaborn as sns
%matplotlib inline
df_diesel_price = pd.read_csv("diesel_price.csv")
df_diesel_price.describe()
```

	Diesel price
count	33.000000
mean	6.205152
std	1.612116
min	3.200000
25%	5.120000
50%	5.950000
75%	7.080000
max	9.590000

Figure 5.3: *Descriptive statistics of the diesel dataset*

Group by price and find the descriptive statistics:

```
grouped_data = df_diesel_price.groupby(["Diesel price"])
grouped_data["Diesel price"].describe().head()
```

	count	mean	std	min	25%	50%	75%	max
Diesel price								
3.20	1.0	3.20	NaN	3.20	3.20	3.20	3.20	3.20
4.00	1.0	4.00	NaN	4.00	4.00	4.00	4.00	4.00
4.60	1.0	4.60	NaN	4.60	4.60	4.60	4.60	4.60
4.80	1.0	4.80	NaN	4.80	4.80	4.80	4.80	4.80
4.99	1.0	4.99	NaN	4.99	4.99	4.99	4.99	4.99

Figure 5.4: *Descriptive statistics of the diesel dataset group by price*

The measure of central tendency

Mean, median, and mode are components of measures of the central tenancy. Each has its characteristics.

```
df_diesel_price["Diesel price"].mean()
```

output

```
6.205151515151515
```

```
df_diesel_price["Diesel price"].median()
```

output

```
5.95
```

```
df_diesel_price["Diesel price"].mode()
```

output

```
0    5.10
1    5.13
```

Measure of variability

We can calculate the measure of the variability of the dataset using the range, variance, standard deviation, and interquartile range.

```
df_diesel_price["Diesel price"].var()
```

Output

```
2.60
```

```
df_diesel_price["Diesel price"].std()
```

Output

```
1.61
```

```
df_diesel_price["Diesel price"].quantile([.25, .5, .75])
```

Output

```
0.25    5.12
0.50    5.95
0.75    7.08
Name: Diesel price, dtype: float64
```

```
df_diesel_price["Diesel price"].max()
```

Output

```
9.59
```

```
df_diesel_price["Diesel price"].min()
```

Output

```
3.2
```

```
print("##############################################")
print("        Measures of central tendency          ")
print("Mean:",np.mean(df_diesel_price["Diesel price"], axis=0))
print("Median:",np.median(df_diesel_price["Diesel price"], axis=0))
#print("Mode:",np.mode(df_diesel_price["Diesel price"], axis=0))
print("##############################################")
print("\n############################################")
```

```
print("              Measures of variability           ")
print("Variance:",df_diesel_price["Diesel price"].var())
print("Standard deviation:", np.std(df_diesel_price["Diesel price"],
axis=0, ddof=1))
print("Range:", np.ptp(df_diesel_price["Diesel price"], axis=0))
print("Interquartile range:",np.quantile(df_diesel_price["Diesel
price"],[.25, .5, .75], axis=0))
print("##############################################")
```

Output

```
##############################################
        Measures of central tendency
Mean: 6.205151515151515
Median: 5.95
##############################################
############################################
            Measures of variability
Variance: 2.5989195075757574
Standard deviation: 1.6121164683656568
Range: 6.39
Interquartile range: [5.12 5.95 7.08]
############################################
```

Boxplots

Boxplot is a descriptive statistical plot to represent how the data is distributed in the dataset across the five different points - minimum, maximum, median, lower quartile, and upper quartile respectively and to identify outliers from the plot easily.

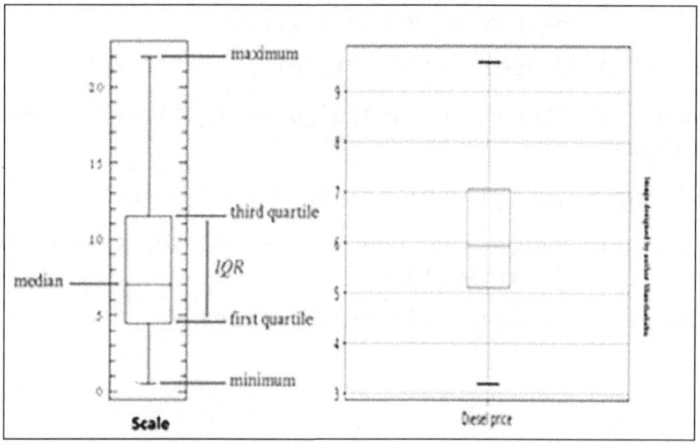

Figure 5.5: *Boxplot for diesel price with its components*

```
sns.boxplot(x="Diesel price",data=df_diesel_price)
```

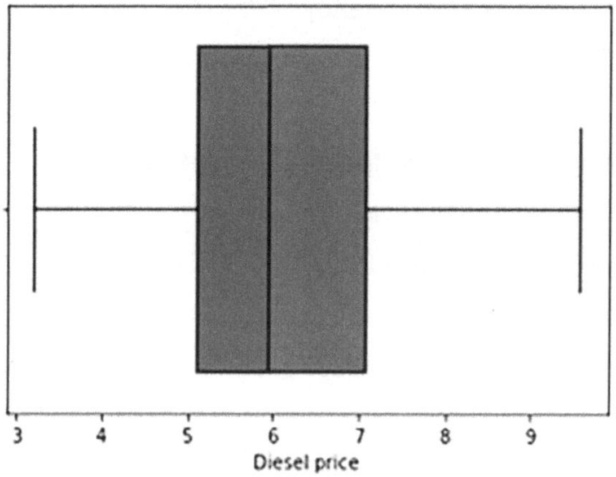

Figure 5.6: *Boxplot for diesel price*

Histogram

The histogram is a descriptive statistical plot to represent how the data is distributed in the dataset as a univariate. It plots frequencies and the variable count in each bin.

```
df_diesel_price["Diesel price"].hist()
```

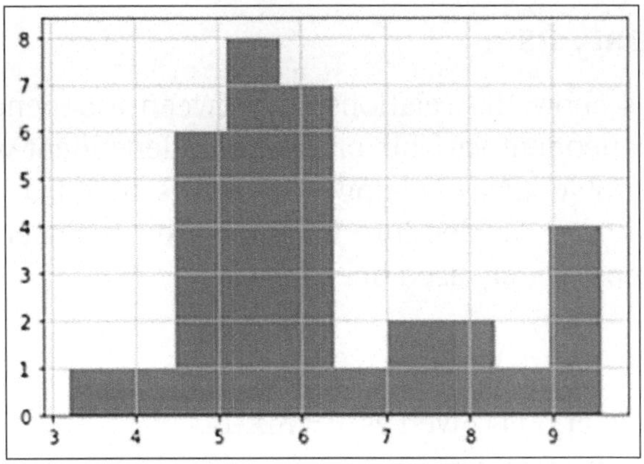

Figure 5.7: *Histogram plot for diesel price*

Inferential Statistics

The meaning of the Inference is **GUESS**timate. The term inferential statistics translates the sample population into predictions from the dataset based on the probabilities. Here is a random sample from the dataset that has been considered as a population to make inferences, this inference will be considered as a prediction for the sample population. In this exercise, the data analyst would work with a small sample rather than the entire population, since the probability is an outcome from the generalized population. We should remember that the accuracy of inferential statistics purely depends on the data sample, and it represents the larger population.

This technique is further divided into three types, which include regression analysis, hypothesis tests, and confidence intervals.

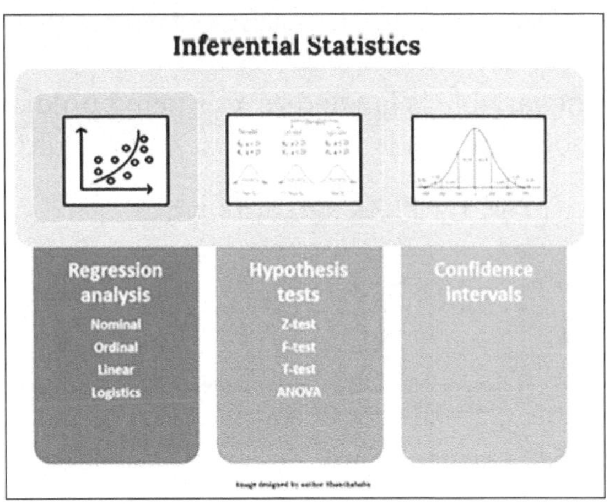

Figure 5.8: *Inferential statistics*

Regression analysis

Regression models show the relationship between a dependent variable and either a single independent variable or a set of independent variables. In which the dependent variable always changes or reacts based on the independent variables. This is further divided into minimal, ordinal, linear-simple, multiple, and logistic. The most widely used one is linear.

Linear model

The straight-line equation is given as Y = mX+b.

Y	=	m	X	+	b
Dependent variable		**Slope**	**Independent variable**		**intercept**

Figure 5.9: *Regression Analysis – Linear equation (simple)*

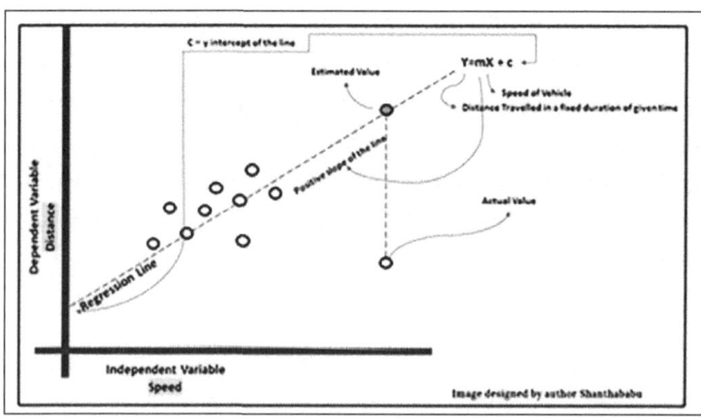

Figure 5.10: *Regression Analysis – Linear graph*

In which a dependent variable is labeled as Y, is being predicted, and other sets of independent variables are labeled as X1, X2.... Xn for multi-regression.

Y = β0 + β1X1 + β2X2 + ··· βkXk +error noise

$y =$	$b_0 + b_1{}^*x_1$	$+ b_2{}^*x_2 + \dots$	$+ b_n{}^*x_n$
↓	↓	↓	↓
Dependent variable	Independent variable	Independent variable	Independent variable

Figure 5.11: *Regression Analysis – Linear equation (multiple)*

Logistic model

In the logistic model, input would be either continuous or discrete and deal with the categorical dependent variables and the nature of the variables could be in binary format yes/no, male/female,0/1, and fitting into the **Sigmoid Curve** and very powerful in the probability-based classification model.

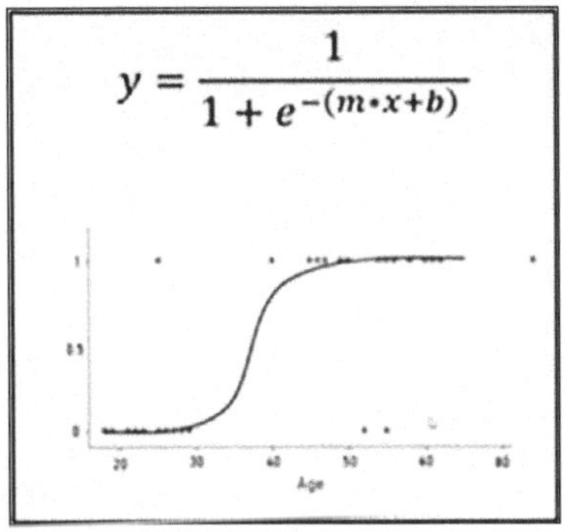

$$y = \frac{1}{1 + e^{-(m \cdot x + b)}}$$

Figure 5.12: *Regression Analysis – Logistic*

Hypothesis testing

Hypothesis testing is used to test assumptions from the sample which are taken from the larger population dataset and make statistical decisions. The final assumption is drawn based on the value of the test results, and it would be a one-tail or two-tail critical region, along with the confidence intervals.

In hypothesis, we have Z, T, and F tests and each test has its characteristics.

T-Test: T-test can be done as a single group or pair of groups based on the situation. Specifically, it is used when the data sample size is less than 30 and used to compare the mean of the sample and population, while the population variance is an unknown scenario.

Condition

- Null Hypothesis (H0): $\mu = \mu_0$
- Alternate Hypothesis (H1): $\mu > \mu_0$

One-Sample T-Test

```
import scipy.stats as stats
import pandas as pd
print("######################")
print("One Sample T-test")
```

```
print("######################")
t_statistic, p_value = stats.ttest_1samp(a=df_diesel_price["Diesel price"], popmean=6.2)
print("Statistic:",round(t_statistic,2))
print("p-value:",round(p_value,2))
```

```
Output
######################
One Sample T-test
######################
Statistics : 0.02
p-value: 0.99
```

One sample t-test observations:

As the p_value is more than 0.05, we accept the **null hypothesis** and reject the **alternative hypothesis**. To understand null and alternative hypothesis – Chapter 3 -Time series analysis and its components.

Two-Sample T-Test

```
import scipy.stats as stats
df_diesel_price_set1 =
np.array([5,6,5.6,5.12,5.1,5.34,5.45,4,6.17,4.6,3.2,5.13,4.99,5.2,6.08,5.95,5.13,4.8])
df_diesel_price_set2  = np.array([5.1,5.67,5.98,6.04,6.89,7.37,7.85,8.64,9.59,9.11,9.27,
9.36,7.69,6.27])
print("################################")
print("Mean for price set 1 and 2")
print("################################")
print(np.mean(df_diesel_price_set1))
print(np.mean(df_diesel_price_set2))
print("\n\n################################")
print("Two-Sample T-Test")
print("################################")
```

```
stats.ttest_ind(a=df_diesel_price_set1, b=df_diesel_price_set2, equal_
var=True)
```

```
Output
##################################
Mean for price set 1 and 2
##################################
5.158888888888889
7.487857142857142


##################################
Two-Sample T-Test
##################################
Ttest_indResult(statistic=-5.684148079534916,
pvalue=3.38088331693646e-06)
```

Two sample t-test observations:

- H(0) => μ1 = μ2 (Mean of set1 is equal to set2)
- H(A) => μ1 ≠μ2 (Mean of set1 is NOT equal to set)

Here, since the p-value (3.38088) is greater than alpha = 0.05

and mean not equal, so we cannot reject the null hypothesis.

Z Test: This test is used while the following conditions exist in the sample population

- If the sample size is greater than or equal to 30
- When the data follows a normal distribution
- Means of the sample and population are equal
- When known population variance

Condition

- Null Hypothesis: H0 μ=μ0
- Alternate Hypothesis: H1 μ>μ0

If the z statistic is greater than the z critical value, then **reject the null hypothesis**.

One-sample Z-test

```
import pandas as pd
from scipy import stats
from statsmodels.stats import weightstats as stests
ztest ,pval = stests.ztest(df_diesel_price["Diesel price"], x2=None, value=6.2)
print("########################")
print("   One-sample Z test    ")
print("########################")
print(float(pval))
if pval<0.05:
    print("p-value <0.05 \nReject null hypothesis")
else:
    print("p-value >0.05 \nAccept null hypothesis")
```

```
Output
########################
   One-sample Z test
########################
0.9853542637672824
p-value >0.05
Accept null hypothesis
```

Two-sample Z-test, similar to the T-test here, decides whether the population sample mean of two groups is equal or not.

```
ztest ,pval1 = stests.ztest(df_diesel_price_set1, x2=df_diesel_price_set2, value=0,alternative='two-sided')
print("########################")
print("   Two-sample Z test    ")
print("########################")
print(float(pval1))
if pval<0.05:
    print("p-value <0.05 \nReject null hypothesis")
```

```
else:
    print("p-value >0.05\nAccept null hypothesis")
```

```
Output
########################
   Two-sample Z test
########################
1.3146633287005285e-08
p-value >0.05
Accept null hypothesis
```

F Test: When there is a difference between the variances of two samples, we have to use the F-Test.

Condition

- Null Hypothesis(H0) $\sigma_1^2=\sigma_2^2$
- Alternate Hypothesis(H1) $\sigma_1^2>\sigma_2^2$

```
import numpy as np
import scipy.stats

print("###########################")
print(" Variance of set 1 and 2")
print("###########################")

print(np.var(df_diesel_price_set1))
print(np.var(df_diesel_price_set2))

f_test = np.var(df_diesel_price_set1, ddof=1)/np.var(df_diesel_price_
set2, ddof=1)
nun = np.array(df_diesel_price_set1).size-1
dun = np.array(df_diesel_price_set2).size-1
p_value = 1-scipy.stats.f.cdf(f_test, nun, dun)
```

```
print("\n########################")
print("   F test   ")
print("########################")
print(float(p_value))
if p_value<0.05:
    print("p-value <0.05 \nReject null hypothesis")
else:
    print("p-value >0.05\nAccept null hypothesis")
```

```
Output

#########################
 The variance between sets 1 and 2
#########################
0.5110987654320989
2.175831122448979

#######################
   F test
#######################
0.9971210073821054
p-value >0.05
Accept null hypothesis
```

The p-value is 0.997, so accept the null hypothesis and the variance of sets 1 and 2 are not equal.

Analysis of Variance (ANOVA) test: This is a parametric test used to test statistically significant differences among three or more groups. We could consider this test as an **Omnibus Test** since it tests the difference in the overall sample as multiple groups and exhibits which group is different.

Condition

- Null Hypothesis: H0 $\mu_1 = \mu_2 = \mu_3 = \ldots = \mu_n$
- Alternate Hypothesis: H1 - One of the group's mean is different from the rest.

```
# Importing library
from scipy.stats import f_oneway

df_diesel_price_set1 = np.array([5,6,5.6,5.12,5.1,5.34,5.45,4,6.17])
df_diesel_price_set2 = np.ar-
ray([4.6,3.2,5.13,4.99,5.2,6.08,5.95,5.13,4.8])
df_diesel_price_set3  = np.array([5.1,5.67,5.98,5.34,5.45,4,6.17])
df_diesel_price_set4 = np.array([7.37,7.85,8.64,9.59,9.11,9.27])

print("################################")
print("      Mean for all 4 sets     ")
print("################################")
print(np.mean(df_diesel_price_set1))
print(np.mean(df_diesel_price_set2))
print(np.mean(df_diesel_price_set3))
print(np.mean(df_diesel_price_set4))

print("\n\n##########################")
print("The one-way ANOVA Test")
print("##########################")
f_oneway(df_diesel_price_set1, df_diesel_price_set2, df_diesel_price_
set3, df_diesel_price_set4)
```

Output

```
################################
      Mean for all 4 sets
################################
5.308888888888889
5.0088888888888885
5.387142857142857
8.638333333333334


##########################
The one-way ANOVA Test
```

```
############################
F_onewayResult(statistic=32.931723147830255,
pvalue=3.6217439172213854e-09)
```

The p-value is greater than 0.05, hence we would accept the null hypothesis.

Note: Statistics is the branch of mathematics and the backbone of data analytics. It can be categorized into two major divisions: descriptive statistics and inferential statistics. This is also known as quantitative analysis. Descriptive Statistics: Distribution, Measure of central tendency and variability Inferential Statistics: Regression, different hypothesis tests and confidence intervals.

Confidence intervals

In statistics, three types of statistical intervals are available: confidence, prediction, and tolerance intervals. Let's focus on confidence intervals in this book. We have intervals between the data and data samples that contain the true population.

This statistical interval is used to estimate an unknown population value of the sample and to estimate the mean. There are two types of confidence intervals, those are z and t intervals.

z- intervals	population standard deviation
t- intervals	sample standard deviation

z- intervals (population standard deviation): This is a parameter, defined as the difference between parameters and statistics, which is calculated from individual samples in the population.

$$\sigma = \sqrt{\frac{\Sigma (x_i - \mu)^2}{n}}$$

Figure 5.13: *Population standard deviation*

x-individual values of the population

n- count of values in the population

μ -population average

t- intervals (sample standard deviation): It has greater variability, calculated from the individuals in a population and depends on the sample. The sample standard deviation is greater than that of the population.

$$S = \sqrt{\frac{\Sigma (x_i - \bar{x})^2}{(n - 1)}}$$

Figure 5.14: *Sample standard deviation*

$\bar{x}$ - sample average

x - individual values of a sample

n- count of values in a sample

Confidence intervals assessment at the speed of the motor

For a simple use case, let's have the speed of the motor in the manufacturing plant and line-1 have the differences are 960 rpm and 980 rpm and in line -2 the differences are 1080 rpm and 1100 rpm.

In both cases, the rpm is the same. As the number of samples increases and the length of the confidence interval decreases.

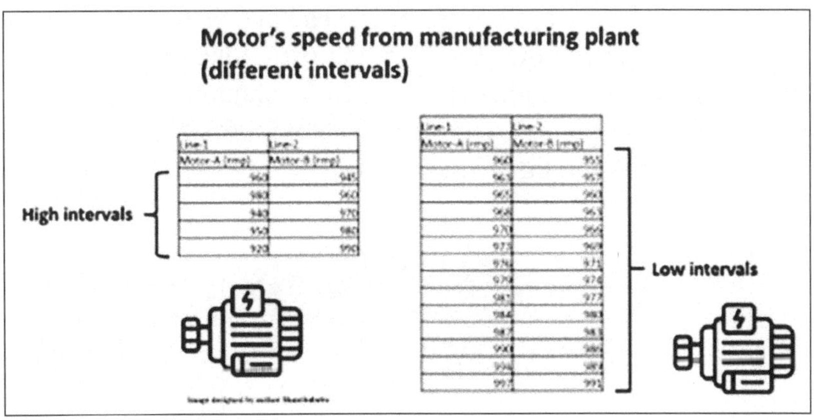

Figure 5.15: *Confidence intervals assessment at the speed of the motor*

Statistical intervals provide a way to quantify the uncertainty about a scalar quantity of a population based on a random sample of data. A statistical interval is a range, comprising a lower bound and an upper bound, which is expected to contain the true population value, with a certain degree of confidence.

Study the shapes of Time Series

In TSA, data points are sequential in quantities prepared from various sources over fixed intervals (or) tracking the changes over a while. We have discussed different visualization techniques on time intervals–minutes, hours, days, weeks, months, and years. When we want to classify the time series data, we have multiple available choices, among them K-Nearest Neighbors (KNN), which supports a larger volume of data along with specific measures of different elasticity distance approaches and to identify classes within the dataset, which are as follows for our reference.

- Dynamic Time Warping (**DTW**)
- Time Warp Edit (**TWE**)
- Complexity Invariant Distance (**CID**)

We are aware that time series data have high dimensionality and require huge training time, space complexity, high computational memory, and classification accuracy to accomplish the requirements to extract insight from the dataset. In that scenario **Shapelets** concept was proposed by Ye and Keogh and addresses these boundaries and challenges. This concept is more accurate and faster than the rest of the classifier algorithms.

In this concept, the shapes can be transformed into a one-dimensional time series data description. In this case, samples of leaves have been taken from different species. *Figure* 5.16 below shows the Verbena urticifolia leaves as shapelets for the time series shape. The detailed study of these shapelets is beyond the scope of this scope since multiple research and development is ongoing. This is just a glimpse of your understanding of shapelets.

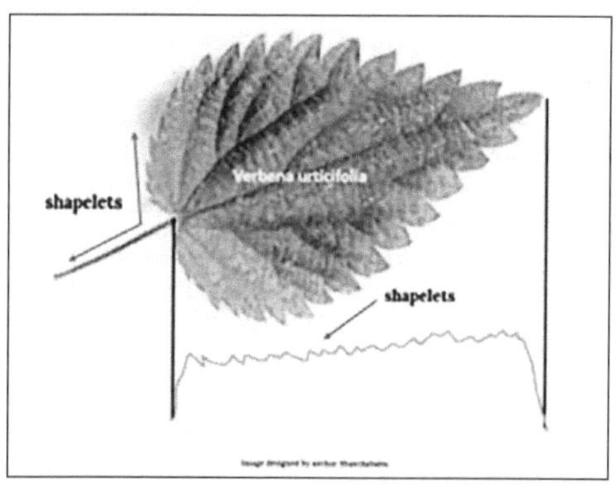

Figure 5.16: *Verbena urticifolia leaves as shapelets for time series shape*

Transforms for TSA&F

Transforming the data is a recommended activity in TSA&F to remove noise and improve time series forecasting. We have discussed various transformations like power transform, log, square root, and cube root in *Chapter 3, Time Series Analysis and Its Components*. In this chapter, we will see few more advanced versions.

In this technique, certain transformations are applied to the time series data, the techniques are as follows:

- Power Transform
    - Log Transfer
    - Square Root
- Cube root

Power Transform: The square root transform and log transform belong to a class of transforms called power transforms.

Square Root: This is a straightforward method of applying the NumPy sqrt function on the diesel price column.

```
#Transformation - Square Root
df_log=np.sqrt(df_diesel_price["Diesel price"])
df_diff_diesel_price=df_log.diff().dropna()
```

New dataframe after applying to Square Root

```
df_diff_diesel_price.head(5)
1     0.213422
2    -0.083058
3    -0.103690
4    -0.004424
5     0.052526
Name: Diesel price, dtype: float64
```

Note: 5 SQRT is 0.213422

Let's plot df_diff_diesel_price

```
df_diff_diesel_price.plot()
```

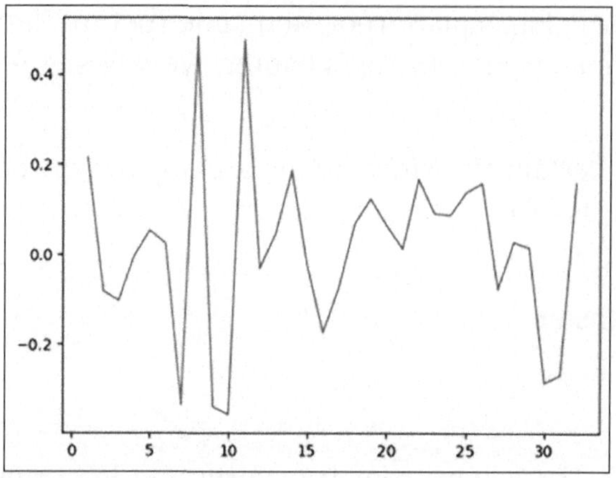

***Figure* 5.17**: *Transformation - Square Root plot (Converting Non-Stationary into Stationary)*

Log Transfer: This is a straightforward method of applying the log function in the diesel price column. Here, each variable x is replaced with a log(x) with and line plot histogram.

```
from matplotlib import pyplot
from math import exp
from the numpy import log

print("\t\t\t**********************************************")
print("\t\t\t    Before and After Log - Transformation      ")
print("\t\t\t              Data Distribution                ")
print("\t\t\t**********************************************")
fig, ax = plt.subplots(2, 2)
# line plot
ax[0,0].plot(df_diesel_price["Diesel price"])
ax[0, 0].set_title('Before Transformation')
# histogram
ax[0,1].hist(df_diesel_price["Diesel price"])
ax[0,1].set_title('Before Transformation - Hist')

ax[1,0].plot(log(df_diesel_price["Diesel price"]))
ax[1,0].set_title('After Log Transformation')
# histogram
```

```
ax[1,1].hist(log(df_diesel_price["Diesel price"]))
ax[1,1].set_title('After Log Transformation - Hist')
#plotting the graphs in a grid format
for axf in ax.flat:
    axf.set(xlabel='x-label', ylabel='y-label')


for axf in ax.flat:
    axf.label_outer()
```

Figure 5.18 shows the plot to view the original and the log-transformed distribution of the data.

```
***********************************************
Before and After Log - Transformation
Data Distribution
***********************************************
```

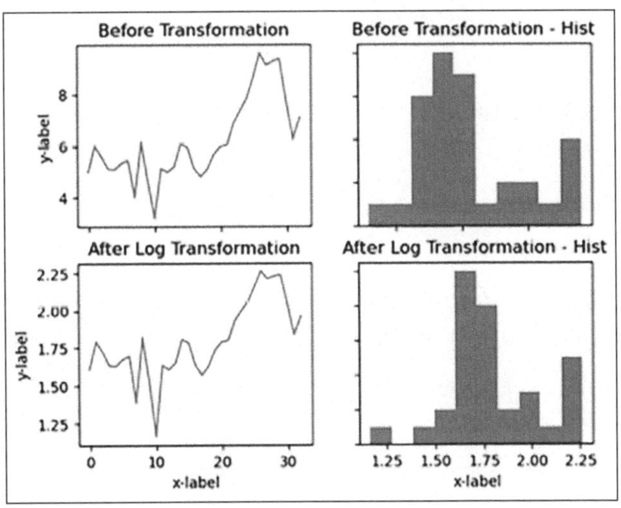

Figure 5.18: *Log Transformation - (Converting Non-Stationary into Stationary) and histogram*

Cube Root: This is also very similar to Log and Sqrt transformation in a variable.

```
print("\t\t\t************************************************")
print("\t\t\t    Before and After Cube root - Transformation ")
print("\t\t\t************************************************")
fig, ax = plt.subplots(2, 2)
# line plot
```

```
ax[0,0].plot(df_diesel_price["Diesel price"])
ax[0,0].set_title('Before Transformation')

# histogram
ax[0,1].hist(df_diesel_price["Diesel price"])
ax[0,1].set_title('Before Transformation - Hist')

ax[1,0].plot(np.cbrt(df_diesel_price["Diesel price"]))
ax[1,0].set_title('After Log Transformation')

# histogram
ax[1,1].hist(np.cbrt(df_diesel_price["Diesel price"]))
ax[1,1].set_title('After Cube Root Transformation - Hist')

#plotting the graphs in grid format
for axf in ax.flat:
    axf.set(xlabel='x-label', ylabel='y-label')

for axf in ax.flat:
    axf.label_outer()
```

The following *Figure* 5.19 shows the plot to view the original and the cube root transformed the distribution of the data.

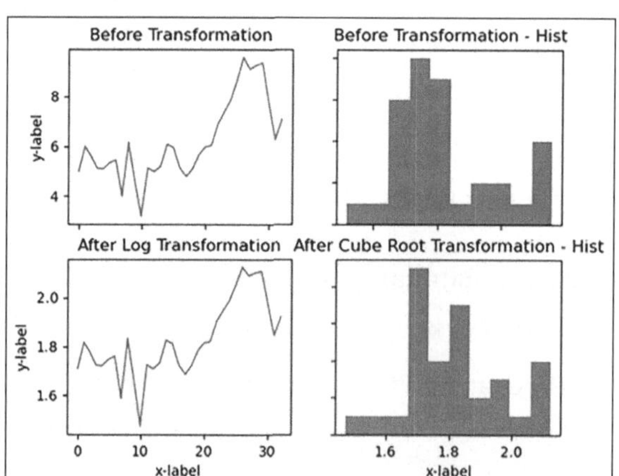

Figure 5.19: *Cube Root Transformation - (Converting Non-Stationary into Stationary) and histogram*

Box-Cox transformation

This transformation is a highly configurable method for transforming the data for different configurations value for lambda (λ) and exhibits the different transformations as results which include log and square transformation, the range for the -1 to 1 with intervals of 0.5. The outcome of the series is linear and uniform distribution, depending on the data generated from the devices or human intervention.

The scipy.stats library provides a **Box-Cox** function and, based on the value of lambda, we can extract different transformations and distributions for the sample dataset.

Lambda (λ) Value	Mode of Transformation
-1.0	Reciprocal transform
-.05	Reciprocal square root transform
0.0	Log transform
0.5	Square root transform
1.0	No transform

Table 5.1: *Box-Cox Transformation*

Box-Cox Transformation Implementation:

```
print("####################################################")
print("Box-Cox Transformation Implementation (Lamda -1)  ")
print("###################################################")
df_diesel_price["Diesel price"] = boxcox(df_diesel_price["Diesel
price"], lmbda=-1)
pyplot.figure(1)
pyplot.subplot(211)
pyplot.plot(df_diesel_price["Diesel price"] )
pyplot.subplot(212)
pyplot.hist(df_diesel_price["Diesel price"] )
pyplot.show()
```

Output

```
#######################################################
Box-Cox Transformation Implementation (Lamda -1)
######################################################
```

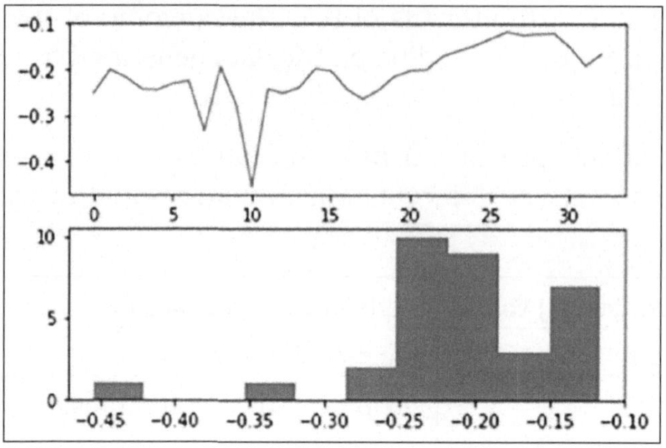

Figure 5.20: *Box-Cox Transformation Implementation (Lamda -1)*

```
print("#########################################################")
print("Box-Cox Transformation Implementation (Lamda -0.5)    ")
print("#########################################################")
df_diesel_price["Diesel price"] = boxcox(df_diesel_price["Diesel
price"], lmbda=-0.5)
pyplot.figure(1)
pyplot.subplot(211)
pyplot.plot(df_diesel_price["Diesel price"] )
pyplot.subplot(212)
pyplot.hist(df_diesel_price["Diesel price"] )
pyplot.show()
```

Output

```
##########################################################
Box-Cox Transformation Implementation (Lamda -0.5)
##########################################################
```

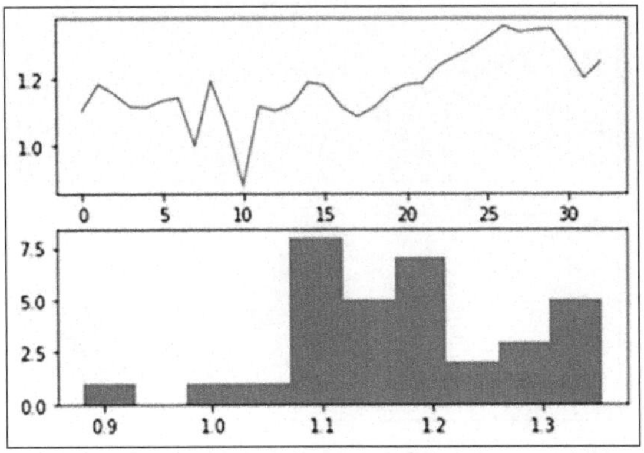

Figure 5.21: *Box-Cox Transformation Implementation (Lamda -0.5)*

```
from scipy.stats import boxcox
from matplotlib import pyplot
print("##########################################################")
print("Box-Cox Transformation Implementation (Lamda 0.0 )   ")
print("##########################################################")
df_diesel_price["Diesel price"] = boxcox(df_diesel_price["Diesel
price"], lmbda=0.0)
pyplot.figure(1)
# line plot
pyplot.subplot(211)
pyplot.plot(df_diesel_price["Diesel price"] )
# histogram
pyplot.subplot(212)
pyplot.hist(df_diesel_price["Diesel price"] )
pyplot.show()
```

Output

```
##########################################################
Box-Cox Transformation Implementation (Lamda 0.0 )
##########################################################
```

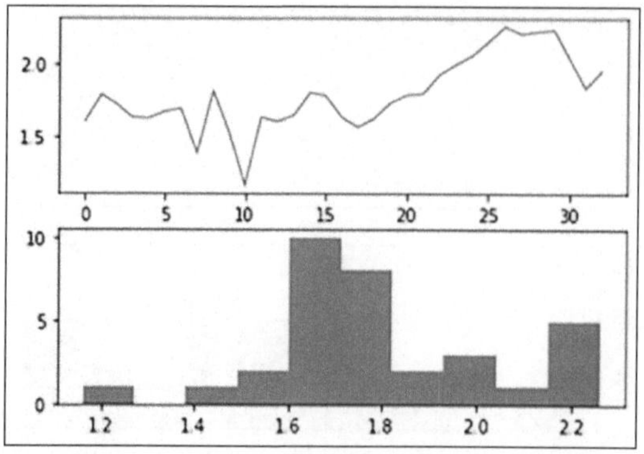

Figure 5.22: Box-Cox Transformation Implementation (Lamda 0.0)

```
print("#####################################################")
print("Box-Cox Transformation Implementation (Lamda 0.5)  ")
print("#####################################################")
df_diesel_price["Diesel price"] = boxcox(df_diesel_price["Diesel
price"], lmbda=0.5)
pyplot.figure(1)
pyplot.subplot(211)
pyplot.plot(df_diesel_price["Diesel price"] )
pyplot.subplot(212)
pyplot.hist(df_diesel_price["Diesel price"] )
pyplot.show()
```

```
#####################################################
Box-Cox Transformation Implementation (Lamda 0.5)
#####################################################
```

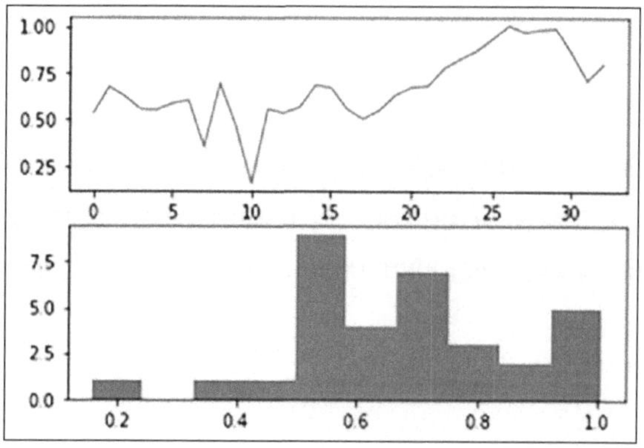

Figure 5.23: Box-Cox Transformation Implementation (Lamda 0.5)

```
print("########################################################")
print("Box-Cox Transformation Implementation (Lamda 1.0)  ")
print("########################################################")
df_diesel_price["Diesel price"] = boxcox(df_diesel_price["Diesel
price"], lmbda=1.0)
pyplot.figure(1)
pyplot.subplot(211)
pyplot.plot(df_diesel_price["Diesel price"] )
pyplot.subplot(212)
pyplot.hist(df_diesel_price["Diesel price"] )
pyplot.show()
```

```
########################################################
Box-Cox Transformation Implementation (Lamda 1.0)
########################################################
```

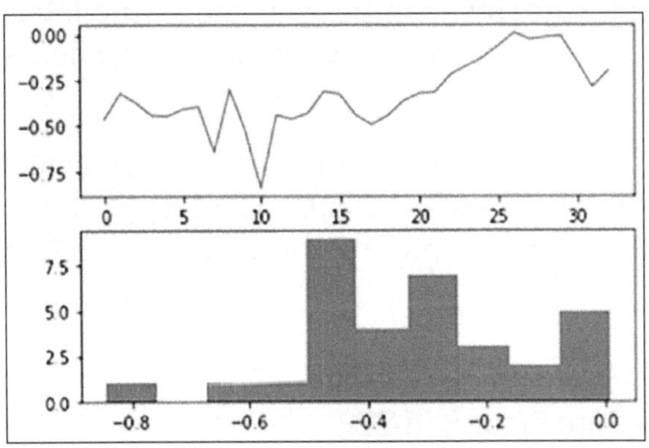

Figure 5.24: *Box-Cox Transformation Implementation (Lamda 1.0)*

Note: Transforming the data is a recommended activity to remove noise and improve time series forecasting. different transformation techniques are available to power transform, log, square root and cube root and box-cox transformation is a highly configurable method to transform the data for different configurations value for lambda (λ) and exhibits the different transformations.

Forecasting metrics: The reliability of a forecast has been determined by the accuracy of the forecasting and the set of metrics used to measure those factors precisely. These types of metrics measure the forecasting error and derive from the difference calculations between an actual value and its expected forecast for the analysis or model outcomes.

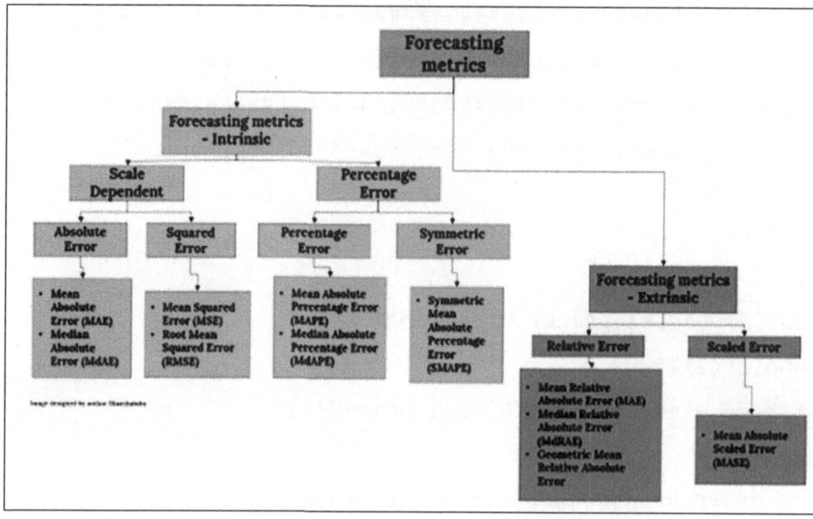

Figure 5.25: *Forecasting metrics*

Forecasting metrics – Intrinsic: In this technique, the internal factors playing a major role, such as the average of company sales, student's height, rainfall in cm, etc.,

Scale-dependent: This is scaling dependency and the error metrics are expressed in terms of units and are easy to calculate and interpret the insights. It would be in sales, units, inches, centimeters, length, and height of the primary data.

Absolute error

- Mean Absolute Error (MAE)
- Median Absolute Error (MdAE)

Squared error

- Mean Squared Error (MSE)
- Root Mean Squared Error (RMSE)

Percentage error: These measures are used to compare different time series factors and are independent of scales and specifically used to compare the performance between different time series factors and assess the forecasting.

Percentage error

- Mean Absolute Percentage Error (MAPE)
- Median Absolute Percentage Error (MdAPE)

Symmetric error

- Symmetric Mean Absolute Percentage Error (SMAPE)

Forecasting metrics – Extrinsic: In this technique, the measures are from the external reference and the forecast has arrived based on the external factors' influence.

Relative error

- Mean Relative Absolute Error (MAE)
- Median Relative Absolute Error (MdRAE)
- Geometric Mean Relative Absolute Error

Scaled error

- Mean Absolute Scaled Error (MASE)

Overview of Naive forecasting

The naïve forecasting method is predicting the same thing will happen again, what had happened in the past. If the sales of the product were 1 million last year, the same expectation will be set as the result of future sales. So, this approach is not accurate and doesn't consider many influencing factors. As you know, we have to calculate the error(s) while forecasting. The calculation for this method is a very simple formula.

Let's consider **`Year`**, **`Month`**, **`Region`**, and **`Mobile Sales (Actuals)`** with some data.

Year	Month	Region	Mobile Sales (Actuals)
2021	January	Chennai	10235
2021	February	Chennai	10336
2021	March	Chennai	10534
2021	April	Chennai	10338
2021	May	Chennai	10139
2021	June	Chennai	10200
2021	July	Chennai	10541
2021	August	Chennai	10602
2021	September	Chennai	10743

***Figure 5.26**: Naive Forecasting – sample dataset*

Mobile Sales (Forecast): As mentioned, predicting the same thing will happen again, what had happened in the past from *Figure* 5.27.

Year	Month	Region	Mobile Sales (Actuals)	Mobile Sales (Forecast)
2021	January	Chennai	10235	
2021	February	Chennai	10336	10235
2021	March	Chennai	10534	10336
2021	April	Chennai	10338	10534
2021	May	Chennai	10139	10338
2021	June	Chennai	10200	10139
2021	July	Chennai	10541	10200
2021	August	Chennai	10602	10541
2021	September	Chennai	10743	10602
2021	October	Chennai	10144	10743
2021	November	Chennai	10245	10144
2022	December	Chennai	10546	10245
2022	January	Chennai	10747	10546
2022	February	Chennai	10848	10747

Figure 5.27: *Naive Forecasting – sample dataset with forecast*

Let's calculate Absolute Percentage Error and Mean Absolute Percentage Error using the Excel formula **`ABS(Dn-En)/Dn*100`** and **`=AVERAGE(Fn:Fn)`**.

The outcome from the above formula is that a new column with **`the Absolute Percentage Error series`** is shown in Figure 5.28:

Year	Month	Region	Mobile Sales (Actuals)	Mobile Sales (Forecast)	Absolute Percentage Error
2021	January	Chennai	10235		
2021	February	Chennai	10336	10235	0.9772
2021	March	Chennai	10534	10336	1.8796
2021	April	Chennai	10338	10534	1.8959
2021	May	Chennai	10139	10338	1.9627
2021	June	Chennai	10200	10139	0.5980
2021	July	Chennai	10541	10200	3.2350
2021	August	Chennai	10602	10541	0.5754
2021	September	Chennai	10743	10602	1.3125
2021	October	Chennai	10144	10743	5.9050
2021	November	Chennai	10245	10144	0.9858
2022	December	Chennai	10546	10245	2.8542
2022	January	Chennai	10747	10546	1.8703
2022	February	Chennai	10848	10747	0.9310
2022	March	Chennai	10280	10848	5.5253
2022	April	Chennai	10550	10280	2.5592
2022	May	Chennai	10751	10550	1.8696
2022	June	Chennai	10252	10751	4.8673
2022	July	Chennai	10345	10252	0.8990

Figure 5.28: *Naive Forecasting – sample dataset with absolute percentage error*

Mean Absolute Percentage Error: **2.2613**

The same method will calculate the Absolute Deviation for the dataset using the **`ABS(Dn-En)`** formula Mean Absolute Deviation **`AVERAGE(Gn:Gn)`**.

Year	Month	Region	Mobile Sales (Actuals)	Mobile Sales (Forecast)	Absolute Percentage Error	Absolute Deviation
2021	January	Chennai	10235			
2021	February	Chennai	10336	10235	0.9772	101
2021	March	Chennai	10534	10336	1.8796	198
2021	April	Chennai	10338	10534	1.8959	196
2021	May	Chennai	10139	10338	1.9627	199
2021	June	Chennai	10200	10139	0.5980	61
2021	July	Chennai	10541	10200	3.2350	341
2021	August	Chennai	10602	10541	0.5754	61
2021	September	Chennai	10743	10602	1.3125	141
2021	October	Chennai	10144	10743	5.9050	599
2021	November	Chennai	10245	10144	0.9858	101
2022	December	Chennai	10546	10245	2.8542	301
2022	January	Chennai	10747	10546	1.8703	201
2022	February	Chennai	10848	10747	0.9310	101
2022	March	Chennai	10280	10848	5.5253	568
2022	April	Chennai	10550	10280	2.5592	270
2022	May	Chennai	10751	10550	1.8696	201
2022	June	Chennai	10252	10751	4.8673	499
2022	July	Chennai	10345	10252	0.8990	93

Figure 5.29: *Naive Forecasting – sample dataset with absolute deviation*

Mean Absolute Deviation: **235.11**

Year	Month	Region	Mobile Sales (Actuals)	Mobile Sales (Forecast)	Absolute Percentage Error	Absolute Deviation	
2021	January	Chennai	10235				
2021	February	Chennai	10336	10235	0.9772	101	
2021	March	Chennai	10534	10336	1.8796	198	
2021	April	Chennai	10338	10534	1.8959	196	
2021	May	Chennai	10139	10338	1.9627	199	
2021	June	Chennai	10200	10139	0.5980	61	
2021	July	Chennai	10541	10200	3.2350	341	
2021	August	Chennai	10602	10541	0.5754	61	
2021	September	Chennai	10743	10602	1.3125	141	
2021	October	Chennai	10144	10743	5.9050	599	
2021	November	Chennai	10245	10144	0.9858	101	
2022	December	Chennai	10546	10245	2.8542	301	
2022	January	Chennai	10747	10546	1.8703	201	
2022	February	Chennai	10848	10747	0.9310	101	
2022	March	Chennai	10280	10848	5.5253	568	
2022	April	Chennai	10550	10280	2.5592	270	
2022	May	Chennai	10751	10550	1.8696	201	
2022	June	Chennai	10252	10751	4.8673	499	
2022	July	Chennai	10345	10252	0.8990	93	
				Mean Absolute Percentage Error	2.2613	235.11	Mean Absolute Deviation

Figure 5.30: *Naive Forecasting – sample dataset with mean absolute deviation*

Conclusion

In this chapter, we have explored various aspects of time series analysis and forecasting, understanding time series analysis concepts. We studied major statistics and its two divisions of descriptive and inferential statistics, along with samples. Under these divisions, we investigated the distribution, a measure of central tendency and variability, and under inferential statistics - regression analysis, various hypotheses, along with sample code and outcomes. We understood the study of the shapes of time series, re-gap the transforms in time series analysis, and box-cox transformation with classical examples.

Overview of forecasting metrics and Naive forecasting techniques. This chapter will provide a solid understanding of statistics and their roles in time series analysis and forecasting.

In the next chapter, we will discuss various time series models and their implementation process, which includes Autoregressive Models - AR(p), Moving Average Models - MA(q), and ARMA (AR +MA) along with classical explanations and examples.

Points to remember

In this chapter, it is important to keep a few things in mind that will be handy throughout this book:

- Understanding time series analysis and its significance with classical examples.
- Detailed study of statistical analysis and its characteristics with a neat sketch.
- Explore descriptive and inferential statistical in-depth analysis along with samples.
- Study the shapes of time series along with verbena urticifolia leaves as shapelets for time series shape analysis.
- Transforms time series analysis and forecasting techniques re-gap (power, log, sqrt) and detailed study of box-cox transformation techniques.
- Explored forecasting metrics such as intrinsic and extrinsic and their hierarchy.
- Confidence intervals explanation and assessment at the speed of motor analysis.
- Overview of Naive forecasting and simple implementation with mobile sales and forecasting.

Chapter 6

Exploring Time Series Models - AR, MA, ARMA, and ARIMA

Introduction

In the previous chapter, we discussed the detailed study of statistical analysis and its characteristics with a neat sketch and explanations and explored descriptive and inferential statistical in-depth analysis along with classical examples. Transforms time series analysis and forecasting techniques and additionally studied box-cox transformation techniques and forecasting metrics. This chapter will help us explore various time series models and their implementation, including Autoregressive, Moving Average, ARMA, and ARIMA. Understanding residual analysis, plot, and scaling techniques.

Structure

In this chapter, we will discuss the following topics:

- Overview and time series models and their benefits
- Detailed study of the following models
    - Autoregressive (AR)

- Moving Average (MA)
- Autoregressive Moving Average (ARMA)
- Autoregressive Integrated Moving Average (ARIMA)

Overview and time series models

So far, we have discussed various aspects of the time series and analyses and forecasting with a historical time series and understand trends, and patterns like seasonal, cyclic and regularity. This chapter will discuss the important areas of machine learning models. A set of machine learning models for time series data can have many forms, processes, and purposes to achieve the end results. All these models are used to investigate how the data points are connected and compared with other variables over the same time.

All these models are used to forecast the values based on historical datasets. They're very common types, which include the following:

- Autoregressive (AR)
- Moving Average (MA)
- Autoregressive Moving Average (ARMA)
- Autoregressive Integrated Moving Average (ARIMA)

We should remember that all these models do not have the same results for the same dataset taken for analysis and forecasting. Before we go to model building, we must consider a few parameters and start working on building models.

- **Data volume:** In data analysis and forecasting, more data volume would create more opportunities to build a stable model with more testing and tuning.
- **Size of time horizons**: Required time horizon of predictions – shorter time horizons are often easier to predict – with higher confidence, than longer ones.
- **Frequency of forecast update:** Forecasts might need to be updated frequently over time or they might need to be made once and remain static. If we need to be more accurate, the forecasting should be updated frequently so that the results are accurate with perfect predictions.
- **Sequential order of frequency**: Sequential of the frequencies, up and down with proper sampling rate offers benefits while modeling.

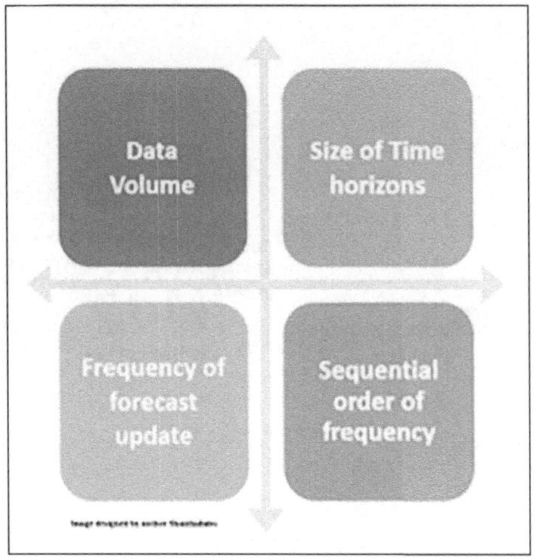

Figure 6.1: *Factors Influencing the time series analysis and forecasting*

Statistical models for TSA&F

We discussed the statistics and how they are closely related to time series analysis in *Chapter* 5, *Exploring various aspects of time series analysis and forecasting*. Here is one step further on how the time series models are related to linear regression and correlation between time series data points, and all these models are conventionally proven techniques of TSA&F methods.

Before our deep dive into all these models, we should understand one key point is that all these models (AR, MA, ARMA, and ARIMA) are extended versions of each other and impoverished capabilities for various beneficial perspectives, *Figure* 6.2 represents the same.

In a simple equation, we can denote these models as follows:

- AR (p-lags)
- MR (q-lags)
- AR+MR=ARMR (p-lags) +(q-lags)
- AR+I+MR=ARIMA [(p-lags) +d-difference in the order+(q-lags)]

Each model has its assumptions, benefits, challenges, and interesting parts in time series analysis and forecasting.

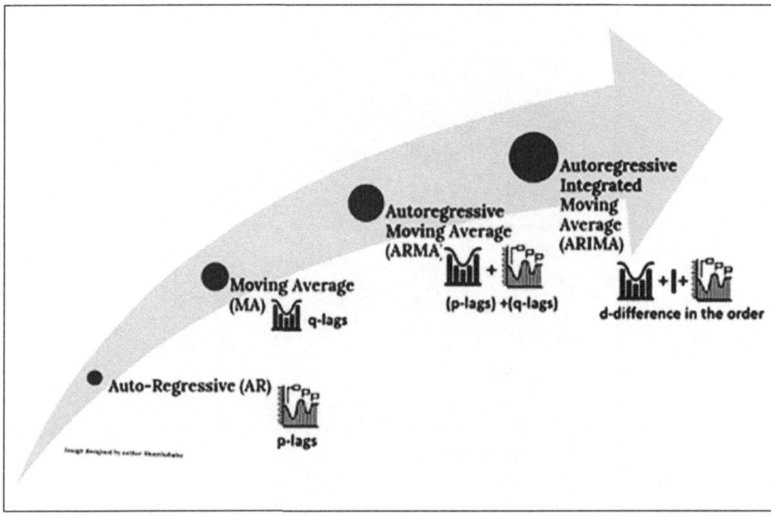

Figure 6.2: *Factors Influencing the time series analysis and forecasting*

Autoregressive (AR) Model

In this model, we can predict the next values in the series, using the past observations as input in terms of the lag value-p from the linear regression model. Purely depends on the p-value. This model is very simple and accurate forecasting. It comes up with the assumption that the observations at previous values help us to predict the next steps and interpret the linear regression model and exhibit the correlation between them, due to this reason this model is also called an **Autocorrelation** and **Serial-Correlation** because of the time series data are arranged in the sequenced structure. This correlation can be **positive, negative,** or **zero**.

The current and previous value changes together in the same direction and then will get a positive correlation. If both are in opposite directions, then it could be a negative correlation, otherwise the correlation would be zero, then no correlation.

The autoregression model assumes that the observations at previous time steps are useful in predicting the value at the next time step. It can be represented by the following mathematical formula:

$$Y_t=C+ \Sigma\ \beta_i Y_t -_i +\varepsilon_t$$

$$Y_t=C+ \alpha_1 Y_t -1+ \alpha_2 Y_{t-1}+ \alpha_3 Y_{t-1}+......+ \alpha_n Y_{t-n} +\varepsilon_t$$

Where,

- Y_{t-1}-> represents the previous value of Y
- n-> past values
- C-> Constant
- α-> Coefficient of each 'n'
- ε_t-> error in time or residual

Benefits of Autoregressive (AR)

- It can prepare recurring patterns from the given dataset
- Suitable for a lower volume of the dataset at hand and predicting forecasting
- The best fitment for lack of randomness in the given dataset
- Appropriate models for investment analysis, qualitative methods, and market research

Limitations of Autoregressive (AR)

- This model is purely dependent on the autocorrelation coefficient, and this factor should be greater than 0.5 for analysis and model. If it is less than 0.5, then not suitable for any further analysis.
- Predictions are dependent on historical data and correlated with economic conditions.

Autoregressive (AR) Implementation

Let's implement the AR model using our diesel price dataset in simple steps.

Given the dataset as shown in Figure 6.3:

Sale_Date	Diesel price
16-04-2022	5
17-04-2022	6
18-04-2022	5.6
18-04-2022	5.12
21-04-2022	5.1
22-04-2022	5.34
24-04-2022	5.45
25-04-2022	4
26-04-2022	6.17
26-04-2022	4.6
29-04-2022	3.2

Figure 6.3: *Diesel price dataset*

Let Y be the price and keep lags (p) is 3 will calculate Y_{t-1}, Y_{t-2}, Y_{t-3} [1,2 and 3] and the outcome as shown in *Figure* 6.4:

Sale_Date	Diesel price	Y_{t-1}	Y_{t-2}	Y_{t-3}
16-04-2022	5			
17-04-2022	6	5		
18-04-2022	5.6	6	5	
18-04-2022	5.12	5.6	6	5
21-04-2022	5.1	5.12	5.6	6
22-04-2022	5.34	5.1	5.12	5.6
24-04-2022	5.45	5.34	5.1	5.12
25-04-2022	4	5.45	5.34	5.1
26-04-2022	6.17	4	5.45	5.34
26-04-2022	4.6	6.17	4	5.45
29-04-2022	3.2	4.6	6.17	4
30-04-2022	5.13	3.2	4.6	6.17
02-05-2022	4.99	5.13	3.2	4.6
03-05-2022	5.2	4.99	5.13	3.2
04-05-2022	6.08	5.2	4.99	5.13
05-05-2022	5.95	6.08	5.2	4.99
06-05-2022	5.13	5.95	6.08	5.2
07-05-2022	4.8	5.13	5.95	6.08
08-05-2022	5.1	4.8	5.13	5.95

Figure 6.4: *Diesel price dataset after applying* Yt-1, Yt-2, Yt-3

After the lags were applied, let me remove the null cells from the proceeding table and the final dataset for our analysis shown in *Figure* 6.5:

Sale_Date	Diesel price	Y_{t-1}	Y_{t-2}	Y_{t-3}
18-04-2022	5.12	5.6	6	5
21-04-2022	5.1	5.12	5.6	6
22-04-2022	5.34	5.1	5.12	5.6
24-04-2022	5.45	5.34	5.1	5.12
25-04-2022	4	5.45	5.34	5.1
26-04-2022	6.17	4	5.45	5.34
26-04-2022	4.6	6.17	4	5.45
29-04-2022	3.2	4.6	6.17	4
30-04-2022	5.13	3.2	4.6	6.17
02-05-2022	4.99	5.13	3.2	4.6
03-05-2022	5.2	4.99	5.13	3.2
04-05-2022	6.08	5.2	4.99	5.13
05-05-2022	5.95	6.08	5.2	4.99
06-05-2022	5.13	5.95	6.08	5.2
07-05-2022	4.8	5.13	5.95	6.08

Figure 6.5: *Diesel price final dataset*

Once the final dataset arrives, we have to do the data analysis. To do this, we have to perform the following steps to enable **`Analysis ToolPak in Excel`**

Step-1: Go to the file menu and select **`Options`** sub-menu.

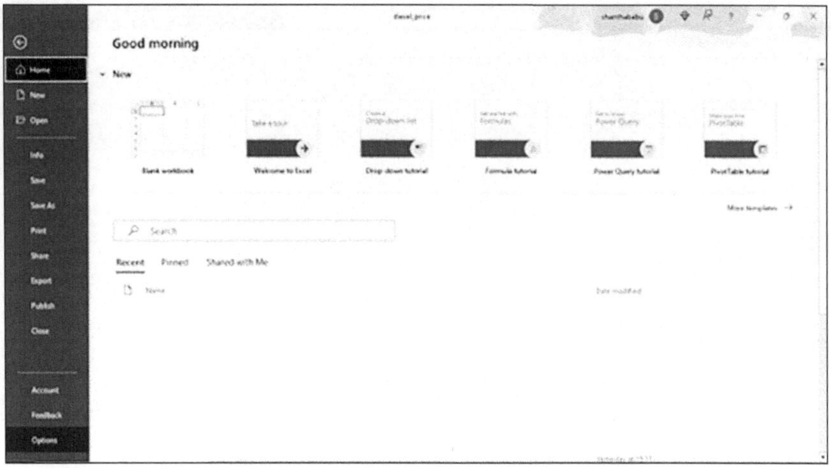

***Figure 6.6** Step-1 Analysis ToolPak in Excel*

Step-2: In the Excel option popup, select **`Add-Ins`** and check **Analysis ToolPak in Excel** under the active or inactive list. Select this add-in and click **`OK`.**

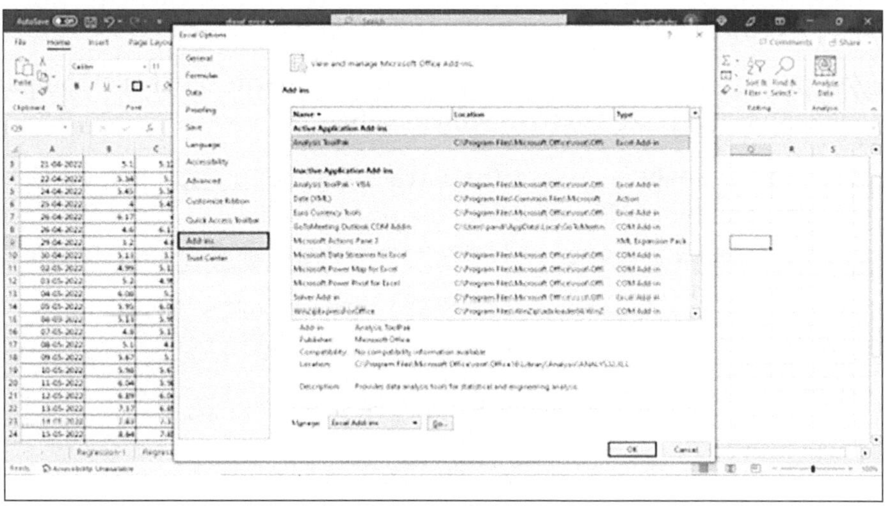

***Figure 6.7:** Step-2 Analysis ToolPak in Excel*

Step-3: Go to the **`Data`** main menu and check the **`Data Analysis`** tab available and you are ready to do the AR analysis.

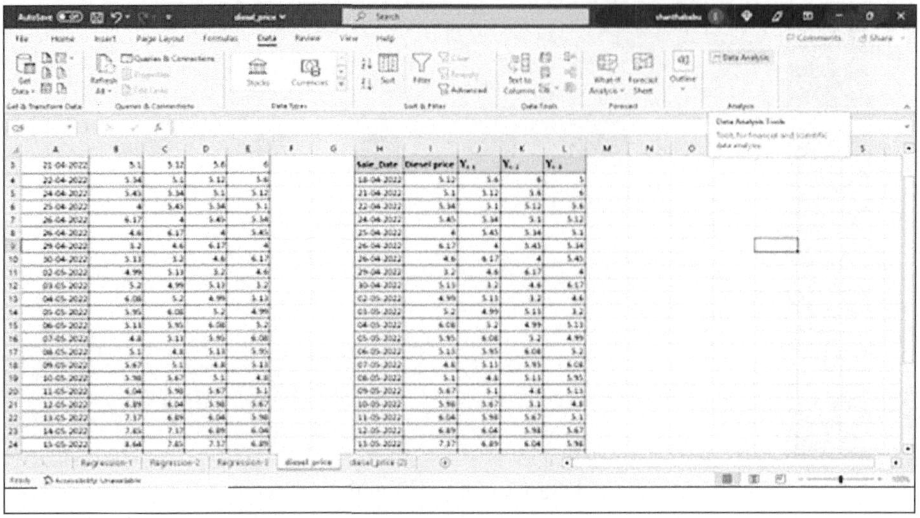

Figure 6.8: *Step-3 Analysis ToolPak in Excel*

For additional reference, please use the following Microsoft (Load the Analysis ToolPak in Excel):

https://support.microsoft.com/en-us/office/load-the-analysis-toolpak-in-excel-6a63e598-cd6d-42e3-9317-6b40ba1a66b4

Let's start our AR analysis. Select the **`Data`** main menu and click on the **`Data Analysis`** tab as shown in *Figure 6.9*:

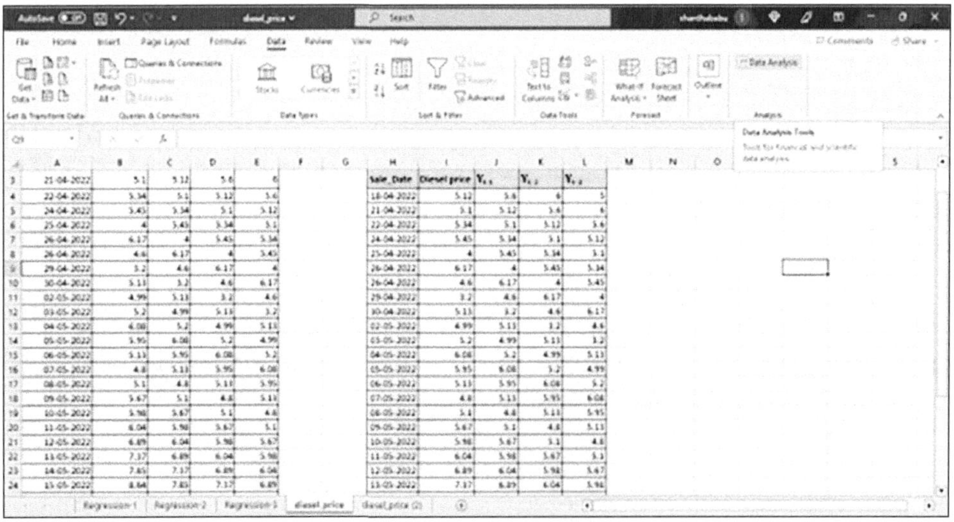

Figure 6.9: *Step-4 Analysis ToolPak in Excel*

After clicking on the **Data Analysis** tab, you will get a **Data Analysis** popup screen showing *Figure 6.10*:

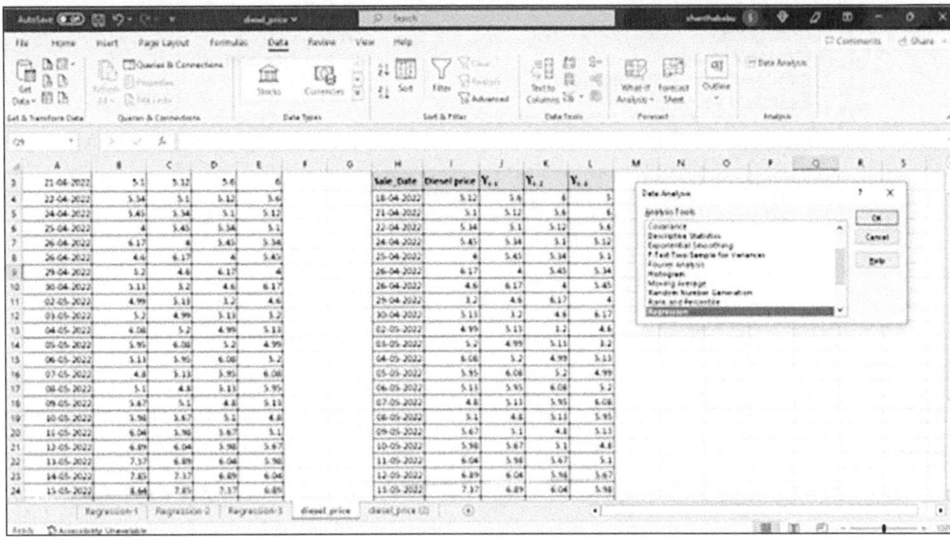

Figure 6.10: *Step-5 Analysis ToolPak in Excel*

Select the dataset we are planning to apply to the **Autoregressive** model and select the **Regression** from the list as shown in *Figure 6.11*:

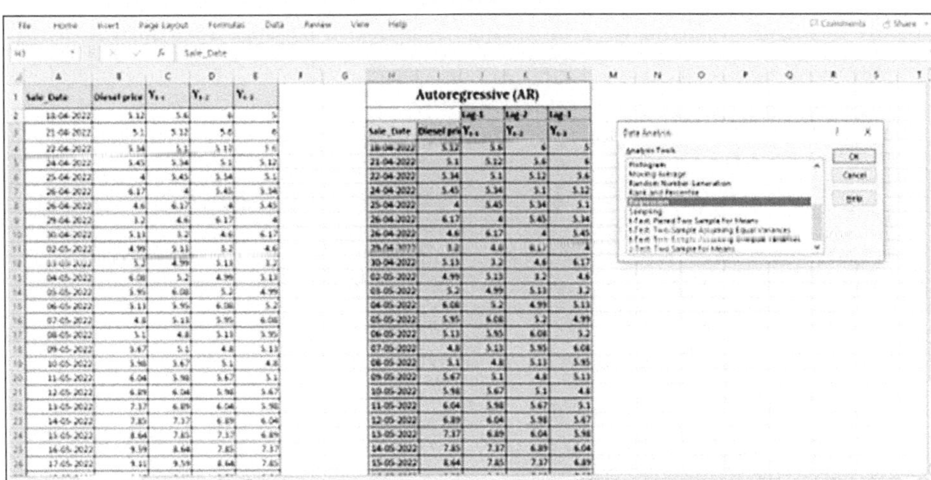

Figure 6.11: *Step-6 Analysis ToolPak in Excel*

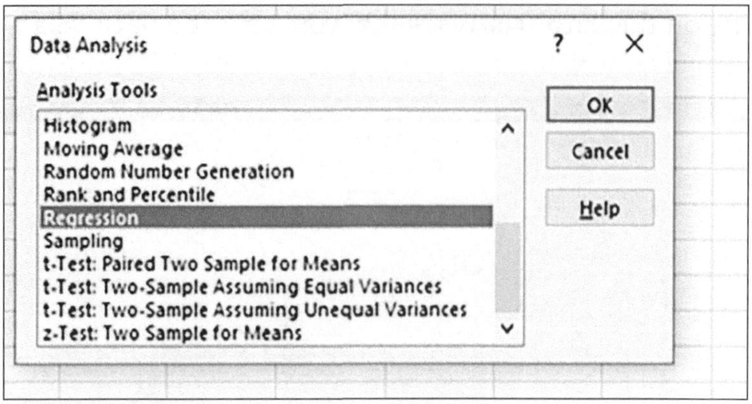

Figure 6.12: *ToolPak – Data analysis options*

Configure the inputs, outputs, residuals, and new worksheet for regression analysis:

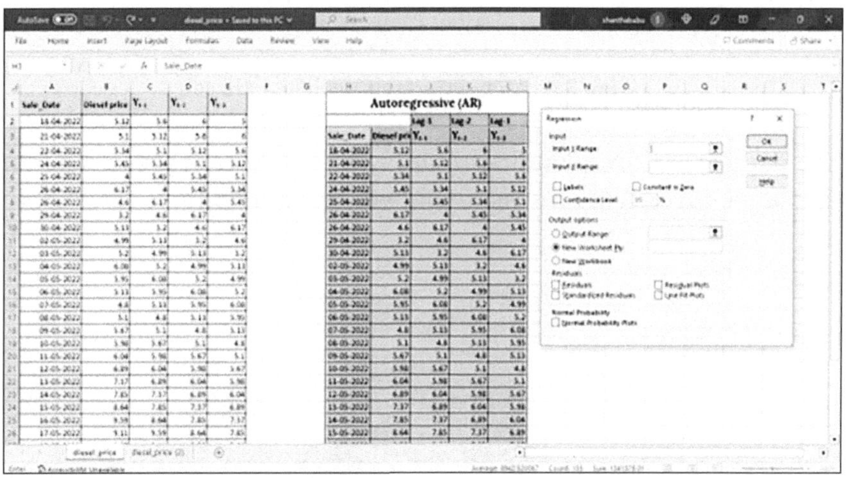

Figure 6.13: *Step-7 Analysis ToolPak in Excel (configuring the regression model)*

For our analysis, we will perform the following configuration:

- Input range -> Diesel price
- Output range -> all three lags
- Labels -> Check
- Confidence intervals -> Check
- Residuals -> Check
- New worksheet Ply -> mention the target new sheet (Regression-1)

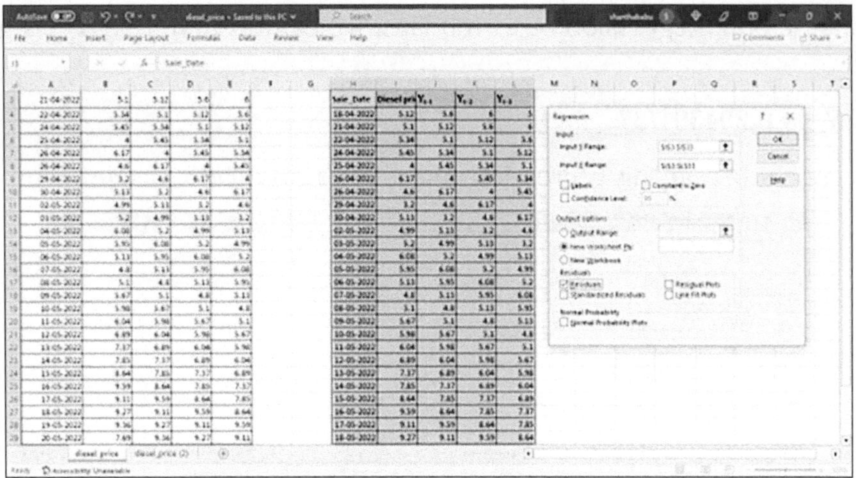

Figure 6.14: *Step-8 Analysis ToolPak in Excel (configuring the regression model)*

After the configuration has been completed, click on **OK**, excel will create *Figure* 6.15 to show you the statistical summary.

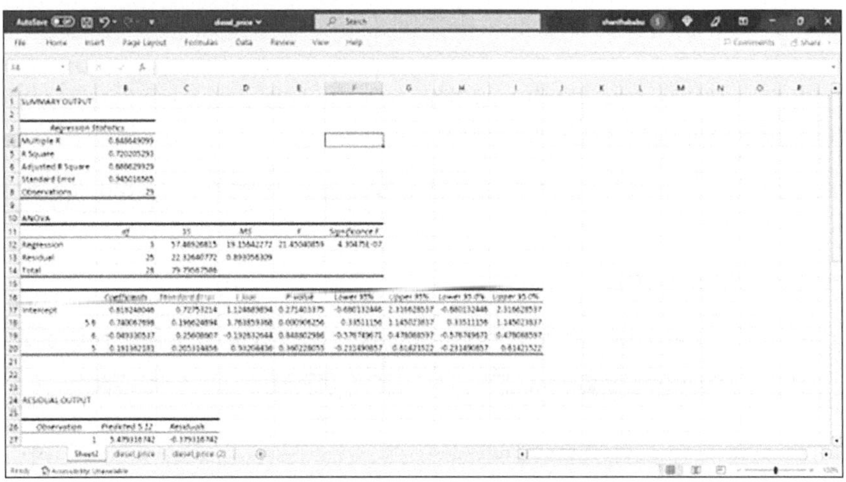

Figure 6.15: AR - *Statistical summary*

Analysis of the P-value

The condition for statistically significant is, p-value < Alpha (α) [α=0.05]

α is the coefficient and it can be described as the autoregressive model with p-value lags. In an AR model, a series of lags will be considered as a predictor and used to fit the dependent variable in the sequence method for the equation of $\mathbf{Y_t}$.

From *Figure* 6.16, Regression -1 with 3 lags, we can observe that $\mathbf{Y_{t-3}}$ is greater than α.

$$\mathbf{Y_{t-3} = 0.294391737}$$

So will conclude that this regression analysis is ***statistically insignificant.***

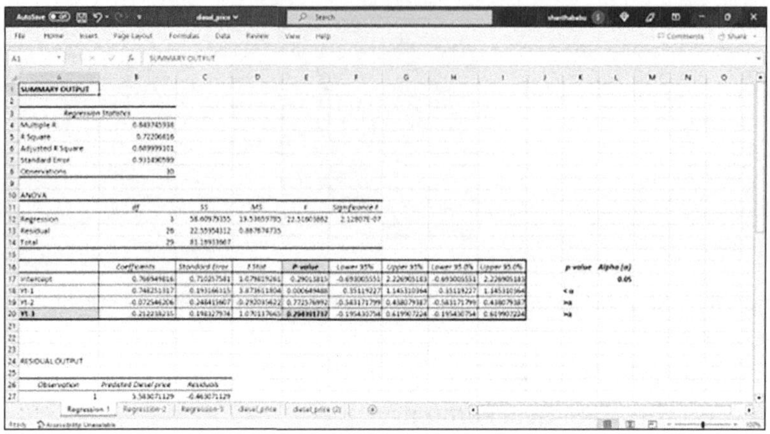

Figure 6.16: AR – *Regression -1, statistical summary analysis with p and α*

Repeat the preceding regression configuration steps for the second regression analysis by ignoring the Y_{t-3} lags range.

In *Figure* 6.17, Regression -2 with 2 lags and we can observe that $\mathbf{Y_{t-2}}$ is greater than α

$$\mathbf{Y_{t-2} = 0.626017112}$$

So will conclude that this regression analysis is ***statistically insignificant.***

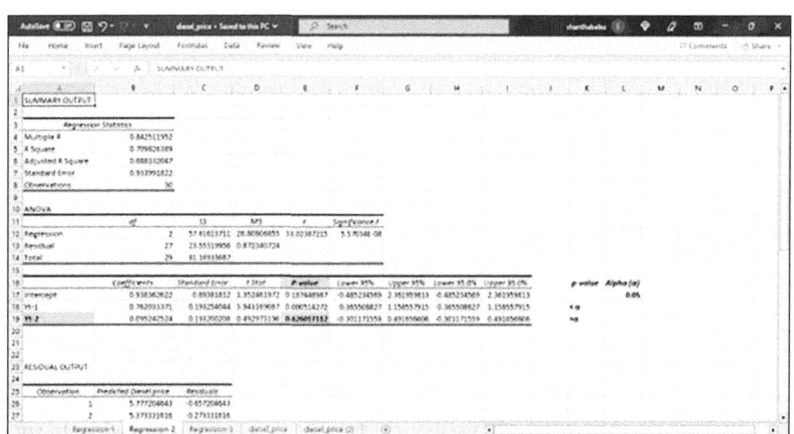

Figure 6.17: AR – *Regression -2, Statistical summary analysis with p and α*

Repeat the preceding regression configuration steps for the third regression analysis by ignoring the Y_{t-2} and Y_{t-3} lags range.

From *Figure* 6.18, Regression -3 with 1 lag and we can observe that $\mathbf{Y_{t-1}}$ is lesser than α

$$\mathbf{Y_{t-1} = 5.96E\text{-}09}$$

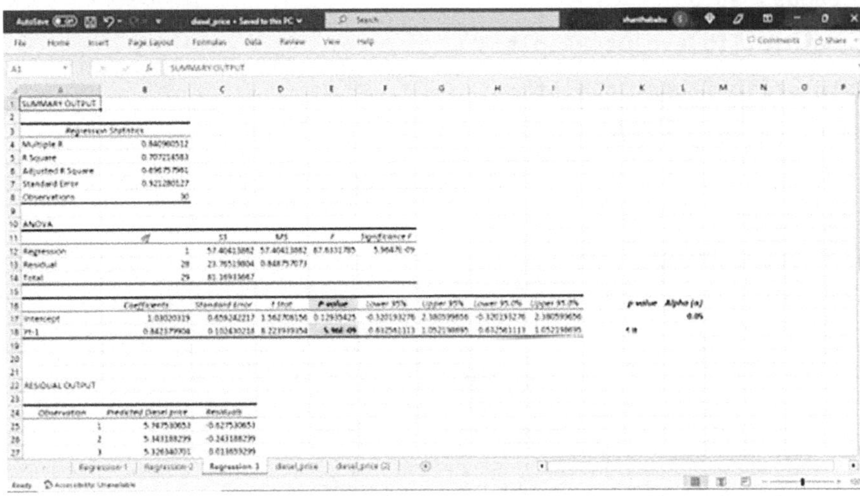

Figure 6.18: AR – *Regression -3, statistical summary analysis with p and α*

So will conclude that this regression analysis is ***statistically significant***

Let's predict the new diesel price by applying values in the following equation:

$$Y_t = C + \alpha_1 Y_{t-1} + \alpha 2\ Y_{t-1} + \alpha 3\ Y_{t-1} + \ldots + \alpha_n\ Y_{t-n} + \varepsilon_t$$

for lag=1

$Y_t = C + \alpha_1 Y_{t-1}$ **(1)**$Y_{t-1} = 7.5$

C= 1.03020319

α1= 0.294391737

apply these values in *Equation* (1):

$$Y_t = 3.238141217$$

Auto-regression model for TSA&F with Python

Let's analyze the autoregression model using Python,

```
#load the required libraries
import numpy as np
import pandas as pd
import matplotlib.pyplot as plt
from matplotlib import pyplot
#load dataset for analysis
df_diesel_price = pd.read_csv('diesel_price AR.csv', header=0, index_
col=0)
df_diesel_price.head()
```

	Diesel price
Sale_Date	
16-04-2022	5.00
17-04-2022	6.00
18-04-2022	5.60
18-04-2022	5.12
21-04-2022	5.10

Figure 6.19: *Diesel price dataset*

Line plot: this plot represents a line plot for the given dataset, to understand the data across different dates in the dataset.

```
print("########################################")
print("    Line Plot for the Diesel Price     ")
print("########################################")
df_diesel_price.plot()
pyplot.show()
```

```
########################################
     Line Plot for the Diesel Price
########################################
```

Figure 6.20: *Line plot for diesel price*

Log plot: this plot represents a logarithmic scale on the x- and y-axis. the diesel prices (t) on the x-axis against diesel prices on the previous day (t-1) on the y-axis. We were able to observe that there is minimal correlation existing in the data. If we have a huge volume, the representation of correlation would be more.

```
from pandas.plotting import lag_plot
print("###########################################")
print("    Lag plot for the Diesel Price     ")
print("###########################################")
lag_plot(df_diesel_price)
pyplot.show()
```

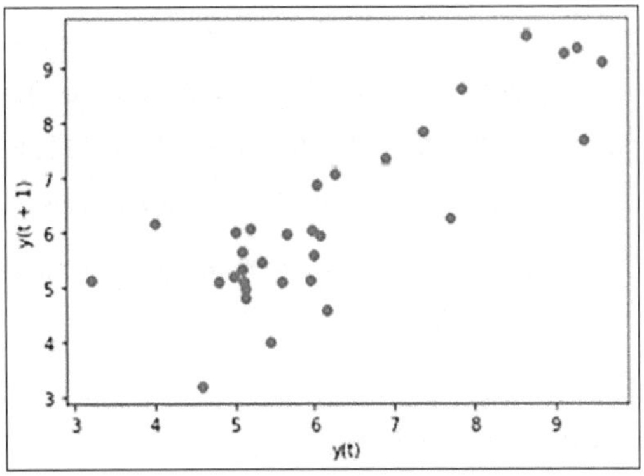

Figure 6.21: *Lag plot for the diesel price*

Autocorrelation using 3 lags: Instead of the plot methods, we can test the correlation using the statistical test. Let's go with the `corr()` function on the dataset and calculate the correlation between the lag variable and observations. This test produces the correlation table for two variables, and this will be exhibited in terms of positive, negative and zero correlations as discussed earlier and with a specific scale range from 0.5 to -0.5.

The following code helps us to create the matrix of the diesel prices (t) against diesel prices on the previous day (t-1)

```
values = pd.DataFrame(df_diesel_price.values)
dataframe = pd.concat([values.shift(3),values.shift(2),values.shift(1),
values], axis=1)
print("##################################################")
print("    Autocorrelation using 3 lags (corr())      ")
print("##################################################")
dataframe.columns = ['t-1', 't+1', 't+2','t+3']
result = dataframe.corr()
print(result)
print("##################################################")
```

Output

```
##################################################
     Autocorrelation using 3 lags (corr())
##################################################
          t-1       t+1       t+2       t+3
t-1  1.000000  0.850301  0.735969  0.698860
t+1  0.850301  1.000000  0.838991  0.737966
t+2  0.735969  0.838991  1.000000  0.836193
t+3  0.698860  0.737966  0.836193  1.000000
##################################################
```

The preceding matrix shows a strong positive correlation (0.85) between the observation and the lag=1 value than other combinations.

Autocorrelation (AR) Plots: Let's plot the correlation coefficient for each lag variable this is best practice for finding the relation between historical data changing over a while and predictive modeling:

```
from pandas.plotting import autocorrelation_plot
print("\t##################################################")
print("           Autocorrelation (AR) Plots          ")
print("\t##################################################")
```

```
autocorrelation_plot(df_diesel_price)
pyplot.show()
```

```
            ##################################################
                    Autocorrelation (AR) Plots
            ##################################################
```

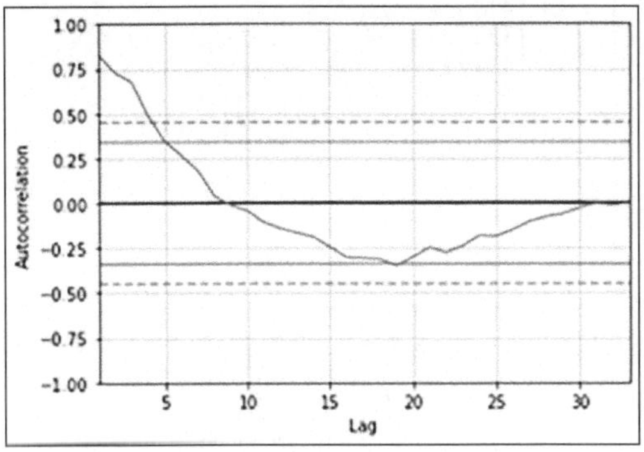

Figure 6.22: *Autocorrelation (AR) plots*

- x-axis -> lag number
- y-axis -> correlation coefficient [Range between -1 and 1]
- solid and dashed lines with 95% and 99% confidence intervals

Observation: Correlation values above solid and dashed lines are more significant than those below.

Let's plot the autocorrelation function using `plot_acf()`, here lags on the horizontal axis and correlations on the vertical axis.

```
from pandas import read_csv
from matplotlib import pyplot
print("\t##################################################")
print("\tAutocorrelation (AR) Plot using ACF function    ")
print("\t##################################################")
from statsmodels.graphics.tsaplots import plot_acf
plot_acf(df_diesel_price, lags=31)
pyplot.show()
```

```
Output####################################################
  Autocorrelation (AR) Plot using ACF function
####################################################
```

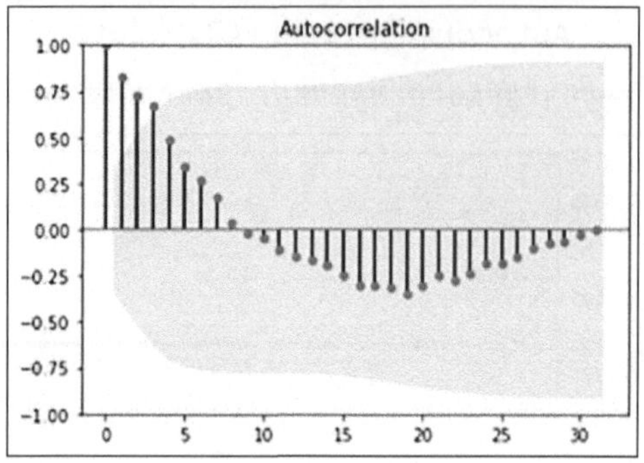

Figure 6.23: *Autocorrelation (AR) plot using ACF function*

Let's do Auto-regression (AR) using code and plot the test and prediction.

Auto-regression (AR)

```
#Including libraries for Auto-regression (AR)
print("\t\tAuto-regression (AR)")
print("\t\t######################\n")
from statsmodels.tsa.ar_model import AutoReg
from sklearn.metrics import mean_squared_error
from math import sqrt
# load dataset
series = pd.read_csv('diesel_price AR.csv', header=0, index_col=0,
parse_dates=True, squeeze=True)
# split dataset for test and train
X = series.values
train, test = X[1:len(X)-5], X[len(X)-5:]
# Implementing Auto-regression using AutoReg algorithm
model = AutoReg(train, lags=10)
model_fit = model.fit()
print("\t################################################")
print("\t    Coefficient for the taken sample for AR    ")
print("\t################################################")
print('\t %s' % model_fit.params)
```

```
# make predictions
start=len(train)
end=len(train)+len(test)-1
predictions = model_fit.predict(start,end, dynamic=False)
#looping the prediction
print("\t##################################################")
print("\t                 Predicted Vs Expected           ")
print("\t##################################################")
for i in range(len(predictions)):
 print('\tpredicted=%f, expected=%f' % (predictions[i], test[i]))
rmse = sqrt(mean_squared_error(test, predictions))
print("\t##################################################")
print("\tTest RMSE: %.3f" % rmse)
print("\t##################################################")
print("\t##################################################")
print('\tTest MSE: %.3f' % test_score)
print("\t##################################################")
```

Output

```
                    Auto-regression (AR)
                    #####################
        ################################################
            Coefficient for the taken sample for AR
        ################################################
[-4.42837797  0.88085754 -0.18652467  0.3274679  -0.32614067  0.3361129
  0.25017828  0.22951608  0.04673161  0.11385048  0.27097321]
        ################################################
                    Predicted Vs Expected
        ################################################
            predicted=9.970689, expected=9.270000
            predicted=11.540870, expected=9.360000
            predicted=12.922754, expected=7.690000
            predicted=15.048094, expected=6.270000
            predicted=17.460997, expected=7.080000
```

```
##############################################
Test RMSE: 6.595
##############################################
##############################################
Test MSE: 0.947
##############################################
```

Plotting Test Vs Predictions

```
print("\t##############################################")
print("\t          Plotting Test Vs predictions          ")
print("\t##############################################")

def plot_test_predict(x):
 return x
predictions = list()
for x in test_X:
 y = plot_test_predict(x)
 predictions.append(y)
test_score = mean_squared_error(test_y, predictions)
# plot predictions vs expected
pyplot.plot(test_y,color="red")
pyplot.plot(predictions, color="green")
plt.legend(["predictions", "test"], loc ="lower right")
pyplot.show()
```

Output

```
##############################################
Plotting Test Vs predictions
##############################################
```

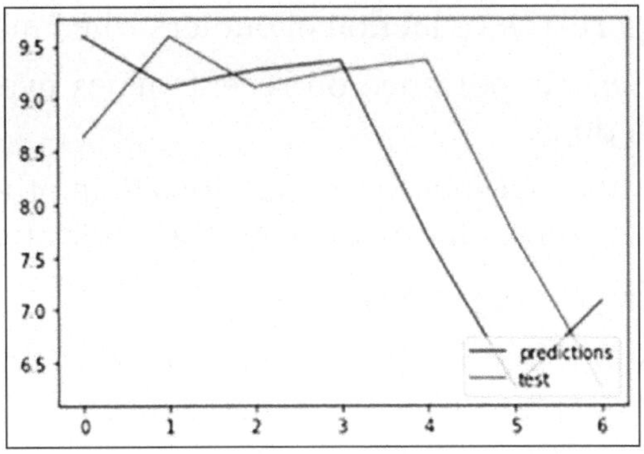

Figure 6.24: AR - *Plotting test Vs predictions*

Note: Using the autoregressive (AR) model, we can predict the next values in the series, using the past observations as input in terms of lag value-p from the linear regression model. Purely depends on the p-value. This model is very simple and accurate forecasting. It assumes that the observations at previous time steps are useful for predicting the value at the next step. It can be represented by the Yt=C+ Σ βiYt-i+εt mathematical formula. Using Analysis ToolPak in Excel, we were able to build the model very quickly.

Moving Average (MA) Model

This model will consider the average of the data in terms of M-value (set of values) taken into account for the prediction, this will be calculated manually using the following formula:

$$MA = \frac{\sum X_t}{n}$$

i □ 1.....n

n □ Number of periods in the Moving Average

X □ Demand for the period

We are following three different methods to apply the MA model. Let's discuss them in detail. Simple Moving Average (**SMA**), Cumulative Moving Average (**CMA**) and Exponential Moving Average (**EMA**).

Benefits of Moving Average (MA)

- Best fit for predicting short-term forecasting, flexible, ease of use and building trends

- It highly supports the reduction of outliers when making predictions by
- It supports more importance on recent values over older values while making predictions
- The SMA method provides faster solutions than other complex methods and it has been proven for many real-time applications

Limitations of Moving Average (MA)

- Operationally, this technique is slower to respond since the rapid changes in the stream data feed from the applications.
- Due to its nature, the cyclical pattern is not captured by future predictions.
- Since the bottom-line past data points are not signs of real-time applications and building the gap over there while predictions.

Moving Average (MA) Implementation

Let's implement the MA model using our diesel price dataset in simple steps. Given the dataset. as shown in *Figure* 6.25.

Sale_Date	Diesel price
16-04-2022	5
17-04-2022	6
18-04-2022	5.6
18-04-2022	5.12
21-04-2022	5.1
22-04-2022	5.34
24-04-2022	5.45
25-04-2022	4
26-04-2022	6.17
26-04-2022	4.6
29-04-2022	3.2
30-04-2022	5.13
02-05-2022	4.99

***Figure* 6.25:** *Diesel price dataset*

Let Y be the price and calculate the simple forecasting after 4 days using the AVERAGE function and the outcome as shown in *Figure* 6.26:

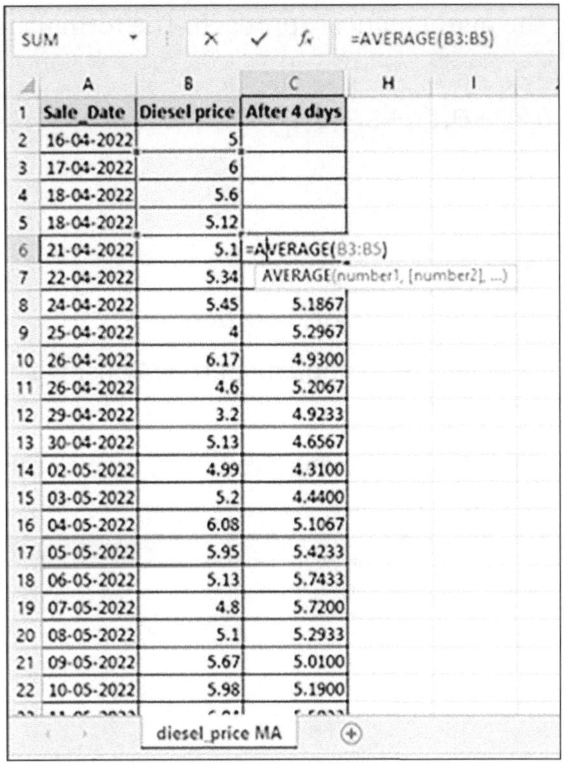

SUM =AVERAGE(B3:B5)

	A	B	C
1	Sale_Date	Diesel price	After 4 days
2	16-04-2022	5	
3	17-04-2022	6	
4	18-04-2022	5.6	
5	18-04-2022	5.12	
6	21-04-2022	5.1	=AVERAGE(B3:B5)
7	22-04-2022	5.34	AVERAGE(number1, [number2], ...)
8	24-04-2022	5.45	5.1867
9	25-04-2022	4	5.2967
10	26-04-2022	6.17	4.9300
11	26-04-2022	4.6	5.2067
12	29-04-2022	3.2	4.9233
13	30-04-2022	5.13	4.6567
14	02-05-2022	4.99	4.3100
15	03-05-2022	5.2	4.4400
16	04-05-2022	6.08	5.1067
17	05-05-2022	5.95	5.4233
18	06-05-2022	5.13	5.7433
19	07-05-2022	4.8	5.7200
20	08-05-2022	5.1	5.2933
21	09-05-2022	5.67	5.0100
22	10-05-2022	5.98	5.1900

diesel_price MA

Figure 6.26: *MA Implementation using Average function*

The line plot for the old and future prices is shown in *Figure 6.27*:

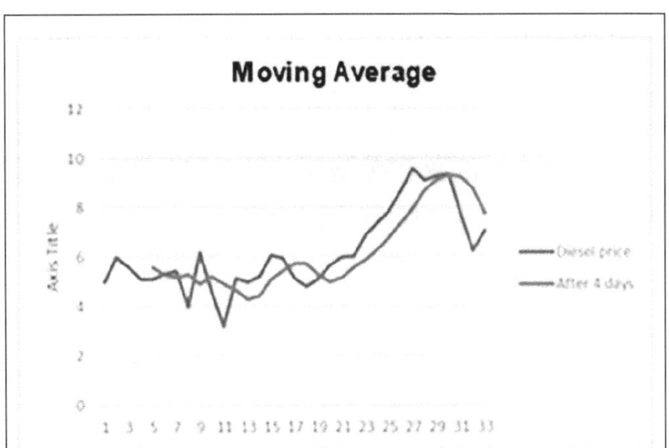

Figure 6.27: *MA Implementation - line plot for old and future prices*

Let's do more with the mathematical approach. The formula for the MA method is as follows:

$$Y_t = C + \varepsilon_t + \theta_1 \varepsilon_{t-1} + \theta_2 \varepsilon_{t-2} + \ldots + \theta_q \varepsilon_{t-q}$$

Where,

- Θ_i -> Coefficient
- ε_t -> white noise
- q -> moving the average model of order

A very simple method would be to implement the MV using an Excel sheet, as we did earlier for the AM model.

Let's start our MA analysis. Select the **`Data`** main menu and click on the **`Data Analysis`** tab as shown in *Figure 6.28*:

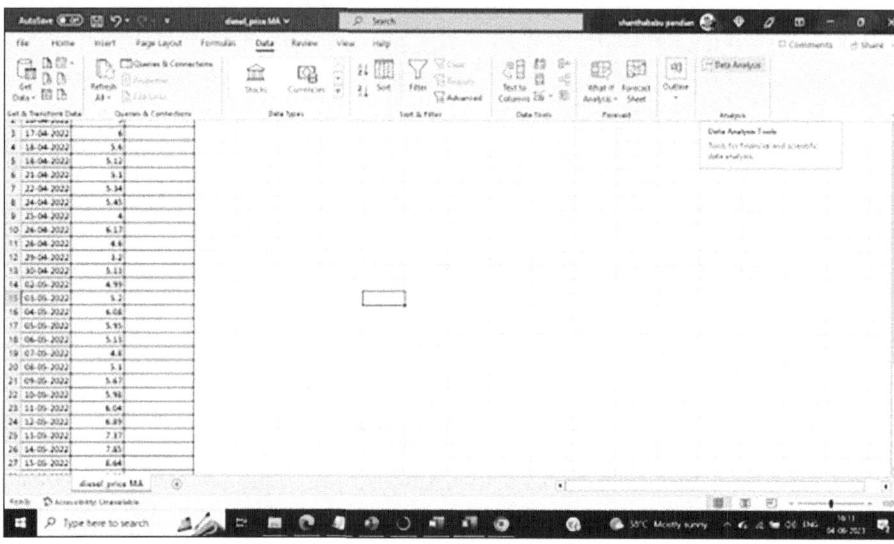

Figure 6.28: *Step-1 Select data analysis options from the Data menu*

After clicking on the Data Analysis tab, you will get a **`Data Analysis`** popup screen shown in *Figure 6.29*.

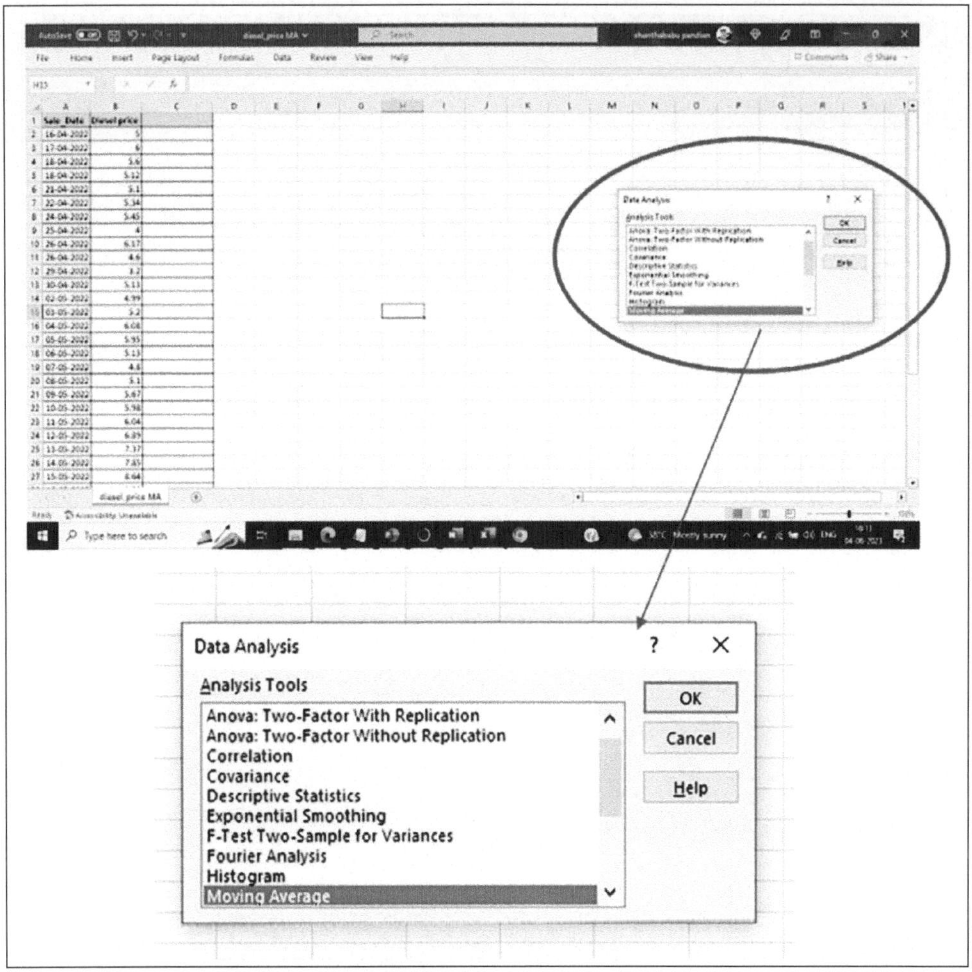

Figure 6.29: *Step-2 Select the Moving Average model from the data analysis*

Configure the input, output, residuals and new worksheet for regression analysis. *Figure* 6.30 shows the moving average model input configuration pop-up window.

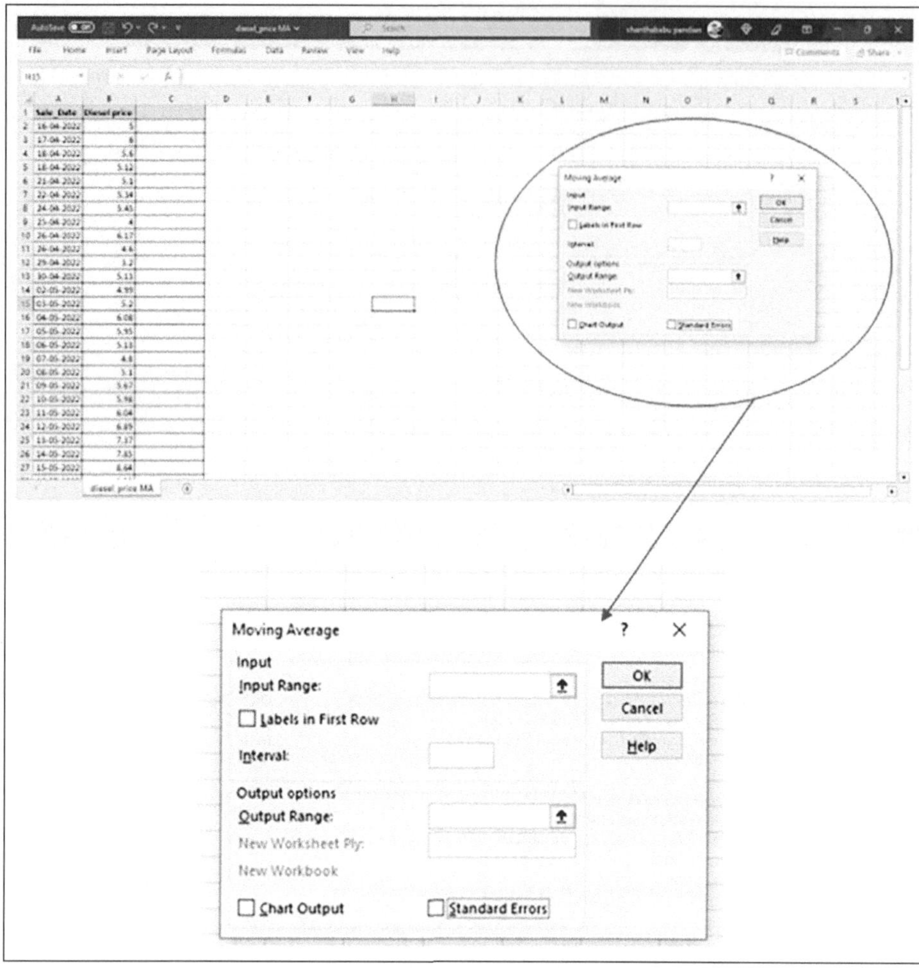

Figure 6.30: *Step-3 Configure Moving Average model*

For our analysis, we will perform the following configuration:

- **`Input range`** -> Diesel price
- **`Output range`** ->
- **`Labels in First Row`** -> Check
- **`Intervals`** -> in numbers
- **`Standard Errors`** -> Check
- **`Chart Output`** -> Check

Figure 6.31 shows the moving average model valid input configuration pop-up window.

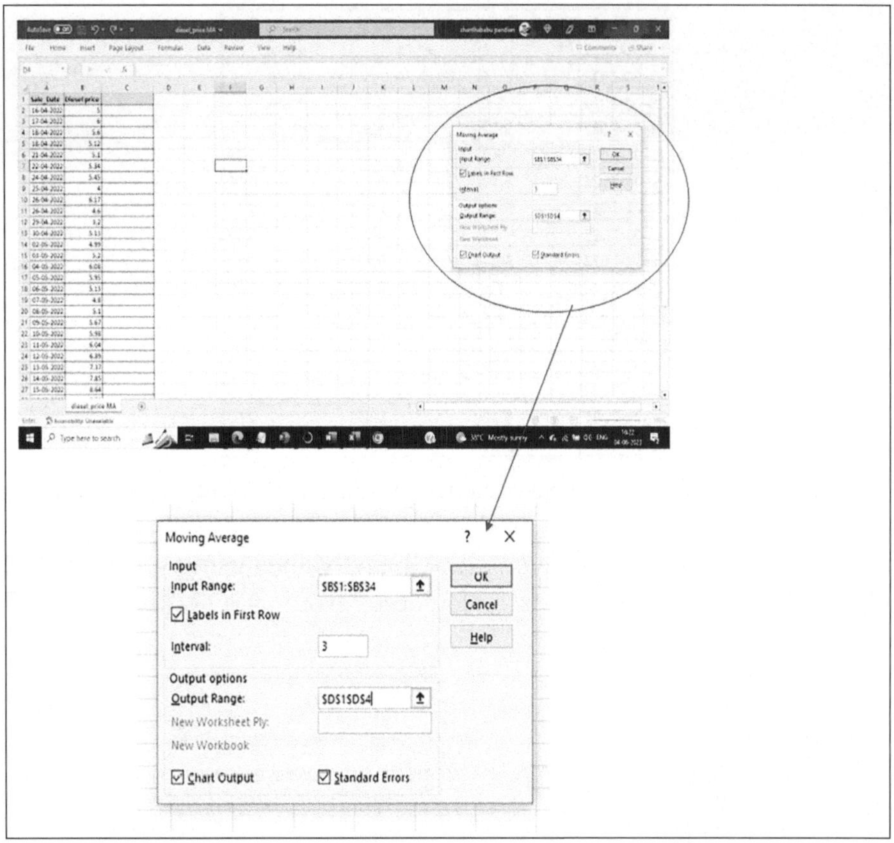

Figure 6.31: *Step-4 Configure the Moving Average model (valid inputs)*

After the configuration has been completed, click on OK, excel will create *Figure* 6.32 to show you the predicted and standard error columns for the intervals along with Chart [Actual Vs Predicted]

Sale_Date	Diesel price	Predicted Price	Standard Errors
16-04-2022	5	#N/A	#N/A
17-04-2022	6	#N/A	#N/A
18-04-2022	5.6	5.53	#N/A
18-04-2022	5.12	5.57	#N/A
21-04-2022	5.1	5.27	0.28
22-04-2022	5.34	5.19	0.29
24-04-2022	5.45	5.30	0.16
25-04-2022	4	4.93	0.55
26-04-2022	6.17	5.21	0.78
26-04-2022	4.6	4.92	0.80
29-04-2022	3.2	4.66	1.03
30-04-2022	5.13	4.31	0.98
02-05-2022	4.99	4.44	1.02
03-05-2022	5.2	5.11	0.57
04-05-2022	6.08	5.42	0.50
05-05-2022	5.95	5.74	0.40

Figure 6.32: *Moving Average model output – predicted price and standard errors*

Prediction is calculated by the average of 3 past values using =AVERAGE(B2:B4) formula and standard error is calculated from =SQRT(SUMXMY2(B4:B6, C4:C6)/3) formula:

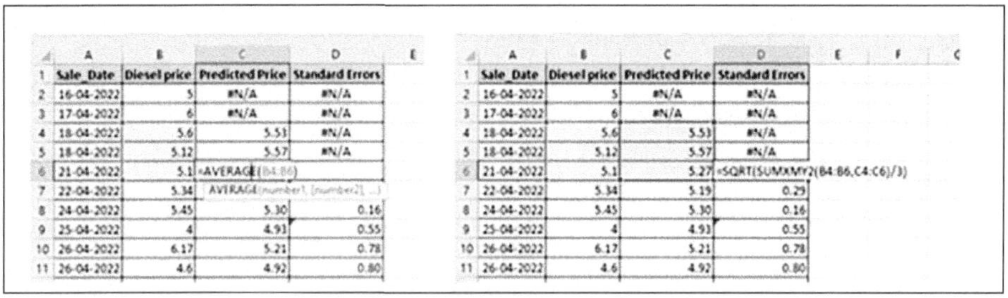

Figure 6.33: *Moving Average model output – predicted price and standard errors along with formulas*

Figure 6.34 shows the: actual vs forecast line plot using the moving average model.

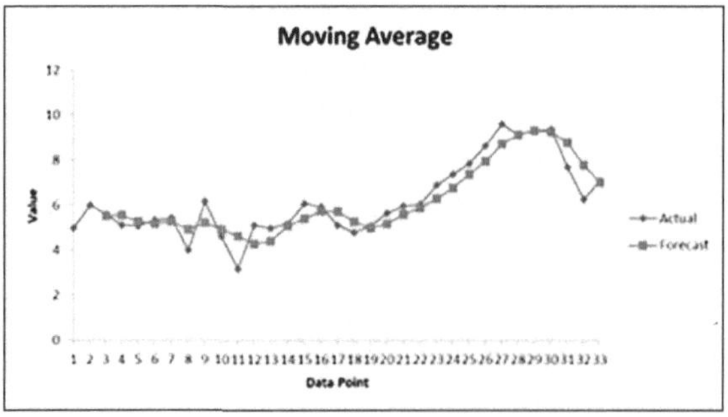

Figure 6.34: *Moving Average model output – line plot*

Using this MV model, we can predict the future in a better way by referring to the chart that the moving average is changing based on the previous values, the same way we can predict the 5th,7th - and 9th -days as intervals and forecasting with a simple process as we did in the previous steps.

In a similar method, we can build Simple Moving Average (**SMA**), Cumulative Moving Average (**CMA**) and Exponential Moving Average (**EMA**) models using Excel sheets and Python code.

Simple Moving Average (SMA): In this model, the number of values within a period is divided by the total number of periods taken into account. In simple terms, the average value over the specified period and a constant size M sliding window during the calculation

$$\text{SMA} = \left\{ \frac{X_1 + X_{t-1} + X_{t-2} + X_{t-3} + \ldots + X_{M-(n-1}}{M} \right\}$$

In the following calculation, M is always 3.

SUM | × ✓ fx | =(B4+B3+B2)/3

	A	B	E
1	Sale_Date	Diesel price	Simple Moving Average (SMA)
2	16-04-2022	5	
3	17-04-2022	6	
4	18-04-2022	5.6	
5	18-04-2022	5.12	=(B4+B3+B2)/3
6	21-04-2022	5.1	5.57
7	22-04-2022	5.34	5.27
8	24-04-2022	5.45	5.19
9	25-04-2022	4	5.30
10	26-04-2022	6.17	4.93
11	26-04-2022	4.6	5.21
12	29-04-2022	3.2	4.92
13	30-04-2022	5.13	4.66
14	02-05-2022	4.99	4.31
15	03-05-2022	5.2	4.44

Figure 6.35: *SMA calculation for diesel price dataset along with formula*

Figure 6.36 shows the actual vs. forecast line plot using the SMA model.

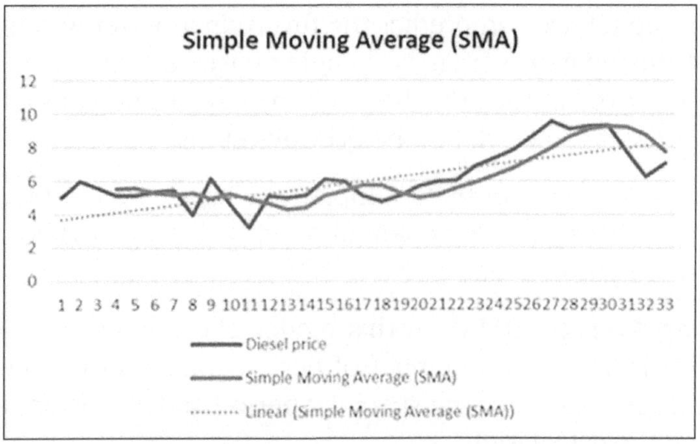

Figure 6.36: *SMA line plot for diesel price dataset*

Here, chart the diesel price movement of protected and disregarded day-to-day price fluctuations from past values.

SMA implementation using Python

Let's implement the SMA model using Python code with a diesel data set and plot the line chart to understand the movements

```
#load the required libraries
import numpy as np
import pandas as pd
import matplotlib.pyplot as plt
from matplotlib import pyplot
#load dataset for SMA model analysis
df_diesel_price_MA = pd.read_csv('diesel_price MA -Python.csv',
header=0, index_col=0)


df_diesel_price_MA['SMA-1'] = df_diesel_price_MA.Diesel_price.rolling(3,
min_periods=1).mean()
df_diesel_price_MA['SMA-2'] = df_diesel_price_MA.Diesel_price.rolling(5,
min_periods=1).mean()
colors = ['green', 'red', 'blue']
df_diesel_price_MA.plot(color=colors, linewidth=3, figsize=(12,6))
plt.xticks(fontsize=14)
plt.yticks(fontsize=14)
```

```
plt.legend(labels =['Diesel Price', '3-Days SMA', '5-Day SMA'], fon-
tsize=14)
plt.title('Diesel_price', fontsize=20)
plt.xlabel('Sale_Date', fontsize=16)
plt.ylabel('Diesel_price', fontsize=16)
print("\t\t\t####################################################")
print("\t\t\t     Simple Moving Average (SMA): - Plot         ")
print("\t\t\t####################################################")
```

```
####################################################
        Simple Moving Average (SMA): - Plot
####################################################
```

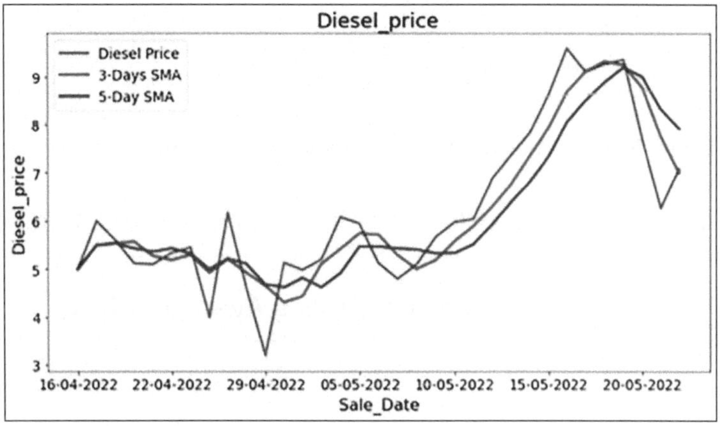

Figure 6.37: *SMA line plot for diesel price using Python code for 3rd and 5th days*

We were able to observe the 3-day and 5-day intervals for SMA, along with the history dataset.

Cumulative Moving Average (CMA): In simple terms, CMA is the unweighted mean of the previous data and running into current data with time interval t. In which the size of the window develops and increases as time passes.

$$CMA = \left\{ \frac{X_1 + X_2 + X_3 + \ldots + X_t}{M} \right\}$$ In the following calculation, M keeps on increasing.

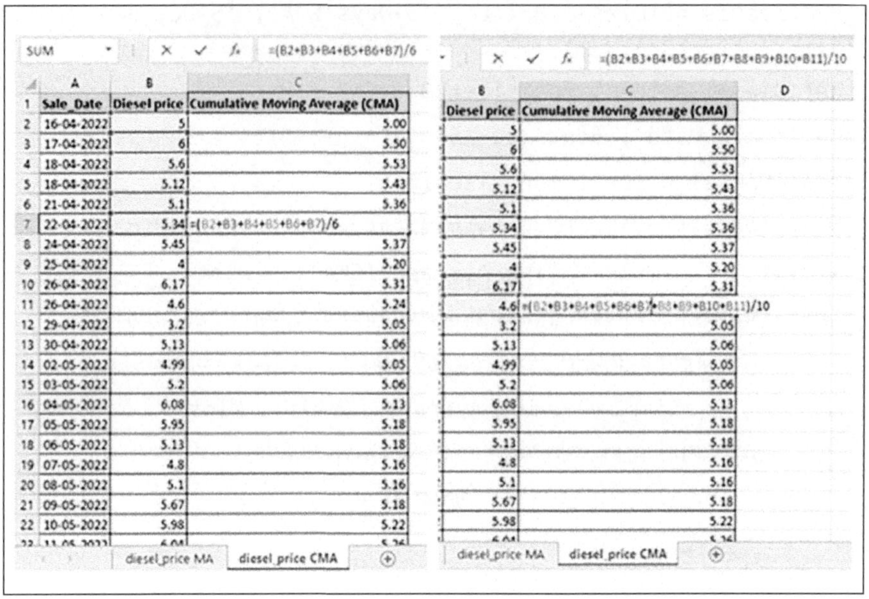

SUM =(B2+B3+B4+B5+B6+B7)/6

	A	B	C
1	Sale_Date	Diesel price	Cumulative Moving Average (CMA)
2	16-04-2022	5	5.00
3	17-04-2022	6	5.50
4	18-04-2022	5.6	5.53
5	18-04-2022	5.12	5.43
6	21-04-2022	5.1	5.36
7	22-04-2022	5.34	=(B2+B3+B4+B5+B6+B7)/6
8	24-04-2022	5.45	5.37
9	25-04-2022	4	5.20
10	26-04-2022	6.17	5.31
11	26-04-2022	4.6	5.24
12	29-04-2022	3.2	5.05
13	30-04-2022	5.13	5.06
14	02-05-2022	4.99	5.05
15	03-05-2022	5.2	5.06
16	04-05-2022	6.08	5.13
17	05-05-2022	5.95	5.18
18	06-05-2022	5.13	5.18
19	07-05-2022	4.8	5.16
20	08-05-2022	5.1	5.16
21	09-05-2022	5.67	5.18
22	10-05-2022	5.98	5.22

diesel_price MA | diesel_price CMA

=(B2+B3+B4+B5+B6+B7+B8+B9+B10+B11)/10

Diesel price	Cumulative Moving Average (CMA)
4.6	=(B2+B3+B4+B5+B6+B7+B8+B9+B10+B11)/10

diesel_price MA | diesel_price CMA

Figure 6.38: CMA model output – *predicted price along with formula*

Figure 6.39 shows the actual vs forecast line plot using the CMA model.

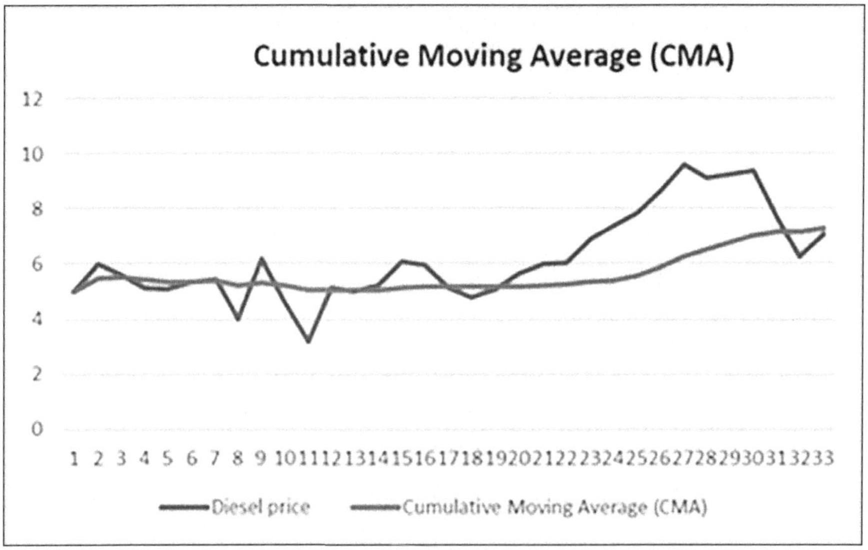

Figure 6.39: *CMA model line plot for diesel price dataset*

CMA implementation using Python

Let's implement the CMA model using the Python code with a diesel data set and plot the line chart to understand the movements.

```
#load the required libraries
import numpy as np
import pandas as pd
import matplotlib.pyplot as plt
from matplotlib import pyplot
#load dataset for CMA model analysis
df_diesel_price_CMA = pd.read_csv("diesel_price CMA.csv", header=0,
index_col=0)
df_diesel_price_CMA.index.name = 'Sale_Date'
df_diesel_price_CMA['average_price'] = df_diesel_price_CMA.mean(axis=1)
df_diesel_price_CMA['CMA'] = df_diesel_price_CMA.average_price.
expanding().mean()
df_diesel_price_CMA[['average_price', 'CMA']].plot(color=colors,
linewidth=3, figsize=(12,6))
plt.xticks(fontsize=14)
plt.yticks(fontsize=14)
plt.legend(labels =['Average price', 'Cumulative Moving Average'],
fontsize=14)
plt.title('Diesel', fontsize=20)
plt.xlabel('Sala_Date', fontsize=16)
plt.ylabel('Diesel Price', fontsize=16)
print("\
t\t#######################################################")
print("\t\t          Cumulative Moving Average Plot for Diesel
")
print("\
t\t#######################################################")
```

```
        #######################################################
                 Cumulative Moving Average Plot for Diesel
        #######################################################
```

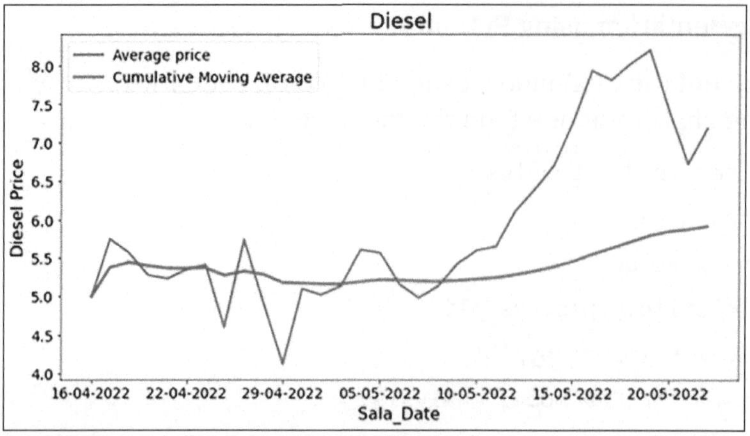

***Figure 6.40:** CMA model line plot for diesel price dataset using Python code*

Exponential Moving Average (EMA): This model reacts faster to changes and is more sensitive than other methods (SMA and CMA). Here the weight of each data point decreases gradually over time since this approach is used to filter out the noises and outline the plots to the recent moments.

The mathematical representation of this method is denoted by the following equation:

$$EMA = \begin{cases} x_0 & t=0 \\ Bx_t + (1-\beta)EMA_{t-1} & t>0 \end{cases}$$

- β is the smoothing factor [value range from 0 to 1].
- x_t is the observation from the dataset during the time(t) period.

In the following calculation, the smoothing factor for the current and previous data points is 0.1 and 0.9:

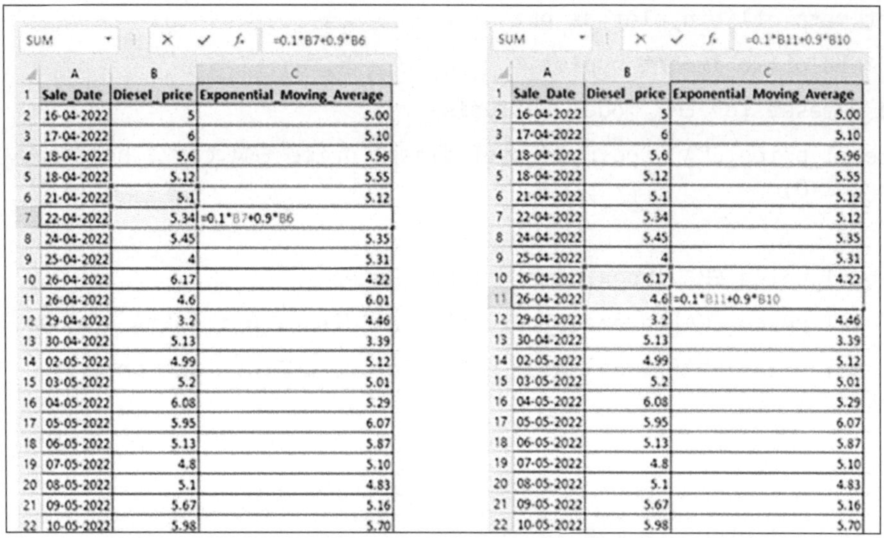

SUM =0.1*B7+0.9*B6

	A	B	C
1	Sale_Date	Diesel_price	Exponential_Moving_Average
2	16-04-2022	5	5.00
3	17-04-2022	6	5.10
4	18-04-2022	5.6	5.96
5	18-04-2022	5.12	5.55
6	21-04-2022	5.1	5.12
7	22-04-2022	5.34	=0.1*B7+0.9*B6
8	24-04-2022	5.45	5.35
9	25-04-2022	4	5.31
10	26-04-2022	6.17	4.22
11	26-04-2022	4.6	6.01
12	29-04-2022	3.2	4.46
13	30-04-2022	5.13	3.39
14	02-05-2022	4.99	5.12
15	03-05-2022	5.2	5.01
16	04-05-2022	6.08	5.29
17	05-05-2022	5.95	6.07
18	06-05-2022	5.13	5.87
19	07-05-2022	4.8	5.10
20	08-05-2022	5.1	4.83
21	09-05-2022	5.67	5.16
22	10-05-2022	5.98	5.70

SUM =0.1*B11+0.9*B10

	A	B	C
1	Sale_Date	Diesel_price	Exponential_Moving_Average
2	16-04-2022	5	5.00
3	17-04-2022	6	5.10
4	18-04-2022	5.6	5.96
5	18-04-2022	5.12	5.55
6	21-04-2022	5.1	5.12
7	22-04-2022	5.34	5.12
8	24-04-2022	5.45	5.35
9	25-04-2022	4	5.31
10	26-04-2022	6.17	4.22
11	26-04-2022	4.6	=0.1*B11+0.9*B10
12	29-04-2022	3.2	4.46
13	30-04-2022	5.13	3.39
14	02-05-2022	4.99	5.12
15	03-05-2022	5.2	5.01
16	04-05-2022	6.08	5.29
17	05-05-2022	5.95	6.07
18	06-05-2022	5.13	5.87
19	07-05-2022	4.8	5.10
20	08-05-2022	5.1	4.83
21	09-05-2022	5.67	5.16
22	10-05-2022	5.98	5.70

Figure 6.41: *EMA model output – predicted price along with formula*

Figure 6.42 shows the actual vs forecast line plot using the EMA model.

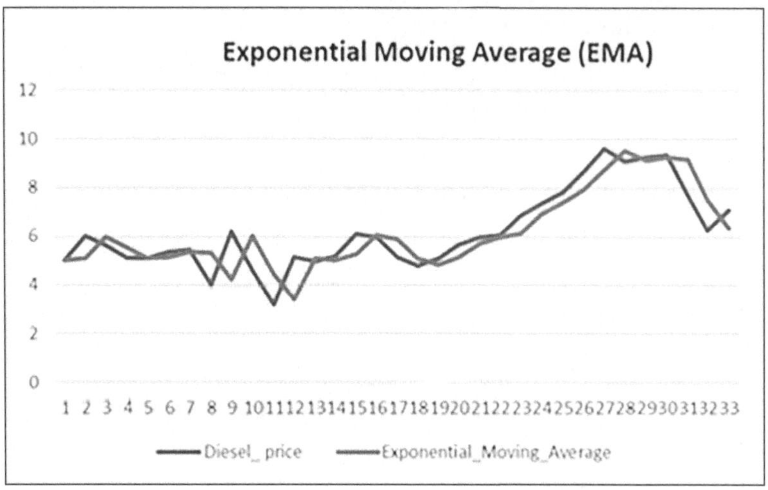

Figure 6.42: *EMA model line plot for diesel price dataset*

EMA implementation using Python

Let's implement the EMA model using Python code with a diesel data set and plot the line chart to understand the movements.

```
#load the required libraries
import numpy as np
import pandas as pd
```

```
import matplotlib.pyplot as plt
from matplotlib import pyplot
#load dataset for EMA model analysis
df_diesel_price_EMA = pd.read_csv("diesel_price EMA.csv", header=0,
index_col=0)

df_diesel_price_EMA.index.name = 'Sale_Date'
df_diesel_price_EMA['average_price'] = df_diesel_price_EMA.mean(axis=1)
df_diesel_price_EMA['EMA'] = df_diesel_price_EMA.average_price.
expanding().mean()


# smoothing factor - 0.1,0.25,.5
df_diesel_price_EMA['EMA_0.1'] = df_diesel_price_EMA.average_price.
ewm(alpha=0.1, adjust=False).mean()
df_diesel_price_EMA['EMA_0.25'] = df_diesel_price_EMA.average_price.
ewm(alpha=0.25, adjust=False).mean()
df_diesel_price_EMA['EMA_0.5'] = df_diesel_price_EMA.average_price.
ewm(alpha=0.5, adjust=False).mean()

colors = ['orange','blue', 'green', 'red']
df_diesel_price_EMA[['average_price', 'EMA_0.1','EMA_0.25','EMA_0.5']].
plot(color=colors, linewidth=3, figsize=(12,6))
plt.xticks(fontsize=14)
plt.yticks(fontsize=14)
plt.legend(labels =['Average price', 'EMA_0.1','EMA_0.25','EMA_0.5'],
fontsize=14)
plt.title('Diesel', fontsize=20)
plt.xlabel('Sala_Date', fontsize=16)
plt.ylabel('Diesel Price', fontsize=16)
print("\
t\t##################################################################")
print("\t\t           Exponential Moving Average Plot for Diesel
")
print("\
t\t##################################################################")
```

```
################################################################
                Exponential Moving Average Plot for Diesel
       ################################################################
```

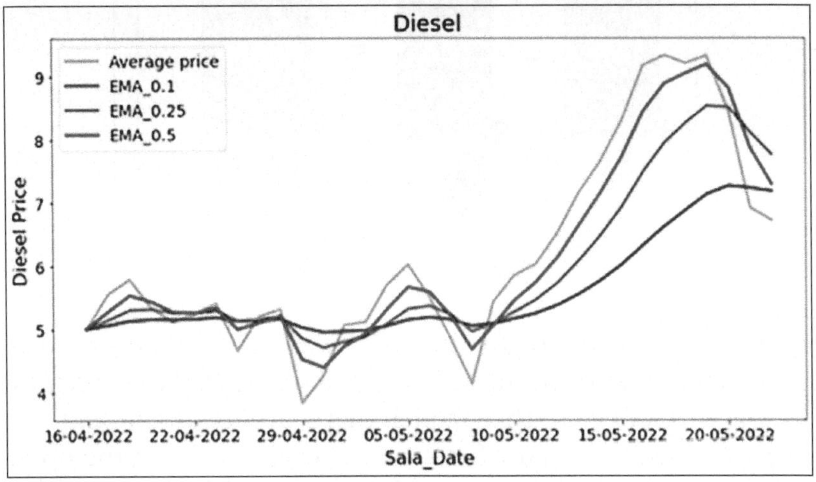

Figure 6.43: *EMA model line plot for diesel price dataset using Python code (EMA .1,.25,.5)*

Figure 6.43 represents the EMA for .1, .25, and .5 smoothing factors and movements.

So far, we have discussed the AR and MA Models and their implementation. Let's focus on the ARMA model now.

Note: The moving average (MA) model always will consider the average of the data in terms of M-value (set of values) taken into account for the prediction, this will be calculated manually using the following formula **MA** = Σ **Xi/n**. We can follow any techniques from its sub-sets- Simple Moving Average (SMA), Cumulative Moving Average (CMA) and Exponential Moving Average (EMA). This model is very simple and accurate forecasting. Similar to the AR model, we can use Analysis ToolPak in Excel and we can build the model very quickly.

ARMA Model

This model uses a combination of autoregression and moving average models and finds the predictions based on past values, which are very similar to AR and MA models and

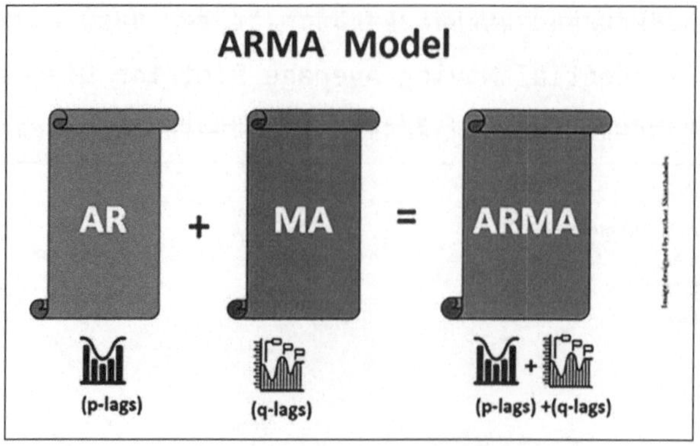

Figure 6.44: *ARMA Model*

Sometimes there were questions with accuracy while using the AR and MA model, that is the reason and brought the ARMA (p,q) is also called the "Auto-Regressive Moving Average" model, in this model there are two different polynomial processes are involved, one part for the auto-regressive and the other one for the moving average. This model is only for stationary data.

The mathematical representation of this model is as follows:

$$Y_t = C + \sum \beta_i Y_{t-i} + \varepsilon_t + \sum_{i=1}^{q} \theta_i \varepsilon_{t-i}$$

Where,

$\sum \beta_i Y_{t-i} + \varepsilon_t$ represents AR model

$\sum_{i=1}^{q} \theta_i \varepsilon_{t-i}$ represents MV model

The ARMA model is best for predicting stationary data series. So, the ARIMA was developed to support both stationary and non-stationary series for high flexibility and accuracy.

Auto-Regressive Integrated Moving Average (ARIMA)

Here we have three major components such as AR, MA and Integration to strengthen the model for both stationary and non-stationary series. We should always remember that in TSA, non-stationary data should be transformed into stationary data for analysis and forecasting.

In this model, the Auto-Regressive(AR) part forms the regression analysis and helps us to indicate the dependent variable strength with other changing factors in the dataset and the Moving Average (MA) helps us to predict the movement of the future time series by investigating on the recent values over older values while making predictions from its own series.

Here the major instrumental process is Integration (I), with the help of differencing steps to generate stationary time series data by removing the seasonal and generating the trend components. Please refer to *Chapter 3, Time Series Analysis and Its Components* for more details.

This model is represented by **ARIMA(p, d, q)** since it is integrated from the AR, MA model and differencing steps.

p-> No of lag observations and log order

d-> Degree of differencing

q-> Order of moving average

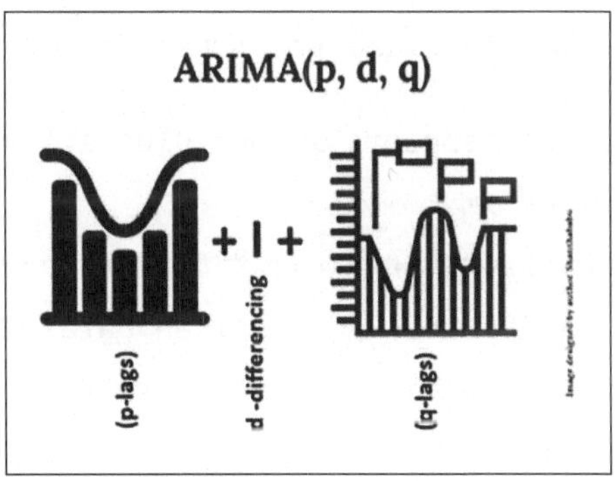

Figure 6.45: ARIMA Model

ARIMA implementation using Python: The implementation is a simple and easy step. We can get the capabilities from statsmodels following are the steps.

- Calling ARIMA() and passing in the p, d, and q parameters to model the object
- Prepare training data by calling the fit() function on the model object
- By calling the predict() function and specifying the required parameters for prediction

```
import numpy as np

import pandas as pd

import matplotlib.pyplot as plt
```

```
%matplotlib inline

df_diesel_price_ARIMA = pd.read_csv("diesel_price ARIMA.csv", header=0,
index_col=0)

df_diesel_price_ARIMA["Diesel_ price"].plot(figsize=(8,5))
```

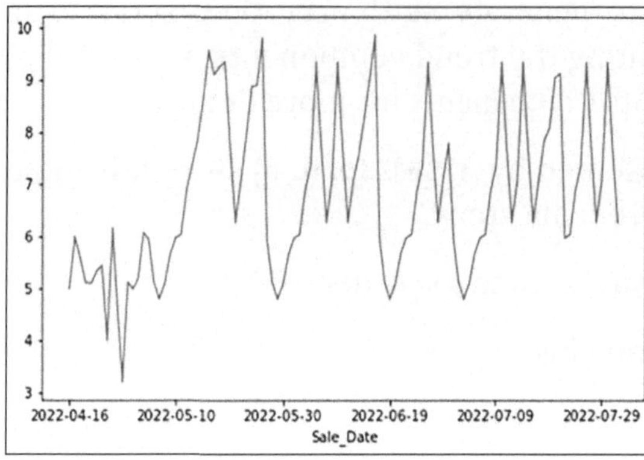

Figure 6.46: *Diesel price dataset line plot*

```
from statsmodels.graphics.tsaplots import plot_acf,plot_pacf
import statsmodels.api as sm
print("#####################################################")
print("        Plotting ACF and PACF - given dataset       ")
print("#####################################################")
fig = plt.figure(figsize=(12,8))
ax1 = fig.add_subplot(211)
fig = sm.graphics.tsa.plot_acf(df_diesel_price_ARIMA["Diesel_ price"].
dropna(),lags=20,ax=ax1)
ax2 = fig.add_subplot(212)
fig = sm.graphics.tsa.plot_pacf(df_diesel_price_ARIMA["Diesel_ price"].
dropna(),lags=25,ax=ax2)
          #####################################################
                  Plotting ACF and PACF - given dataset
          #####################################################
```

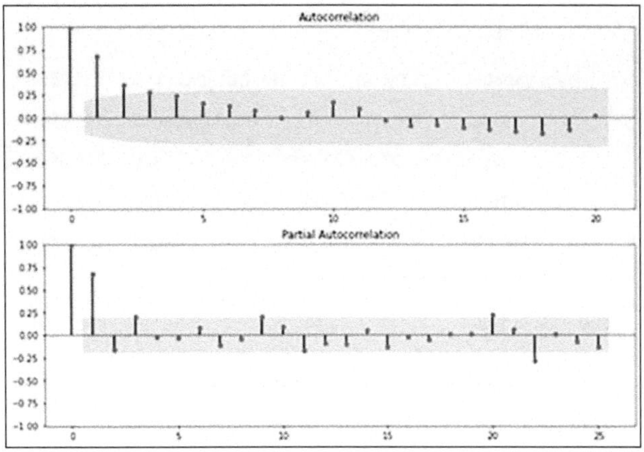

Figure 6.47: *Diesel price dataset Autocorrelation and Partial Autocorrelation plot*

By building the ARIMA model using statsmodels with (p=1, q=0, d=0), you can perform a similar trial for different values of p, q, and d.

```
from statsmodels.tsa.arima.model import ARIMA
print("######################################################")
print("                 ARIMA Model Building                 ")
print("######################################################")
model = ARIMA(df_diesel_price_ARIMA['Diesel_ price'], order=(1,0,0))
model_fit=model.fit()
model_fit.summary()
```

```
######################################################
                 ARIMA Model Building
######################################################
```

SARIMAX Results

Dep. Variable:	Diesel_ price	**No. Observations:**	260
Model:	ARIMA(1, 0, 0)	**Log Likelihood**	-159.659
Date:	Thu, 08 Jun 2023	**AIC**	325.319
Time:	00:35:33	**BIC**	336.001
Sample:	0	**HQIC**	329.613
	- 260		
Covariance Type:	opg		

	coef	std err	z	P>|z|	[0.025	0.975]
const	6.7619	0.372	18.154	0.000	6.032	7.492
ar.L1	0.6760	0.075	8.999	0.000	0.529	0.823
sigma2	1.2544	0.186	6.761	0.000	0.891	1.618

Ljung-Box (L1) (Q):	3.15	**Jarque-Bera (JB):**	202.66
Prob(Q):	0.08	**Prob(JB):**	0.00
Heteroskedasticity (H):	0.00	**Skew:**	-0.02
Prob(H) (two-sided):	0.00	**Kurtosis:**	7.32

Figure 6.48: *ARIMA output using Python code*

```
model_fit.forecast(100)
```

Output

```
260    6.761891
261    6.761891
262    6.761891
263    6.761891
264    6.761891
         ...
355    6.761891
356    6.761891
357    6.761891
358    6.761891
359    6.761891
Name: predicted_mean, Length: 100, dtype: float64
```

Actual vs. Forecasting plot-based outcomes

```
df_diesel_price_EMA['forecast']=model_fit.predict(start=10,end=100,
dynamic=True)
df_diesel_price_EMA[['Diesel_ price','forecast']].plot(figsize=(12,8))
print("\t\t\t##########################################################")
print("\t\t\t          Actual Vs Forecasting plot                        ")
print("\t\t\t##########################################################")
```

```
##########################################################
                 Actual Vs Forecasting plot
##########################################################
```

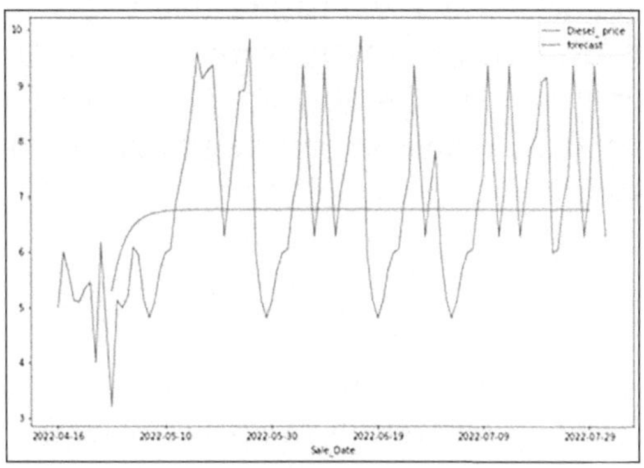

Figure 6.49: *ARIMA Actual vs. Forecasting plot*

Time Series Analysis and Forecasting Process Workflow

So far, we have discussed the various TSA&F and classical examples. *Figure* 6.53 represents the overall time series analysis and forecasting process workflow for a clear understanding.

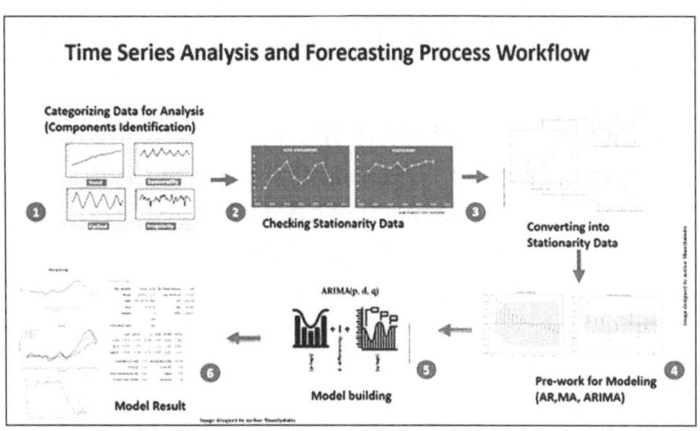

Figure 6.50: *Time Series Analysis and Forecasting Process Workflow*

Pertinency of the model

In the TSA&F model, we have multiple choices, but we must choose the right model in the right place, which is a key task for data scientists and machine learning engineers. Here are the quick bites.

If you trust that in the time series data, the previous values $\mathbf{Y_{t-1}}$ have an immediate effect on the given time series for the next value, then you will opt for the Auto-regression **(AR)** model.

If you trust that the weighted sum of differences $\mathbf{\Sigma\ \theta_i \varepsilon_t}$ has an immediate effect on the given time series, then you will opt for the Moving Average **(MA)** model.

Concerning ARIMA, we have discussed earlier that in **ARIMA** [$\Sigma\ \beta i Y_{t-i} + \varepsilon_t + \Sigma\ \theta_i \varepsilon_{t-i}$] the combination of **AR**, **MA**, and **Integration aspects** strengthens the overall model for both stationary and non-stationary series. We should remember that in TSA, non-stationary data should always be transformed into stationary data for analysis and forecasting.

Conclusion

In this chapter, we have discussed the detailed studies of statistical models for TSA&F and their significance with clear examples. We explored the consideration of key parameters and how to start working on building models.

We explored the various statistical models right from AR, MR, ARMR, and ARIMA and their benefits and limitations with neat explanations.

We experimented and implemented AR, MR, and ARIMA models with sample dataset and their visualization using Excel and Python code.

This chapter will provide a solid understanding of the statistical models for TSA&F, limitations, benefits, characteristics, and various techniques to implement them with the data.

In the next chapter, we will discuss the Exponential Smoothing and ETS Methods in time series analysis and their qualities, significance, and various types. Following this will explore ETS (Error, Trend, Seasonal), Exponentially Weighted Moving Averages (EWMA), Single Exponential Smoothing (SES), Holt's Linear Trend, and Winters models.

Points to remember

In this chapter, it is important to keep a few things in mind that will be handy throughout this book:

- Understanding the different statistical models for TSA&F and their significance with clear examples.
- Explored the various parameters which are closely connected with statistical models, which includes data volume, size of time horizons, frequency of forecast updates and sequential order of frequency.
- Understanding of different statistical models for TSA&F and its benefits and limitations.
    - AR (p-lags)
    - MR (q-lags)
    - AR+MR=ARMR (p-lags) +(q-lags)
    - AR+I+MR=ARIMA [(p-lags) +d-difference in the order+(q-lags)]
- Detailed study of the Moving Average (MA) model and its sub-types of Simple Moving Average (SMA), Cumulative Moving Average (CMA) and Exponential Moving Average (EMA) models.
- How the Auto-Regressive Integrated Moving Average (ARIMA) works, time series analysis and forecasting process workflow.

Chapter 7

Understanding Exponential Smoothing and ETS Methods in TSA

Introduction

In the previous chapter, we discussed the detailed studies of statistical models for TSA&F and their significance with clear examples. We explored the consideration of key parameters and how to start working on building models. We explored the various statistical models right from AR, MR, ARMR, and ARIMA and their benefits and limitations with neat explanations. We experimented and implemented AR, MR, and ARIMA models with sample dataset and their visualization using Excel and Python code. This chapter will help us explore Exponential Smoothing and ETS Methods in Time Series Analysis, and their characteristics and various types. ETS (Error, Trend, Seasonal). Discuss a few more models - Simple Moving Average (SMA), Exponentially Weighted Moving Averages (EWMA), Single Exponential Smoothing (SES), Holt's Linear Trend Model, and Winters.

Structure

In this chapter, we will discuss the following topics:

- Understanding Exponential Smoothing and its types
- ETS techniques
- ETS Characteristics and types
- Detailed study of SMA, EWMA, and SES
- Holt's Linear Trend Model

Understanding Exponential Smoothing

Exponential smoothing is among the powerful time series analysis and forecasting methods using univariate time series data and it uses the exponential window function. This works by assigning exponentially decreasing weight(s) from past observations as predictions about a weighted linear sum of the lags with the assumption that future values will be, to some degree of the recent past values. This method best fits when the time series factors vary slowly over time, which is why it could be seasonality or systematic trends in terms of patterns. This method is noise free or very low noise.

This technique requires just three quantities of data

- Needs forecasting data points for the most recent period.
- Needs actual data points for that period.
- Needs the appropriate smoothing constant.

At the end of the process, a **weighting factor** reflects the given data point weight to the recent data value(s).

Mathematically, we can represent this method using the following formula:

$$F_t = \alpha A_{t-1} + (1 - \alpha)F_{t-1}$$

- Ft-> Forecast demand
- α-> Smoothing constant
- At-1-> actual demand [previous period]
- Ft-1-> forecast demand [previous period]

Benefits of Exponential Smoothing

- It produces accurate forecasts from the given data series by considering the difference between the actual forecasts and what occurred.

- Recent observations play a significant role in this method, since the random and noise variations are neglected.
- It is straightforward to learn and apply using univariant time series data, with a smoothing constant.

Limitations of Exponential Smoothing

- Suitable for short-term forecasting purposes along with the data series in the absence of cyclical variations.
- It exhibits inaccurate results while forecasting seasonal variation data points that are present with the given time series data.

Exponential Smoothing implementation using Excel

Let's implement the AR model using our diesel price dataset in simple steps.

Given the dataset, as shown in *Figure 7.1*:

Sale_Date	Diesel price
16-04-2022	5
17-04-2022	6
18-04-2022	5.6
18-04-2022	5.12
21-04-2022	5.1
22-04-2022	5.34
24-04-2022	5.45
25-04-2022	4
26-04-2022	6.17
26-04-2022	4.6
29-04-2022	3.2

Figure 7.1: *Diesel price dataset*

Once the dataset is ready, we have to start doing the data analysis. To do this, we must follow these steps to enable **`Analysis ToolPak in Excel`**. We have discussed this in *Chapter 6, Exploring Time Series Models* - AR, MA, ARMA, *and* ARIMA in detail.

MS-Excel also provides the option to implement **Exponential Smoothing**. Let's explore how to do this.

Let's start our exponential smoothing analysis. Select the **`Data`** main menu and click on the **`Data Analysis`** tab as shown in *Figure 7.2*:

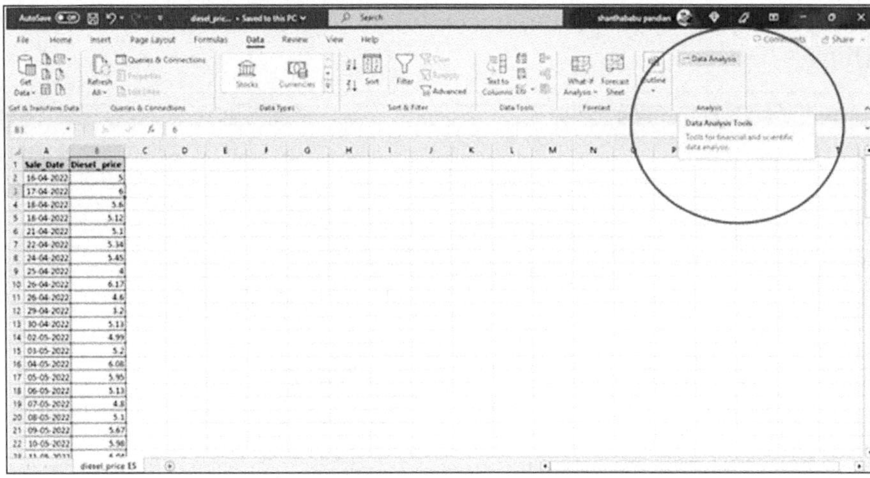

Figure 7.2: *Step-1 Select Data Analysis Options from the Data menu*

After clicking on the `Data Analysis` tab, you will get a `Data Analysis` popup screen shown in *Figure 7.3*:

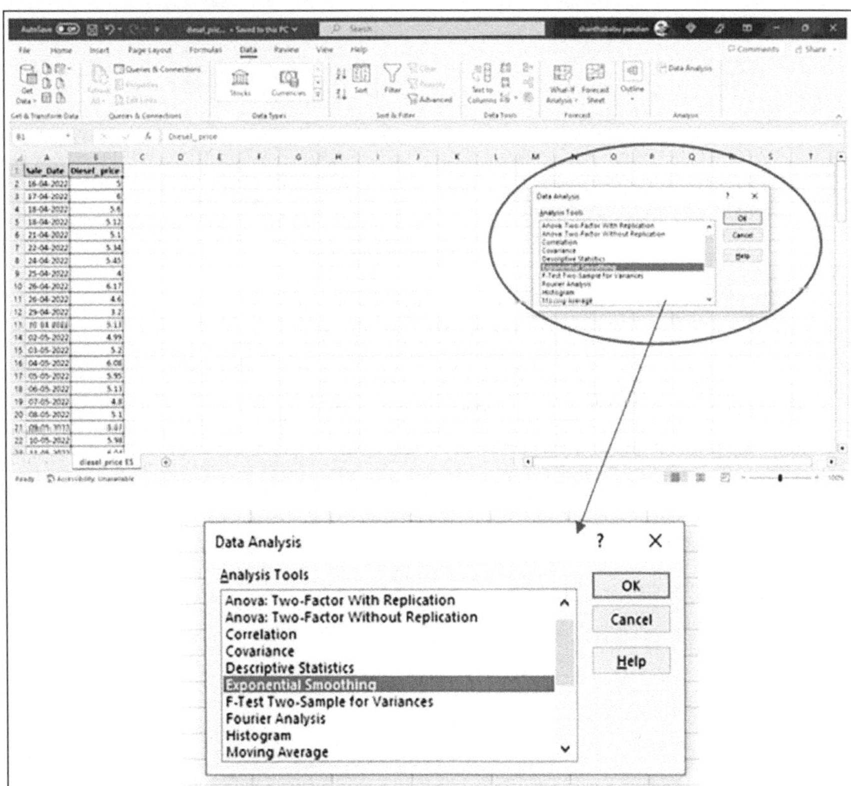

Figure 7.3: *Step-2 Select the Exponential Smoothing model from Data Analysis*

Configure the input, output, damping factor, and new worksheet for Exponential Smoothing.

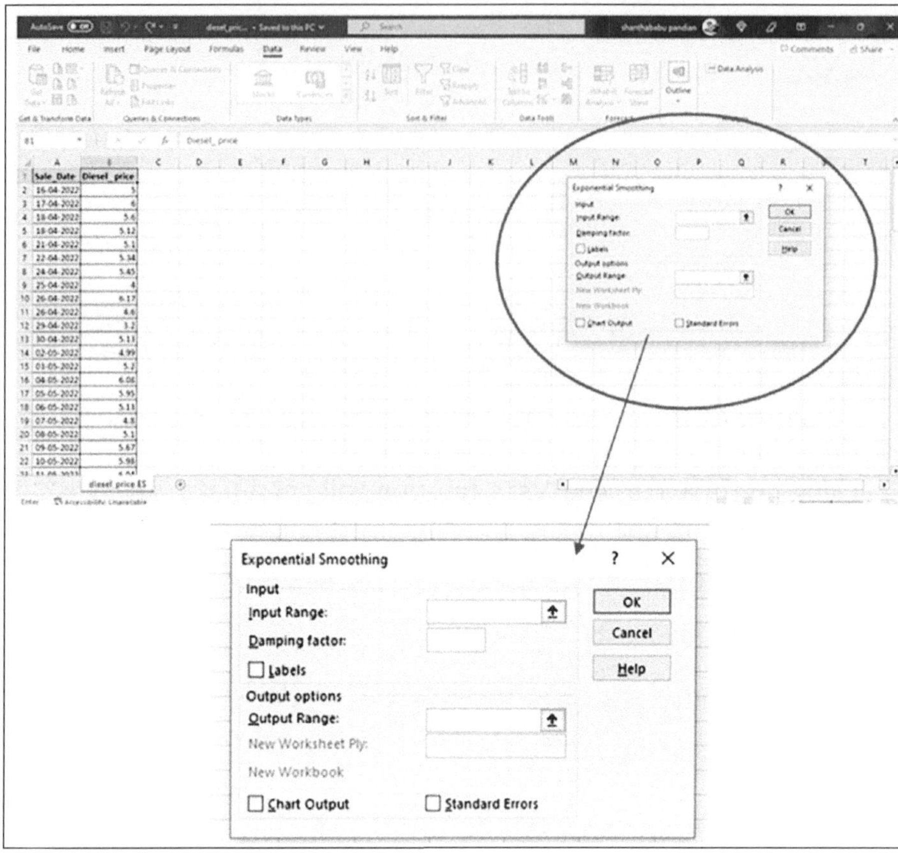

Figure 7.4: *Step-3 Configuration Exponential Smoothing model*

For our analysis, we will follow the following configuration:

- Input range -> Diesel price
- Output range -> Depends on input
- Damping factor -> Range between 0 and 1 (smooth out the graph)
- Standard Errors -> Check
- Chart Output -> Check

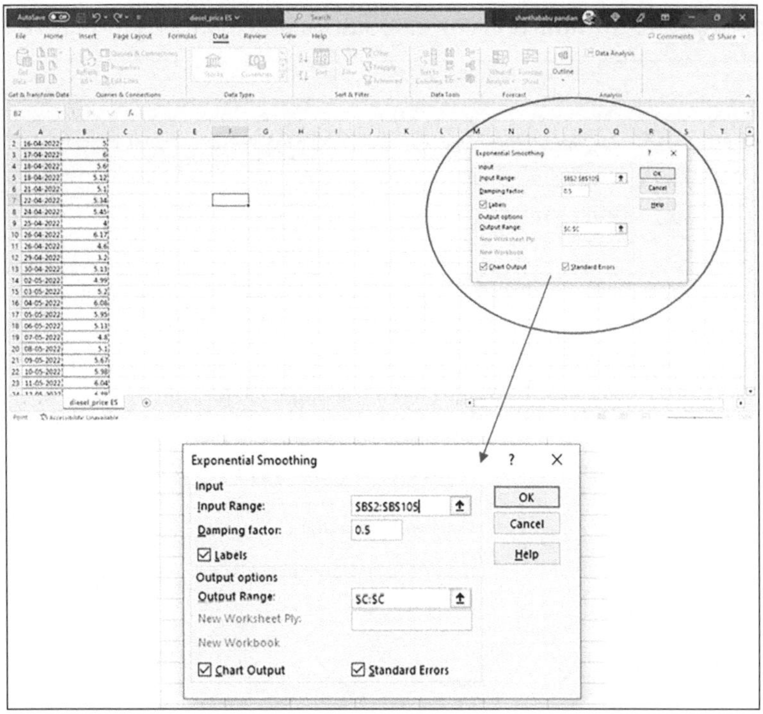

Figure 7.5: *Step-4 Configure the Exponential Smoothing model (valid inputs)*

After the configuration has been completed, click on **OK**, excel will create *Figure 7.6* to show you the predicted and standard error columns for the intervals along with Chart [Actual Vs Predicted]

Prediction is calculated by using =0.5*B4+0.5*C3 formula and standard error is calculated from =SQRT(SUMXMY2(B5:B7,C4:C6)/3) formula.

Sale_Date	Diesel_price	Forecasting	Standard Errors
16-04-2022	5	#N/A	#N/A
17-04-2022	6	6.00	#N/A
18-04-2022	5.6	5.80	#N/A
18-04-2022	5.12	5.46	#N/A
21-04-2022	5.1	5.28	0.50
22-04-2022	5.34	5.31	0.45
24-04-2022	5.45	5.38	0.23
25-04-2022	4	4.69	0.80
26-04-2022	6.17	5.43	1.17
26-04-2022	4.6	5.02	1.26
29-04-2022	3.2	4.11	1.43
30-04-2022	5.13	4.62	1.29
02-05-2022	4.99	4.80	1.22
03-05-2022	5.2	5.00	0.67
04-05-2022	6.08	5.54	0.70
05-05-2022	5.95	5.75	0.70
06-05-2022	5.13	5.44	0.75
07-05-2022	4.8	5.12	0.56
08-05-2022	5.1	5.11	0.51

Figure 7.6: *Exponential Smoothing model output – forecasting price and standard errors*

The forecasting and standard error calculations are shown in *Figure 7.7*:

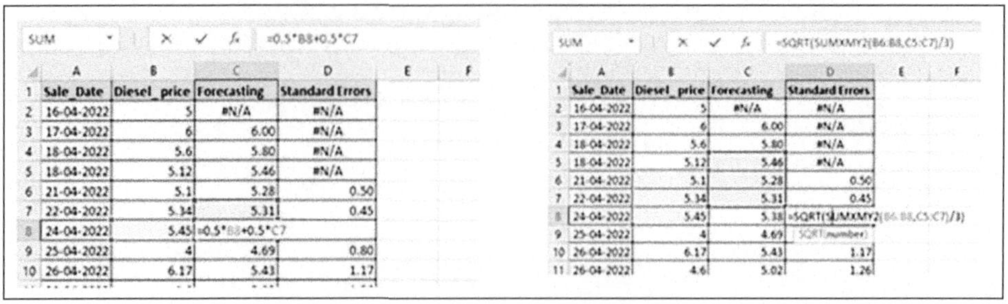

=0.5*B8+0.5*C7

	A	B	C	D
1	Sale_Date	Diesel_price	Forecasting	Standard Errors
2	16-04-2022	5	#N/A	#N/A
3	17-04-2022	6	6.00	#N/A
4	18-04-2022	5.6	5.80	#N/A
5	18-04-2022	5.12	5.46	#N/A
6	21-04-2022	5.1	5.28	0.50
7	22-04-2022	5.34	5.31	0.45
8	24-04-2022	5.45	=0.5*B8+0.5*C7	
9	25-04-2022	4	4.69	0.80
10	26-04-2022	6.17	5.43	1.17

=SQRT(SUMXMY2(B6:B8,C5:C7)/3)

	A	B	C	D
1	Sale_Date	Diesel_price	Forecasting	Standard Errors
2	16-04-2022	5	#N/A	#N/A
3	17-04-2022	6	6.00	#N/A
4	18-04-2022	5.6	5.80	#N/A
5	18-04-2022	5.12	5.46	#N/A
6	21-04-2022	5.1	5.28	0.50
7	22-04-2022	5.34	5.31	0.45
8	24-04-2022	5.45	5.38	=SQRT(SUMXMY2(B6:B8,C5:C7)/3)
9	25-04-2022	4	4.69	
10	26-04-2022	6.17	5.43	1.17
11	26-04-2022	4.6	5.02	1.26

Figure 7.7: *Exponential Smoothing model output – predicted price and standard errors along with formulas*

Figure 7.8 shows the exponential smoothing model line plot (Actual vs. Forecast).

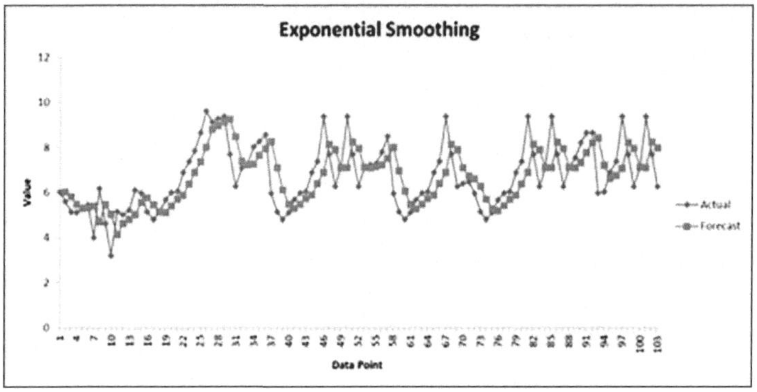

Figure 7.8: *Exponential Smoothing model output – line plot (Actual vs. Forecast)*

Try this to change the damping factors 0.7 and 0.9 and run exponential smoothing. Based on the damping factor, the alpha value will adjust and the graph's line becomes smooth as the damping factor value increases.

- **More Volatility Data**
    - If the damping factor is low (~0.1), then the alpha is high(~0.9)
- **Less Volatility Data**
    - If the damping factor is more (~0.9), then the alpha is low(!0.1)

Exponential Smoothing types

The exponential smoothing method is further classified into three methods, to estimate exponential smoothing. They are as follows:

- Single Exponential Smoothing
- Double Exponential Smoothing
- Triple exponential smoothing

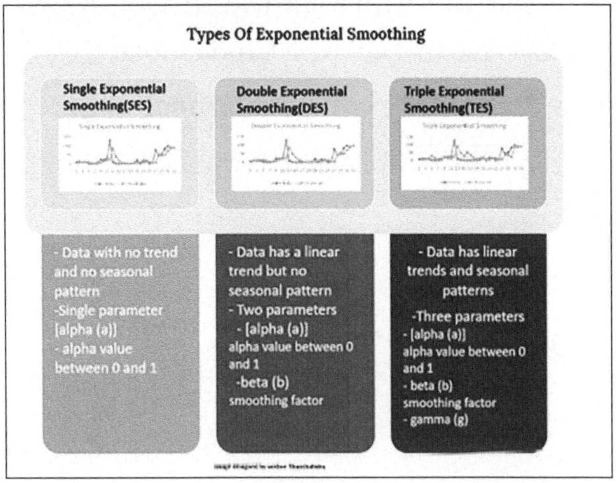

Figure 7.9: *Types of Exponential Smoothing Method*

- **Single Exponential Smoothing (SES):** This method is used with univariate time series data with no seasonal patterns or trends. It has a single parameter called the smoothing factor, which is denoted by alpha (a) and ranges between 0 and 1, and it is used to control the influence of past observations, which decreases exponentially as the base method exponential smoothing method.

Mathematically written with the following formula:

$$s_t = \alpha x_t + (1 - \alpha)s_{t-1}$$

where,

- s_t -> current smoothed statistic (of xt)
- s_{t-1} -> previously smoothed statistics
- α -> smoothing factor (range 0 to 1)
- t -> time

Double Exponential Smoothing (DES): The name implies that two parameters play a vital role in this smoothing method and are best suited for data that has a linear trend but no seasonal patterns. These parameters are alpha(α) and beta(β), the first one for the level and the second one for the trend.

This method exhibits smoothing with both linear and exponential trends. It supports both trends in separate approaches as an additive and a multiplicative, respectively.

- o Additive Trend: DES with a linear.
- o Multiplicative Trend: DES with exponential.

This is also called the **2nd-order exponential smoothing** technique.

Mathematically written with the following formula:

$$Y_{t+1} = L_t + (h)T_t$$

$$L_t = \alpha Y_t + (1 - \alpha)(L_{t-1} + T_{t-1})$$

$$T_t = \beta(L_t - L_{t-1}) + (1 - \beta)T_{t-1}$$

where,

- L -> Level
- T -> Trend
- $\mathbf{Y_{t+1}}$ -> value at time t+1
- L_t -> level value time at time t
- T_t -> trend value at time t
- Alpha(α) -> Level parameter
- Beta(β) -> Trend parameter
- h -> forecast horizon
- **Triple Exponential Smoothing (TES)**: This is the most This is also one of the extensions of the exponential smoothing technique, and in addition to alpha(α), and beta(β) there is gamma(g). It supports seasonality to the univariate time series data with a trend and seasonal pattern and controls the effect on the seasonal component. This method is also known as **Holt-Winters** exponential smoothing.
- Additive Trend: TES with linear seasonality.
- Multiplicative Trend: TES with exponential seasonality.

Mathematically written with the following formula:

$$S_0 = x_0$$

$$S_t = \alpha\, x_t / C_t - L + (1 - \alpha)(S_{t-1} + b_{t-1})$$

$$b_t = \beta(S_t - S_{t-1}) + (1 - \beta)b_{t-1}$$

$$C_t = \gamma x_t / S_t + (1 - \gamma)C_{t-1}$$

where,

- α -> Smoothing factor (Range 0 to 1)
- β -> Trend smoothing factor (Range 0 to 1)
- γ -> Seasonal change smoothing factor (Range 0 to 1)
- t -> Time period
- b_t -> Best estimate of a trend at a time **"t"**
- C_t -> Seasonal correction factor at a time **"t"**
- S_t -> Smoothed statistic
- S_{t-1} -> Previous smoothed statistics

Triple Exponential Smoothing Model for TSA&F using Excel

The seasonal diesel dataset is shown in *Figure 7.10*:

DATE	Diesel_price
16-04-2022	7.25
17-04-2022	7.07
18-04-2022	6.25
19-04-2022	5.75
20-04-2022	5.53
21-04-2022	5.81

Figure 7.10: *Seasonal diesel dataset*

Figure 7.11 shows the diesel dataset line plot to understand the time series data

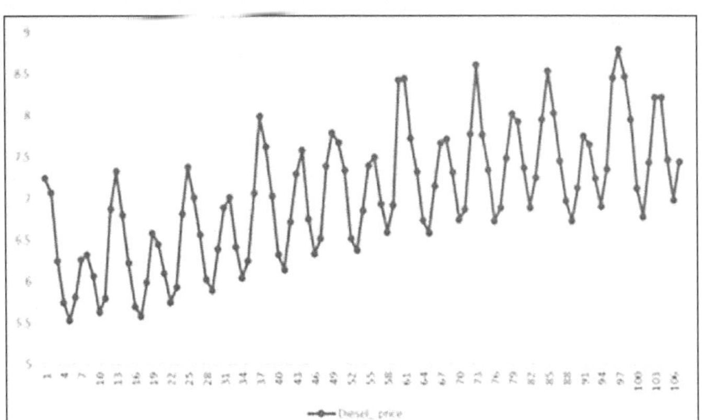

Figure 7.11: *Seasonal graph diesel dataset*

The TES technique uses season-1 and finds some of the initial values to find the forecasting for season-2.

Step -1: Bring the period and find how long is season is. In our case, one season has four periods. The end of season-1 is the fourth period.

Step-2: Let's start with 5.5 L_t and T_t 1.2 and calculate $L_t + T_t$.

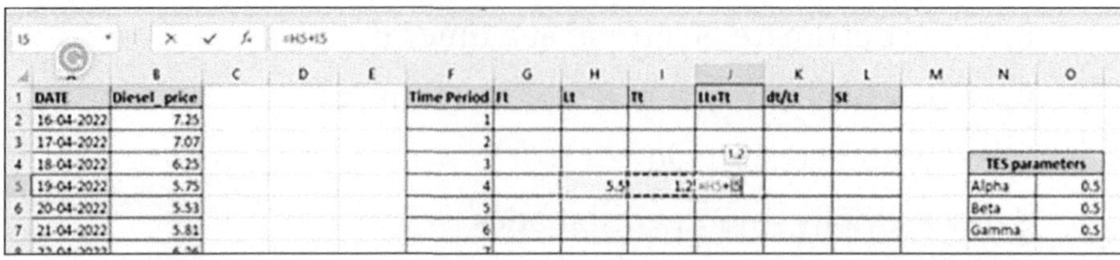

Figure 7.12: *Initializing the Lt, Tt and Lt+Tt for the diesel dataset*

Step-3: Find the seasonality as follows, using `=B2/AVERAGE(B2:B5)` formula:

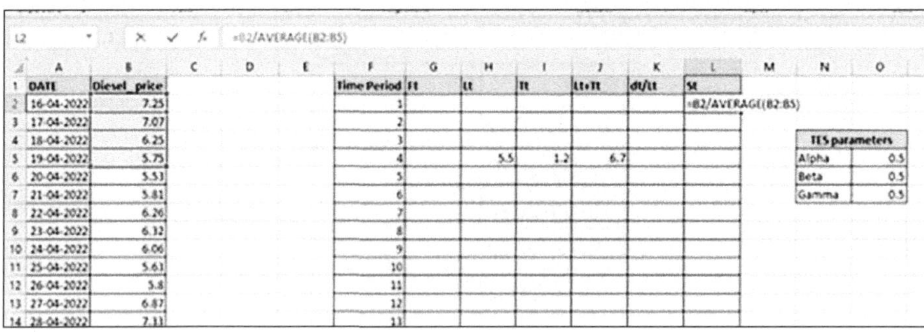

Figure 7.13: *Finding the first seasonality from the diesel dataset*

The first Seasonality factors arrive in Step 3:

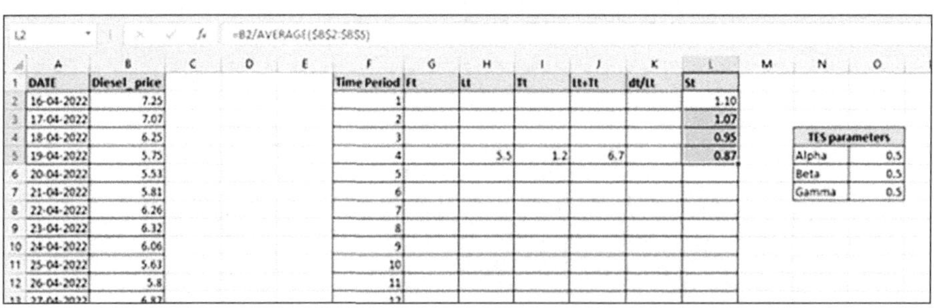

Figure 7.14: *First seasonality has arrived from the diesel dataset*

Step-4: Find the forecast for the second season.

Let's calculate the Level(Lt), Trend(Lt), Sum of Lt, Tt and dt/Lt

Level(Lt): using `=(05*B6)/L2+(1-05)*J5` formula:

Formula bar: =(O5*B6)/L2+(1-O5)*J5

B	C	D	E	F	G	H	I	J	K	L
Diesel_price				Time Period	Ft	Lt	Tt	Lt+Tt	dt/Lt	St
7.25			Season -1	1						1.10
7.07				2						1.07
6.25				3						0.95
5.75				4		5.5	1.2	6.7		0.87
5.53			Season -2	5	7.38	=(O5*B6)/L2+(1-O5)*J5				
5.81				6						
6.26				7						
6.32				8						

TES parameters	
Alpha	0.5
Beta	0.5
Gamma	0.5

Figure 7.15: *Level (Lt) calculation from the diesel dataset*

The Level (Lt) calculated for the seasonal diesel dataset is shown in *Figure 7.16*:

	A	B	E	F	G	H	I	J	K	L
1	DATE	Diesel_price		Time Period	Ft	Lt	Tt	Lt+Tt	dt/Lt	St
2	16-04-2022	7.25	Season -1	1						1.10
3	17-04-2022	7.07		2						1.07
4	18-04-2022	6.25		3						0.95
5	19-04-2022	5.75		4		5.5	1.2	6.7		0.87
6	20-04-2022	5.53	Season -2	5	7.38	5.86				
7	21-04-2022	5.81		6						
8	22-04-2022	6.26		7						
9	23-04-2022	6.32		8						

Figure 7.16: *Level (Lt) arrived from the diesel dataset*

Trend(Lt): Using =O6*(H6-H5)+(1-O6)*I5 formula:

Formula bar: =O6*(H6-H5)+(1-O6)*I5

	A	B	E	F	G	H	I	J	K	L
1	DATE	Diesel_price		Time Period	Ft	Lt	Tt	Lt+Tt	dt/Lt	St
2	16-04-2022	7.25	Season -1	1						1.10
3	17-04-2022	7.07		2						1.07
4	18-04-2022	6.25		3						0.95
5	19-04-2022	5.75		4		5.5	1.2	6.7		0.87
6	20-04-2022	5.53	Season -2	5	7.38	5.86	=O6*(H6-H5)+(1-O6)*I5			
7	21-04-2022	5.81		6						
8	22-04-2022	6.26		7						
9	23-04-2022	6.32		8						
10	24-04-2022	6.06		9						

TES parameters	
Alpha	0.5
Beta	0.5
Gamma	0.5

Figure 7.17: *Trend (Tt) calculation from the diesel dataset*

The Trend (Tt) calculated for the seasonal diesel dataset is shown in *Figure 7.18*:

=O6*(H6-H5)+(1-O6)*I5

Diesel_price		Time Period	Ft	Lt	Tt	Lt+Tt	dt/Lt	St
7.25		1						1.10
7.07	Season -1	2						1.07
6.25		3						0.95
5.75		4		5.5	1.2	6.7		0.87
5.53		5	7.38	5.86	0.78			
5.81	Season -2	6						
6.26		7						
6.32		8						
6.06		9						

Figure 7.18: *Trend (Tt) arrived from the diesel dataset*

Lt+Tt: Using =H6+I6 formula:

SUM =H6+I6

	A	B	C	D	E	F	G	H	I	J	K	L
1	DATE	Diesel_price				Time Period	Ft	Lt	Tt	Lt+Tt	dt/Lt	St
2	16-04-2022	7.25				1						1.10
3	17-04-2022	7.07			Season -1	2						1.15
4	18-04-2022	6.25				3						1.07
5	19-04-2022	5.75				4		5	0.5	5.50		0.99
6	20-04-2022	5.53				5	6.06	5.26	0.38	=H6+I6	1.05	0.92

Figure 7.19: *Level(Lt)+ Trend (Tt) calculation from the diesel dataset*

dt/Lt: Using =B6/H6 formula:

SUM =B6/H6

	A	B	C	D	E	F	G	H	I	J	K	L
1	DATE	Diesel_price				Time Period	Ft	Lt	Tt	Lt+Tt	dt/Lt	St
2	16-04-2022	7.25				1						1.10
3	17-04-2022	7.07			Season -1	2						1.15
4	18-04-2022	6.25				3						1.07
5	19-04-2022	5.75				4		5	0.5	5.50		0.99
6	20-04-2022	5.53				5	6.06	5.26	0.38	5.64	=B6/H6	0.92

Figure 7.20: *dt/Lt calculation from the diesel dataset*

The dt/Lt calculated for the seasonal diesel dataset is shown in *Figure 7.21*:

I10 =O10*(H10-H9)+(1-O10)*I9

	A	B	C	D	E	F	G	H	I	J	K	L
1	DATE	Diesel_price				Time Period	Ft	Lt	Tt	Lt+Tt	dt/Lt	St
2	16-04-2022	7.25				1						1.10
3	17-04-2022	7.07			Season -1	2						1.15
4	18-04-2022	6.25				3						1.07
5	19-04-2022	5.75				4		5	0.5	5.50		0.99
6	20-04-2022	5.53				5	6.06	5.26	0.38	5.64	1.05	0.92

Figure 7.21: *dt/Lt arrived from the diesel dataset*

Seasonality factor for the second season =07*K6+(1-07)*L2

L6 =07*K6+(1-07)*L2

	A	B	E	F	G	H	I	J	K	L
1	DATE	Diesel_price		Time Period	Ft	Lt	Tt	Lt+Tt	dt/Lt	St
2	16-04-2022	7.25	Season -1	1						1.10
3	17-04-2022	7.07		2						1.07
4	18-04-2022	6.25		3						0.95
5	19-04-2022	5.75		4		5.5	1.2	6.7		0.87
6	20-04-2022	5.53	Season -2	5	7.38	5.86	0.78	6.64	0.94	=07*K6+(1-07)*L2
7	21-04-2022	5.81		6						

TES parameters	
Alpha	0.5
Beta	0.5
Gamma	0.5

Figure 7.22: *Seasonality factor for the second season arrived from the diesel dataset*

All values are ready to be calculated for the rest of the rows in the dataset.

Clipboard Font Alignment Number

G6 =J5*L2

	A	B	E	F	G	H	I	J	K	L
1	DATE	Diesel_price		Time Period	Ft	Lt	Tt	Lt+Tt	dt/Lt	St
2	16-04-2022	7.25	Season -1	1						1.10
3	17-04-2022	7.07		2						1.07
4	18-04-2022	6.25		3						0.95
5	19-04-2022	5.75		4		5.5	1.2	6.7		0.87
6	20-04-2022	5.53		5	7.38	5.86	0.78	6.64	0.94	1.02

Figure 7.23: *Level (Lt), Trend (Lt), Sum of Lt, Tt, dt/Lt and Seasonality factor is ready*

Step-6: Drag the cell until the bottom of the dataset.

	Time Period	Ft	Lt	Tt	Lt+Tt	dt/Lt	St
Season -1	1						1.10
	2						1.07
	3						0.95
	4		5.5	1.2	6.7		0.87
Season -2	5	7.38	5.86	0.78	6.64	0.94	1.02
	6	7.13	5.86	0.39	6.25	0.99	1.02
	7	5.94	5.86	0.39	6.25	1.07	1.02
	8	5.46	5.86	0.39	6.25	1.08	1.02
Season -3	9	6.39	5.86	0.39	6.25	1.03	1.02
	10	6.39	5.86	0.39	6.25	0.96	1.02
	11	6.39	5.86	0.39	6.25	0.99	1.02
	12	6.39	5.86	0.39	6.25	1.17	1.02
Season -4	13	6.39	5.86	0.39	6.25	1.25	1.02
	14	6.39	5.86	0.39	6.25	1.16	1.02
	15	6.39	5.86	0.39	6.25	1.06	1.02
	16	6.39	5.86	0.39	6.25	0.97	1.02

Figure 7.24: *TES dataset*

Now, let's add the forecast value to the line plot and see the results.

Figure 7.25 shows the forecast in terms of triple exponential smoothing from preceding calculations.

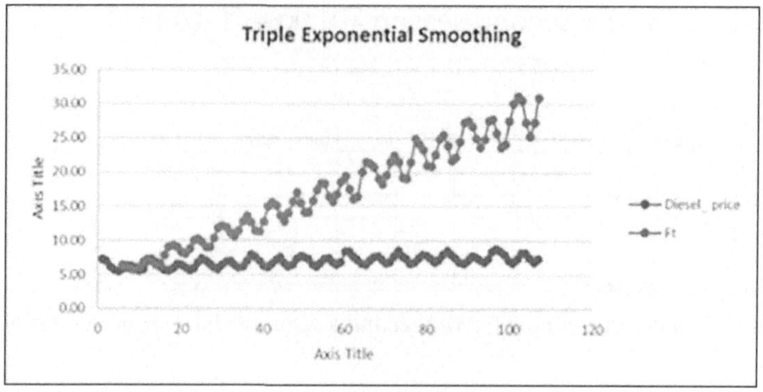

Figure 7.25: *TES line plot*

SES and DES Model implementation using Python

Using diesel_price TES - Python.CSV file will implement the SES and DES

```
#load basic libraries
import numpy as np
import pandas as pd
import matplotlib.pyplot as plt
#load statsmodels
from statsmodels.tsa.api import ExponentialSmoothing,
SimpleExpSmoothing, Holt


%matplotlib inline
df_diesel_price = pd.read_csv('diesel_price TES - Python.CSV', header=0,
index_col=0)
df_diesel_price.head()
```

output

DATE	Diesel_ price
16-04-2022	7.25
17-04-2022	7.07
18-04-2022	6.25
19-04-2022	5.75
20-04-2022	5.53

Figure 7.26: *Diesel price dataset*

```
pl = df_diesel_price.plot()
pl.set_xlabel("Year")
pl.set_ylabel("Diesel Price")
```

output

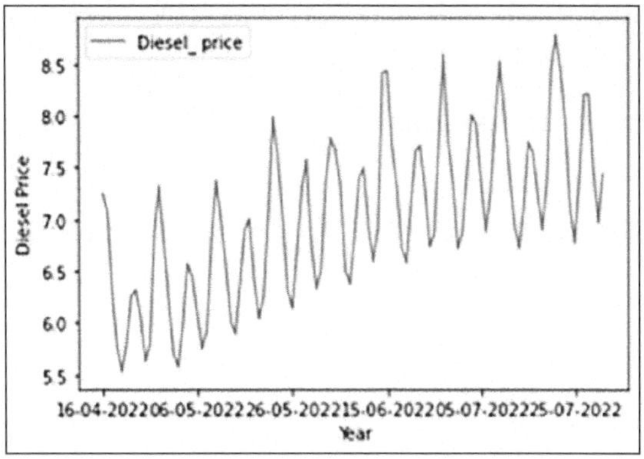

Figure 7.27: *Diesel price dataset line plot (understand the linearity and seasonality)*

Calculating SES, DES, and forecasting

```
#α Smoothing factor (Range  0 to 1)
alpha = 0.90
#β Trend smoothing factor (Range  0 to 1)
beta = 0.10

print("############################################")
print("Smoothing factor :",alpha)
print("Trend smoothing factor  :",beta)
print("############################################")

print("###################################################")
print("Adding two columns for this analysis -  SES and DES")
print("###################################################")

#SES column initialization
df_diesel_price["SES"] = 0.00
```

```
#DES column initialization
df_diesel_price["DES"] = 0.00

#DES column
df_diesel_price["SES"][0] = df_diesel_price["Diesel_ price"][0]

#SES and DES column calculations

df_diesel_price["DES"][0] = df_diesel_price["Diesel_ price"][1] - df_
diesel_price["Diesel_ price"][0]
x = 1
while x < 50:
 x += 1
 for i in range(1,50):
#SES calculation
#Lt = αYt + (1 – α)(Lt-1 + Tt-1) ==> Calculation
    df_diesel_price["SES"][i] = alpha * df_diesel_price["Diesel_ price"]
[i] + (1-alpha) * (df_diesel_price["SES"][i-1] + df_diesel_price["DES"]
[i-1])

#DES calculation
#Tt = β(Lt – Lt-1) + (1 – β)Tt-1 ==> Calculation
    df_diesel_price["DES"][i] = beta * ( df_diesel_price["SES"][i] - df_
diesel_price["SES"][i-1] ) + (1-beta) * df_diesel_price["DES"][i-1]

df_diesel_price["Forecast"] = 0.00

#Forecasting Calculation

for i in range(2,50):
#Yt+1 =Lt +(h)Tt
     df_diesel_price["Forecast"][i] = df_diesel_price["SES"][i-1] + df_
diesel_price["DES"][i-1]
df_diesel_price.head(5)
```

output

```
#############################################
Smoothing factor : 0.9
Trend smoothing factor  : 0.1
#############################################
#####################################################
Adding two columns for this analysis -  SES and DES
#####################################################
```

	Diesel_ price	SES	DES	Forecast
DATE				
16-04-2022	7.25	7.250000	-0.180000	0.000000
17-04-2022	7.07	7.070000	-0.180000	0.000000
18-04-2022	6.25	6.314000	-0.237600	6.890000
19-04-2022	5.75	5.782640	-0.266976	6.076400
20-04-2022	5.53	5.528566	-0.265686	5.515664

Figure 7.28: *Diesel price dataset with SES, DES, and Forecast*

Calculating Absolute Error

```
print("#######################################################
###################")
print("Adding Absolute Error column for this analysis using Actuals and
Forecast")
print("#######################################################
###################")
#new Absolute-Error column
df_diesel_price["Absolute-Error"] = 0.00


for i in range(1,50):
     df_diesel_price["Absolute-Error"][i] = abs(df_diesel_price["Diesel_
price"][i] - df_diesel_price["Forecast"][i] )
df_diesel_price.head(10)
##############################################################
Adding an Absolute Error column for this analysis using Actuals and
Forecast
```

```
##########################################################################
```

	Diesel_ price	SES	DES	Forecast	Absolute-Error
DATE					
16-04-2022	7.25	7.250000	-0.180000	0.000000	0.000000
17-04-2022	7.07	7.070000	-0.180000	0.000000	7.070000
18-04-2022	6.25	6.314000	-0.237600	6.890000	0.640000
19-04-2022	5.75	5.782640	-0.266976	6.076400	0.326400
20-04-2022	5.53	5.528566	-0.265686	5.515664	0.014336
21-04-2022	5.81	5.755288	-0.216445	5.262881	0.547119
22-04-2022	6.26	6.187884	-0.151541	5.538843	0.721157
23-04-2022	6.32	6.291634	-0.126012	6.036343	0.283657

Figure 7.29: *Diesel Price Dataset with Absolute Error*

```
pl = df_diesel_price.plot()
pl.set_xlabel("Year")
pl.set_ylabel("Diesel Price")
```

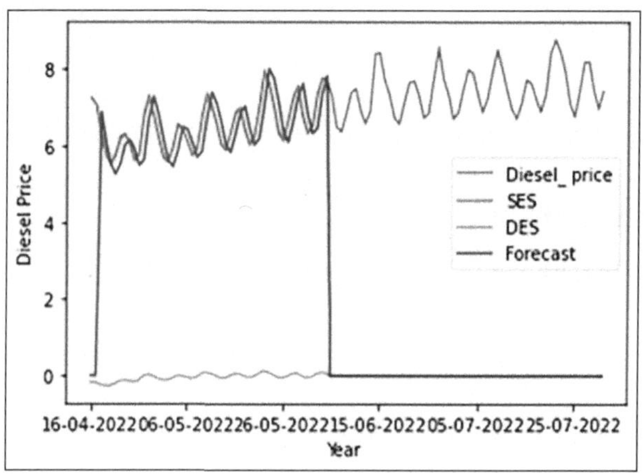

Figure 7.30: *Line plot for various columns from the final dataset*

NOTE:

- The exponential Smoothing technique requires three major quantities of data for analysis and forecasting - data points for the most recent period, actual data points for that period, and the appropriate smoothing constant. Each exponential smoothing type is unique and has specific parameters (alpha, beta, and gamma).
- Exponential Smoothing has major benefits and limitations since the time series data is smoother and doesn't get affected much by outliers. It produces accurate forecasts from the given data series by considering the difference between actual forecasts and what occurred.

It is straightforward to learn and apply using univariant time series data, with a smoothing constant. Concerning the limitations, this is suitable for short-term forecasting purposes along with the data series in the absence of cyclical variations and it exhibits inaccurate results while forecasting seasonal variation data points that are present with the given time series data.

Error - Trend-Seasonality (ETS)

The error-trend-seasonality model is used for time series decomposition. It decomposes the time series into three components: **Error (E)**, **Trend(T)** and **Seasonality(S)**. Specifically used for univariate forecasting and focusing on trend and seasonal components. All these factors are used for smoothing the time series data and predicting the forecasting.

The ETS models are a family of time series models with an underlying state space model consisting of a level component, a trend component (T), a seasonal component (S), and an error term (E).

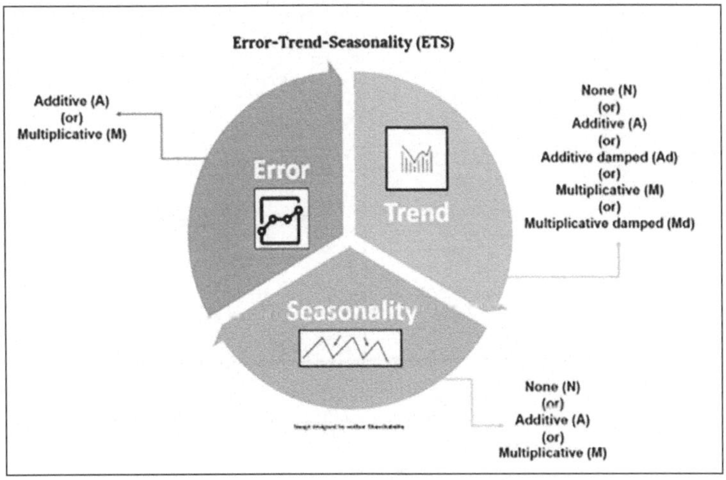

Figure 7.31: *Error-Trend-Seasonality*

While doing time series analysis and forecasting, this ETS method that helps us to better understand the time series data in terms of decomposed components such as trend, seasonality and noise.

ETS Characteristics

Error-Trend-Seasonality has a defined taxonomy concerning each component having its characteristics. The taxonomies are Additive(A), Multiplicative(M), Additive damped(Ad) and Multiplicative damped(Md).

Additive (A): When the seasonal variation is relatively constant over the recorded time.

Multiplicative (M): When seasonal data variation increases over the recorded time.

Additive/ Multiplicative damping (Ad/Md): When the data is with a trend and with seasonality components and able to separate seasonality, level and damped trend.

- **Error**: It could be Additive or Multiplicative.
- **Trend**: It could be None or Additive or Additive damped or Multiplicative or Multiplicative damped.
- **Seasonality**: It could be None or Additive or Multiplicative.

Based on the taxonomies components, we can develop 30 ETS models with different types of errors, trends, and seasonality.

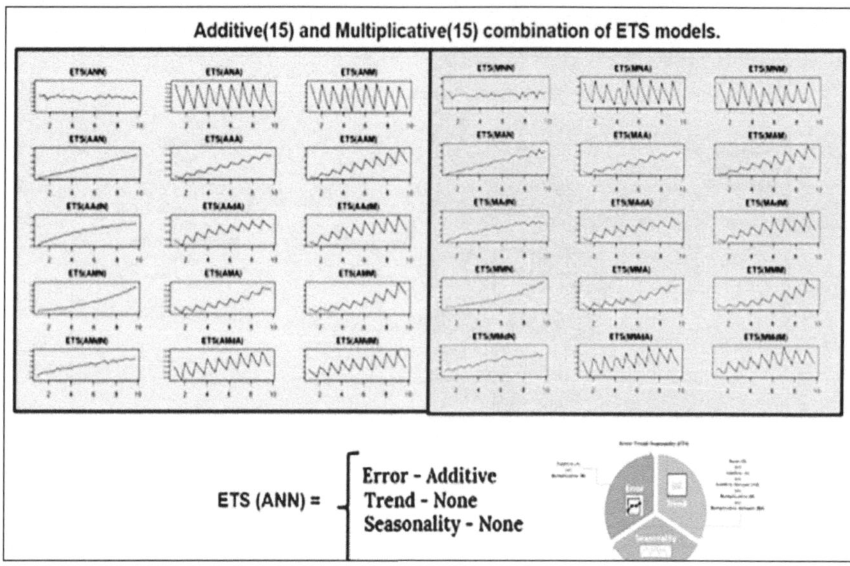

Figure 7.32: *Additive(15) and Multiplicative(15) combination of ETS models*

Different time series scenarios which ETS supports on time series analysis and forecasting.

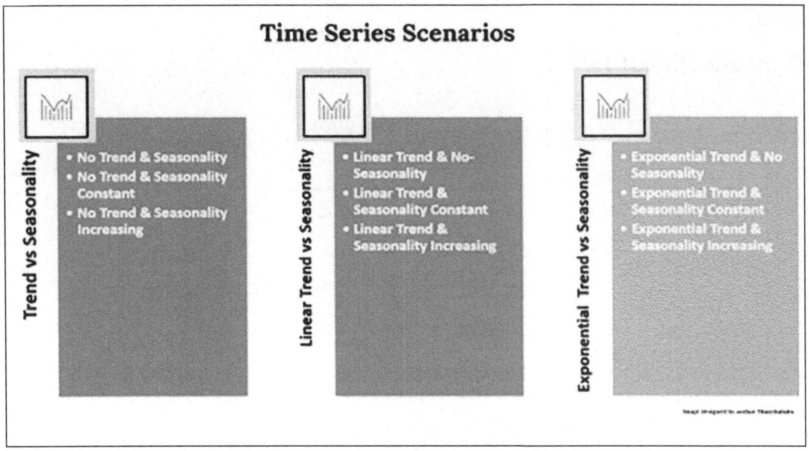

Figure 7.33: *Time Series Scenarios*

Types of ETS Models

- Exponential Trend Method: It is also called the **Exponential Smoothing Method**.
- Simple Exponential Smoothing Method: It is also called **Single Exponential Smoothing**.
- Holtz-Winter Seasonal Method: It is also called **Triple Exponential Smoothing**.
- Holt's Linear Trend Method: It is also called **Double Exponential Smoothing**.

Since all these techniques use the seasonality of the univariate time series data with a trend, error and seasonal patterns, this would be considered under ETS models, and all methods are discussed in detail in this chapter earlier with classical examples.

ETS Model implementation using Python

```
#load basic libraries
import numpy as np
import matplotlib.pyplot as plt
import pandas as pd
from statsmodels.tsa.exponential_smoothing.ets import ETSModel
%matplotlib inline
#load diesel_price ETS - Python.csv file
df_diesel_price = pd.read_csv("diesel_price ETS - Python.csv", header=0,
```

```
index_col=0)
df_diesel_price.head()
```

	Diesel price
DATE	
16-04-2022	7.25
17-04-2022	7.07
18-04-2022	6.25
19-04-2022	5.75
20-04-2022	5.53

Figure 7.34: *Diesel Price dataset*

```
print("##############################################")
print("        Diesel Price  line plot              ")
print("##############################################")
df_diesel_price.plot()
```

```
##############################################
           Diesel Price  line plot
##############################################
```

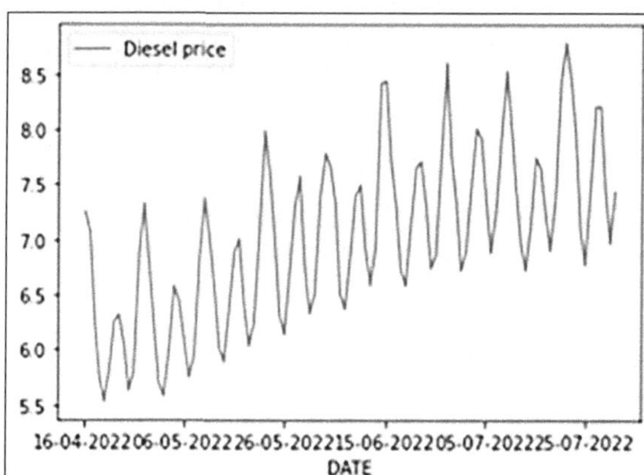

Figure 7.35: *Diesel Price line plot*

```
import statsmodels as sm
import statsmodels.api as sm
import matplotlib.pyplot as plt
import pandas as pd
%matplotlib inline
```

```
print("################################################################")
print("    Diesel Price - Decomposition ETS (additive)        ")
print("################################################################")
decomposition = sm.tsa.seasonal_decompose(df_diesel_price["Diesel price"], model = 'additive',extrapolate_trend='freq', period=2)
fig = decomposition.plot()
plt.rcParams['figure.figsize'] = [10,5]
```

```
############################################################
        Diesel Price - Decomposition ETS (additive)
############################################################
```

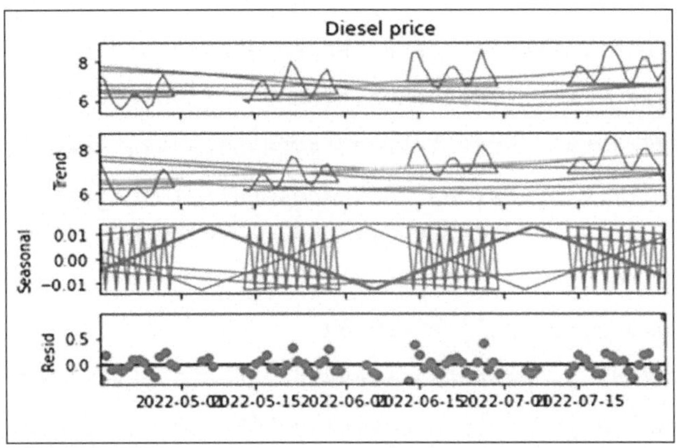

Figure 7.36: *Diesel Price - Decomposition ETS (additive)*

```
print("################################################################")
print("    Diesel Price - Decomposition ETS (multiplicative)        ")
print("################################################################")
decomposition = sm.tsa.seasonal_decompose(df_diesel_price["Diesel price"], model = 'multiplicative',extrapolate_trend='freq', period=2)
fig = decomposition.plot()
plt.rcParams['figure.figsize'] = [10,5]
```

```
################################################################
        Diesel Price - Decomposition ETS (multiplicative)
################################################################
```

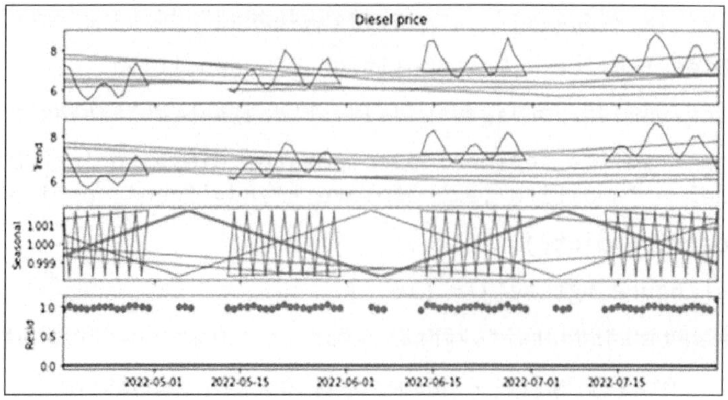

Figure 7.37: *Diesel Price - Decomposition ETS (multiplicative)*

```
print("####################################################################")
print("    Diesel Price - Decomposition ETS (additive damped)       ")
print("####################################################################")
decomposition = sm.tsa.seasonal_decompose(df_diesel_price["Diesel
price"], model = 'additivedamped',extrapolate_trend='freq', period=2)
fig = decomposition.plot()
plt.rcParams['figure.figsize'] = [10,5]
     ####################################################################
          Diesel Price - Decomposition ETS (additive damped)
     ####################################################################
```

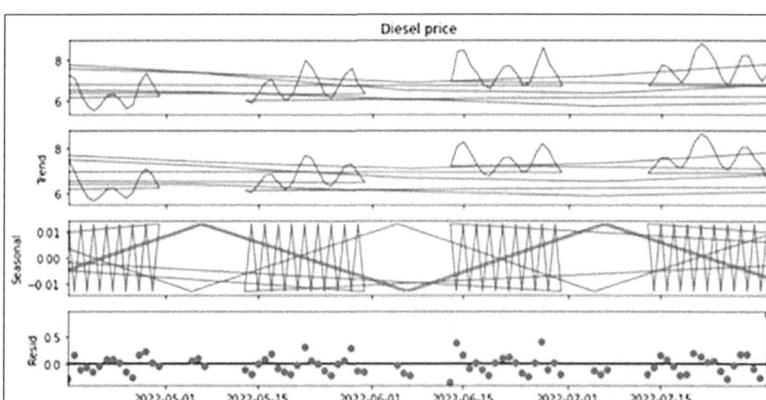

Figure 7.38: *Diesel Price - Decomposition ETS (additive damped)*

```
print("##############################################################
###########")
print("    Diesel Price - Decomposition ETS (multiplicativedamped)
```

```
")
print("######################################################################
###########")
decomposition = sm.tsa.seasonal_decompose(df_diesel_price["Diesel
price"], model = 'multiplicativedamped',extrapolate_trend='freq', peri-
od=2)
fig = decomposition.plot()
plt.rcParams['figure.figsize'] = [10,5]
```

```
##########################################################################
        Diesel Price - Decomposition ETS (multiplicativedamped)
##########################################################################
```

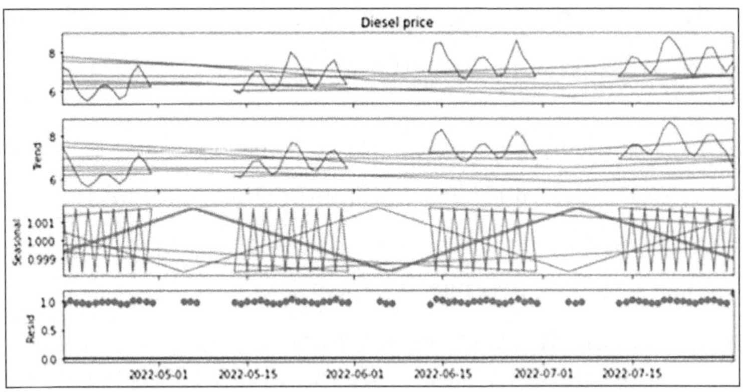

Figure 7.39: *Diesel Price - Decomposition ETS (multiplicative damped)*

Note: The ETS model decomposes the time series into three components: Error (E), Trend(T) and Seasonality(S) and this is specifically used for univariate forecasting and focusing on trend and seasonal components. All these factors are used for smoothing the time series data and predicting the forecasting.

Types of ETS Models

- Exponential Trend Method: it is also called the **Exponential Smoothing Method**
- Simple Exponential Smoothing Method: it is also called **Single Exponential -Smoothing**
- Holtz-Winter Seasonal Method: it is also called **Triple Exponential Smoothing**
- Holt's Linear Trend Method: it is also called **Double Exponential Smoothing**

Exponentially Weighted Moving Averages (EWMA)

We discussed the EMA in *Chapter 6, Exploring Time Series Models - AR, MA, ARMA, and ARIMA* and EWMA is an extension of the EMA and statistical measure and assumed that the observations are normally distributed in the given dataset. This method is considered past data based on their weightage. When the data is getting aged then the moving average gives lower weights, and it decreases exponentially over the period.

The exponentially weighted came into the picture along with the parameter alpha(α) and it decides the current data point in EWMA calculation, which is used to build the volatility modelling using time series analysis data.

Mathematically, we can represent this method using the following formula:

$$EWMA(t) = \alpha * x(t) + (1-\alpha) * EWMA_{(t-1)}$$

- EWMA(t) -> moving average at time t
- Alpha(α) -> Degree of mixing parameter [Range 0 and 1]
- x(t) -> value of signal
- $EWMA_{(t-1)}$ -> moving average at time t-1

This method is a recursive function in nature so that the current observation is calculated using the previous observation and this helps to decrease exponentially weights over the period.

$$EWMA(t) = \alpha * x(t) + (1-\alpha) * (\alpha * x(t-1)+(1-\alpha)* EWMA_{(t-2)})$$

$$EWMA(t) = \alpha * x(t) + (1-\alpha) * (\alpha * x(t-1)+(1-\alpha)*(\alpha * x(t-2)+(1-\alpha)*EWMA_{(t-3)})$$

Benefits of EWMA

- It reduces the noise in the given time series dataset and makes the data smoother.
- They are highly capable of detecting minor shifts quickly, but larger shifts will take slower responses.
- The outcome data doesn't get affected much by outliers, since each data point is calculated in the exponentially weighted and moving average approach.

Limitations of EWMA

- The dataset should have continuous data for model-building
- This is suitable for small shifts and not fit for larger shifts process
- It reduces the noise in the given time series dataset and makes the data smoother

EWMA Model for TSA&F with Excel (simple method)

EWMA implementation using Excel with diesel dataset with Alpha(α) 0.3.

DATE	Diesel price
16-04-2022	7.25
17-04-2022	7.07
18-04-2022	6.25
19-04-2022	5.75
20-04-2022	5.53
21-04-2022	5.81
22-04-2022	6.26

Figure 7.40: *Diesel dataset*

Step -1:

Apply the formula EWMA(t) = $\alpha * x(t) + (1- \alpha) * EWMA_{(t-1)}$ in the given dataset. `=G1*C4+(1-G1)*C3`.

	A	B	C	D	E	F	G
1	DATE	Diesel price	EWMA (0.3)	EWMA (0.97)		Alpha(α)	0.3
2	16-04-2022	7.25	7.25				
3	17-04-2022	7.07	7.20				
4	18-04-2022	6.25	6.91	6.92			
5	19-04-2022	5.75	6.56	6.57			
6	20-04-2022	5.53	6.25	6.26			
7	21-04-2022	5.81	6.12	6.12			
8	22-04-2022	6.26	6.16	6.16			
9	23-04-2022	6.32	6.21	6.21			
10	24-04-2022	6.06	6.16	6.17			

Figure 7.41: *Diesel dataset – EWMA calculation (Alpha =0.3)*

Figure 7.42 shows the actual vs. forecast line plot using the EWMA line plot (Alpha =0.3).

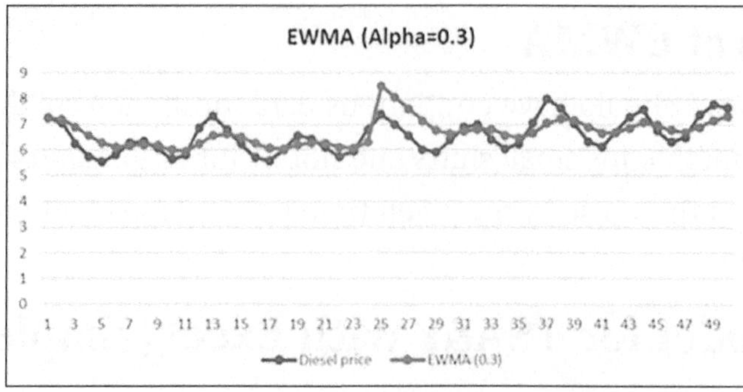

Figure 7.42: *Diesel dataset – EWMA line plot (Alpha =0.3)*

Step -2:

D5 =0.97*C5+(1-0.97)*C4

	A	B	C	D	E
1	DATE	Diesel price	EWMA (0.3)	EWMA (0.97)	
2	16-04-2022	7.25	7.25		
3	17-04-2022	7.07	7.20		
4	18-04-2022	6.25	6.91	6.92	
5	19-04-2022	5.75	6.56	6.57	
6	20-04-2022	5.53	6.25	6.26	
7	21-04-2022	5.81	6.12	6.12	
8	22-04-2022	6.26	6.16	6.16	
9	23-04-2022	6.32	6.21	6.21	
10	24-04-2022	6.06	6.16	6.17	
11	25-04-2022	5.63	6.00	6.01	
12	26-04-2022	5.8	5.94	5.94	

Figure 7.43: *Diesel dataset – EWMA calculation (Alpha =0.97)*

Figure 7.44 shows the actual vs. forecast line plot using the EWMA line plot (Alpha =0.97).

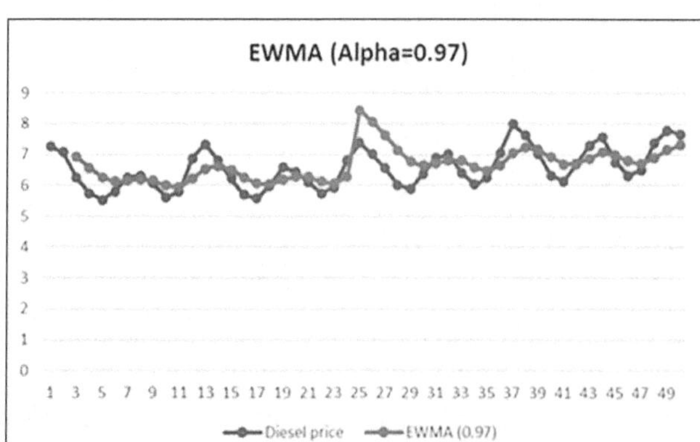

Figure 7.44: *Diesel dataset – EWMA line plot (Alpha =0.97)*

EWMA Model implementation using Python

```
#load required libraries
import numpy as np
import pandas as pd
from statsmodels.tsa.seasonal import seasonal_decompose
df_diesel_price = pd.read_csv("diesel_price EWMA - Python.csv",
header=0, index_col=0)
df_diesel_price.plot()
```

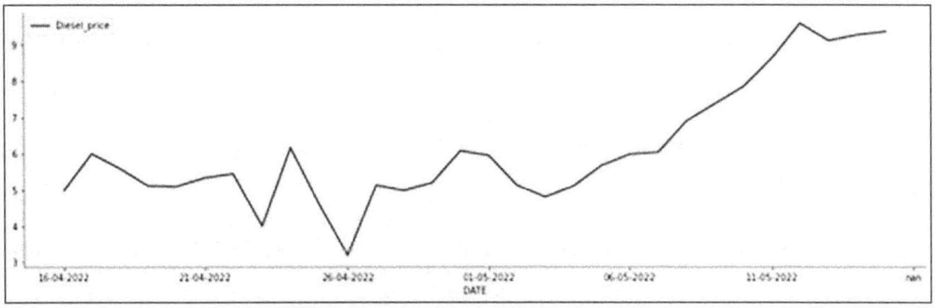

Figure 7.45: *Diesel dataset –line plot*

```
print("###########################################################")
print("    Diesel Price - EWMA (alpha=0.3,0.6 and 0.9)        ")
print("###########################################################")
df_diesel_price["EWMA(0.3)"] = df_diesel_price["Diesel_price"].ewm
(alpha=.3, adjust=False).mean()
df_diesel_price["EWMA(0.5)"] = df_diesel_price["Diesel_price"].ewm
(alpha=.5, adjust=False).mean()
df_diesel_price["EWMA(0.9)"] = df_diesel_price["Diesel_price"].ewm
(alpha=.9, adjust=False).mean()
df_diesel_price.head(5)
```

```
###########################################################
        Diesel Price - EWMA (alpha=0.3,0.6 and 0.9)
###########################################################
```

DATE	Diesel_price	EWMA(0.3)	EWMA(0.5)	EWMA(0.9)
16-04-2022	5.00	5.0000	5.0000	5.0000
17-04-2022	6.00	5.3000	5.5000	5.9000
18-04-2022	5.60	5.3900	5.5500	5.6300
19-04-2022	5.12	5.3090	5.3350	5.1710
20-04-2022	5.10	5.2463	5.2175	5.1071

Figure 7.46: *Diesel dataset – EWMA values*

```
print("################################################################")
print("     Diesel Price - EWMA (alpha=0.3,0.6 and 0.9) line plot    ")
print("################################################################")
df_diesel_price.plot()
```

```
################################################################
     Diesel Price - EWMA (alpha=0.3,0.6 and 0.9) line plot
################################################################
```

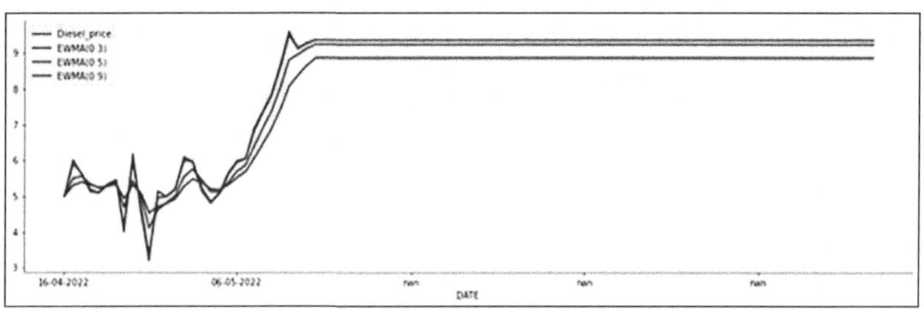

Figure 7.47: *Diesel dataset – EWMA values (line plot)*

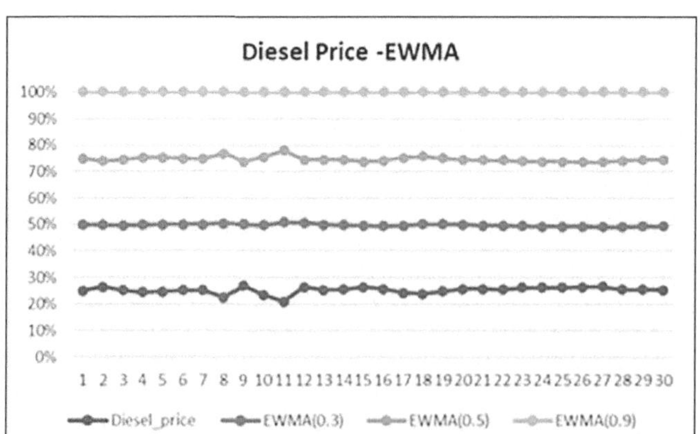

Figure 7.48: *Diesel dataset – EWMA values (line plot from Excel)*

Note: The EWMA method considered past data based on its weightage. When the data is getting aged then the moving average gives lower weights, and it decreases exponentially over the period.

The exponentially weighted came into the picture along with the parameter alpha(α) and it decides the current data point in EWMA calculation, which is used to build the volatility modelling using time series analysis data.

Conclusion

In this chapter, we have discussed the detailed studies of various powerful time series analysis and forecasting methods using univariate time series data, which includes Exponential Smoothing and its subtypes SES, DES and TES and their implementation using Excel and Python.

We explored all the techniques and requirements for TSA&F like needs forecast data points for the most recent period, actual data points for that period and the appropriate smoothing constant to build the models.

Benefits and limitations of exponential smoothing, exponentially weighted moving averages and model implementation using Excel tool "Analysis ToolPak in Excel" and using Python code,

We studied in detail Error - Trend- Seasonality (ETS), its characteristics, taxonomies and types. Different time series scenarios which ETS supports on time series analysis and forecasting.

This chapter will provide a solid understanding of the exponential smoothing of statistical models for TSA&F, limitations, benefits, characteristics, and various techniques to implement them with the data.

In the next chapter, we will discuss the various vector autoregression methods and basic requirements for using the VAR model for time series problems. How VAR distinguishes from AR. The sub-types are characteristics of vector autoregression and implementation.

Points to remember

In this chapter, it is important to keep a few things in mind that will be handy throughout this book:

- Understanding the exponential smoothing models for TSA&F and their significance with clear examples.
- Exploring various exponential smoothing methods and they are further classified into three sub-type methods to estimate exponential smoothing. They are as follows:
    - Single Exponential Smoothing
    - Double Exponential Smoothing
    - Triple exponential smoothing
- Error - Trend-Seasonality (ETS) and its characteristics. Taxonomies of ETS such as Additive(A), Multiplicative(M), Additive damped(Ad) and Multiplicative damped(Md). The combination of Additive (15) and Multiplicative(15) across ETS components.
- Understanding different time series scenarios which ETS supports in time series analysis and forecasting.
- Detailed study of the Exponentially Weighted Moving Averages (EWMA) model, its benefits, limitations, and implementation using Excel and Python.

CHAPTER 8

Exploring Vector Autoregression and its Subsets (VAR, VMA, and VARMA)

Introduction

In the previous chapter, we discussed the detailed studies of Exponential Smoothing, ETS, and EWMA models in time series analysis and their characteristics, sub-types of SES, DES, and TES and their implementations using sample datasets and their visualization using Excel and Python code. This chapter will help us explore Vector Auto-Regression (VAR) methods and basic requirements to use the VAR model for time series problems. Its sub-types, detailed study of its characteristics and implementation and extension of ARIMA - Seasonal Auto-Regressive Integrated Moving Average (SARIMA) with exogenous variables and Fractional Auto-Regressive Integrated Moving Average (FARIMA).

Structure

In this chapter, we will discuss the following topics:

- Vector autoregression methods and basic requirements
- Difference between AR and VAR
- Multivariate time series analysis and forecasting
    - VAR
    - VMA
    - VARMA
    - VARMAX
- SARIMA and FARIMA

So far, we have discussed various univariate time series analyses, forecasting techniques and their benefits and limitations. When we need to handle a multivariate time series, we have specific techniques; they are **VAR, VMA,** and **VARMA**.

Understanding Vector Autoregression

We have discussed univariate time series data, which contains only a single time-dependent variable and have analyzed them and derived the forecasting. While in the multivariate discussion, the time series data has more than one time-dependent variable, and each variable purely depends on the other and not only on its past observations and has current observations as well. The VAR model has strong requirements, as follows "More than two or more time series variables and the relationship between them."

This chapter is mainly focused on Vector Autoregressive (VAR) models and their subtypes, and this model is the best fit when dealing with more than two or more time series variables that influence each other. That is the dynamic relationships between the time series data involved and bidirectional movement behaviors, especially to design forecasting tools for examining "Macro Economic" based forecasting.

The VAR model is best for forecasting multiple variables by understanding them through lively collaborations and providing effective suggestions for dependent variables. This model effectively deals with the stock exchange, economic, and money inflation rate behavior since it has the capability to demonstrate forecasting any time series variables that are stationary or non-stationary.

Difference between VAR and other TSA&F models

The VAR model differs from other major models like AR, MA and ARIMA, all these models are used for univariate time series data and unidirectional models, and dependent variables are influenced by their past, whereas the VAR models work with multivariate time series data and bi-directional model, and the dependent variable is influenced by its past value or variable.

Mathematically deriving VAR from AR equation

The autoregression (AR) model can be represented by the following equation. We have discussed this in *Chapter 6: Exploring Time Series Models* - AR, MA, ARMA, *and* ARIMA.

$$Y_t = C + \alpha_1 Y_{t-1} + \alpha_2 Y_{t-1} + \alpha_3 Y_{t-1} + \ldots\ldots + \alpha_n Y_{t-n} + \varepsilon_t$$

We understand that VAR is a multivariate time series with more than two or more time series variables that influence each other. Therefore, the VAR model equation can be written as expansions with two or more dependent variables in the time series dataset.

Let's consider Y1 and Y2 as time series variables, and while calculating the Y1(t) variable, the model will use the lags of both variables (Y1 and Y2).

For example, the equation for the VAR(1) model with two time-series variables (Y1 and Y2) will write the following equations:

$$Y_{1,t} = C_1 + \alpha_{11,1} Y_{1,t-1} + \alpha_{12,1} Y_{2,t-1} + \varepsilon_{1,t}$$

$$Y_{2,t} = C_2 + \alpha_{21,1} Y_{1,t-1} + \alpha_{22,1} Y_{2,t-1} + \varepsilon_{2,t}$$

Where,

- $Y_{\{1,t-1\}}$ -> First lag value for YY1
- $Y_{\{2,t-1\}}$ -> First lag value for YY2
- n-> past values
- C-> Constant
- α -> Coefficient of each 'n'
- ε_t-> error in time or residual

We can write Y1 and Y2 in vector representation:

$$ft = \begin{pmatrix} C_1 \\ C_2 \end{pmatrix} \begin{pmatrix} \alpha_{11} & \alpha_{12} \\ \alpha_{21} & \alpha_{22} \end{pmatrix} \begin{pmatrix} Y_{t-1} \\ Y_{t-2} \end{pmatrix} \begin{pmatrix} \varepsilon_1 \\ \varepsilon_2 \end{pmatrix}$$

The equations of the model are as follows for VAR(2) with Y1 and Y2 time series variables:

$$Y_{1,t}=C_1+ \alpha_{11,1}Y_{1,t-1}+ \alpha_{12,1}Y_{2,t-1}+ \alpha_{11,2}Y_{1,t-2}+ \alpha_{12,2}Y_{2,t-2}+ \varepsilon_{1,t}$$

$$Y_{2,t}=C_{2+} \alpha_{21,1}Y_{1,t-1}+ \alpha_{22,1}Y_{2,t-1}+ \alpha_{21,2}Y_{1,t-2}+ \alpha_{22,1}Y_{2,t-2}+ \varepsilon_{2,t}$$

From the preceding equations, we can understand how the model's equations are increasing with variables and the lag/p values. So the length of the equation increases based on the number of variables increasing in directly proportional ways.

Benefits of Vector Autoregressive (VAR)

- Has the ability to work on the dynamics of interconnected VAR(1) and VAR(2) of time series data
- Suitable for better forecasting performance since multivariate
- Highly flexible method for getting complex time series data behavior
- Appropriate model for forecasting finance, marketing strategy, and economic growth forecasting

Limitations of Vector Autoregressive (VAR)

- The VAR model does not take responsibility for non-linearities and base-structural changes in the data
- To handle the preceding situation, we need additional efforts to test stability and non-linearity

VAR implementation using Python

Let's build the VAR model using Python; here, we have taken stock buy and sell data for analysis. The VAR implementation involves the following steps:

1. Analyze the time series data and its characteristics
2. Test for data stationarity using the ADF method
3. Train-test split

4. Re-run ADF test
5. Optimal order (p) selection process
6. Apply the VAR algorithm
7. Analysis of Serial Correlation of Residuals [ScoR]
8. Building forecast VAR model
9. Model evaluation

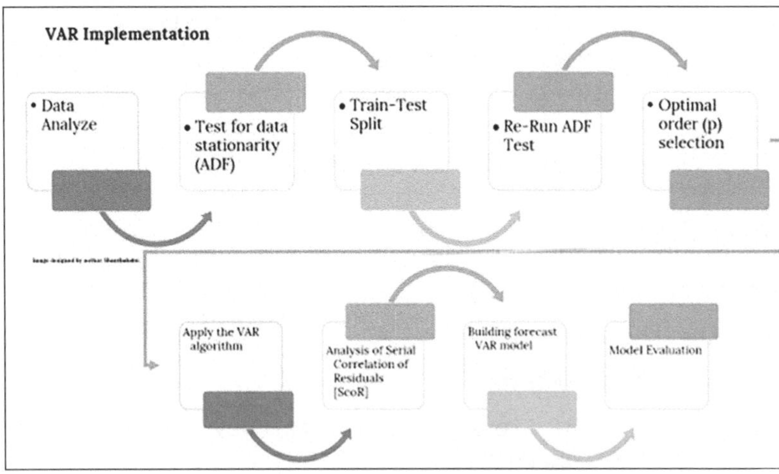

Figure 8.1: *VAR Implementation Process*

1. Analyze the time series data and its characteristics

Import all the required libraries:

```
#####################################
#Import all the required libraries#
#####################################
# Import pandas,numpy and matplot libraries
import pandas as pd
import numpy as np
import matplotlib.pyplot as plt
%matplotlib inline

# Import Statsmodels,adf and eval measures libraries
from statsmodels.tsa.api import VAR
```

```
from statsmodels.tsa.stattools import adfuller
from statsmodels.tools.eval_measures import rmse, aic
df_Stock_Buy_Selling = pd.read_csv('Stock_Buy_Selling.csv')
df_Stock_Buy_Selling.head()
```

	Date	Buy_stock_amount	Selling_stock_amount
0	01-01-2021	1518.43	3593.48
1	02-01-2021	1517.35	3593.19
2	03-01-2021	1517.87	3618.81
3	04-01-2021	1521.39	3622.37
4	05-01-2021	1532.26	3654.15

Figure 8.2: *Stock Buy Selling dataset*

Preparing the dataset:

```
print("####################")
print("Preparing the dataset")
print("####################")
df_Stock_Buy_Selling = df_Stock_Buy_Selling[["Buy_stock_
amount","Selling_stock_amount"]]
df_Stock_Buy_Selling.head()
```

```
######################
Preparing the dataset
######################
```

	Buy_stock_amount	Selling_stock_amount
0	1518.43	3593.48
1	1517.35	3593.19
2	1517.87	3618.81
3	1521.39	3622.37
4	1532.26	3654.15

Figure 8.3: *Stock Buy Selling dataset*

Visualization of dataset:

```
print("\t\t\t\t*****************************************")
print("\t\t\t\t   Visualization of Stock Buy and Selling    ")
print("\t\t\t\t*****************************************")
```

```
df_Stock_Buy_Selling.plot()
```

```
        *****************************************
            Visualization of Stock Buying and Selling
        *****************************************
```

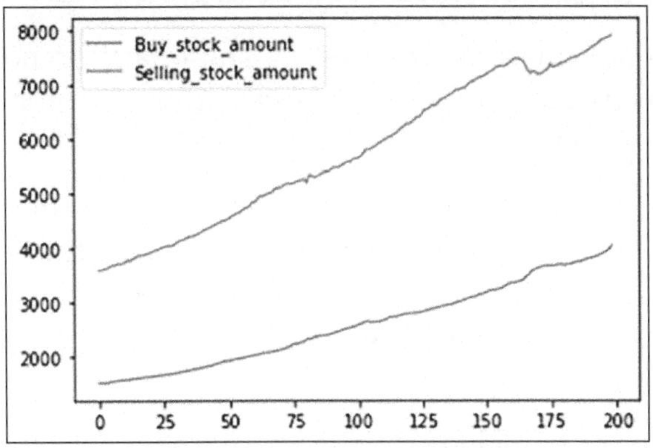

Figure 8.4: Stock Buy-Selling Plot

Here we can see that both Buy and Selling amounts have a high correlation. We understand that both variables are steadily growing, and the selling amount has some decrement. Check the time series pattern along with their log values.

```
print("\t\t\
t\t*************************************************************")
print("\t\t\t\t Pattern of TS in their log values of Stock Buy and
Selling data ")
print("\t\t\
t\t*************************************************************")
data = np.log(df_Stock_Buy_Selling).diff().dropna()
data.plot()
```

Figure 8.5: Stock Buy-Selling Plot

Here we can observe the relationship between buying and selling is as strong and follows the same line pattern and indicates both are dependent on each other.

2. Test for data stationarity using the ADF method

The time series data must be checked as stationary or not before they are analyzed and forecasted. We have discussed this in *Chapter 3: Time Series Analysis and Its Components.*

Stationarity is the base characteristic of time series; as the name implies, it is stable to analyze, in which the mean and variance of a time series data do not change over time. All basic and advanced time series data modelling referring to the time series should be **stationary**, which will be discussed in very detail in upcoming chapters.

Stationarity enables us to include the time base frequency effect of the series, as mentioned earlier, in terms of years, months, weeks, days, hours, and minutes.

Augmented Dickey-Fuller (ADF) test

The ADF test is an extensively used test for checking the stationarity of time series data, and it checks for the null hypothesis presence of a unit root in the data with the following assumptions:

- Null Hypothesis (H0)
    - The series has a **unit root**, or else the series is non-stationary
- Alternate Hypothesis (HA)
    - The series has **no unit root**, or else the series is stationary

Here the p-value is the marginal significance for a hypothesis test and the probability of the event; there are two possibilities for this p-value concerning "α", in the stationarity of time series data analysis. α= 0.05 (well-defined level of significance).

- p-value >0.05 Fail to reject (**H0**)
- p-value <= 0.05 Accept (**H1**)

Let's try to find out the p-value using the Stock Buy Selling dataset.

```
print("*********************************************")
print("Dickey-fuller Test - Result- Buy_stock_amount")
print("*********************************************")
```

```
df_adftest = adfuller(df_Stock_Buy_Selling["Buy_stock_amount"],
autolag='AIC')
dfoutput=pd.Series(df_adftest[0:4],index=['Test Statistic','
p-value','#lags used','Observation numbers for test'])
for key,value in df_adftest[4].items():
    dfoutput['critical value (%s)'%key]= value
print(dfoutput)


print("**************************************************")
print("Dickey-fuller Test - Result (Selling_stock_amount)")
print("**************************************************")
df_adftest = adfuller(df_Stock_Buy_Selling["Selling_stock_amount"],
autolag='AIC')
dfoutput=pd.Series(df_adftest[0:4],index=['Test Statistic','
p-value','#lags used','Observation numbers for test'])
for key,value in df_adftest[4].items():
    dfoutput['critical value (%s)'%key]= value
print(dfoutput)
```

Output

```
*********************************************
Dickey-fuller Test - Result- Buy_stock_amount
*********************************************
Test Statistics                   2.727828
p-value                          0.999088
#lags used                       4.000000
Observation numbers for test   194.000000
critical value (1%)             -3.464515
critical value (5%)             -2.876556
critical value (10%)            -2.574775
dtype: float64
```

Observation

Test statistics are 2.727828

Critical Value (1%) is -3.464515, (5%) is -2.876556, (10%) is -2.574775

p-value is 0.1

Test Statistic > Critical Value

p-value > 0.05.

Based on the results, the null hypothesis cannot be rejected. Hence, the series is non-stationary.

Output

```
************************************************

Dickey-fuller Test - Result (Selling_stock_amount)

************************************************

Test Statistics                    -0.345914

p-value                             0.918745

#lags used                          4.000000

Observation numbers for test      194.000000

critical value (1%)                -3.464515

critical value (5%)                -2.876556

critical value (10%)               -2.574775

dtype: float64
```

Observation

Test statistics are -0.345914

Critical Value (1%) is -3.464515, (5%) is -2.876556, (10%) is -2.574775

p-value is 0.918745

Test Statistic > Critical Value

p-value > 0.05.

Based on the results, the null hypothesis cannot be rejected. Hence, the series is non-stationary.

Since both variables are non-stationary, we will split the dataset and take the train dataset and first-order difference of the dataset and re-run the ADF test.

3. Train-test split

```
print("###################################")
print("          Train-Test Split         ")
print("###################################")
test_split = 70
train = df_Stock_Buy_Selling[:-test_split]
test = df_Stock_Buy_Selling[-test_split:]
# Check size
print("Train dataset size:",df_train.shape)
print("Test dataset size:",df_test.shape)
```

Output

```
##################################
          Train-Test Split
##################################
Train dataset size: : (129, 2)
Test dataset size: : (70, 2)
```

Apply the diff() function to calculate the 1st-order discrete difference in the train dataset along the given axis.

```
print("###################################")
print("   Applying 1st difference        ")
print("###################################")
df_differ = df_train.diff().dropna()
df_differ.head()
```

Output

```
##################################
  Applying 1st difference
##################################
```

	Buy_stock_amount	Selling_stock_amount
1	-1.08	-0.29
2	0.52	25.62
3	3.52	3.56
4	10.87	31.78
5	10.74	32.89

Figure 8.6: *Stock Buy-Selling 1st difference dataset*

4. Re-run the ADF test

```
print("****************************************************")
print("Re-run Dickey-fuller Test - Result- Buy_stock_amount")
print("****************************************************")

df_adftest = adfuller(df_differ["Buy_stock_amount"],autolag='AIC')
dfoutput=pd.Series(df_adftest[0:4],index=['Test Statistic','p-value','#lags used','Observation numbers for test'])
for key,value in df_adftest[4].items():
    dfoutput['critical value (%s)'%key]= value
print(dfoutput)

print("*********************************************************")
print("Re-run Dickey-fuller Test - Result (Selling_stock_amount)")
print("*********************************************************")
df_adftest = adfuller(df_differ["Selling_stock_amount"],autolag='AIC')
dfoutput=pd.Series(df_adftest[0:4],index=['Test Statistic','p-value','#lags used','Observation numbers for test'])
for key,value in df_adftest[4].items():
    dfoutput['critical value (%s)'%key]= value
print(dfoutput)
```

Output

```
****************************************************
Re-run Dickey-fuller Test - Result- Buy_stock_amount
****************************************************
Test Statistics                  -5.352843
p-value                           0.000004
#lags used                        3.000000
Observation numbers for test    124.000000
critical value (1%)              -3.484220
critical value (5%)              -2.885145
critical value (10%)             -2.579359
```

```
dtype: float64
```

Observation

Test statistics are -5.352843

Critical Value (1%) is -3.484220, (5%) is -2.885145, (10%) is -2.579359

p-value is 0.000004

Test Statistic < Critical Value

p-value < 0.05.

Based on the results, the null hypothesis is rejected. Hence, the series is stationary.

```
*****************************************************
Re-run Dickey-fuller Test - Result (Selling_stock_amount)
*****************************************************
Test Statistics                  -1.104614
p-value                           0.713228
#lags used                        9.000000
Observation numbers for test    118.000000
critical value (1%)              -3.487022
critical value (5%)              -2.886363
critical value (10%)             -2.580009
dtype: float64
```

Observation

Test statistics are -1.104614

Critical Value (1%) is -3.487022, (5%) is -2.886363, (10%) is -2.580009

p-value is 0.713228

Test Statistic > Critical Value

p-value > 0.05.

Based on the results, the null hypothesis cannot be rejected. Hence, the series is non-stationary.

5. Apply the VAR algorithm

```
print("****************************************")
print("      Building VAR model and summary     ")
print("****************************************")
var_model = VAR(train)
VAR_results = var_model .fit(5)
VAR_results.summary()
```

```
****************************************
      Building VAR model and summary
****************************************
```

```
  Summary of Regression Results
==================================
Model:                         VAR
Method:                        OLS
Date:           Fri, 30, Jun, 2023
Time:                     01:34:44
--------------------------------------------------------------------
No. of Equations:         2.00000    BIC:                    10.5841
Nobs:                     125.000    HQIC:                   10.3423
Log likelihood:          -972.789    FPE:                    26301.2
AIC:                      10.1769    Det(Omega_mle):         22886.8
--------------------------------------------------------------------
Results for equation Buy_stock_amount
==========================================================================================
                            coefficient       std. error           t-stat            prob
------------------------------------------------------------------------------------------
const                         -8.054644         6.241317           -1.291           0.197
L1.Buy_stock_amount            1.104450         0.091551           12.064           0.000
L1.Selling_stock_amount        0.029362         0.032138            0.914           0.361
L2.Buy_stock_amount           -0.106893         0.139745           -0.765           0.444
L2.Selling_stock_amount       -0.067499         0.036673           -1.841           0.066
L3.Buy_stock_amount            0.166618         0.140154            1.189           0.235
L3.Selling_stock_amount       -0.011132         0.037068           -0.300           0.764
L4.Buy_stock_amount           -0.192696         0.090272           -2.135           0.033
L4.Selling_stock_amount        0.065118         0.032926            1.978           0.048
==========================================================================================

Results for equation Selling_stock_amount
==========================================================================================
                            coefficient       std. error           t-stat            prob
------------------------------------------------------------------------------------------
const                         -1.515808        18.081774           -0.084           0.933
L1.Buy_stock_amount            0.256539         0.265232            0.967           0.333
L1.Selling_stock_amount        0.539063         0.093106            5.790           0.000
L2.Buy_stock_amount           -0.373243         0.404857           -0.922           0.357
L2.Selling_stock_amount        0.266555         0.106246            2.509           0.012
L3.Buy_stock_amount           -0.536521         0.406040           -1.321           0.186
L3.Selling_stock_amount        0.169385         0.107389            1.577           0.115
L4.Buy_stock_amount            0.651524         0.261529            2.491           0.013
L4.Selling_stock_amount        0.035254         0.095391            0.370           0.712
==========================================================================================

Correlation matrix of residuals
                        Buy_stock_amount  Selling_stock_amount
Buy_stock_amount                1.000000             -0.213597
Selling_stock_amount           -0.213597              1.000000
```

Figure 8.7: *VAR model summary*

6. Optimal order (p) selection process

The selection of the optimal order of the VAR model either iteratively fits the increasing orders of the VAR model or the `select_order(maxlags)` method and followed picks the order that gives a VAR model with the tiniest AIC or where AIC drops is the best fit.

Let's try both here.

iterative method

```
print("**************************************************************
**")
print("       Select the Order (P) of VAR model using iterative method
")
print("**************************************************************
**")
for i in range(1,10):
    VAR_results = var_model.fit(i)
    print("******************************")
    print("Order =", i)
    print("AIC: ", VAR_results.aic)
    print("BIC: ", VAR_results.bic)
    print("******************************")
```

```
****************************************************************
      Select the Order (P) of VAR model using iterative method
****************************************************************
******************************
Order = 1
AIC:  10.349366797840396
BIC:  10.483055716461628
******************************
******************************
Order = 2
AIC:  10.206042474464235
BIC:  10.429994213555464
******************************
******************************
Order = 3
AIC:  10.225571325080146
BIC:  10.540713759185866
******************************
******************************
Order = 4
AIC:  10.176869167828809
BIC:  10.58414634600034
******************************
******************************
Order = 5
AIC:  10.149485037266157
BIC:  10.649857573099307
******************************
```

Figure 8.8: *Optimal order (p) selection process VAR -I*

```
******************************
Order = 6
AIC:  10.155201687131003
BIC:  10.74964716062436
******************************
******************************
Order = 7
AIC:  10.168084326759509
BIC:  10.857597698415228
******************************
******************************
Order = 8
AIC:  10.221372940824974
BIC:  11.006966978430668
******************************
******************************
Order = 9
AIC:  10.290962763511747
BIC:  11.173668482059394
******************************
```

Figure 8.9: *Optimal order (p) selection process VAR -II*

In the preceding output, the AIC drops to lowest at lag 5, then increases from lag 6 and goes with lag 5.

Select_order(maxlags) method

Optimal order (p) □ (* highlights the minimums) in the Figure

```
print("**********************************************************
**")
print("       Select the Order (P) of the VAR model using select_order
")
print("**********************************************************
**")
Order_of_VAR_model= var_model.select_order()
Order_of_VAR_model.summary()
    **********************************************************
          Select the Order (P) of the VAR model using select_order
    **********************************************************
```

VAR Order Selection (* highlights the minimums)

	AIC	BIC	FPE	HQIC
0	21.13	21.18	1.508e+09	21.15
1	10.47	10.61	3.516e+04	10.53
2	10.34	10.58*	3.095e+04	10.44*
3	10.36	10.69	3.148e+04	10.49
4	10.29	10.72	2.948e+04	10.46
5	10.26	10.78	2.862e+04	10.47
6	10.25*	10.87	2.839e+04*	10.50
7	10.26	10.98	2.877e+04	10.55
8	10.30	11.11	2.997e+04	10.63

Figure 8.10: VAR Order Selection for optimal order (p)

7. Analysis of Serial Correlation of Residuals [ScoR]

The analysis of the serial correlation of residuals using the **Durbin Watson Statistic (DWS)** method is used to check any remaining pattern in the residuals, mainly used to strengthen the model and forecasting.

The value of DWS can vary between 0 and 4.

- DWS -> closer to 2, -> there is no serial correlation.
- DWS -> closer to 0 -> there is a positive serial correlation.
- DWS -> closer to 4 -> there is a negative serial correlation.

```
print("**********************************************************
***************")

print("Analysis of Serial-Correlation of Residuals using Durbin
Watson-Statistic")

print("**********************************************************
***************")

from statsmodels.stats.stattools import durbin_watson

ScoR_DWS = durbin_watson(VAR_results.resid)

for col, val in zip(df_Stock_Buy_Selling.columns, ScoR_DWS):

    print(adjust(col), ':', round(val, 2))

*******************************************************************
***********

Analysis of Serial Correlation of Residuals  using Durbin Watson
Statistics
```

```
**********************************************************************
***********
Buy_stock_amount : 1.87
Selling_stock_amount : 2.04
```

Analysis of serial correlation if it looks fine for both variables

8. Building forecast VAR model

Find the lag order from the previous data to predict the forecast.

```
print("*************************************")
print("Get the lag order from the VAR model ")
print("*************************************")
lag_order = VAR_results.k_ar
print("lag order :",lag_order)
```

Output

```
*************************************
Get the lag order from the VAR model
*************************************
lag order : 4

print("*******************************")
print("Building Forecasting using lag ")
print("*******************************")
forecast_input = df_differ.values[-lag_order:]
forecast_input

*******************************
Building Forecasting using lag
*******************************
array([[14.08, 59.92],
       [13.74, 77.56],
       [14.26,  2.15],
       [14.7 , 39.55]])
print("*********************************")
```

```
print("Forecasting Dataset for analysis ")
print("********************************")
fc_Stock_Buy_Selling = VAR_results.forecast(y=forecast_input,
steps=test_split)
df_Stock_Buy_Selling_forecast = pd.DataFrame(fc_Stock_Buy_Selling,
index=df_Stock_Buy_Selling.index[-test_split:], columns=df_Stock_Buy_
Selling.columns + '_2d')
df_Stock_Buy_Selling_forecast
********************************
Forecasting Dataset for analysis
********************************
```

	Buy_stock_amount_2d	Selling_stock_amount_2d
129	10.287239	35.877458
130	4.874545	29.918678
131	-5.912631	29.765257
132	-15.193986	30.697767
133	-24.478311	31.694967
...	...	...
194	-227.615044	85.000887
195	-227.969646	84.974838
196	-228.306695	84.942605
197	-228.627264	84.904524
198	-228.932362	84.860906

70 rows × 2 columns

Figure 8.11: *Forecasting Dataset*

```
print("********************************************")
print("    Stock_Buy_Selling  Forecasting Plot       ")
print("********************************************")
df_Stock_Buy_Selling_forecast.plot()
```

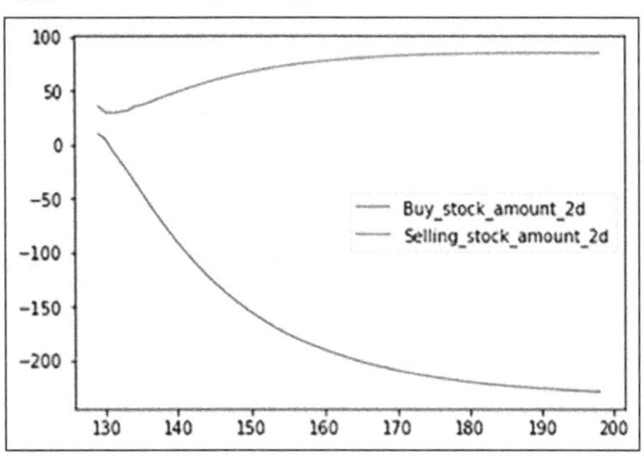

Figure 8.12: *Stock_Buy_Selling Forecasting plot*

9. Model evaluation

```
forcast_actual=df_Stock_Buy_Selling_forecast["Buy_stock_amount_2d"]
- df_Stock_Buy_Selling["Buy_stock_amount"]
forcast_data=df_Stock_Buy_Selling_forecast["Buy_stock_amount_2d"]
actual_data=df_Stock_Buy_Selling["Buy_stock_amount"]
me = np.mean(forcast_actual)
mae = np.mean(np.abs(forcast_actual))
mpe = np.mean((forcast_actual)/actual_data)   # MPE
rmse = np.mean((forcast_actual)**2)**.5  # RMSE

print("***************************")
print("       Model Evaluation    ")
print("***************************")
print("Mean :",me)
print("MAE (Mean absolute error)  :",mae)
print("MPE (Mean Percentage Error) :",mpe)
print("RMSE (Root Mean Squared Error) :",rmse)
```

Output

```
***************************
       Model Evaluation
***************************
Mean : -3585.6982402764497
MAE (Mean absolute error)  : 3585.6982402764497
MPE (Mean Percentage Error) : -1.0477819392347547
RMSE (Root Mean Squared Error) : 3607.4479295363303
```

Note: The VAR model is best for forecasting multiple variables; this model effectively deals with the stock exchange, economic, and money inflation rate behavior since it has the capability to demonstrate forecasting of any time series variables that are stationary or non-stationary. There are other versions which include threshold VAR, Vector and error correction models. In this model, the predictions are dependent on historical data and correlated with economic conditions. This model does not take responsibility for non-linearities and base-structural changes in the data.

Vector Autoregression Moving - Average (VARMA)

The VARMA model is the extension of the "ARMA" model, but this model is specifically for multivariate time-series data and determining their forecasting. It encompasses two major components, such as the **Vector Auto-Regressive (VAR)** and the **Vector Moving Average (VMA),** like the ARMA model. The simplified format of ARMA is used to analyze the multivariate time series.

The Vector Autoregression Moving-Average (VARMA) model can also be used to build the **Vector Autoregression (VAR)** or **Vector Moving-Average (VMA)** models.

The **VAR model** is a typically generalized model of the **AR model** and is specific to multivariate time series modelling by considering the **lag order 'p'** while building the model and where the time series is stationary.

The **VMA model** is a typically generalized model of the **MA model** and is specific to multivariate time series modelling by considering the **order-of-moving-average 'q'** while building the model and where the time series is stationary.

The VARMA model is a combination of VAR and VMA models, and is specific to multivariate time series modelling by considering both the lag order, the moving average, and the order while building the model.

To build the **VARMA** model as **VAR** and **VMA** models, the simple configuration of the VARMA model as follows:

- **The VAR model** -> Setting the **q** parameter as 0, the **VARMA** model acts as VAR
- **VMA model** -> Setting the **p** parameter as 0, the **VARMA** model acts as VMA

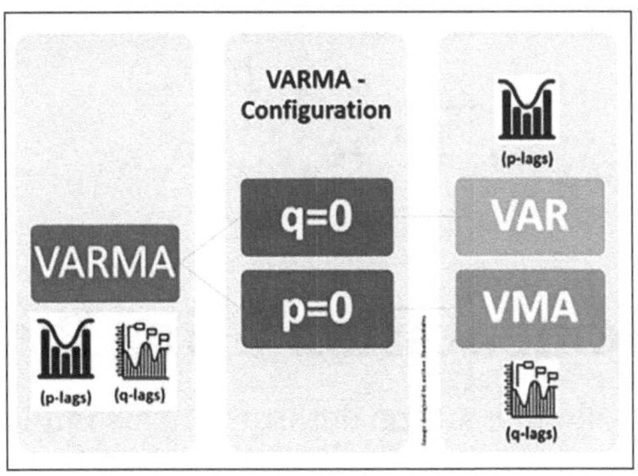

Figure 8.13: *VARMA configuration to build VAR and VMA*

Benefits of Vector Autoregressive (VARMA)

- Suitable for multivariate time series data exclusive to trend and seasonal components
- Has the ability to increase the performance of the model with a reduction of time frame compared with other models
- Highly flexible method for getting complex multivariate time series data behavior
- An appropriate model for microeconomics analysis and strategic planning, highly complex qualitative methods and market research

Limitations of Vector Autoregressive (VARMA)

- The data requirement for VARMA analysis is a huge volume of data to build and demonstrate the model.
- There should be major considerations when selecting the lag length (p or q).
- Depending on the volume of the lags, either low or high volume would impact the model accuracy and inaccurate forecast results.

Mathematically deriving VARMA from AR and MA equations

As we know, VAR is a generalized model of AR

$$\mathbf{Y_t = C + \alpha_1 Y_{t-1} + \alpha_2 Y_{t-1} + \alpha_3 Y_{t-1} + \ldots\ldots + \alpha_n Y_{t-n} + \varepsilon_t \ (AR)}$$

$$\mathbf{Y_{1,t} = C_1 + \alpha_{11,1} Y_{t-1,1} + \alpha_{12,1} Y_{t-1,2} + \varepsilon_{1,t} \ (VAR)}$$

As we know, VMA is a generalized model from MA

$$\mathbf{Y_t = C + \Theta_1 \varepsilon_{t-1} + \Theta_2 \varepsilon_{t-2} + + \Theta_n \varepsilon_{t-n} \ (MA)}$$

$$\mathbf{Y_{1,t} = C_{11} + \Theta_{11} \varepsilon_{t-1,1} + \Theta_{12} \varepsilon_{t-2} \ (VMA)}$$

VARMA(p,q) □ VAR + VMA

$$Y_t = C + \sum \beta_i Y_{t-1} + \varepsilon_t + \sum_{i=1}^{q} \theta_i \varepsilon_{t-i} \quad \textbf{(ARMA)}$$

$$Y_{1,t} = C + \mathbf{C_1 + \alpha_{11,1} Y_{t-1,1} + \alpha_{12,1} Y_{t-1,2} + \varepsilon_{1,t} + C_{11} + \Theta_{11} \varepsilon_{t-1,1} + \Theta_{12} \varepsilon_{t-2}}$$

(VARMA)

VARMA implementation using Python

Let us use the stock exchange status dataset for this implementation.

##

```
#Import all the required libraries#
########################################
import pandas as pd
import numpy as np
import statsmodels.api as sm
from statsmodels.tsa.stattools import adfuller
from statsmodels.tsa.api import VAR
from statsmodels.tools.eval_measures import rmse, aic
from pmdarima import auto_arima
from statsmodels.tsa.stattools import adfuller
from statsmodels.tools.eval_measures import mse,rmse
from statsmodels.tsa.statespace.varmax import VARMAX,VARMAXResults
import matplotlib.pyplot as plt
%matplotlib inline
print("*********************************************")
print("      Load Stock Exchange Status Data        ")
print("*********************************************")
df_Stock_Exchange_Status = pd.read_csv("Stock_Exchange_Status.csv")
df_Stock_Exchange_Status.head()
```

```
*********************************************
        Load Stock Exchange Status Data
*********************************************
```

	Date	Open_Stock_Rate	Max__Stock_Rate	Min__Stock_Rate	Close__Stock_Rate
0	06/30/2023	17134.96	17233.68	17134.96	17203.80
1	06/29/2023	16927.29	17073.84	16914.32	17061.21
2	06/28/2023	16940.69	16951.88	16877.96	16926.33
3	06/27/2023	16869.52	16987.83	16865.20	16963.37
4	06/26/2023	16865.40	16909.75	16805.16	16857.36

Figure 8.14: *Stock Exchange Status dataset*

Prepare the dataset for further analysis.

```
print("########################################")
print("            Preparing the dataset      ")
```

```
print("############################################")
df_Stock_Exchange_Status = df_Stock_Exchange_Status[["Open_Stock_
Rate","Max__Stock_Rate","Min__Stock_Rate","Close__Stock_Rate"]]
df_Stock_Exchange_Status.head()
```

```
############################################
                Preparing the dataset
############################################
```

	Open_Stock_Rate	Max__Stock_Rate	Min__Stock_Rate	Close__Stock_Rate
0	17134.96	17233.68	17134.96	17203.80
1	16927.29	17073.84	16914.32	17061.21
2	16940.69	16951.88	16877.96	16926.33
3	16869.52	16987.83	16865.20	16963.37
4	16865.40	16909.75	16805.16	16857.36

Figure 8.15: *Stock Exchange Status dataset – Prepared for VARMA*

```
print("*********************************************")
print("   Visualization of Stock Exchange Status     ")
print("*********************************************")
df_Stock_Exchange_Status.plot()
```

```
*********************************************
    Visualization of Stock Exchange Status
*********************************************
```

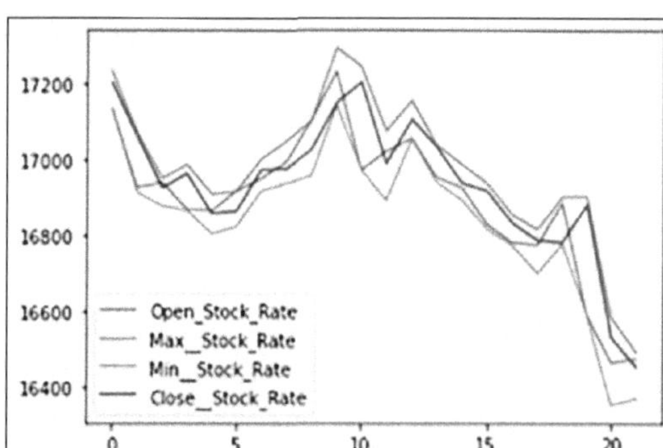

Figure 8.16: *Stock Exchange Status Plot*

Check for Stationarity -Dickey-fuller test

```
print("*********************************************")
print("Dickey-fuller Test - Result- Open_Stock_Rate")
```

```
print("********************************************")
df_adftest = adfuller(df_Stock_Exchange_Status["Open_Stock_Rate"], autolag='AIC')
dfoutput=pd.Series(df_adftest[0:4],index=['Test Statistic','p-value','#lags used','Observation numbers for test'])
for key,value in df_adftest[4].items():
    dfoutput['critical value (%s)'%key]= value
print(dfoutput)
print("\n")
print("************************************************")
print("Dickey-fuller Test - Result (Max__Stock_Rate )")
print("************************************************")
df_adftest = adfuller(df_Stock_Exchange_Status["Max__Stock_Rate"], autolag='AIC')
dfoutput=pd.Series(df_adftest[0:4],index=['Test Statistic','p-value','#lags used','Observation numbers for test'])
for key,value in df_adftest[4].items():
    dfoutput['critical value (%s)'%key]= value
print(dfoutput)
print("\n")
print("********************************************")
print("Dickey-fuller Test - Result- Min__Stock_Rate ")
print("********************************************")
df_adftest = adfuller(df_Stock_Exchange_Status["Min__Stock_Rate"], autolag='AIC')
dfoutput=pd.Series(df_adftest[0:4],index=['Test Statistic','
p-value','#lags used','Observation numbers for test'])
for key,value in df_adftest[4].items():
    dfoutput['critical value (%s)'%key]= value
print(dfoutput)
print("\n")
print("************************************************")
print("Dickey-fuller Test - Result (Close__Stock_Rate)")
print("************************************************")
```

```
df_adftest = adfuller(df_Stock_Exchange_Status["Close__Stock_Rate"],
autolag='AIC')
dfoutput=pd.Series(df_adftest[0:4],index=['Test Statistic','
p-value','#lags used','Observation numbers for test'])
for key,value in df_adftest[4].items():
    dfoutput['critical value (%s)'%key]= value
print(dfoutput)
```

```
*******************************************
Dickey-fuller Test - Result- Open_Stock_Rate
*******************************************
Test Statistic                  7.137927
p-value                         1.000000
#lags used                      9.000000
Observation numbers for test   12.000000
critical value (1%)            -4.137829
critical value (5%)            -3.154972
critical value (10%)           -2.714477
dtype: float64
```

Observation

Test statistics are 7.137927

Critical Value (1%) is -4.137829, (5%) is -3.154972, (10%) is -2.714477

p-value is 1.00

Test Statistic > Critical Value

p-value > 0.05.

Based on the results, the null hypothesis cannot be rejected. Hence, the series is non-stationary.

```
************************************************
Dickey-fuller Test - Result (Max__Stock_Rate  )
************************************************
Test Statistic                  1.318857
p-value                         0.996712
#lags used                      9.000000
```

```
Observation numbers for test    12.000000
critical value (1%)             -4.137829
critical value (5%)             -3.154972
critical value (10%)            -2.714477
dtype: float64
```

Observation

```
Test statistics are 1.318857
Critical Value (1%) is -4.137829, (5%) is -3.154972, (10%) is -2.714477
p-value is 0.996712
Test Statistic > Critical Value
p-value > 0.05.
```

Based on the results, the null hypothesis cannot be rejected. Hence, the series is non-stationary.

```
********************************************
Dickey-fuller Test - Result- Min__Stock_Rate
********************************************
Test Statistic                   1.182309
p-value                          0.995861
#lags used                       9.000000
Observation numbers for test    12.000000
critical value (1%)             -4.137829
critical value (5%)             -3.154972
critical value (10%)            -2.714477
dtype: float64
```

Observation

Test statistics are 1.182309

Critical Value (1%) is -4.137829, (5%) is -3.154972, (10%) is -2.714477

p-value is 0.995861

Test Statistic > Critical Value

p-value > 0.05.

Based on the results, the null hypothesis cannot be rejected. Hence, the series is non-stationary.

```
*********************************************

Dickey-fuller Test - Result (Close__Stock_Rate)

*********************************************

Test Statistic                   1.934322
p-value                          0.998581
#lags used                       9.000000
Observation numbers for test    12.000000
critical value (1%)             -4.137829
critical value (5%)             -3.154972
critical value (10%)            -2.714477
dtype: float64
```

Observation

Test statistics are 1.934322

Critical Value (1%) is -4.137829, (5%) is -3.154972, (10%) is -2.714477

p-value is 0.998581

Test Statistic > Critical Value

p-value > 0.05.

Based on the results, the null hypothesis cannot be rejected. Hence, the series is non-stationary.

Let's decide the order of the VARMA(p,q) for the dataset.

```
print("************************************************")
print(" Auto ARIMA Test - on (Open_Stock_Rate)")
print("************************************************")
auto_arima(df_Stock_Exchange_Status["Open_Stock_Rate"], error_
action='ignore', trace=True,suppress_warnings=True, maxiter=10,
seasonal=True, m=4)
```

```
*********************************************

 Auto ARIMA Test - on (Open_Stock_Rate)

*********************************************

Perform stepwise search to minimize aic
```

```
 ARIMA(2,1,2)(1,0,1)[4] intercept   : AIC=272.419, Time=0.12 sec
 ARIMA(0,1,0)(0,0,0)[4] intercept   : AIC=262.261, Time=0.01 sec
 ARIMA(1,1,0)(1,0,0)[4] intercept   : AIC=264.982, Time=0.05 sec
 ARIMA(0,1,1)(0,0,1)[4] intercept   : AIC=264.675, Time=0.07 sec
 ARIMA(0,1,0)(0,0,0)[4]             : AIC=261.820, Time=0.01 sec
 ARIMA(0,1,0)(1,0,0)[4] intercept   : AIC=264.233, Time=0.04 sec
 ARIMA(0,1,0)(0,0,1)[4] intercept   : AIC=264.161, Time=0.04 sec
 ARIMA(0,1,0)(1,0,1)[4] intercept   : AIC=265.641, Time=0.08 sec
 ARIMA(1,1,0)(0,0,0)[4] intercept   : AIC=263.096, Time=0.03 sec
 ARIMA(0,1,1)(0,0,0)[4] intercept   : AIC=262.758, Time=0.05 sec
 ARIMA(1,1,1)(0,0,0)[4] intercept   : AIC=264.825, Time=0.05 sec
Best model:  ARIMA(0,1,0)(0,0,0)[4]
Total fit time: 0.602 seconds
print("**************************************************")
print(" Auto ARIMA Test - on (Max__Stock_Rate)")
print("**************************************************")
auto_arima(df_Stock_Exchange_Status["Max__Stock_Rate"], error_
action='ignore', trace=True,
             suppress_warnings=True, maxiter=10,seasonal=True, m=4)
**************************************************
 Auto ARIMA Test - on (Max__Stock_Rate)
**************************************************
Perform stepwise search to minimize aic
 ARIMA(2,0,2)(1,0,1)[4] intercept   : AIC=465.598, Time=0.17 sec
 ARIMA(0,0,0)(0,0,0)[4] intercept   : AIC=296.526, Time=0.02 sec
 ARIMA(1,0,0)(1,0,0)[4] intercept   : AIC=301.230, Time=0.08 sec
 ARIMA(0,0,1)(0,0,1)[4] intercept   : AIC=282.941, Time=0.05 sec
 ARIMA(0,0,0)(0,0,0)[4]             : AIC=492.981, Time=0.01 sec
 ARIMA(0,0,1)(0,0,0)[4] intercept   : AIC=280.356, Time=0.03 sec
 ARIMA(0,0,1)(1,0,0)[4] intercept   : AIC=286.232, Time=0.03 sec
 ARIMA(0,0,1)(1,0,1)[4] intercept   : AIC=292.787, Time=0.06 sec
 ARIMA(1,0,1)(0,0,0)[4] intercept   : AIC=279.698, Time=0.03 sec
 ARIMA(1,0,1)(1,0,0)[4] intercept   : AIC=290.370, Time=0.07 sec
```

```
 ARIMA(1,0,1)(0,0,1)[4] intercept   : AIC=279.870, Time=0.05 sec
 ARIMA(1,0,1)(1,0,1)[4] intercept   : AIC=307.377, Time=0.07 sec
 ARIMA(1,0,0)(0,0,0)[4] intercept   : AIC=278.525, Time=0.04 sec
 ARIMA(1,0,0)(0,0,1)[4] intercept   : AIC=279.082, Time=0.10 sec
 ARIMA(1,0,0)(1,0,1)[4] intercept   : AIC=316.621, Time=0.08 sec
 ARIMA(2,0,0)(0,0,0)[4] intercept   : AIC=279.409, Time=0.04 sec
 ARIMA(2,0,1)(0,0,0)[4] intercept   : AIC=2987.952, Time=0.03 sec
 ARIMA(1,0,0)(0,0,0)[4]             : AIC=inf, Time=0.01 sec
Best model:  ARIMA(1,0,0)(0,0,0)[4] intercept
Total fit time: 0.985 seconds
print("**************************************************")
print(" Auto ARIMA Test - on (Min__Stock_Rate)")
print("**************************************************")
auto_arima(df_Stock_Exchange_Status["Min__Stock_Rate"], error_ac-
tion='ignore', trace=True,
           suppress_warnings=True, maxiter=10,seasonal=True, m=4)
**************************************************
 Auto ARIMA Test - on (Min__Stock_Rate)
**************************************************
Perform stepwise search to minimize aic
 ARIMA(2,1,2)(1,0,1)[4] intercept   : AIC=269.834, Time=0.13 sec
 ARIMA(0,1,0)(0,0,0)[4] intercept   : AIC=261.359, Time=0.01 sec
 ARIMA(1,1,0)(1,0,0)[4] intercept   : AIC=264.497, Time=0.05 sec
 ARIMA(0,1,1)(0,0,1)[4] intercept   : AIC=264.064, Time=0.06 sec
 ARIMA(0,1,0)(0,0,0)[4]             : AIC=261.512, Time=0.01 sec
 ARIMA(0,1,0)(1,0,0)[4] intercept   : AIC=263.216, Time=0.03 sec
 ARIMA(0,1,0)(0,0,1)[4] intercept   : AIC=262.796, Time=0.04 sec
 ARIMA(0,1,0)(1,0,1)[4] intercept   : AIC=264.544, Time=0.05 sec
 ARIMA(1,1,0)(0,0,0)[4] intercept   : AIC=262.515, Time=0.03 sec
 ARIMA(0,1,1)(0,0,0)[4] intercept   : AIC=262.118, Time=0.03 sec
 ARIMA(1,1,1)(0,0,0)[4] intercept   : AIC=264.499, Time=0.03 sec
Best model:  ARIMA(0,1,0)(0,0,0)[4] intercept
Total fit time: 0.492 seconds
```

```
print("*************************************************")
print(" Auto ARIMA Test - on (Close__Stock_Rate)")
print("*************************************************")
auto_arima(df_Stock_Exchange_Status["Close__Stock_Rate"], error_ac-
tion='ignore', trace=True,
          suppress_warnings=True, maxiter=10,seasonal=True, m=4)
*************************************************
 Auto ARIMA Test - on (Close__Stock_Rate)
*************************************************
Perform stepwise search to minimize aic
 ARIMA(2,1,2)(1,0,1)[4] intercept   : AIC=271.551, Time=0.13 sec
 ARIMA(0,1,0)(0,0,0)[4] intercept   : AIC=263.004, Time=0.01 sec
 ARIMA(1,1,0)(1,0,0)[4] intercept   : AIC=266.085, Time=0.06 sec
 ARIMA(0,1,1)(0,0,1)[4] intercept   : AIC=265.776, Time=0.07 sec
 ARIMA(0,1,0)(0,0,0)[4]             : AIC=262.925, Time=0.01 sec
 ARIMA(0,1,0)(1,0,0)[4] intercept   : AIC=264.904, Time=0.06 sec
 ARIMA(0,1,0)(0,0,1)[4] intercept   : AIC=263.647, Time=0.07 sec
 ARIMA(0,1,0)(1,0,1)[4] intercept   : AIC=266.137, Time=0.09 sec
 ARIMA(1,1,0)(0,0,0)[4] intercept   : AIC=264.204, Time=0.03 sec
 ARIMA(0,1,1)(0,0,0)[4] intercept   : AIC=263.978, Time=0.04 sec
 ARIMA(1,1,1)(0,0,0)[4] intercept   : AIC=266.035, Time=0.06 sec
Best model:  ARIMA(0,1,0)(0,0,0)[4]
Total fit time: 0.659 seconds
```

Try the 1st order difference stock exchange status.

```
print("*************************************************")
print("    1st order difference Stock Exchange Status     ")
print("*************************************************")
df_SES_transformed = df_Stock_Exchange_Status.diff().dropna()
df_SES_transformed.head()
```

```
*********************************************
   1nd order difference Stock Exchange Status
*********************************************
```

	Open_Stock_Rate	Max__Stock_Rate	Min__Stock_Rate	Close__Stock_Rate
1	-207.67	-159.84	-220.64	-142.59
2	13.40	-121.96	-36.36	-134.88
3	-71.17	35.95	-12.76	37.04
4	-4.12	-78.08	-60.04	-106.01
5	52.43	8.08	18.09	6.36

Figure 8.17: *Stock Exchange Status transformed*

Will split the dataset:

```
print("******************************")
print("    Split Test and Train       ")
print("******************************")
tt_split = 12
train = df_SES_transformed[0:-tt_split]
test = df_SES_transformed[-tt_split:]
test.head()
```

```
******************************
   Split Test and Train
******************************
```

	Open_Stock_Rate	Max__Stock_Rate	Min__Stock_Rate	Close__Stock_Rate
10	-259.02	-49.85	-169.86	54.47
11	49.36	-168.78	-81.21	-214.36
12	33.19	79.43	162.21	116.39
13	-102.14	-116.22	-114.76	-72.89
14	-27.18	-51.26	-45.65	-94.78

Figure 8.18: *Stock Exchange Status test data*

```
train.head()
```

	Open_Stock_Rate	Max__Stock_Rate	Min__Stock_Rate	Close__Stock_Rate
1	-207.67	-159.84	-220.64	-142.59
2	13.40	-121.96	-36.36	-134.88
3	-71.17	35.95	-12.76	37.04
4	-4.12	-78.08	-60.04	-106.01
5	52.43	8.08	18.09	6.36

Figure 8.19: *Stock Exchange Status test data*

Build a VARMA model using SES_transformed data.

```
print("*******************************")
print("     Build VARMS model          ")
print("*******************************")
model = VARMAX(df_SES_transformed, order=(1,2), trend='c')
SES_results = model.fit(maxiter=1000, disp=False)
SES_results.summary()
```

Statespace Model Results

Dep. Variable:	['Open_Stock_Rate', 'Max__Stock_Rate', 'Min__Stock_Rate', 'Close__Stock_Rate']	**No. Observations:**	21
Model:	VARMA(1,2)	**Log Likelihood**	-359.424
	+ intercept	**AIC**	842.849
Date:	Sun, 02 Jul 2023	**BIC**	907.609
Time:	20:01:21	**HQIC**	856.903
Sample:	0		
	- 21		
Covariance Type:	opg		

Ljung-Box (L1) (Q):	0.12, 0.01, 0.54, 0.78	**Jarque-Bera (JB):**	0.48, 0.79, 0.18, 0.54
Prob(Q):	0.73, 0.91, 0.46, 0.38	**Prob(JB):**	0.79, 0.67, 0.91, 0.76
Heteroskedasticity (H):	0.89, 1.46, 4.23, 0.82	**Skew:**	0.02, -0.31, -0.22, 0.32
Prob(H) (two-sided):	0.88, 0.63, 0.08, 0.80	**Kurtosis:**	2.26, 2.28, 3.13, 2.53

Figure 8.20: *Stock Exchange Status Summary -I*

Results for equation Open_Stock_Rate

	coef	std err	z	P>|z|	[0.025	0.975]
intercept	-26.4423	0.022	-1228.810	0.000	-26.484	-26.400
L1.Open_Stock_Rate	0.3801	0.178	2.132	0.033	0.031	0.729
L1.Max__Stock_Rate	-2.0393	0.137	-14.883	0.000	-2.308	-1.771
L1.Min__Stock_Rate	-0.2523	0.111	-2.274	0.023	-0.470	-0.035
L1.Close__Stock_Rate	0.9941	0.080	12.451	0.000	0.838	1.151
L1.e(Open_Stock_Rate)	1.5728	0.065	24.324	0.000	1.446	1.700
L1.e(Max__Stock_Rate)	-0.6907	0.029	-24.203	0.000	-0.747	-0.635
L1.e(Min__Stock_Rate)	-1.6018	0.041	-38.748	0.000	-1.683	-1.521
L1.e(Close__Stock_Rate)	3.5070	0.028	123.260	0.000	3.451	3.563
L2.e(Open_Stock_Rate)	2.6029	0.058	44.759	0.000	2.489	2.717
L2.e(Max__Stock_Rate)	-1.6251	0.048	-34.164	0.000	-1.718	-1.532
L2.e(Min__Stock_Rate)	-2.3133	0.137	-16.836	0.000	-2.583	-2.044
L2.e(Close__Stock_Rate)	5.7198	0.080	71.407	0.000	5.563	5.877

Results for equation Max__Stock_Rate

	coef	std err	z	P>|z|	[0.025	0.975]
intercept	-7.2487	0.017	-428.247	0.000	-7.282	-7.216
L1.Open_Stock_Rate	1.7647	0.063	28.028	0.000	1.641	1.888
L1.Max__Stock_Rate	-0.2821	0.045	-6.304	0.000	-0.370	-0.194
L1.Min__Stock_Rate	-1.2963	0.073	-17.798	0.000	-1.439	-1.154
L1.Close__Stock_Rate	0.6506	0.142	4.577	0.000	0.372	0.929
L1.e(Open_Stock_Rate)	0.0676	0.035	1.913	0.056	-0.002	0.137
L1.e(Max__Stock_Rate)	-0.0421	0.069	-0.612	0.541	-0.177	0.093
L1.e(Min__Stock_Rate)	-0.1588	0.119	-1.339	0.180	-0.391	0.074
L1.e(Close__Stock_Rate)	0.9156	0.032	28.856	0.000	0.853	0.978
L2.e(Open_Stock_Rate)	-0.9347	0.073	-12.826	0.000	-1.078	-0.792
L2.e(Max__Stock_Rate)	0.9743	0.043	22.556	0.000	0.890	1.059
L2.e(Min__Stock_Rate)	1.0277	0.122	8.404	0.000	0.788	1.267
L2.e(Close__Stock_Rate)	-1.7293	0.113	-15.299	0.000	-1.951	-1.508

Figure 8.21: *Stock Exchange Status Summary - II*

Results for equation Min__Stock_Rate

	coef	std err	z	P>|z|	[0.025	0.975]
intercept	-24.6559	0.027	-899.122	0.000	-24.710	-24.602
L1.Open_Stock_Rate	1.6445	0.090	18.333	0.000	1.469	1.820
L1.Max__Stock_Rate	-1.2831	0.068	-18.799	0.000	-1.417	-1.149
L1.Min__Stock_Rate	-1.2497	0.074	-16.781	0.000	-1.396	-1.104
L1.Close__Stock_Rate	0.9347	0.114	8.191	0.000	0.711	1.158
L1.e(Open_Stock_Rate)	0.6536	0.171	3.815	0.000	0.318	0.989
L1.e(Max__Stock_Rate)	-1.1483	0.055	-20.764	0.000	-1.257	-1.040
L1.e(Min__Stock_Rate)	-0.6665	0.060	-11.019	0.000	-0.785	-0.548
L1.e(Close__Stock_Rate)	2.7675	0.072	38.390	0.000	2.626	2.909
L2.e(Open_Stock_Rate)	0.5008	0.140	3.586	0.000	0.227	0.774
L2.e(Max__Stock_Rate)	0.1768	0.059	2.988	0.003	0.061	0.293
L2.e(Min__Stock_Rate)	0.1713	0.076	2.258	0.024	0.023	0.320
L2.e(Close__Stock_Rate)	0.9466	0.066	14.424	0.000	0.818	1.075

Results for equation Close__Stock_Rate

	coef	std err	z	P>|z|	[0.025	0.975]
intercept	-9.0389	0.041	-220.847	0.000	-9.119	-8.959
L1.Open_Stock_Rate	1.7605	0.074	23.752	0.000	1.615	1.906
L1.Max__Stock_Rate	0.6448	0.048	13.411	0.000	0.551	0.739
L1.Min__Stock_Rate	-1.2578	0.152	-8.261	0.000	-1.556	-0.959
L1.Close__Stock_Rate	-0.0925	0.237	-0.391	0.696	-0.557	0.372
L1.e(Open_Stock_Rate)	-0.6065	0.138	-4.385	0.000	-0.878	-0.335
L1.e(Max__Stock_Rate)	-0.4047	0.205	-1.978	0.048	-0.806	-0.004
L1.e(Min__Stock_Rate)	1.1238	0.075	15.018	0.000	0.977	1.271
L1.e(Close__Stock_Rate)	-0.2348	0.082	-2.871	0.004	-0.395	-0.075
L2.e(Open_Stock_Rate)	-1.2457	0.146	-8.550	0.000	-1.531	-0.960
L2.e(Max__Stock_Rate)	1.2852	0.151	8.539	0.000	0.990	1.580
L2.e(Min__Stock_Rate)	1.3698	0.069	19.778	0.000	1.234	1.506
L2.e(Close__Stock_Rate)	-2.5765	0.077	-33.654	0.000	-2.727	-2.426

Figure 8.22: *Stock Exchange Status Summary -III*

Error covariance matrix

	coef	std err	z	P>|z|	[0.025	0.975]
sqrt.var.Open_Stock_Rate	81.4816	0.022	3772.846	0.000	81.439	81.524
sqrt.cov.Open_Stock_Rate.Max__Stock_Rate	30.4300	0.031	984.839	0.000	30.369	30.491
sqrt.var.Max__Stock_Rate	14.7340	0.018	798.987	0.000	14.698	14.770
sqrt.cov.Open_Stock_Rate.Min__Stock_Rate	47.7842	0.022	2127.105	0.000	47.740	47.828
sqrt.cov.Max__Stock_Rate.Min__Stock_Rate	4.3539	0.011	391.094	0.000	4.332	4.376
sqrt.var.Min__Stock_Rate	20.9913	0.047	450.008	0.000	20.900	21.083
sqrt.cov.Open_Stock_Rate.Close__Stock_Rate	5.3082	0.051	103.409	0.000	5.208	5.409
sqrt.cov.Max__Stock_Rate.Close__Stock_Rate	13.7195	0.021	663.374	0.000	13.679	13.760
sqrt.cov.Min__Stock_Rate.Close__Stock_Rate	12.1041	0.066	182.105	0.000	11.974	12.234
sqrt.var.Close__Stock_Rate	0.5482	0.154	3.569	0.000	0.247	0.849

Figure 8.23: *Stock Exchange Status Summary -IV*

Find the forecast values from the model results.

```
print("**************************************************")
print("     Stock Exchange Status Forecasting values        ")
print("**************************************************")
df_SES_forecast = SES_results.forecast(10)
df_SES_forecast
```

```
*************************************************
        Stock Exchange Status Forecasting value
*************************************************
```

	Open_Stock_Rate	Max__Stock_Rate	Min__Stock_Rate	Close__Stock_Rate
21	-166.116682	-26.563700	-121.755816	-0.688856
22	-21.655558	-129.591574	-98.744912	-155.538566
23	99.897015	17.895678	84.040938	7.874464
24	-38.340346	60.177035	18.990617	71.927074
25	-97.024531	-69.704042	-121.424809	-68.276510
26	41.587529	-45.829864	-6.838464	-65.741920
27	19.198573	45.161337	49.637914	49.308549
28	-74.748739	-18.371234	-66.978750	-13.119605
29	-13.534122	-55.690468	-52.562275	-67.014948
30	28.625492	9.110713	27.597134	3.541514

Figure 8.24: *Stock Exchange Status Forecasting dataset*

```
print("**************************************************")
print("     Stock Exchange Status Forecasting Plot          ")
print("**************************************************")
```

```
df_SES_forecast.plot()
```

```
******************************************************
          Stock Exchange Status Forecasting Plot
******************************************************
```

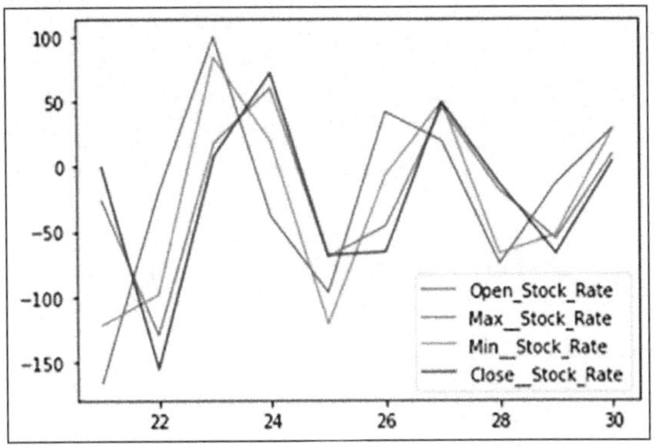

***Figure 8.25**: Stock Exchange Status Forecasting plot*

Process of inverting the transformation

We used the 1st order difference for forecasting; the dataset needs to be inverted to compare the actual and forecasting.

```
print("******************************************************")
print(" Build the forecast values from the Ist  difference   ")
print("******************************************************")
df_SES_forecast['Open_Stock_Rate1d'] = (df_Stock_Exchange_Status
['Open_Stock_Rate'].iloc[-tt_split-1]-df_Stock_Exchange_Status
['Open_Stock_Rate'].iloc[-tt_split-2]) + df_SES_forecast
['Open_Stock_Rate'].cumsum()
df_SES_forecast['Open_Stock_Rate_Forecast'] = df_Stock_Exchange_
Status['Open_Stock_Rate'].iloc[-tt_split-1] + df_SES_forecast
['Open_Stock_Rate'].cumsum()
df_SES_forecast['Max__Stock_Rate1d'] = (df_Stock_Exchange_Status
['Max__Stock_Rate'].iloc[-tt_split-1]-df_Stock_Exchange_Status
['Max__Stock_Rate'].iloc[-tt_split-2]) + df_SES_forecast
['Max__Stock_Rate'].cumsum()
df_SES_forecast['Max__Stock_Rate_Forecast'] = df_Stock_Exchange_
Status['Max__Stock_Rate'].iloc[-tt_split-1] + df_SES_forecast
['Max__Stock_Rate'].cumsum()
df_SES_forecast['Min__Stock_Rate1d'] = (df_Stock_Exchange_Status
['Min__Stock_Rate'].iloc[-tt_split-1]-df_Stock_Exchange_Status
```

```
['Min__Stock_Rate'].iloc[-tt_split-2]) + df_SES_forecast['Min__Stock_Rate'].cumsum()

df_SES_forecast['Min__Stock_Rate_Forecast'] = df_Stock_Exchange_Status['Min__Stock_Rate'].iloc[-tt_split-1] + df_SES_forecast['Min__Stock_Rate'].cumsum()

df_SES_forecast['Close__Stock_Rate1d'] = (df_Stock_Exchange_Status['Close__Stock_Rate'].iloc[-tt_split-1]-df_Stock_Exchange_Status['Close__Stock_Rate'].iloc[-tt_split-2]) + df_SES_forecast['Close__Stock_Rate'].cumsum()

df_SES_forecast['Close__Stock_Rate_Forecast'] = df_Stock_Exchange_Status['Close__Stock_Rate'].iloc[-tt_split-1] + df_SES_forecast['Close__Stock_Rate'].cumsum()
print("************************************************************************")

print(Stock Exchange Status Forecasting - After Invert Transformation Process  ")

print("************************************************************************")

df_SES_forecast

print("*******************************************************************")

print("   Stock Exchange Status Actual Vs Forecasting - Open_Stock_Rate ")

print("*******************************************************************")

df_Stock_Exchange_Status['Open_Stock_Rate'][-tt_split:].plot(figsize=(10,5),legend=True).autoscale(axis='x',tight=True)

df_SES_forecast["Open_Stock_Rate_Forecast"].plot(legend=True)
```

```
*******************************************************************
     Stock Exchange Status Actual Vs Forecasting - Open_Stock_Rate
*******************************************************************
```

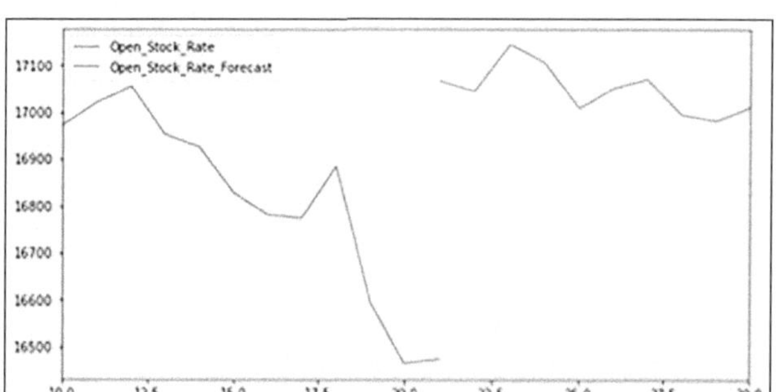

Figure 8.26: *Stock Exchange Status Actual Vs Forecasting - Open_Stock_Rate*

```
print("**********************************************************
**********")
print("   Stock Exchange Status Actual Vs Forecasting - Max__Stock_Rate
")
print("**********************************************************
**********")
df_Stock_Exchange_Status['Max__Stock_Rate'][-tt_split:].plot
(figsize=(10,5),legend=True).autoscale(axis='x',tight=True)
df_SES_forecast["Max__Stock_Rate_Forecast"].plot(legend=True)
```

```
******************************************************************
      Stock Exchange Status Actual Vs Forecasting - Max__Stock_Rate
******************************************************************
```

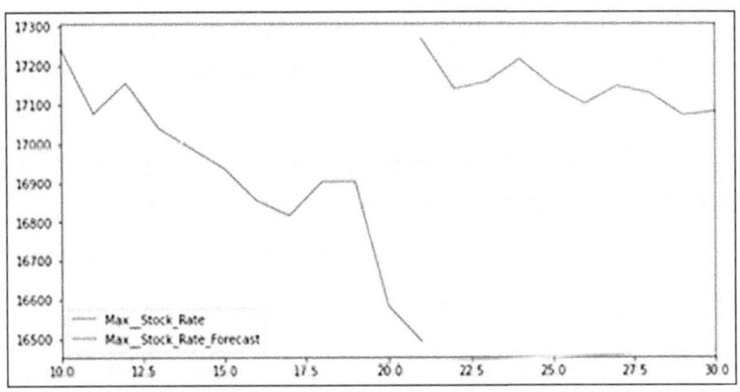

Figure 8.27: *Stock Exchange Status Actual Vs Forecasting - Max__Stock_Rate*

```
print("**********************************************************
**********")
print("   Stock Exchange Status Actual Vs Forecasting - Max__Stock_Rate
")
print("**********************************************************
**********")
df_Stock_Exchange_Status['Min__Stock_Rate'][-tt_split:].plot(fig-
size=(10,5),legend=True).autoscale(axis='x',tight=True)
df_SES_forecast["Min__Stock_Rate_Forecast"].plot(legend=True)
```

```
******************************************************************
      Stock Exchange Status Actual Vs Forecasting - Max__Stock_Rate
******************************************************************
```

Figure 8.28: *Stock Exchange Status Actual Vs Forecasting - Max__Stock_Rate*

```
print("************************************************************
**********")
print("    Stock Exchange Status Actual Vs Forecasting - Close__Stock_
Rate     ")
print("************************************************************
**********")
df_Stock_Exchange_Status['Close__Stock_Rate'][-nobs:].plot(fig-
size=(10,5),legend=True).autoscale(axis='x',tight=True)
df_SES_forecast["Close__Stock_Rate_Forecast"].plot(legend=True)
```

```
**********************************************************************
     Stock Exchange Status Actual Vs Forecasting - Close__Stock_Rate
**********************************************************************
```

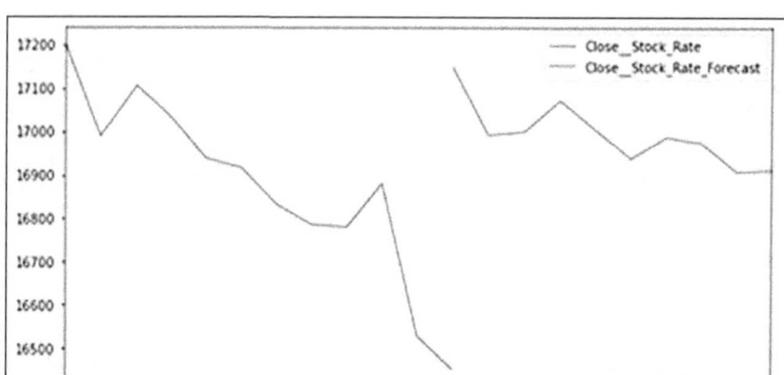

Figure 8.29: *Stock Exchange Status Actual Vs Forecasting - Close__Stock_Rate*

Model Evaluation Stock Exchange Status with actual and forecasting values

```
print("************************************************************
**********")
print("    Model Evaluation (Stock Exchange Status)    - Open_Stock_
Rate1d    ")
```

```
print("*************************************************************
*********")
forcast_actual=df_SES_forecast["Open_Stock_Rate1d"] - df_Stock_Exchange_
Status["Open_Stock_Rate"]
forcast_data=df_SES_forecast["Open_Stock_Rate1d"]
actual_data=df_Stock_Exchange_Status["Open_Stock_Rate"]
me = np.mean(forcast_actual)
mae = np.mean(np.abs(forcast_actual))
mpe = np.mean((forcast_actual)/actual_data)
rmse = np.mean((forcast_actual)**2)**.5
print("Mean :",me)
print("MAE (Mean absolute error)  :",mae)
print("MPE (Mean Percentage Error) :",mpe)
print("RMSE (Root Mean Squared Error) :",rmse)
 ********************************************************************
       Model Evaluation (Stock Exchange Status)   - Open_Stock_Rate1d
 ********************************************************************
Mean : -16511.796682144053
MAE (Mean absolute error)  : 16511.796682144053
MPE (Mean Percentage Error) : -1.0022724210314726
RMSE (Root Mean Squared Error) : 16511.796682144053
print("*************************************************************
**********")
print("    Model Evaluation (Stock Exchange Status)   - Max__Stock_Rate
")
print("*************************************************************
**********")
forcast_actual=df_SES_forecast["Max__Stock_Rate1d"] - df_Stock_Exchange_
Status["Max__Stock_Rate"]
forcast_data=df_SES_forecast["Max__Stock_Rate1d"]
actual_data=df_Stock_Exchange_Status["Max__Stock_Rate"]
me = np.mean(forcast_actual)
mae = np.mean(np.abs(forcast_actual))
mpe = np.mean((forcast_actual)/actual_data)
rmse = np.mean((forcast_actual)**2)**.5
```

```
print("Mean :",me)
print("MAE (Mean absolute error)  :",mae)
print("MPE (Mean Percentage Error) :",mpe)
print("RMSE (Root Mean Squared Error) :",rmse)
*******************************************************************
    Model Evaluation (Stock Exchange Status)   - Max__Stock_Rate
*******************************************************************
Mean : -16327.973700180823
MAE (Mean absolute error)  : 16327.973700180823
MPE (Mean Percentage Error) : -0.9900289769591621
RMSE (Root Mean Squared Error) : 16327.973700180823
print("*********************************************************
**********")
print("    Model Evaluation (Stock Exchange Status)   - Min__Stock_Rate
")
print("*********************************************************
**********")
forcast_actual=df_SES_forecast["Min__Stock_Rate1d"] - df_Stock_Exchange_
Status["Min__Stock_Rate"]
forcast_data=df_SES_forecast["Min__Stock_Rate1d"]
actual_data=df_Stock_Exchange_Status["Min__Stock_Rate"]
me = np.mean(forcast_actual)
mae = np.mean(np.abs(forcast_actual))
mpe = np.mean((forcast_actual)/actual_data)
rmse = np.mean((forcast_actual)**2)**.5
print("Mean :",me)
print("MAE (Mean absolute error)  :",mae)
print("MPE (Mean Percentage Error) :",mpe)
print("RMSE (Root Mean Squared Error) :",rmse)
*******************************************************************
Model Evaluation (Stock Exchange Status)   - Min__Stock_Rate
*******************************************************************
Mean : -16306.745815538612
MAE (Mean absolute error)  : 16306.745815538612
MPE (Mean Percentage Error) : -0.9961438799171045
```

```
RMSE (Root Mean Squared Error) : 16306.745815538612
print("***********************************************************
**********")
print("    Model Evaluation (Stock Exchange Status)    - Close__Stock_
Rate     ")
print("***********************************************************
**********")
forcast_actual=df_SES_forecast["Close__Stock_Rate1d"] - df_Stock_Ex-
change_Status["Close__Stock_Rate"]
forcast_data=df_SES_forecast["Close__Stock_Rate1d"]
actual_data=df_Stock_Exchange_Status["Close__Stock_Rate"]
me = np.mean(forcast_actual)
mae = np.mean(np.abs(forcast_actual))
mpe = np.mean((forcast_actual)/actual_data)
rmse = np.mean((forcast_actual)**2)**.5
print("Mean :",me)
print("MAE (Mean absolute error)  :",mae)
print("MPE (Mean Percentage Error) :",mpe)
print("RMSE (Root Mean Squared Error) :",rmse)
*********************************************************************
    Model Evaluation (Stock Exchange Status)    - Close__Stock_Rate
*********************************************************************
Mean : -16332.20885554582
MAE (Mean absolute error)  : 16332.20885554582
MPE (Mean Percentage Error) : -0.9925896373524122
RMSE (Root Mean Squared Error) : 16332.20885554582
```

Note: The VARMA model is the extension of the "ARMA" model for multivariate time-series data. It encompasses two major components, such as Vector Auto-Regressive (VAR)

and Vector Moving Average (VMA) like the ARMA model. Vector Autoregression

The Move-Average (VARMA) model can also be used to build Vector Autoregression

(VAR) and Vector Moving-Average (VMA) models. From VARMA.

We can build a VAR or VMA model with simple configuration changes in the model parameters.

- The VAR model => Setting the **q** parameter as 0, and the VARMA model acts as VAR.
- The VMA model => Setting the **p** parameter as 0, and the VARMA model acts as VMA.

Vector Autoregression Moving-Average with Exogenous Regressors (VARMAX)

VARMAX is a further extension of the ARMA and VARMA model along with variables called **exogenous** and also called covariates. The exogenous variable is a special variable, and this is determined outside the model separately and then passed on to the primary model. Here, "X" is represented as an exogenous variable. The primary model is the actual multivariate time series data taken for our analyses that are referred to as **endogenous** data to distinguish from the exogenous sequence. This VAMAX can also be used to model VARX and VMAX with exogenous variables and without trend and seasonal components.

The VARMAX model helps to build dynamic relationships between endogenous variables in the system, which would be the dependent variables and also the dependent and independent variables. This helps many micro-economic and financial-based multivariate time series since all these applications have contemporaneous relationships between exogenous and endogenous components of the vector time series data.

In this model, orders can be automatically determined by the collection of options since these models are defined in terms of order of AR or MA and both along with exogenous variables and also possible for non-automatic selection of order options as shown in the following Figure 8.30.

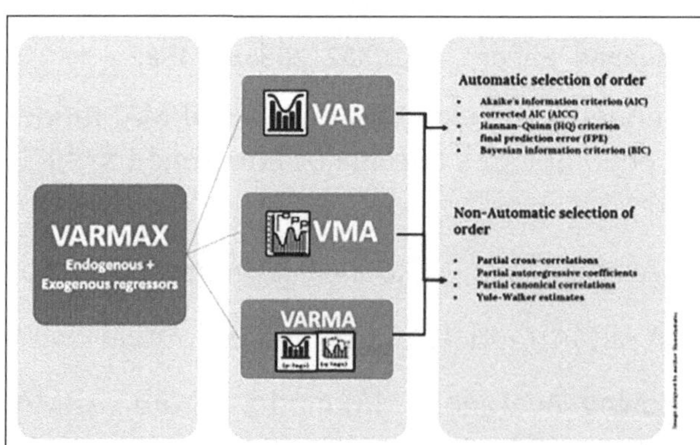

Figure 8.30: *VARMAX structure*

VARMAX implementation using Python

Let's use Stock Buy Selling dataset and keep p=1 q=2 for VARMAX model building; consider the `df_train` dataset from the VAR model implementation code.

```
VARMAX_results=VARMAX(df_train, order=(1, 2))

VARMAX_model=VARMAX_results.fit(disp=False)

VARMAX_model.summary()
```

Statespace Model Results

Dep. Variable:	['Buy_stock_amount', 'Selling_stock_amount']	**No. Observations:**	129
Model:	VARMA(1,2)	**Log Likelihood**	-2511.970
	+ intercept	**AIC**	5057.939
Date:	Mon, 03 Jul 2023	**BIC**	5106.556
Time:	01:57:50	**HQIC**	5077.693
Sample:	0		
	- 129		
Covariance Type:	opg		

Ljung-Box (L1) (Q):	9.27, 81.09	**Jarque-Bera (JB):**	20.25, 2.89
Prob(Q):	0.00, 0.00	**Prob(JB):**	0.00, 0.24
Heteroskedasticity (H):	3.80, 6.63	**Skew:**	0.14, 0.23
Prob(H) (two-sided):	0.00, 0.00	**Kurtosis:**	4.92, 2.43

Figure 8.31: VARMAX - *Stock Buy Selling – Summary I*

Results for equation Buy_stock_amount

	coef	std err	z	P>|z|	[0.025	0.975]
intercept	2124.6367	20.133	105.529	0.000	2085.176	2164.097
L1.Buy_stock_amount	2.9376	0.064	46.220	0.000	2.813	3.062
L1.Selling_stock_amount	-1.3025	0.029	-45.590	0.000	-1.358	-1.246
L1.e(Buy_stock_amount)	-2.8548	0.058	-48.840	0.000	-2.969	-2.740
L1.e(Selling_stock_amount)	1.4301	0.035	41.440	0.000	1.362	1.498
L2.e(Buy_stock_amount)	-4.5204	0.098	-46.052	0.000	-4.713	-4.328
L2.e(Selling_stock_amount)	2.6746	0.053	50.867	0.000	2.572	2.778

Results for equation Selling_stock_amount

	coef	std err	z	P>|z|	[0.025	0.975]
intercept	4927.9871	11.513	428.053	0.000	4905.423	4950.551
L1.Buy_stock_amount	4.8525	0.144	33.632	0.000	4.570	5.135
L1.Selling_stock_amount	-2.1752	0.064	-33.858	0.000	-2.301	-2.049
L1.e(Buy_stock_amount)	-6.6424	0.141	-47.017	0.000	-6.919	-6.366
L1.e(Selling_stock_amount)	3.3892	0.055	61.133	0.000	3.281	3.498
L2.e(Buy_stock_amount)	-8.3567	0.242	-34.523	0.000	-8.831	-7.882
L2.e(Selling_stock_amount)	4.8850	0.099	49.224	0.000	4.691	5.080

Figure 8.32: VARMAX - *Stock Buy Selling – Summary II*

Error covariance matrix

	coef	std err	z	P>|z|	[0.025	0.975]
sqrt.var.Buy_stock_amount	15.1218	0.497	30.415	0.000	14.147	16.096
sqrt.cov.Buy_stock_amount.Selling_stock_amount	16.9644	1.601	10.598	0.000	13.827	20.102
sqrt.var.Selling_stock_amount	29.7222	0.521	57.007	0.000	28.700	30.744

Figure 8.33: VARMAX - Stock Buy Selling – Summary III

Forecasting and Plot

```
VARMAX_model_forecast=VARMAX_model.forecast(10)
VARMAX_model_forecast
```

	Buy_stock_amount	Selling_stock_amount
129	2910.386358	6447.970162
130	2946.983160	6259.374810
131	2628.796908	5612.640483
132	2536.471245	5475.438487
133	2443.963178	5325.875418
134	2367.019529	5202.315160
135	2301.928896	5097.718987
136	2246.956685	5009.388187
137	2200.522469	4934.775986
138	2161.300788	4871.753191

Figure 8.34: VARMAX - Stock Buy Selling – Forecasting

```
VARMAX_model_forecast.plot()
```

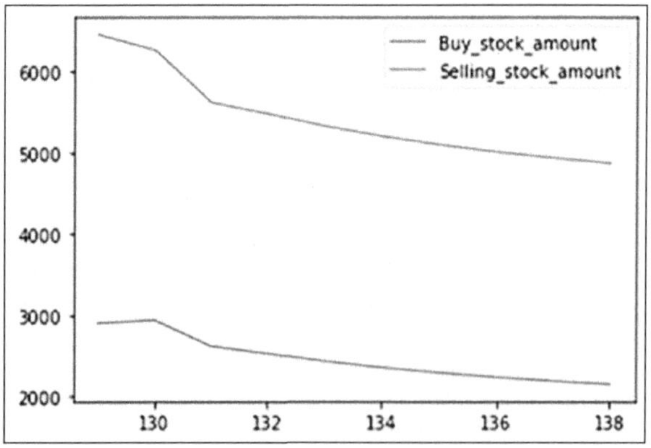

Figure 8.35: VARMAX - Stock Buy Selling – plot

Seasonal Autoregressive Integrated Moving-Average (SARIMA)

SARIMA is another statistical technique used for univariate time series analysis and forecasting and extension of ARIMA; it is used with time series with seasonality. As the name implies, they combine the ARIMA model with the seasonal level. It consists of autoregression(P), differencing(D), and moving average(Q) components along at the seasonal level(s).

The set of parameters is **AR(p), I(d)**, and **MA(q)** like ARIMA, and additionally, the parameter m or s represents the **Length of the seasonal cycle.**

SARIMA models have few advantages over ARIMA models when dealing exhibits strong seasonal patterns in the dataset. The data is capable of handling complex seasonality, and multiple seasonal patterns such as weekly, monthly, quarterly, and yearly patterns exist.

On the other hand, it requires more parameters during model building, which is a challenging part of extending the computational speed of the model, not suitable for fundamental data trends and seasonal changes and always in the assumption of consistent seasonal pattern levels over time.

We have the SARIMAX model, which is an extension of the SARIMA model, which includes the exogenous variables while building the model.

SARIMA implementation using Python

Let's have the `Stock_Buy_SARIMAX` as univariate time series data and in the assumption of seasonal pattern level over time in the dataset.

```
#load SARIMA libraries
from statsmodels.tsa.statespace.sarimax import SARIMAX
from random import random
#load Stock_Buy_SARIMA data
df_Stock_Buy_SARIMA = pd.read_csv("Stock_Buy_SARIMAX.csv")
print("*********************")
print(" Stock Buy data      ")
print("*********************")
df_Stock_Buy_SARIMA.head()
```

```
********************
Stock Buy data
********************
```

	Date	Buy_stock_amount
0	01-01-2021	1518.43
1	02-01-2021	1517.35
2	03-01-2021	1517.87
3	04-01-2021	1521.39
4	05-01-2021	1532.26

Figure 8.36: *Stock Buy dataset*

```
print("*********************************************")
print(" Visualization of Stock Buy plot (Actual)     ")
print("*********************************************")
df_Stock_Buy_SARIMA["Buy_stock_amount"].plot()
```

```
*********************************************
Visualization of Stock Buy plot (Actual)
*********************************************
```

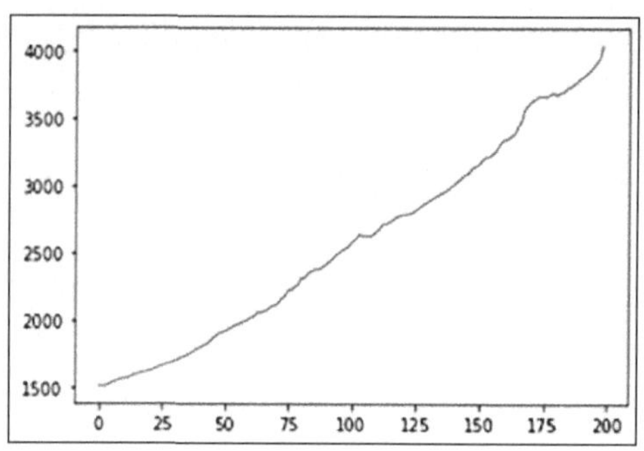

Figure 8.37: *Stock Buy (Actual) – plot*

```
#apply SARIMAX model on df_Stock_Buy_SARIMA
SARIMA_results=SARIMAX(df_Stock_Buy_SARIMAX['Buy_stock_amount'],
order=(1, 1, 1), seasonal_order=(1, 1, 1, 2))
SARIMA_results_fit = SARIMA_results.fit(disp=False)
SARIMA_results_forecast=SARIMA_results_fit.forecast(10)
SARIMAX_results_forecast
199    4085.218820
```

```
200    4118.427420
201    4151.800550
202    4173.171884
Name: predicted_mean, dtype: float64
print("**************************************************")
print(" Visualization of Stock Buy plot (Forecasting)     ")
print("**************************************************")
SARIMA_results_forecast.plot()
```

```
             ************************************************
                Visualization of Stock Buy plot (Forecasting)
             ************************************************
```

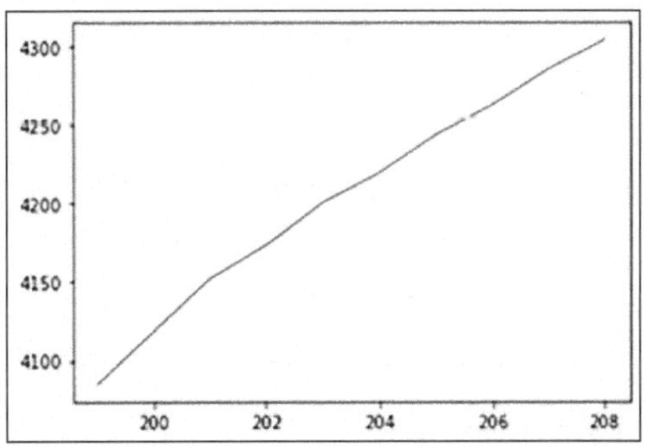

***Figure 8.38**: Stock Buy (Forecast) – plot (SARIMA)*

SARIMAX implementation using Python

Let's consider the `Stock_Buy_SARIMA` dataset as an endogenous variable and `Stock_Sell_SARIMAX` dataset as an exogenous variable for this analysis and model building.

```
#load SARIMA libraries
from statsmodels.tsa.statespace.sarimax import SARIMAX
from random import random
#load Stock_Buy_SARIMAX data
df_Stock_Buy_SARIMA = pd.read_csv("Stock_Buy_SARIMA.csv")
#load Stock_Buy_SARIMAX data [exogenous variable]
df_Stock_Sell_SARIMAX = pd.read_csv("Stock_Sell_SARIMAX.csv")
#apply SARIMAX model on df_Stock_Buy_SARIMA and df_Stock_Sell_SARIMAX
[exogenous ]
```

```
SARIMAX_results=SARIMAX(df_Stock_Buy_SARIMA['Buy_stock_amount'],
exog=df_Stock_Sell_SARIMAX['Selling_stock_amount'], order=(1, 1, 1),
seasonal_order=(0, 0, 0, 0))

SARIMAX_results_fit = SARIMAX_results.fit(disp=False)

SARIMAX_results_forecast=SARIMAX_results_fit.predict(len(df_Stock_Buy_
SARIMA['Buy_stock_amount']), len(df_Stock_Buy_SARIMA['Buy_stock_
amount']) + len(df_Stock_Sell_SARIMAX['Selling_stock_amount']) - 1,
exog=df_Stock_Buy_SARIMA['Buy_stock_amount'].values)

SARIMAX_results_forecast

199    4501.191145
200    4540.925977
201    4580.115347
203    4655.400355
        ...
393    8345.656679
Name: predicted_mean, Length: 199, dtype: float64

print("**************************************************")
print(" Visualization of Stock Buy plot (Forecasting)      ")
print("**************************************************")
SARIMAX_results_forecast.plot()

        **************************************************
            Visualization of Stock Buy plot (Forecasting)
        **************************************************
```

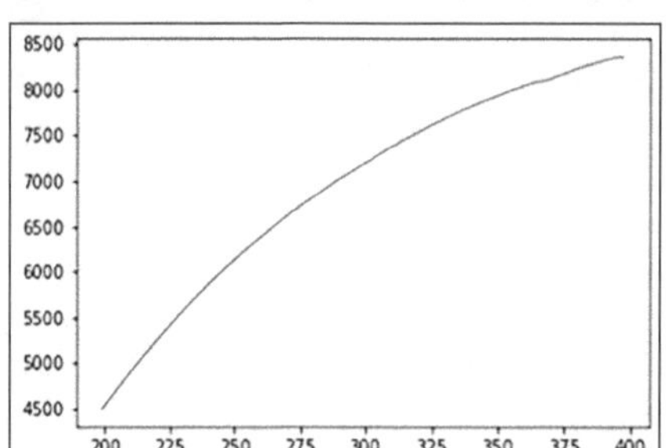

***Figure 8.39**: Stock Buy and Sell (Forecast) – plot (SARIMAX)*

Fractional-Autoregressive-Integrated-Moving Average model (FARIMA)

A fractional autoregressive integrated moving average model (FARIMA) is a time series model and generalized form of ARIMA by allowing non-integer differencing parameter values with non-Gaussian features in the time series data. This model is specifically for modeling time series forecasting with **"LONG MEMORY"**, in which the long memory mean value deterioration will take place much slower than an exponential deterioration process. It can be called either FARIMA or ARFIMA.

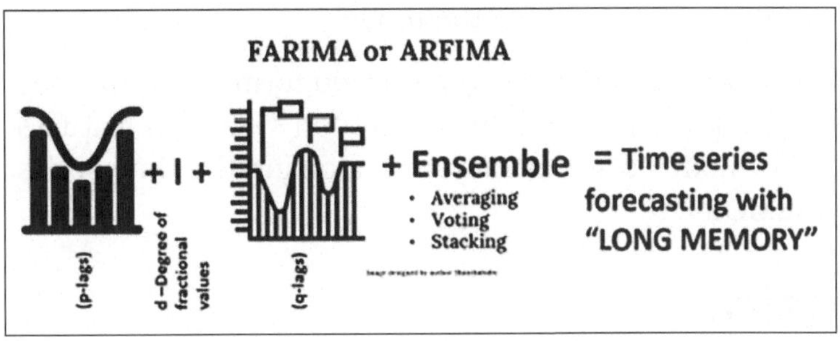

Figure 8.40: *FARIMA with ensemble option*

The set of parameters is **AR(p), I(d),** and **MA(q),** like ARIMA and by simply allowing the differencing(d) to take fractional values while building the model. In simple terms, it allows a fractional degree of integration **I(d),** since fractionally integrating short-memory processes leads to obtaining the long-memory processes.

Mathematical representation of AR and MA in the following equations:

$$Y_t = C + \Sigma\, \beta_i Y_{t-i} + \varepsilon t \quad \text{(AR)}$$

$$Y_t = C + \Sigma\, \Theta_i\, \varepsilon_{t-i} \quad \text{(MA)}$$

Mathematical representation of FARIMA in the following equations

$$(1 - \sum_{i=1}^{n} \beta i\, Y^i)\,(1 - Y)^d\, X_t = (1 - \sum_{i=1}^{n} \Theta i\, Y^i) + \varepsilon_t$$

- $(1 - \sum_{i=1}^{n} \beta i\, Y^i)$ represents the AR model.
- $(1 - \sum_{i=1}^{n} \Theta i\, Y^i)$represents the MA model.

- **d** represents fractional differencing.
- $\mathbf{X_t}$ represents generated time series.

Overcome excessive differences in the given time series data. It also proposes an ensemble learning strategy by establishing averaging, voting and stacking and then combines the prediction results to improve the model concurrency and accuracy.

Note: SARIMA is for univariate and extension of ARIMA; it is used with time series with seasonality. Where a set of parameters are AR(p), I(d), and MA(q) as like ARIMA, and additionally, the parameter **m** or **s** represents the **Length of the seasonal cycle.**

The SARIMAX model is an extension of the SARIMA model, which includes the exogenous variables while building the model.

FARIMA is a time series model and generalized form of ARIMA that allows non-integer differencing parameter values with non-Gaussian features in the time series data. This model is specifically for modeling the time series forecasting with **LONG MEMORY.**

Conclusion

In this chapter, we have discussed the detailed studies of various extended versions of time series analysis and forecasting models using univariate and multivariant time series data which includes VAR, VMA, VARMA and their benefits, limitations and implementation using Python code.

Discussed SARIMA statistical technique and how it is used for univariate time series analysis and forecasting, detailed study of its components like autoregression, differencing, and moving average along with the seasonal level and its representation of Length of the seasonal cycle concepts, its implementation using Python code.

We explored exogenous regressors along with VARMAX and SARIMAX models, and this VAMAX can also be used to model VARX and VMAX with exogenous variables and without trend and seasonal components and its implementation using Python code.

We understand how FARIMA is a time series model and how this is generalized from ARIMA by allowing non-integer differencing parameter values with non-Gaussian features in the time series data for long memory and how this model works in terms of the slow deterioration process.

This chapter will provide a solid understanding of VAR, VMA, VARMA, VARMAX, SARIMA, SARIMAX, and FARIMA time series models, their limitations, benefits, and various methods to implement them with the dataset.

In the next chapter, we will discuss deep learning for time series forecasting, and promises from deep learning for TSA&F. Understanding activation functions and deep learning techniques (ANNs, CNNs, RNNs, and LSTMs) for time series forecasting along with the multilayer perceptron, CNN, Long Short-Term Memory Networks (LSTMs) and Hybrids.

Points to remember

In this chapter, it is important to keep a few things in mind that will be handy throughout this book:

- VAR models work with multivariate time series data and bi-directional models, and the dependent variable is influenced by its past value or by another variable.
    - o There are other versions which include threshold VAR and Vector error correction models.
    - o The VAR model does not take responsibility for non-linearities and base-structural changes in the data.
- The VARMA model is the extension of the **ARMA** model, but this model is specifically for multivariate time-series data and determining their forecasting.
- VRAMA encompasses two major components, such as Vector Auto-Regressive (VAR) and Vector Moving Average (VMA), like the ARMA model.
- The VARMA model can also be used to build Vector Autoregression (VAR) or Vector Moving-Average (VMA) models.
- The VAR model is typically a generalized model of the AR model.
- The VMA model is typically a generalized model of the MA model.
- Building VAR and VMA from the VARMA model.
    - o VAR model -> Setting the "q" parameter as 0, the VARMA model acts as VAR
    - o VMA model -> Setting the "p" parameter as 0, the VARMA model acts as VMA
- VARMAX is a further extension of the ARMA and VARMA model along with variables called exogenous and also called covariates. Here, "X" is represented as an exogenous variable.

- VAMAX can also be used to model VARX and VMAX with exogenous variables and without trend and seasonal components.
- SARIMA models have few advantages over ARIMA models when dealing exhibits strong seasonal patterns in the dataset. The data is capable of handling complex seasonality, and multiple seasonal patterns such as weekly, monthly, quarterly, and yearly patterns exist.
- The SARIMAX method is capable of building other models with exogenous variables, such as ARX, MAX, ARMAX, and ARIMAX.
- FARIMA is a generalized form of ARIMA that allows non-integer differencing parameter values with non-Gaussian features in the time series data and for long memory. It can also be called ARFIMA.
- In simple terms, it allows fractional degrees of integration I(d), since fractionally integrating the short-memory process leads to obtaining the long-memory processes.

CHAPTER 9

Deep Learning for Time Series Analysis and Forecasting

Introduction

In the previous chapter, we discussed the detailed studies of Vector Auto-Regression (VAR) methods and their sub-types, followed by the study of implementation. We have explored various extended versions of time series analysis and forecasting models using univariate and multivariant time series data which includes VAR, VMA, and VARMA and their benefits, limitations and implementation. Furthermore, we experimented with VARMAX SARIMAX and FARIMA models.

This chapter will help us explore how deep learning is good for time series forecasting. This chapter will cover the basic concepts of activation functions and a detailed study of deep learning models - ANNs, CNNs, RNNs, and LSTMs for time series forecasting and use cases for the above models and sample code snippets.

Structure

In this chapter, we will discuss the following topics:

- Deep learning in time series analysis
- Activation functions
- Exploring various deep learning models for time series forecasting

- ANN
- CNN
- RNN
- LSTM

Deep learning in time series analysis

Before we explore why deep learning in TSA&F, let's understand what deep learning is and why so that we can get some clarity on this and focus on deep learning in time series.

Introduction to deep learning

Deep learning is a subset of artificial intelligence and part of machine learning, it deals with structured and unstructured data formats such as images, videos, text, and so on. It can recognize the complex patterns from the given data, and the raw data could be text, images, audio, video, and other complex data to produce insights and predictions very accurately with enhanced performance.

Deep learning works closely with neural networks. The structure replicates the human brain, which works and thinks. Recent technological developments and cloud services provide powerful networks, high speed, and computational capacity to help data analytics and machine learning algorithms execute exponentially. Concerning deep learning model building, which facilitated a vast set of image classification, speech recognition and translation.

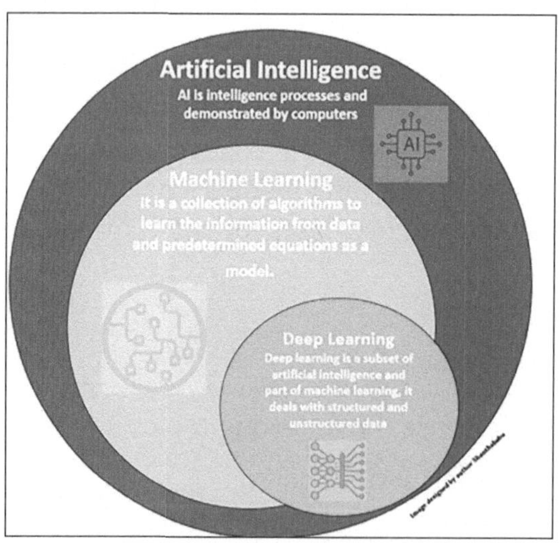

Figure 9.1: AI *family*

Overall, deep learning is very effective when it deals with sophisticated dimensional model approaches because the complicity with feature selection is challenging while dealing with machine learning models and performance-wise, deep learning is much better than machine learning.

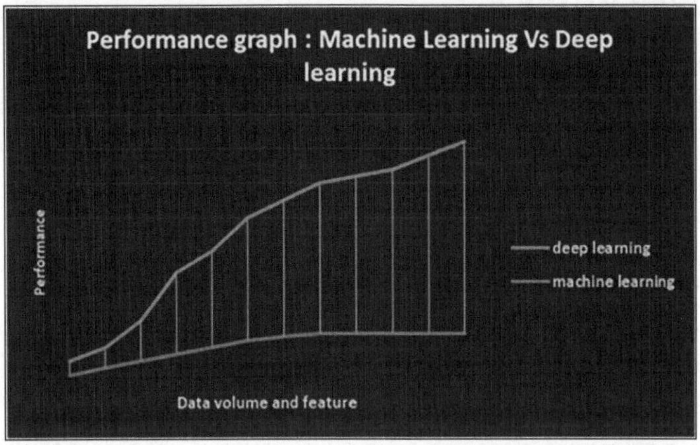

Figure 9.2: *Performance graph: Machine learning vs. Deep learning*

Deep learning came into the picture of time series analysis when the volume of data increases exponentially, the data with highly complex and the nature of the data is non-linearity, It is necessary for deep learning for TSA&F since machine learning techniques become inefficient in terms of model performance and its accuracy, whereas Deep learning performs much better in such cases because of following reasons.

- In the first case, there is no major requirement for data stationarity for analysis and forecasting.
- It is not essential to assess the missing data and data seasonality for the given dataset, Deep learning algorithms are capable of handling missing data, making seasonality and making predictions.
- There is no need to find the order of p, like in AR, MA ARIMA and VARMA time series models.
- It is capable of learning complex mappings automatically and supports from simple I/O to multiple I/O while implementing the models.
- It can automatically learn features from the dataset, and it doesn't require the feature engineering stage.
- It is capable of handling non-linear relationships between features while dealing with multivariate.

- It is capable of handling sequential data while dealing with time series analysis and forecasting using Recurrent Neural Networks (RNNs) and Long Short-term Memory (LSTM) algorithms.

Neural Networks

In artificial intelligence concepts, the neural network is the critical component that helps build the models using data and guides the decision-making in a way inspired by the human brain. This network is interconnected by the nodes, or it could be neurons in a layered structure that typically resembles the human brain.

Activation functions

The activation function plays a vital role in neural networks, predominately, it helps the model to decide whether a neuron should be activated or not by complex calculation internally in terms of the weighted sum and additionally adding bias for different reasons to it. The output of this activation function could be a small or, more significant value. If the inputs exhaust the limits, it does not trigger; otherwise, it works fine.

We should understand the purpose of the activation function first. It introduces the non-linearity into the output of a neuron network to help learn the highly complex patterns in the dataset, which is not feasible in machine learning models and supporting semi-structured and unstructured datasets.

How does it work?

We know that any function used to take the values and execute the set of actions whenever we invoke the function in any programming language, similarly, the activation function takes in the output signal from the previous cell in the network and converts them into some form that can be fed as input to the next cell in the network.

It takes responsibility to define how the weighted sum of the input is received from one cell and how it is transformed into an output.

We know that we have the input, hidden and output layers in the network layer. All these layers are tightly coupled, and all the hidden layers typically use the same activation function, and the output layer typically uses a different activation function from the preceding layers. This methodology is dependent upon the objective of the prediction required to build the model.

All these functions are typical mathematical equations that govern the output of a neural network and act as a switch to activate or deactivate the neurons to get the desired output. In a neural network, the weighted summation of inputs is passed through the activation function and represented in the following equation:

$$Y = AF\ (\Sigma\ (WTs * I/P + B))$$

Where,

- AF->Activation function
- WTs->weights
- I/P->input
- B->bias

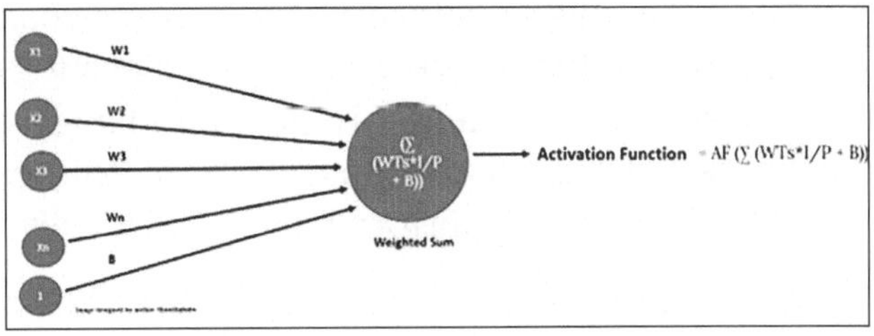

Figure 9.3: *Simple activation function*

Let's focus on the major activation functions for our clarity before we apply them in the upcoming sections specifically while we are dealing with hidden layers:

Linear Activation Function: This activation function is an essential, and simple straight-line function directly proportional to the input of the sum of weighted neurons and represented by the following equation.

$$F(x) = Kx$$

where K is a constant value.

It gives a range of activations for neurons and connects the set of neurons together. The descent will be on a constant gradient based on the activations. If any prediction error, the changes are completed by backpropagation is constant and does not depend on the input changes to kill the gradients.

The linear activation function is represented by *Figure* 9.4:

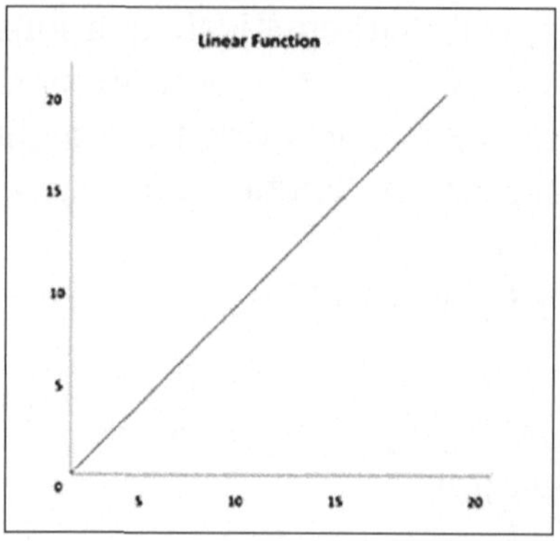

Figure 9.4: *Linear activation function*

Sigmoid Function (Logistic activation function): The sigmoid function is a special function in "Deep Learning engineering", due to its characteristics. It is nonlinear, ranges from 0,1, and is not zero-centered. Because of its saturated gradients in nature, it kills the gradients. Hence, no change during gradient descent, and it simplifies during backpropagation. In this case, the neural network refuses to learn further and performance is drastically slow.

In specific conditions, the large negative numbers become "0" and large positive numbers become "1". It is suitable for logistics regression models where we have to predict the binary form of output either 0 or 1.

Mathematically represented by the following equation:

$$Sigmoid(z) = 1/1 + e^{-z}$$

The sigmoid function is represented by *Figure* 9.5.

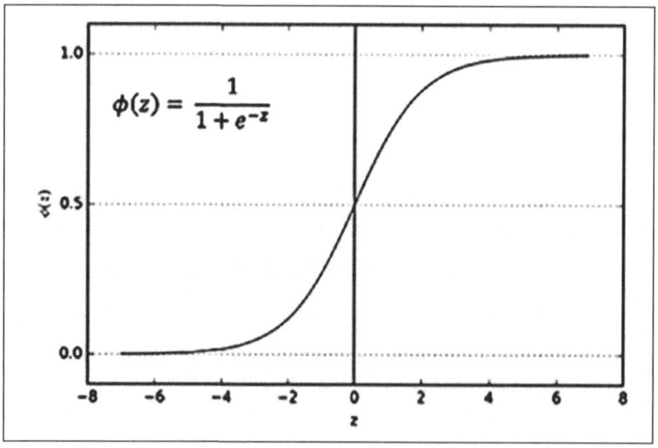

Figure 9.5: *Sigmoid function*

Softmax activation function (Logistic activation function): This one another activation function in a generalized format that is used for multiclass classification. The output (e^{zj}) is in a vector notation with probabilities of each possible outcome as follows:

$$\sigma(z)_{)i} = \frac{e^{zi}}{\sum_{j=i}^{k} e^{zj}}$$

- for i=1,2,3,........ K
- $z = (z_1, z_2, ...z_k)$

Where,

- σ ->Softmax AF
- z->input vector
- e^{zi} ->standard exponential function for an input vector
- K->no. of class in multi-class classifier
- e^{zj} ->standard exponential function for output vector

This function should be stabilized against underflow(~0) and overflow(~ larger value) and is represented in Figure 9.6.

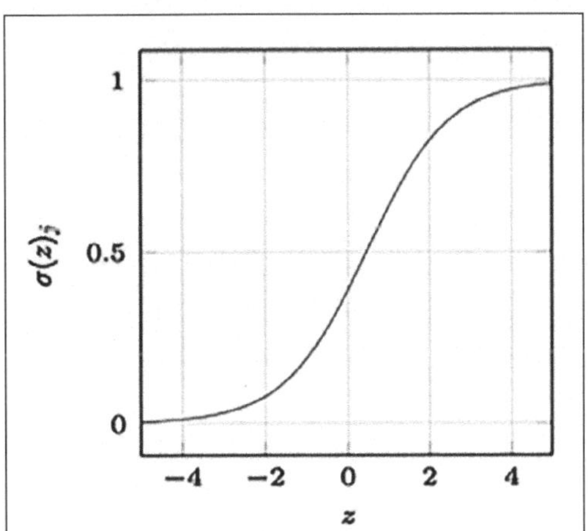

Figure 9.6: *Softmax function*

Characteristics-wise, Sigmoid and Softmax are similar, but still, there is a difference between them the **Sigmoid** activation function is specific to where the output of the neural network needs to be continuous and the other one is categorical (**Softmax**).

Tanh function: This function is also like the logistic **Sigmoid** activation function and the range of the tanh function is from -1 to 1. It is nonlinear in nature and ranges from -1,1 and is zero-centered, hence you can map the output values as strongly from negative, neutral, and positive. The hidden layers of a neural network as its values lie between -1 and 0 or very close to it help in cantering the data and making learning the next layer much easier than other functions. Due to this characteristic, this non-linearity is always.

$$\sigma(z) = \frac{e^{z} - e^{-z}}{e^{z} + e^{-z}}$$

Where,

- σ -> Softmax AF
- z -> input vector

Tanh function is represented in *Figure* 9.7:

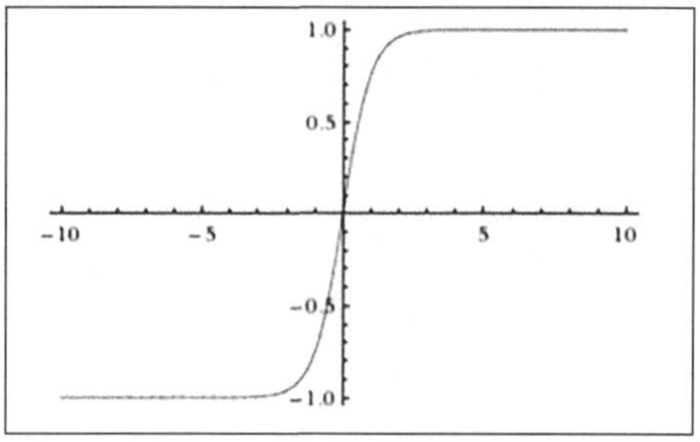

***Figure* 9.7:** *Tanh function*

Rectified Linear Unit (ReLU) function: This is a very simple function, and it helps address some problems of optimizations observed with the sigmoid activation function. This is the most common and used for hidden layers and is less susceptible to vanishing gradients.

It is defined as the following equation:

Relu(x)= Max(0,x)

In which the function is zero for negative values and then it grows linearly for positive values, and it is represented in *Figure* 9.8.

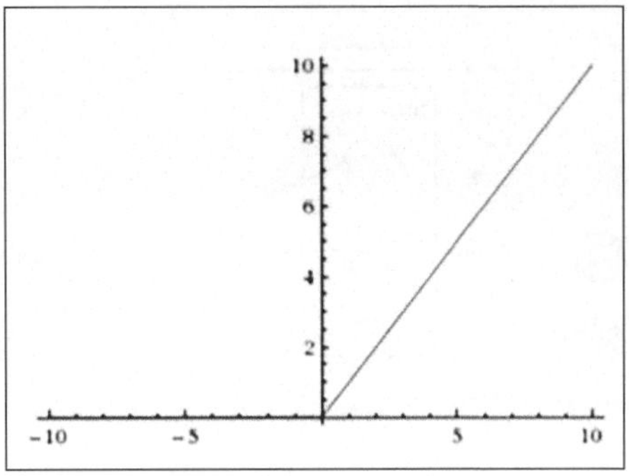

Figure 9.8: *Relu function*

There are two additional activation functions in ReLU, they are defined as follows:

- Leaky ReLU
- Exponential Linear Unit (ELU)

Leaky ReLU: This version of ReLU has all the properties of ReLU and is much improved, and it will never have a dead ReLU problem.

ELU (Exponential Linear Units): ELU is also a much-improved variation of ReLU, in which no dead ReLU situation and closer to zero mean outputs.

Artificial neural networks (ANN)

The ANN algorithm always works with structured data and functions similar to the human brain. It performs sophisticated computations on the large value of data and comes under the machine learning and deep learning model. It is developed from the concept of the human brain system, and how it works in biological neural networks format and even though they are not equivalent, there might be pros and cons are there.

It consists of multiple interconnected and well organized nodes into different layers. All the information flows through these nodes and strengthens the connections during training to learn patterns, predictions, and classification from the input data.

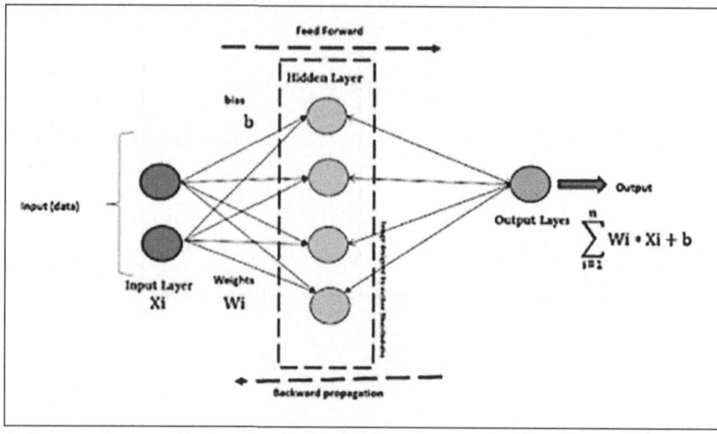

Figure 9.9: *Simple architecture of ANN*

The architecture of ANN is shown in *Figure* 9.9. The ANN consists of three layers. These are as follows:

- Input
- Hidden
- Output

Input Layer: The input for the network and it could be different formats that feed into the hidden layer.

Hidden Layer: This is the middle layer, and it would be one or more than one layer based on the configuration. It performs all types of calculations to extract the hidden features and patterns from the input feed.

Output Layer: The output from the hidden layer is fed into the output layer after a bunch of transformations take place in the hidden layer, which finally feeds the results into this layer as the output that is conveyed to this layer.

The overall performance of the flow is represented in the form of a transfer function, in terms of the sum of the inputs and with weights and includes a bias and is represented by the following formula

$$\sum_{i=1}^{n} (wi * xi) + b$$

Feedforward propagation: This is a very basic ANN, and the data travels in a single direction and only in the forward direction passing through the input layer, hidden layer and exits through the output layer, this way of propagation is called feedforward propagation and usually does not have backpropagation in this neural network.

Back-propagation: If the output from the neural network is identified with any errors, then the backpropagation is applied to whatever it has learned during forward and adjusting the weights of the connections in the network based on the error rate obtained from the forward propagation. The back-and-forth feed process will continue until the neural network gets the correct output with minimal rates of errors.

Long short-term memory (LSTM)

Generally, LSTM contains information in a memory much similar to computer memory, and it has the capabilities to write, read and delete information.

LSTM is used to build a building block for an RNN since it has its own memory capabilities rather than an RNN. It adjusts the weights during backward propagation, which helps RNNs to include new information in the network. We would say this approach gives an extension of RNN and that extends the memory. Eventually, this add-on feature enables RNNs to remember inputs over a long period during training.

Note: Deep learning has its advantages over machine learning techniques, It can handle missing data, find the features and learn on its own, so there is no need for specific EDA and features engineering processes, and it is also capable of handling complex and large data. Along with that, it can handle structured, semi-structured and unstructured data, handling sequential data. The ANN algorithm is a very basic deep learning model that works with structured data and functions similar to the human brain.

Let's do the diesel price prediction using ANN and LSTM models. The dataset is shown in the following figure:

Sale_Date	Diesel_price
2022-04-16	3.65
2022-04-17	3.95
2022-04-18	3.86
2022-04-18	4.06
2022-04-21	3.83
2022-04-22	4.38
2022-04-24	4.48
2022-04-25	4.52
2022-04-26	4.79
2022-04-26	4.52
2022-04-29	4.05
2022-04-30	4.73
2022-05-02	4.42
2022-05-03	4.02
2022-05-04	4.06

Figure 9.10: *Diesel price .csv file*

```
#fundamental libraries
import pandas as pd
import numpy as np
import tensorflow as tf
import matplotlib.pyplot as plt
#Keras libraries
from keras.models import Sequential
from keras.layers import Dense
from keras.callbacks import EarlyStopping
from keras.optimizers import Adam
from keras.layers import LSTM
from tensorflow.keras.callbacks import EarlyStopping

#sscikit learn  libraries
from sklearn.preprocessing import MinMaxScaler
from sklearn.metrics import r2_score

%matplotlib inline
print("###################################")
print("Importing all required libraries")
print("###################################")
```

output

```
##################################
Importing all required libraries
##################################
```

```
print("######################################")
print("loading data from drive successfully")
print("#####################################")
df_diesel_price = pd.read_csv('/content/drive/MyDrive/diesel_price.csv')
```

```
output
##############################################
loading data from the drive successfully
##############################################
df_diesel_price.head()
```

	Sale_Date	Diesel_price
0	2022-04-16	3.65
1	2022-04-17	3.95
2	2022-04-18	3.86
3	2022-04-18	4.06
4	2022-04-21	3.83

Figure 9.11: *Diesel price dataset*

```
print("#######################################")
print("Line Plotthe Diesel price")
print("#######################################")
plt.figure(figsize=(8,5))
plt.plot(df_diesel_price["Diesel_price"])
plt.xlabel('Observation')
plt.ylabel('Diesel price')
plt.title('Day vs Diesel Price')
```

```
######################################
Line Plot the Diesel price
######################################
```

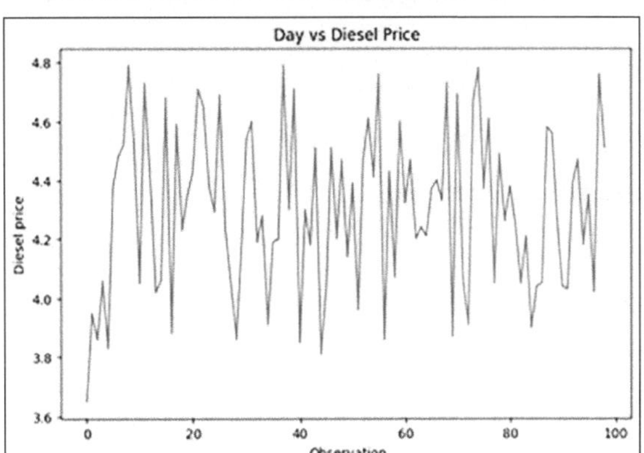

Figure 9.12: *Diesel price line plot*

```
print("############################")
print("Box Plot the Diesel price")
print("############################")
plt.figure(figsize=(8,5))
plt.boxplot(df_diesel_price["Diesel_price"])
plt.xlabel('Observation')
plt.ylabel('diesel_price')
plt.title('Day vs Diesel Price')
```

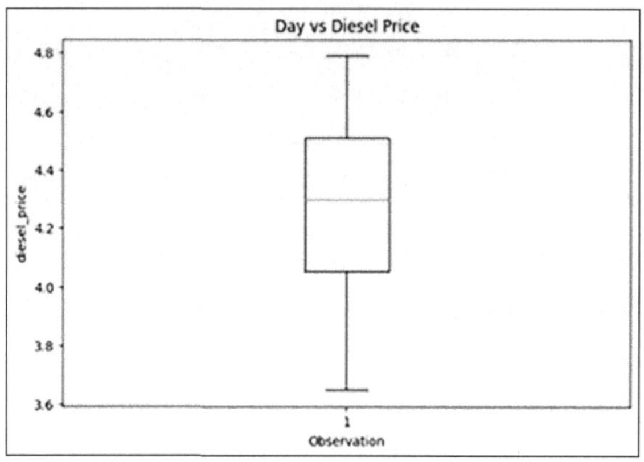

Figure 9.13: *Diesel price box plot*

```
print("###################################")
print("        Diesel Dataset Split       ")
print("###################################")
train_ds = df_diesel_price["Diesel_price"].iloc[0:49].values
test_ds = df_diesel_price["Diesel_price"].iloc[49:99].values

###################################
        Diesel Dataset Split
###################################

print("###################################")
print("        Diesel train dataset       ")
print("###################################")
train_ds
```

output

```
####################################
        Diesel train dataset
####################################
array([3.65, 3.95, 3.86, 4.06, 3.83, 4.38, 4.48, 4.52, 4.79, 4.52, 4.05,
       4.73, 4.42, 4.02, 4.06, 4.68, 3.88, 4.59, 4.23, 4.35, 4.43, 4.71,
       4.65, 4.38, 4.29, 4.69, 4.23, 4.05, 3.86, 4.18, 4.54, 4.6 , 4.19,
       4.28, 3.91, 4.19, 4.2 , 4.79, 4.3 , 4.71, 3.85, 4.3 , 4.18, 4.51,
       3.81, 4.03, 4.51, 4.2 , 4.47])
```

```
print("####################################")
print("        Diesel test dataset      ")
print("####################################")
test_ds
```

output

```
####################################
        Diesel test dataset
####################################
array([4.14, 4.39, 3.96, 4.47, 4.61, 4.41, 4.76, 3.86, 4.43, 4.07, 4.6 ,
       4.32, 4.47, 4.2 , 4.24, 4.21, 4.37, 4.4 , 4.33, 4.73, 3.87, 4.69,
       4.06, 3.91, 4.67, 4.78, 4.37, 4.61, 4.05, 4.49, 4.26, 4.38, 4.25,
       4.05, 4.21, 3.9 , 4.04, 4.05, 4.58, 4.56, 4.25, 4.04, 4.03, 4.39,
       4.47, 4.18, 4.35, 4.02, 4.76, 4.51])
```

```
print("##############################################################
##########")
print("        For Model build X_train,Y_train,X_test and Y_test
")
print("##############################################################
##########")
X_train = train_ds[:-1]
```

```
y_train = train_ds[1:]
X_test = test_ds[:-1]
y_test = test_ds[1:]

##########################################################################

        For Model build X_train,Y_train,X_test and Y_test
##########################################################################
print("X_train")
X_train


X_train
array([3.65, 3.95, 3.86, 4.06, 3.83, 4.38, 4.48, 4.52, 4.79, 4.52, 4.05,
       4.73, 4.42, 4.02, 4.06, 4.68, 3.88, 4.59, 4.23, 4.35, 4.43, 4.71,
       4.65, 4.38, 4.29, 4.69, 4.23, 4.05, 3.86, 4.18, 4.54, 4.6 , 4.19,
       4.28, 3.91, 4.19, 4.2 , 4.79, 4.3 , 4.71, 3.85, 4.3 , 4.18, 4.51,
       3.81, 4.03, 4.51, 4.2 ])

print("Y_train")


Y_train
array([3.95, 3.86, 4.06, 3.83, 4.38, 4.48, 4.52, 4.79, 4.52, 4.05, 4.73,
       4.42, 4.02, 4.06, 4.68, 3.88, 4.59, 4.23, 4.35, 4.43, 4.71, 4.65,
       4.38, 4.29, 4.69, 4.23, 4.05, 3.86, 4.18, 4.54, 4.6 , 4.19, 4.28,
       3.91, 4.19, 4.2 , 4.79, 4.3 , 4.71, 3.85, 4.3 , 4.18, 4.51, 3.81,
       4.03, 4.51, 4.2 , 4.47])

print("X_test")

X_test
array([4.14, 4.39, 3.96, 4.47, 4.61, 4.41, 4.76, 3.86, 4.43, 4.07, 4.6 ,
```

```
        4.32, 4.47, 4.2 , 4.24, 4.21, 4.37, 4.4 , 4.33, 4.73, 3.87, 4.69,
        4.06, 3.91, 4.67, 4.78, 4.37, 4.61, 4.05, 4.49, 4.26, 4.38, 4.25,
        4.05, 4.21, 3.9 , 4.04, 4.05, 4.58, 4.56, 4.25, 4.04, 4.03, 4.39,
        4.47, 4.18, 4.35, 4.02, 4.76])
print("Y_test")
Y_test
array([4.39, 3.96, 4.47, 4.61, 4.41, 4.76, 3.86, 4.43, 4.07, 4.6 , 4.32,
        4.47, 4.2 , 4.24, 4.21, 4.37, 4.4 , 4.33, 4.73, 3.87, 4.69, 4.06,
        3.91, 4.67, 4.78, 4.37, 4.61, 4.05, 4.49, 4.26, 4.38, 4.25, 4.05,
        4.21, 3.9 , 4.04, 4.05, 4.58, 4.56, 4.25, 4.04, 4.03, 4.39, 4.47,
        4.18, 4.35, 4.02, 4.76, 4.51])

print("###########################################################")
print("         Model build using various parameters               ")
print("###########################################################")
annmodel = Sequential()
annmodel.add(Dense(12, input_dim=1, activation='relu'))
annmodel.add(Dense(1))
annmodel.compile(loss='mean_squared_error', optimizer='adam')
early_stop = EarlyStopping(monitor='loss', patience=2, verbose=1)
history = annmodel.fit(X_train, y_train, epochs=200, batch_size=1, ver-
bose=1, callbacks=[early_stop], shuffle=False)
        ###########################################################
                  Model build using various parameters
        ###########################################################
Epoch 1/200
48/48 [==============================] - 1s 2ms/step - loss: 31.2311
Epoch 2/200
48/48 [==============================] - 0s 2ms/step - loss: 17.1333
Epoch 3/200
48/48 [==============================] - 0s 1ms/step - loss: 8.4328
Epoch 4/200
48/48 [==============================] - 0s 2ms/step - loss: 3.5479
```

```
Epoch 5/200
48/48 [==============================] - 0s 1ms/step - loss: 1.2557
Epoch 6/200
48/48 [==============================] - 0s 2ms/step - loss: 0.4139
Epoch 7/200
48/48 [==============================] - 0s 1ms/step - loss: 0.1802
Epoch 8/200
48/48 [==============================] - 0s 1ms/step - loss: 0.1311
Epoch 9/200
48/48 [==============================] - 0s 1ms/step - loss: 0.1229
Epoch 10/200
48/48 [==============================] - 0s 1ms/step - loss: 0.1217
Epoch 11/200
48/48 [==============================] - 0s 1ms/step - loss: 0.1216
Epoch 12/200
48/48 [==============================] - 0s 2ms/step - loss: 0.1215
Epoch 13/200
48/48 [==============================] - 0s 2ms/step - loss: 0.1215
Epoch 14/200
48/48 [==============================] - 0s 1ms/step - loss: 0.1214
Epoch 15/200
48/48 [==============================] - 0s 1ms/step - loss: 0.1214
Epoch 16/200
48/48 [==============================] - 0s 1ms/step - loss: 0.1214
Epoch 17/200
48/48 [==============================] - 0s 1ms/step - loss: 0.1213
Epoch 18/200
48/48 [==============================] - 0s 2ms/step - loss: 0.1213
Epoch 19/200
48/48 [==============================] - 0s 1ms/step - loss: 0.1212
Epoch 20/200
48/48 [==============================] - 0s 1ms/step - loss: 0.1212
Epoch 21/200
```

```
48/48 [==============================] - 0s 1ms/step - loss: 0.1211
Epoch 22/200
48/48 [==============================] - 0s 1ms/step - loss: 0.1211
Epoch 23/200
48/48 [==============================] - 0s 1ms/step - loss: 0.1210
Epoch 24/200
48/48 [==============================] - 0s 1ms/step - loss: 0.1210
Epoch 25/200
48/48 [==============================] - 0s 1ms/step - loss: 0.1209
.
.
.
.
.
.
.
.
.
.
.
.
.
Epoch 198/200
48/48 [==============================] - 0s 1ms/step - loss: 0.0977
Epoch 199/200
48/48 [==============================] - 0s 2ms/step - loss: 0.0976
Epoch 200/200
48/48 [==============================] - 0s 2ms/step - loss: 0.0975

print("################################################")
print("         Model Prediction process              ")
print("################################################")
y_pred_test_nn = annmodel.predict(X_test)
```

```
y_train_pred_nn = annmodel.predict(X_train)
print("R Square score (Train set):\t{:0.2f}".format(r2_score(y_train,
y_train_pred_nn)))
print("R Square (Test set):\t{:0.2f}".format(r2_score(y_test, y_pred_
test_nn)))
print("#############################################")
```

```
#############################################
         Model Prediction process
#############################################
2/2 [==============================] - 0s 5ms/step
2/2 [==============================] - 0s 6ms/step
R Square score (Train set):      -0.17
R Square (Test set):      -0.43
#############################################
```

```
print("#################################################")
print("         LSTM - Dataset preparations            ")
print("################################################")
X_train_lmse = X_train.reshape(X_train.shape[0], 1, 1)
X_test_lmse = X_test.reshape(X_test.shape[0], 1, 1)
print("###################################################")
print('Train shape for LSTM: ', X_train_lmse.shape)
print('Test shape: for LSTM', X_test_lmse.shape)
print("###################################################")
```

```
#################################################
         LSTM - Dataset preparations
################################################
###################################################
Train shape for LSTM:  (48, 1, 1)
Test shape: for LSTM (49, 1, 1)
###################################################
```

```
print("##############################################################")
print("        Model build using various parameters (LSTM)         ")
print("##############################################################")
lstm_model = Sequential()
lstm_model.add(LSTM(7, input_shape=(1, X_train_lmse.shape[1]), acti-
vation='relu', kernel_initializer='lecun_uniform', return_sequences=-
False))
lstm_model.add(Dense(1))
lstm_model.compile(loss='mean_squared_error', optimizer='adam')
early_stop = EarlyStopping(monitor='loss', patience=2, verbose=1)
history_lstm_model = lstm_model.fit(X_train_lmse, y_train, epochs=200,
batch_size=1, verbose=1, shuffle=False, callbacks=[early_stop])
```

```
##############################################################
        Model build using various parameters
##############################################################
Epoch 1/200
48/48 [==============================] - 1s 2ms/step - loss: 42.7310
Epoch 2/200
48/48 [==============================] - 0s 2ms/step - loss: 37.0054
Epoch 3/200
48/48 [==============================] - 0s 2ms/step - loss: 32.5832
Epoch 4/200
48/48 [==============================] - 0s 2ms/step - loss: 29.0786
Epoch 5/200
48/48 [==============================] - 0s 2ms/step - loss: 26.2598
Epoch 6/200
48/48 [==============================] - 0s 2ms/step - loss: 23.9736
Epoch 7/200
48/48 [==============================] - 0s 2ms/step - loss: 22.1074
Epoch 8/200
48/48 [==============================] - 0s 2ms/step - loss: 20.5729
Epoch 9/200
48/48 [==============================] - 0s 2ms/step - loss: 19.2985
```

```
Epoch 10/200
48/48 [==============================] - 0s 2ms/step - loss: 18.2255
Epoch 11/200
48/48 [==============================] - 0s 2ms/step - loss: 17.3053
Epoch 12/200
48/48 [==============================] - 0s 2ms/step - loss: 16.4963
Epoch 13/200
48/48 [==============================] - 0s 2ms/step - loss: 15.7568
Epoch 14/200
48/48 [==============================] - 0s 2ms/step - loss: 15.0284
Epoch 15/200
48/48 [==============================] - 0s 2ms/step - loss: 14.1705
Epoch 16/200
48/48 [==============================] - 0s 2ms/step - loss: 12.7024
Epoch 17/200
48/48 [==============================] - 0s 2ms/step - loss: 9.5004
Epoch 18/200
48/48 [==============================] - 0s 2ms/step - loss: 4.8610
Epoch 19/200
48/48 [==============================] - 0s 2ms/step - loss: 1.6010
Epoch 20/200
48/48 [==============================] - 0s 2ms/step - loss: 0.4225
.
.
.
.
.
.
.
.
.
Epoch 190/200
48/48 [==============================] - 0s 3ms/step - loss: 0.0964
```

```
Epoch 191/200
48/48 [==============================] - 0s 2ms/step - loss: 0.0961
Epoch 192/200
48/48 [==============================] - 0s 2ms/step - loss: 0.0958
Epoch 193/200
48/48 [==============================] - 0s 2ms/step - loss: 0.0955
Epoch 194/200
48/48 [==============================] - 0s 2ms/step - loss: 0.0952
Epoch 195/200
48/48 [==============================] - 0s 2ms/step - loss: 0.0949
Epoch 196/200
48/48 [==============================] - 0s 2ms/step - loss: 0.0946
Epoch 197/200
48/48 [==============================] - 0s 2ms/step - loss: 0.0943
Epoch 198/200
48/48 [==============================] - 0s 2ms/step - loss: 0.0940
Epoch 199/200
48/48 [==============================] - 0s 2ms/step - loss: 0.0938
Epoch 200/200
48/48 [==============================] - 0s 2ms/step - loss: 0.0935
```

```
print("##############################")
print("        The R2 score         ")
print("##############################")

y_pred_test_lstm = lstm_model.predict(X_test_lmse)
y_train_pred_lstm = lstm_model.predict(X_train_lmse)
print("The R2 score on the Train set is:\t{:0.3f}".format(r2_score(y_
train, y_train_pred_lstm)))
print("The R2 score on the Test set is:\t{:0.3f}".format(r2_score(y_
test, y_pred_test_lstm)))
```

```
output
################################
       The R2 score
################################

2/2 [==============================] - 0s 7ms/step
2/2 [==============================] - 0s 5ms/step
The R2 score on the Train set is:      -0.128
The R2 score on the Test set is: -0.369

anntest_mse = annmodel.evaluate(X_test, y_test, batch_size=1)
lstm_test_mse = lstm_model.evaluate(X_test_lmse, y_test, batch_size=1)
print("############################################################")
print("        Model Evaluation process (ANN and LSTM)             ")
print("############################################################")
print('ANN: %f'%anntest_mse)
print('LSTM: %f'%lstm_test_mse)
print("############################################################")

output

49/49 [==============================] - 0s 1ms/step - loss: 0.0942
49/49 [==============================] - 0s 1ms/step - loss: 0.0900

############################################################
        Model Evaluation process (ANN and LSTM)
############################################################
ANN: 0.094176
LSTM: 0.090001
############################################################

print("############################################################")
print("        Model Prediction process (ANN and LSTM)             ")
```

```
print("###################################################################")
ann_y_pred_test = annmodel.predict(X_test)
lstm_y_pred_test = lstm_model.predict(X_test_lmse)
print("###################################################################")
```

output

```
############################################################
        Model Prediction process (ANN and LSTM)
###########################################################
2/2 [==============================] - 0s 6ms/step
2/2 [==============================] - 0s 5ms/step
###########################################################
```

```
print("###############################################################
##########")
print("        Line plot for ANN's Prediction for Diesel price
")
print("###############################################################
##########")
plt.figure(figsize=(8, 5))
plt.plot(y_test, label='True')
plt.plot(y_pred_test_nn, label='ANN')
plt.title("ANN's Prediction for Diesel price")
plt.xlabel('Observation')
plt.ylabel('Diesel price')
plt.legend()
plt.show();
```

output

```
###################################################################
        Line plot for ANN's Prediction for Diesel price
###################################################################
```

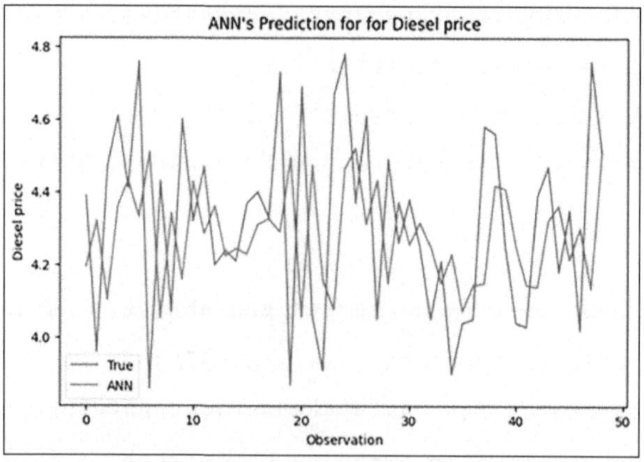

Figure 9.14: *Line plot for ANN's Prediction for Diesel price*

```
print("##################################################################
##########")
print("         Line plot for LSTM's Prediction for Diesel price
")
print("##################################################################
##########")
plt.figure(figsize=(8, 5))
plt.plot(y_test, label='True')
plt.plot(lstm_y_pred_test, label='LSTM')
plt.title("LSTM's Prediction for Diesel price ")
plt.xlabel('Observation')
plt.ylabel('Diesel price')
plt.legend()
plt.show();
```

```
output
############################################################################
        Line plot for LSTM's Prediction for Diesel price
############################################################################
```

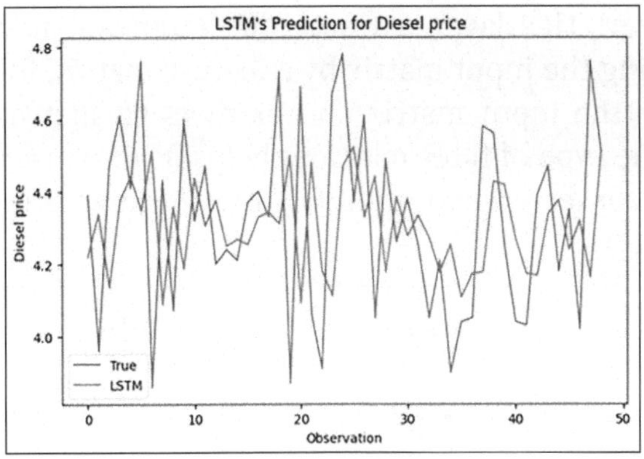

Figure 9.15: *Line plot for LSTM's Prediction for Diesel price*

Convolutional neural networks (CNN)

CNN model architecture is specially designed for semi-structured and unstructured data processing and prediction applications using images, audio, and video. Time series analysis and forecasting typically depend on the quality of the dataset. We have discussed the time series data significance and components in *Chapter 3, Time Series Analysis and its Components.*

In computer science, the image is a matrix of huge pixel values depending on the size of the image and the color in it. Each pixel value depends on the pixel's strength and the image's color composition. The pixel can range from 0 to 255, this is a well-known understanding of the image (or) frame. Furthermore, it depends on the channels, either one or three. Let's say the grey image has just one channel and the colored image has three channels comprising RED, BLUE, and GREEN colors. The CNN model can recognize each image as a matrix of pixel values in terms of the number of channels and the dimension of image width and length.

Concerning CNN input could be changed for Computer Vision - image matrix as input and for Time Series Analysis Forecast - 1D array as input.

Let's understand the components of CNN and use them for time series analyses and forecasting:

- Convolutional layer
- Pooling layer
- Fully connected layer

Convolutional layer: This layer extracts the important features of the input image by multiplying the input matrix by a feature matrix, followed by the filter matrix slides over the input matrix and extracts smaller sub-sections of the image. Based on the type of filter matrices helps us to extract different types of features from the earlier stage output. *Figure* 9.16 shows a filter operation for a 6×6 image.

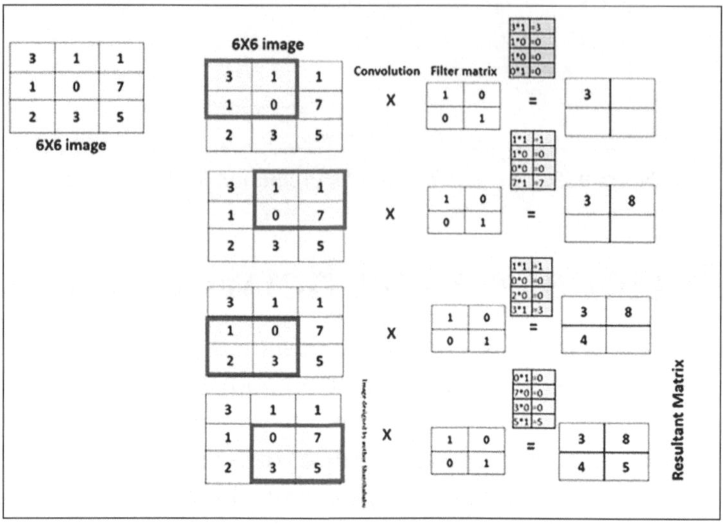

***Figure* 9.16:** CNN - *Convolutional Layer*

Stage -1: Extract features from an input image and maintain the pixel relationship.

Stage 2: Learning the features using slides over input data in the form of small squares.

Padding: While we are doing this shrinking process, there might be data lost from the image corners, so we have to pad them by adding additional borders of "ZEROS" This process is called "Padding" in the CNN model. We could consider this zero padding as hyperparameter tuning. This helps to control the size of the output image appropriately. We have a simple formula to find the output size of the image.

The output size of the image $\left(\frac{N-F+2P}{S}\right)+1$

- N->Size of the image
- F->Size of the filter
- P->Amount of padding
- S->Strides

Stride is a parameter of the CNN's filter, that decides the movement over the image or video. If the stride is set to 1, then the filter will move one pixel or unit at a time preferred in *Figure* 9.16:

Pooling layer

Pooling techniques: helps us to reduce the resultant matrix further if the image size is larger, using different pooling techniques, which are as follows:

- Sum pooling
- Average pooling
- Max Pooling

After pooling, the image is significantly compressed in size.

Sum pooling: This pooling method is the summing of all elements in the feature map as a straightforward method.

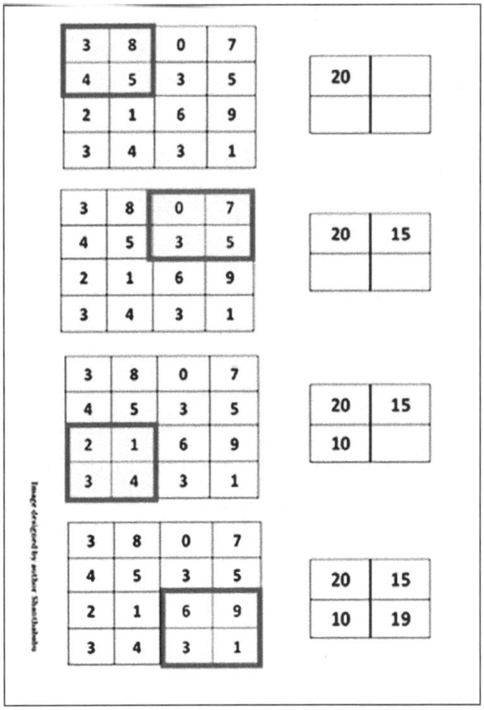

***Figure* 9.17:** CNN - *Pooling Layer (sum pooling)*

Max pooling: The basic idea of this technique is finding the maximum pixels from the image and down the sample an input image and hidden-layer output matrix. Where we are reducing the image by its dimensionality. Here, the pooling technique simply throws the minimum value and picks up the maximum value.

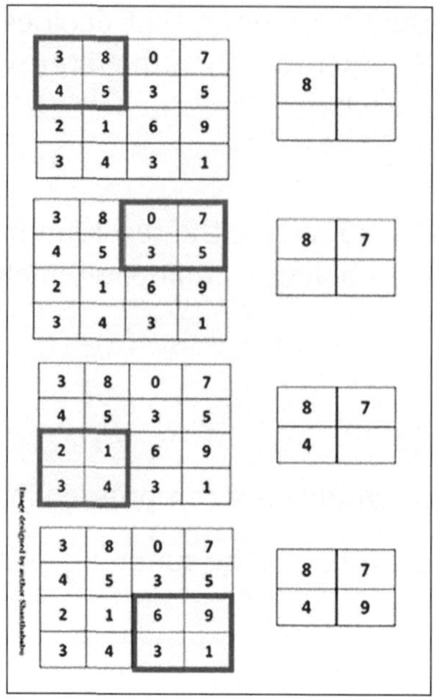

Figure 9.18: CNN - *Pooling Layer (max pooling)*

Average pooling: Average pooling is straightforward forward finding the average pixels and retaining all information from the elements of a block. This technique considers all information in the pixels.

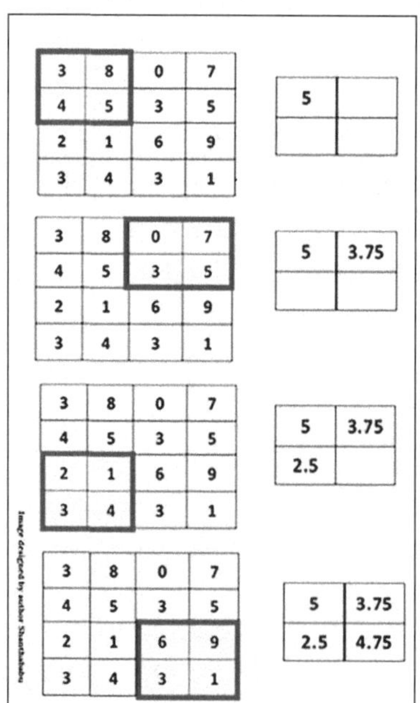

Figure 9.19: CNN - *Pooling Layer (Avg pooling)*

Fully connected layer: After the pooling process, the pooled matrix is then flattened, and the resultant matrix is fed to the **Fully Connected layer** which discovers the images through its neural networks. From the fully connected layers, we could combine all these features to create a model.

Adding activation function: Finally, we have to add an activation function based on our problem statement such as **SIGMOID** or **SOFTMAX to** classify the final outputs.

Figure 9.20 shows the CNN Architecture.

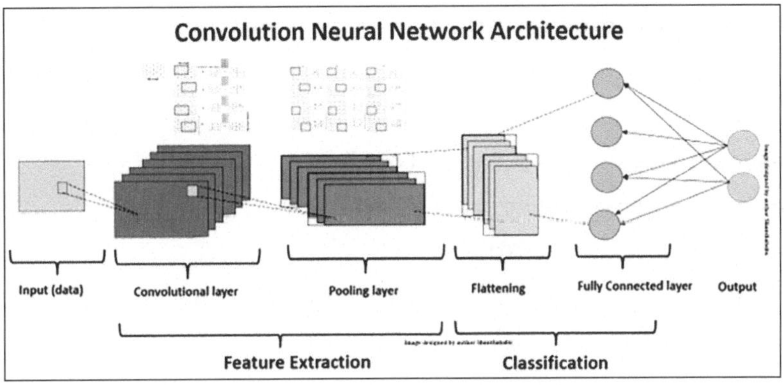

Figure 9.20: *CNN Architecture*

Let's do the diesel price prediction using ANN and LSTM models. The dataset is shown in the following figure:

Sale_Date	Diesel_price
2022-04-16	3.65
2022-04-17	3.95
2022-04-18	3.86
2022-04-18	4.06
2022-04-21	3.83
2022-04-22	4.38
2022-04-24	4.48
2022-04-25	4.52
2022-04-26	4.79
2022-04-26	4.52
2022-04-29	4.05
2022-04-30	4.73
2022-05-02	4.42
2022-05-03	4.02
2022-05-04	4.06

Figure 9.21: *Diesel price .csv file*

```
#fundamental libraries
import tensorflow as tf
import matplotlib.pyplot as plt
import matplotlib.pyplot as plt
%matplotlib inline
import warnings
import numpy as np
import pandas as pd
import matplotlib.pyplot as plt

#Keras libraries
from keras.callbacks import EarlyStopping
from keras.optimizers import Adam
from keras.layers import LSTM
from tensorflow.keras.callbacks import EarlyStopping
from keras import optimizers
from keras.utils import plot_model
from keras.models import Sequential, Model
from keras.layers.convolutional import Conv1D, MaxPooling1D
from keras.layers import Dense, LSTM, RepeatVector, TimeDistributed,
Flatten
from sklearn.metrics import mean_squared_error
from sklearn.model_selection import train_test_split
import plotly.graph_objs as go
from plotly.offline import init_notebook_mode, iplot

%matplotlib inline
warnings.filterwarnings("ignore")
init_notebook_mode(connected=True)

import itertools
import warnings
```

```
warnings.filterwarnings('ignore')
print("###################################")
print("Importing all required libraries")
print("###################################")
```

Output

```
###################################
Importing all required libraries
###################################
```

```
print("#######################################")
print("loading data from drive successfully")
print("######################################")
df_diesel_price = pd.read_csv('/content/drive/MyDrive/diesel_price.csv')
```

Output

```
######################################
loading data from drive successfully
#####################################
```

```
df_diesel_price.head()
```

	Sale_Date	Diesel_price
0	2022-04-16	3.65
1	2022-04-17	3.95
2	2022-04-18	3.86
3	2022-04-18	4.06
4	2022-04-21	3.83

Figure 9.22: *Diesel price dataset*

```
print("###################################")
print("Line Plot the Diesel price")
print("###################################")
```

```
plt.figure(figsize=(8,5))
plt.plot(df_diesel_price["Diesel_price"])
plt.xlabel('Observation')
plt.ylabel('Diesel price')
plt.title('Day vs Diesel Price')
```

```
                    ####################################
                        Line Plot the Diesel price
                    ####################################
```

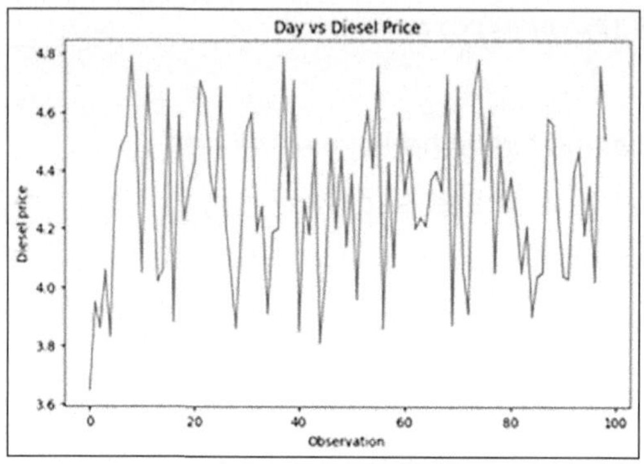

Figure 9.23: *Diesel price dataset*

```
print("####################################")
print("         Split the dataset         ")
print("####################################")
X_train, X_test, Y_train, Y_test = train_test_split(df_diesel_
price["Diesel_price"],df_diesel_price["Diesel_price"], test_size=0.5,
random_state=0)
print("Train Dataset Shape ", X_train.shape)
print('Test Dataset  Shape', X_test.shape)
X_train.head()
```

```
Output
####################################
         Split the dataset
####################################
Train Dataset Shape  (49,)
Test Dataset  Shape (50,)
```

```
90    4.04
59    4.60
0     3.65
34    3.91
28    3.86
Name: Diesel_price, dtype: float64

print("###########################################################")
print("        Shaping the Dataset for model building             ")
print("###########################################################")
X_train_series = X_train.values.reshape((X_train.shape[0], 1))
X_test_series = X_test.values.reshape((X_test.shape[0], 1))
```

Output

```
print("###########################################################")
print("        Model build using various parameters               ")
print("###########################################################")

model_cnn = Sequential()
model_cnn.add(Conv1D(filters=64, kernel_size=2, activation='relu',
input_shape=(X_train_series.shape[0],X_train_series.shape[1])))

model_cnn.add(MaxPooling1D(pool_size=2))
model_cnn.add(Flatten())
model_cnn.add(Dense(50, activation='relu'))
model_cnn.add(Dense(1))
lr = 0.0003
adam = optimizers.Adam(lr)
model_cnn.compile(loss='mse', optimizer=adam)
model_cnn.summary()
```

```
##########################################################
       Model build using various parameters
##########################################################
Model: "sequential_12"
_________________________________________________________________
 Layer (type)                Output Shape              Param #
=================================================================
 conv1d_2 (Conv1D)           (None, 48, 64)            192

 max_pooling1d_6 (MaxPooling  (None, 24, 64)           0
 1D)

 flatten_6 (Flatten)        (None, 1536)              0

 dense_27 (Dense)            (None, 50)                76850

 dense_28 (Dense)            (None, 1)                 51
=================================================================
Total params: 77,093
Trainable params: 77,093
Non-trainable params: 0
_________________________________________________________________
print("################################")
print("         Model fit              ")
print("###############################")
model_cnn = tf.keras.Sequential([tf.keras.layers.Dense(100),tf.keras.
layers.Dense(10),tf.keras.layers.Dense(1)])
model_cnn.compile(loss=tf.keras.losses.mae, optimizer=tf.keras.
optimizers.Adam(),metrics=['mae'])
model_cnn.fit(X_train, Y_train, epochs=100)
```

```
#################################
        Model fit
################################
Epoch 1/100
2/2 [==============================] - 1s 6ms/step - loss: 4.0077 - mae:
4.0077
Epoch 2/100
2/2 [==============================] - 0s 8ms/step - loss: 3.5000 - mae:
3.5000
Epoch 3/100
2/2 [==============================] - 0s 9ms/step - loss: 2.9875 - mae:
2.9875
Epoch 4/100
2/2 [==============================] - 0s 7ms/step - loss: 2.4793 - mae:
2.4793
Epoch 5/100
2/2 [==============================] - 0s 5ms/step - loss: 1.9655 - mae:
1.9655
Epoch 6/100
2/2 [==============================] - 0s 4ms/step - loss: 1.4470 - mae:
1.4470
Epoch 7/100
2/2 [==============================] - 0s 7ms/step - loss: 0.9223 - mae:
0.9223
Epoch 8/100
2/2 [==============================] - 0s 6ms/step - loss: 0.3900 - mae:
0.3900
Epoch 9/100
2/2 [==============================] - 0s 7ms/step - loss: 0.1297 - mae:
0.1297
Epoch 10/100
2/2 [==============================] - 0s 9ms/step - loss: 0.4401 - mae:
0.4401
Epoch 11/100
2/2 [==============================] - 0s 8ms/step - loss: 0.5539 - mae:
0.5539
```

```
Epoch 12/100

2/2 [==============================] - 0s 7ms/step - loss: 0.5197 - mae:
0.5197

Epoch 13/100

2/2 [==============================] - 0s 7ms/step - loss: 0.3762 - mae:
0.3762

Epoch 14/100

2/2 [==============================] - 0s 5ms/step - loss: 0.1500 - mae:
0.1500

Epoch 15/100

2/2 [==============================] - 0s 5ms/step - loss: 0.1143 - mae:
0.1143

Epoch 16/100

2/2 [==============================] - 0s 6ms/step - loss: 0.2522 - mae:
0.2522

Epoch 17/100

2/2 [==============================] - 0s 6ms/step - loss: 0.2610 - mae:
0.2610

Epoch 18/100

2/2 [==============================] - 0s 7ms/step - loss: 0.1675 - mae:
0.1675

Epoch 19/100

2/2 [==============================] - 0s 6ms/step - loss: 0.0474 - mae:
0.0474

Epoch 20/100

2/2 [==============================] - 0s 7ms/step - loss: 0.1626 - mae:
0.1626

.

.

.

.

.

Epoch 95/100

2/2 [==============================] - 0s 5ms/step - loss: 0.0089 - mae:
0.0089

Epoch 96/100
```

```
2/2 [==============================] - 0s 5ms/step - loss: 0.0084 - mae: 0.0084
Epoch 97/100
2/2 [==============================] - 0s 5ms/step - loss: 0.0103 - mae: 0.0103
Epoch 98/100
2/2 [==============================] - 0s 5ms/step - loss: 0.0112 - mae: 0.0112
Epoch 99/100
2/2 [==============================] - 0s 5ms/step - loss: 0.0096 - mae: 0.0096
Epoch 100/100
2/2 [==============================] - 0s 7ms/step - loss: 0.0110 - mae: 0.0110
<keras.callbacks.History at 0x7ef371546140>
```

```
print("################################")
print("    Model Evaluation          ")
print("################################")
model_cnn.evaluate(X_test, Y_test)
model_evaluation_cnn = model_cnn.evaluate(X_test, Y_test, verbose=1)
print('CNN Model Test accuracy:', model_evaluation_cnn[1])
```

Output

```
################################
    Model Evaluation
################################
2/2 [==============================] - 0s 4ms/step - loss: 0.0167 - mae: 0.0167
2/2 [==============================] - 0s 8ms/step - loss: 0.0167 - mae: 0.0167
CNN Model Test accuracy: 0.016665244475007057
```

```
print("########################################")
```

```
print("        Model prediction                 ")
print("########################################")
y_pred = model_cnn.predict(X_test, verbose=0)
print(y_pred)
```

Output

```
########################################
        Model prediction
########################################
[[4.2193966]
 [4.047749 ]
 [3.8665652]
 [4.724805 ]
 [4.352901 ]
 [4.3719726]
 [3.8856373]
 [4.638981 ]
 [4.3910446]
 [4.171717 ]
 [4.5817647]
 [4.0286775]
 [4.467333 ]
 [4.019141 ]
 [4.49594  ]

      .
      .
      .
      .
      .
[4.3624377]]
```

Recurrent Neural Network (RNN)

RNN is one of the major models of deep learning and a powerful type of neural network, which is perfectly adapted to work for time series data or sequence data. It helps us to deliver predictive results effectively in time series data or sequence data than other deep learning models. Basically, this is derived from feedforward networks, and it demonstrates similar behavior to how human brains function. RNN models show up in our everyday life, for example, Siri and Google Translate.

This RNN is a perfect fit for sequential data, it means the ordered data are related to each other in a sequential order. The most accepted type of sequential data is time series data, in which a series of data points that are related to each other in regular intervals would be minutes, hours, days, weeks, months and years.

RNN is derived from feedforward. Based on the characteristics of the feed-forward neural network, the information moves in one direction, which means from the input layer to the output layer and via the hidden layers. In simple terms, the information moves straight through the neural network.

We know that feedforward neural networks have no memory of the input that they have received and no capabilities of predicting what comes next and earlier details than the other neural networks we discussed. This keeps the details of the current input and not any other details.

But RNN keeps the current input alongside what it has learned from the previous input, since the information cycles through a loop exists in this model, this capability helps this model to make a decision. *Figure 9.24* shows the structure of FF-NN and R-NN.

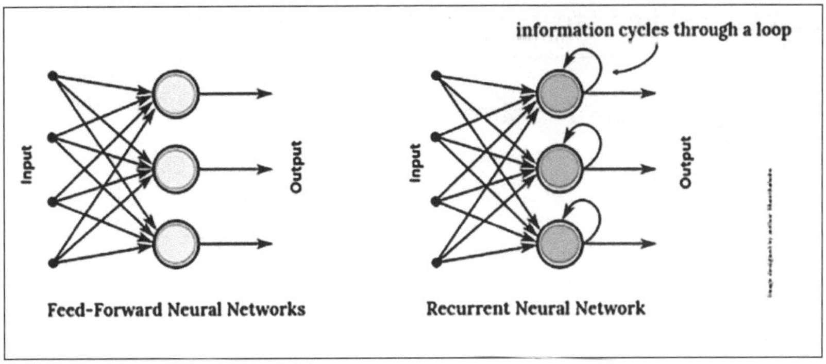

Figure 9.24: *Structure of the F-F and Recurrent-Neural Network*

Here, we can observe that the RNN has two inputs: the present and the recent past, respectively. This is an important feature because the sequence input data contains crucial information, and the loop input contains past information. Additionally, RNNs apply weights to the current and previous inputs, and they can tweak the weights for both backpropagation and gradient descent over time. All these major features are not feasible with other deep learning models.

The RNN has a short-term memory. To implement the model, we could combine it with an LSTM since they have a long-term memory. The final model would have the capability of learning long-term dependencies and this feature makes the RNN model smarter than earlier and remembers information about the past to help decide on the next estimate reasonably.

RNN along with LSTM is used to sort time-series data and predictions accurately.

Depending on the inputs and outputs, RNN is classified into the following types.

- **One-to-One**
- **One-to-Many**
- **Many-to-One**
- **Many-to-Many**

One-to-One: This is a very simple architecture used in traditional neural networks. The name implies that there is only one for input and output.

One-to-Many: This is also a simple architecture with a single input and many outputs.

Many-to-One: This is just opposite to the earlier one. It means that it has a single output produced by many inputs on or after time steps.

Many-to-Many: This is a robust network that has multiple inputs and the output and complexity are higher than the other types we discussed.

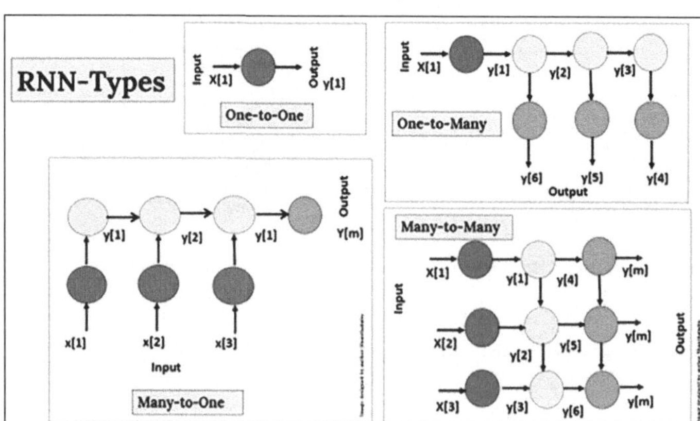

Figure 9.25: *Recurrent Neural Network – Types*

Backpropagation through time (BPTT)

When we apply RNN in time series analysis and forecasting problem statements, we must incorporate a back-propagation algorithm with RNN, this specific process is called **"Backpropagation Through Time"**

Before we understand the concept of BPTT, we must understand how forward and backpropagation works. In general, the neural networks, forward propagation is used to get the output from the model and validate and collect the error(derivative error), followed by backpropagation used to go backwards through our neural network to find an error and adjust the weights and decrease the error concerning the weights, fundamentally it subtracts this error value from the weights, this is how the neural network learns during the training process back-and-forth movements. Refer to the neural network *Figure* 9.9: *Simple architecture of* ANN for a better understanding.

When dealing with time series data, let's assume one-on-one type RNN, the one input is sent into the neural network at a time and one output is obtained. During backpropagation, it uses both the current and prior inputs as input to the neural network, this is referred to as a **TIMESTEP**. So, there are multiple time series data points entering the "RNN" at the same time.

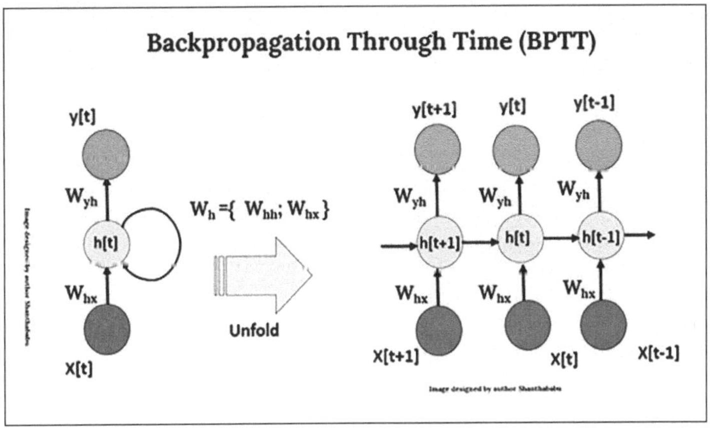

***Figure* 9.26:** *Backpropagation Through Time* (BPTT)

Let's do the diesel price prediction using RNN and LSTM models. The dataset is shown in the following figure.

Sale_Date	Diesel_price
2022-04-16	3.65
2022-04-17	3.95
2022-04-18	3.86
2022-04-18	4.06
2022-04-21	3.83
2022-04-22	4.38
2022-04-24	4.48
2022-04-25	4.52
2022-04-26	4.79
2022-04-26	4.52
2022-04-29	4.05
2022-04-30	4.73
2022-05-02	4.42
2022-05-03	4.02
2022-05-04	4.06

Figure 9.27: *Diesel price .csv file*

```
#fundamental libraries
import numpy as np
import pandas as pd
import matplotlib.pyplot as plt
import tensorflow as tf
from tensorflow import keras
from tensorflow.keras import layers
%matplotlib inline
import warnings

#Keras libraries

from keras.layers import Dense,LSTM
from keras import metrics
from sklearn.preprocessing import MinMaxScaler
from sklearn.metrics import r2_score
from keras.callbacks import EarlyStopping
```

```
from keras.optimizers import Adam
from keras.layers import LSTM
from keras import optimizers
from keras.utils import plot_model
from keras.models import Sequential, Model
from sklearn.metrics import mean_squared_error
from sklearn.model_selection import train_test_split
import plotly.graph_objs as go
warnings.filterwarnings('ignore')

print("###################################")
print("Importing all required libraries")
print("###################################")
```

output

```
##################################
Importing all required libraries
##################################
print("#####################################")
print("loading data from drive successfully")
print("####################################")
df_diesel_price = pd.read_csv('/content/drive/MyDrive/diesel_price.csv')
```

output

```
#####################################
loading data from drive successfully
####################################

df_diesel_price.head()
```

	Sale_Date	Diesel_price
0	2022-04-16	3.65
1	2022-04-17	3.95
2	2022-04-18	3.86
3	2022-04-18	4.06
4	2022-04-21	3.83

Figure 9.28: *Diesel price dataset*

```
print("###################################")
print("Line Plot the Diesel price")
print("###################################")
plt.figure(figsize=(8,5))
plt.plot(df_diesel_price["Diesel_price"])
plt.xlabel('Observation')
plt.ylabel('Diesel price')
plt.title('Day vs Diesel Price')
```

```
###################################
Line Plot the Diesel price
###################################
```

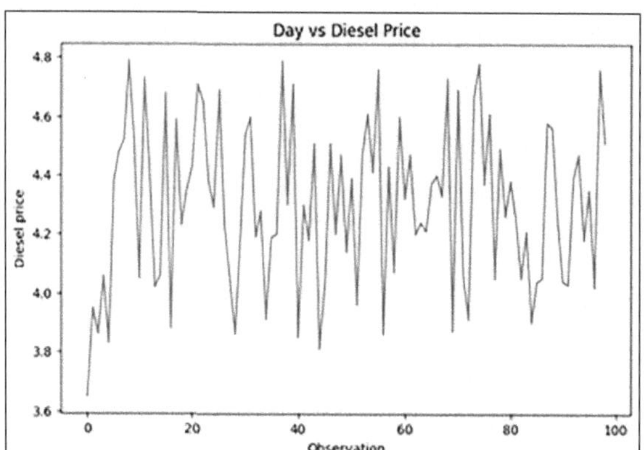

Figure 9.29: *Diesel price line plot*

```
print("###################################")
print("        Diesel Dataset Split      ")
print("###################################")
train_ds = df_diesel_price["Diesel_price"].iloc[0:50].values
test_ds = df_diesel_price["Diesel_price"].iloc[50:100].values
```

```
####################################
        Diesel Dataset Split
####################################

print("######################################################################
##########")
print("        For Model build X_train,Y_train,X_test and Y_test
")
print("######################################################################
##########")
X_train = train_ds[:-1]
y_train = train_ds[1:]
X_test = test_ds[:-1]
y_test = test_ds[1:]

##########################################################################
        For Model build X_train,Y_train,X_test and Y_test
##########################################################################


print("#######################################################
##########")
print("        Model build using various parameters              ")
print("#######################################################
##########")
rnnmodel = Sequential()
rnnmodel.add(LSTM(5,activation = 'tanh',input_shape = (1,1),recurrent_
activation= 'hard_sigmoid'))
rnnmodel.add(Dense(1))
rnnmodel.compile(loss= 'mean_squared_error',optimizer = 'rmsprop',
metrics=[metrics.mae])
rnnmodel.summary()
```

Output

```
##########################################################
       Model build using various parameters
##########################################################
Model: "sequential_20"
_________________________________________________________________
 Layer (type)                Output Shape              Param #
=================================================================
 lstm_17 (LSTM)              (None, 5)                 140


 dense_20 (Dense)            (None, 1)                 6

=================================================================
Total params: 146
Trainable params: 146
Non-trainable params: 0

print("########################################")
print("       Fitting the Model                ")
print("########################################")
rnnmodel.fit(tf.expand_dims(X_test, axis=-1), y_test, epochs=100)

########################################
       Fitting the Model
########################################
Epoch 1/100
2/2 [==============================] - 0s 11ms/step - loss: 16.3245
- mean_absolute_error: 4.0320
Epoch 2/100
2/2 [==============================] - 0s 10ms/step - loss: 16.2496
- mean_absolute_error: 4.0227
Epoch 3/100
2/2 [==============================] - 0s 9ms/step - loss: 16.1750
- mean_absolute_error: 4.0134
```

```
Epoch 4/100
2/2 [==============================] - 0s 10ms/step - loss: 16.1006
- mean_absolute_error: 4.0041
Epoch 5/100
2/2 [==============================] - 0s 10ms/step - loss: 16.0266
- mean_absolute_error: 3.9949
Epoch 6/100
2/2 [==============================] - 0s 9ms/step - loss: 15.9527
- mean_absolute_error: 3.9856
Epoch 7/100
2/2 [==============================] - 0s 12ms/step - loss: 15.8791
- mean_absolute_error: 3.9764
Epoch 8/100
2/2 [==============================] - 0s 9ms/step - loss: 15.8056
- mean_absolute_error: 3.9671
Epoch 9/100
2/2 [==============================] - 0s 9ms/step - loss: 15.7322
- mean_absolute_error: 3.9579
Epoch 10/100
'
'
'
'
'
'
Epoch 95/100
2/2 [==============================] - 0s 11ms/step - loss: 10.7414
- mean_absolute_error: 3.2671
Epoch 96/100
2/2 [==============================] - 0s 13ms/step - loss: 10.6940
- mean_absolute_error: 3.2599
Epoch 97/100

2/2 [==============================] - 0s 12ms/step - loss: 10.6466
- mean_absolute_error: 3.2526
Epoch 98/100
```

```
2/2 [==============================] - 0s 11ms/step - loss: 10.5991
- mean_absolute_error: 3.2452
Epoch 99/100
2/2 [==============================] - 0s 10ms/step - loss: 10.5517
- mean_absolute_error: 3.2379
Epoch 100/100
2/2 [==============================] - 0s 10ms/step - loss: 10.5038
- mean_absolute_error: 3.2306
<keras.callbacks.History at 0x799c4af8e140>

print("#############################################")
print("         Model Prediction process            ")
print("#############################################")
y_pred_test_nn = rnnmodel.predict(X_test)
y_train_pred_nn = rnnmodel.predict(X_train)
print("R Square score (Train set):\t{:0.2f}".format(r2_score(y_train,
y_train_pred_nn)))
print("R Square (Test set):\t{:0.2f}".format(r2_score(y_test, y_pred_
test_nn)))
print("#############################################")

#############################################
         Model Prediction process
#############################################
2/2 [==============================] - 0s 6ms/step
2/2 [==============================] - 0s 6ms/step
R Square score (Train set):      -0.85
R Square (Test set):      -1.21
#############################################

test_mse = model.evaluate(X_test, y_test, batch_size=1)
print("#############################################################")
print("         Model Evaluation process (ANN and LSTM)             ")
print("#############################################################")
print('ANN: %f',rnntest_mse)
```

```
print("####################################################################")
```

Output

```
49/49 [==============================] - 0s 2ms/step - loss: 0.3066
- mae: 0.3066
##################################################################
        Model Evaluation process (ANN and LSTM)
#################################################################
ANN: %f [0.3065764307975769, 0.3065764307975769]
#################################################################
```

```
plt.figure(figsize=(8,5))
plt.plot(y_test,label = 'Test')
plt.plot(Predict, label = 'Prediction')
plt.legend(loc='best')
plt.show()
```

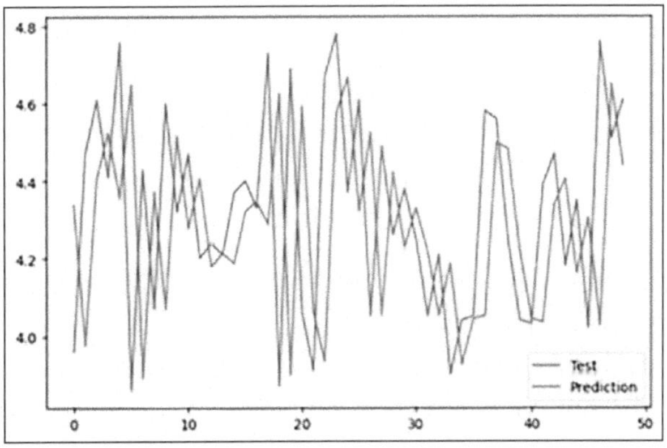

Figure 9.30: *Line plot for RNN's Prediction for Diesel price*

Conclusion

In this chapter, we have discussed the detailed studies of deep learning and its algorithms, such as ANN, LSTM, CNN and RNN, along with different activation functions.

Discussed what deep learning is and its performance, we were able to understand how it deals with structured and unstructured data formats such as images, videos, text, and so on. We can relate and see how deep learning works closely with neural networks. How its structure replicates the human brain, which works and thinks.

We explored how activation functions work and their different types such as linear activation, Sigmoid, Softmax, Tanh and rectified linear unit (ReLU) functions.

We explored Artificial Neural Networks (ANN) architecture and how it works with structured data and functions similar to the human brain and its implementation using Python code.

We understand how the CNN model works along with a neat architecture diagram and the components of CNN and use them for time series analyses and forecasting. convolutional, pooling and fully connected layer. We demonstrate the CNN implementation with the diesel price dataset in the classical method using Python code.

We comprehend how the RNN model plays a major role in deep learning of its powerful characteristics and how this is perfectly adapted to work for time series data or sequence data. It helps us to deliver predictive results effectively in time series data or sequence data than other deep learning models along with implementation using Python code.

This chapter will provide a solid understanding of activation functions, ANN, CNN and RNN models, along with time series data. their limitations, benefits, and various types and their implementation.

In the next chapter, we will explore and understand the Microsoft Azure time series insights component and its significance. How Azure TSI is functioning as a fully managed analytics, storage, and visualization service for near real-time data from IoT and how to scale them in the cloud environment for industry benefits. Further discussion on Azure time series insights Gen2 for industrial IoT concerning various industries. Data exploration and visual anomaly detection using Azure Time Series Insights. Best practices for planning and preparation for Azure time series insights Gen2 environment. Comparison of Gen1 and Gen2. Exploring a list of capabilities, key benefits, and key jobs.

Points to remember

In this chapter, it is important to keep a few things in mind that will be handy throughout this book:

- What is deep learning?
  - Deep learning is a subset of artificial intelligence and part of machine learning, it deals with structured and unstructured data formats such as images, videos, text, and so on.
- How does deep learning work?
  - The structure replicates the human brain, which works and thinks. Recent technological developments and cloud services provide powerful networks, high speed, and computational capacity to help data analytics and machine learning algorithms execute exponentially.
- How deep learning performs much better than machine learning models?
  - It is not essential to assess the missing data and data seasonality for the given dataset, Deep learning algorithms are capable of handling missing data, making seasonality and making predictions.
  - There is no need to find the order of p, like in AR, MA ARIMA and VARMA time series models.
  - It is capable of learning complex mappings automatically and supports from simple I/O to multiple I/O while implementing the models.
  - It can automatically learn features from the dataset, and it doesn't require the feature engineering stage.
- What are the Activation functions and their types?
  - The activation function plays a vital role in neural networks, predominately it helps the model to decide whether a neuron should be activated or not by complex calculation internally in terms of the weighted sum and additionally adding bias for different reasons to it.
    - Linear Activation Function
    - Sigmoid Function (Logistic activation function)
    - Softmax activation function (Logistic activation function):
    - Tanh function
    - Rectified Linear Unit (ReLU) function
      - Leaky ReLU
      - Exponential Linear Unit (ELU)
- How do the activation functions work?
  - The activation function takes in the output signal from the previous cell in the network and converts it into some form that can be fed as input to the next cell in the network.

- What is Artificial Neural Network (ANN)
    - The ANN algorithm always works with structured data and functions similar to the human brain.
    - It consists of multiple nodes which are interconnected and well organized into different layers.
    - All the information flows through these nodes and strengthens the connections during the training period to learn patterns, predictions, and classification from the input data.
- What is Convolutional Neural Networks (CNN)
    - CNN model architecture is specially designed for semi-structured and unstructured data processing and prediction applications using images, audio, and video. Time series analysis and forecasting typically depend on the quality of the dataset.
    - Components of CNN
        - Convolutional Layer
        - Pooling Layer
        - Fully Connected Layer
- What is Recurrent Neural Network (RNN)
    - RNN is one of the major models of deep learning and a powerful type of neural network, which is perfectly adapted to work for time series data or sequence data.
    - Basically, this is derived from feedforward networks, and it demonstrates similar behavior to how human brains function.
    - RNN is classified into the following types
        - One-to-One
        - One-to-Many
        - Many-to-One
        - Many-to-Many
- What is Backpropagation Through Time (BPTT)
    - When we apply RNN in time series analysis and forecasting problem statements, we must incorporate a back-propagation algorithm with RNN, this specific process is called "Backpropagation Through Time".

CHAPTER 10

Azure Time Series Insights

Introduction

In the previous chapter, we discussed detailed studies of deep learning and how this is effective for time series analysis and forecasting, and why deep learning for time series forecasting characteristics. We explored the basic concepts of activation functions and comprehensive learning of deep learning models - ANNs, CNNs, RNNs, and LSTMs specifically for time series forecasting.

This chapter would help us explore and understand the Microsoft Azure time series insights component and its significance. We will learn how Azure TSI functions as a fully managed analytics, storage, and visualization service for near real-time data from IoT and how to scale them in the cloud environment for industry benefits. Further, we will have a discussion on Azure time series insights Gen2 for industrial IoT concerning various industries. The chapter also covers data exploration and visual anomaly detection using Azure Time Series Insights. At the end of the chapter, we will learn about the best practices for planning and preparation for Azure time series insights Gen2 environment, draw a comparison between Gen1 and Gen2, and explore a list of capabilities, key benefits, and key jobs.

Structure

- In this chapter, we will discuss the following topics:
- Understanding Azure - Time Series Insights (Azure TSI) component
- Azure-TSI components significance and exploring Azure-TSI Gen2
- Azure-TSI Gen2 for industrial IoT – Data Analytics Architecture
- Best practices for planning and preparation of Azure-TSI Gen2 environment

Prerequisites

Concerning the chapter, we are assuming that the readers have a good understanding of cloud environments, such as Azure and AWS, because *Chapters* 10 and 11 focus on time series-based components. Let's discuss them in detail.

Understanding Azure - Time Series Insights (Azure-TSI) Gen2 component

Microsoft Azure provides various services for multiple platforms, such as data analytics, data science, machine learning, AI end, and so on, with highly capable components.

Azure TSI is an Azure cloud service that effectively integrates with live data that continually varies with time stamps and is generated from various industry-specific sensors that are well connected with machinery and equipment. This data can be generated on a very large scale and have opportunities for data analysis and prediction. This can be demonstrated with the help of Azure TSI.

Azure TSI Gen2 is an analytics service designed specifically for Industrial Internet of Things (IIoT) deployments. Azure TSI provides a set of powerful APIs for explicit industry manufacturing data from shop floor applications to integrate with the current workflow stream to demonstrate various data analytics functions, especially time series analysis.

Azure TSI is used to build data storage, data visualization, and query for the collected data through IIoT, leading to time series analyses and forecasting.

Azure TSI collects and stores the data and processes it, followed by querying and building various visualizations of IoT data at different levels of scaling, *Figure* 10.1 shows the simple architecture for Azure TSI.

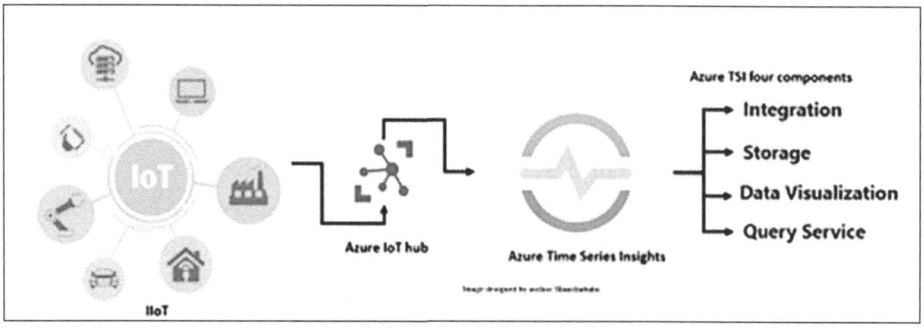

Figure 10.1: *Azure TSI workflow*

Azure TSI is a fully managed analytics solution in the cloud that provides storage, data visualization, and query services that help to explore and analyze various events of IoT concurrently in near real-time. It can optimize our time series data and its analysis and help detect hidden trends, recognize anomalies, and perform root-cause analysis (RCA) for various industry problem statements.

Azure Time Series Model

The Azure time series model is a core unit of Azure TSI, which helps us to collect, consolidate, manage, maintain, and improve time series datasets for analysis in the Azure environment.

The following are the major capabilities:

- Helping us to create and manage all mathematical calculation aspects, such as statistics and probability functions.
- Defining and provisioning the dataset relationship and instance

Components of Azure TSI and its major jobs

Azure TSI provides the following four components that are used to consume the data from various data sources to demonstrate the time series data analysis and use the data which is consumed through the IIoT and applications (event-based).

- **Integration**: Data integration activity from on-premises to the cloud environment is most significant. Azure TSI provides this facilitation extensively, especially by integrating the data generated using IIoT devices by allowing connection between two ends with the help of Azure IoT Hub with well-structured data in clean rows and columns format. The Azure Event Hub connects with the application and collects events from sources, and parses them in JSON format from the message queues, and converts them into structures that have data in clean rows and columns. It has the capability of linking and indexing the metadata along with data in a columnar store.
- **Storage**: Data from the on-premises are consumed in specific formats such as CSV, XML, and JSON structures, and following this, the data has to be cleaned, wrangled, and then stored in a columnar store. The Azure TSI also takes care of the fine-tuned data that is to be retained in the system by building visualization and querying the data. In Azure TSI data is stored on the SSD storage model by default with Data Lake Storage Gen2 and has a faster data retrieval and efficient data retention policy of 400 days, which supports querying the data historically for up to a period of 400 days.

- **Data Visualization:** With the help of integration and storage components, the required data is fetched from the on-premises data sources and stored in SSD storage as the columnar stores, then it is ready to build the visualization charts for easy visual analysis, Azure TSI provides this feature via TSI explorer.
- **Query Service:** However, the Azure TSI also provides a query service using TSI explorer and APIs, which are helping us to integrate your time series data into custom applications as a server layer.

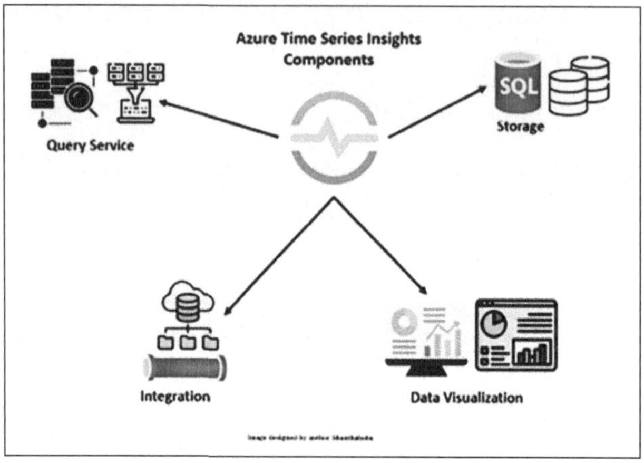

***Figure 10.2**: Components of Azure TSI*

Note: Azure TSI offers platform-as-a-service (PaaS), which will enable the collection of data, processing, and storing it appropriately, followed by analyzing and querying the data from IoT devices at different scales.

In Azure TSI, a Solid-State Device **(SSD)** storage model is used, and this is more advanced than HDD, in which all data is stored in flash-memory chips and here the data can be retained even without any power supply. There are no moving parts in it, and it is more energy-efficient and resistant to wear and tear.

Azure TSI – versions (Gen 1 and Gen 2)

The current Azure TSI version is Gen 2, earlier we had Gen 1, but the support for this version is until March 2025 (reference https://learn.microsoft.com/en-us/azure/time-series-insights/time-series-insights-overview).

Let's focus on Gen 2, instead of Gen 1.

Azure TSI Gen2 provides highly scalable and end-to-end solutions for IoT-specific analytics services with rich visualization and APIs to integrate customer applications.

Azure TSI Gen2 is responsible for fine-tuning the data with highly contextualized and optimized time series analysis and forecasting. It collects data faster from on-premises and processes it in appropriate techniques and stores it for the right usage purposes, and accelerates the building of complex queries and rich visualization charts from the data generated by various IoT devices and event-based applications.

Azure TSI Gen2 is designed to be very flexible and offers ad hoc data exploration and operational analysis such as suppressed trends and anomalies, as well as experiments root-cause analysis, which is a high need for industrial IoT deployments and enhancements.

The data generated by IoT/IIoT devices are collected, and stored by Azure TSI and used to build queries and visualize substantial amounts of time series data.

Azure TSI - Capabilities

In the Azure environment, each component has its capabilities, Azure TSI has its specific capabilities to fulfil the industry demands. *Figure* 10.3 shows the capabilities precisely.

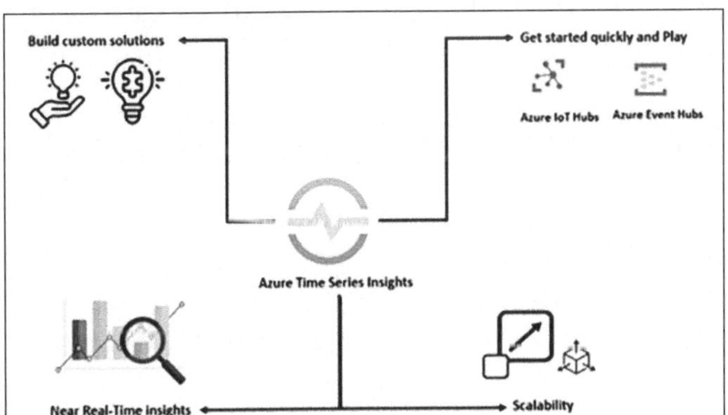

Figure 10.3: *Capabilities of Azure TSI*

- **Quick Start and Play:** Concerning Azure TSI, it doesn't require a straightforward data preparation process, it is much faster to connect to an IoT hub or Event hub with loads of events. After you get connected, you can start interacting with the sensor data, validate your IoT solutions, and visualize them without writing code. Azure TSI provides a very granulated, free-text query environment for users.
- **Near real-time insights analytics:** Azure TSI is capable of ingesting millions of data generated by IoT and application events per day with

very little latency. Azure TSI analytics helps you extract and explore insights from sensor data collected and stored. Ultimately, it is used to spot hidden trends and anomalies, do root-cause analysis experiments, and extremely avoid costly downtime which is the expensive capability of Azure TSI. It supports finding hidden trends in the data with the powerful features of cross-correlation techniques on top of historical and real-time data.

- **Innovative Custom Solutions:** By connecting Azure TSI with customer key application data, you can create new and innovative analytical custom solutions with Azure TSI's REST APIs. In the consuming layer, customers can explore insights and build new solutions through personalized visualization and exercise.
- **Scalability**: Azure TSI is designed to support IoT at different scales and retention spans. Ingress can range from 1 million to 100 million events per day, with a retention span of 31 days.

Note: In Azure TSI, we have the following components, with each performing a major task: integration, storage, data visualization, and Query Service. With the help of all these components, Azure TSI has excellent capabilities in the time series analysis domain, such as quick start and play with data, performing near real-time insights analytics, building new innovative custom solutions, and high scalability to existing solutions.

Exploring Azure TSI Data Storage

Azure TSI works very similarly to other storage like Azure SQL, Azure DW, and so on, along with the Azure Storage account. As we study the various aspects of the time series datasets that have to be for TSA&F, this is not exceptional in Azure and keeps some major considerations while storing data into Azure TSI.

Azure TSI facilitates two different storage capabilities to handle the data in a cloud environment, such as warm and cold storage with in-built Data Lake Storage Gen2, each storage has its strengths.

- **Cold storage:** We can create a new Azure storage resource as a usual method in the subscription and specific region based on our choice and attach the Azure TSI Gen2. IoT and Event data will be sent to cold storage at regular intervals, and this will be kept as two copies each in the Azure storage account in chronological order and stored in the Azure storage account indefinitely and partitioned appropriately to optimize high-performance queries during operations.

- **Warm storage:** This is optional storage so that it can be enabled or disabled based on the necessities. You can disable and utilize the data from cold storage where the data retention time can be configured between 7 and 31 days, and based on demand, we can adjust these timelines.

The data available in this storage is accessible through time series query APIs, TSI Explorer, or Power BI Connectors. Access charges are free of cost, and there are no allocated limits, but in one instance, only 30 concurrent requests are allowable.

Whenever warm storage is enabled, all available data is streamed into your environment regardless of event timestamp, and the streaming data ingestion pipeline is built in such a way as to ingest near-real-time streaming data and not historical data.

The data is no longer available in warm stores after the retention period has elapsed. The calculation of the retention period is based on when the event was indexed storage.

If you configure the retention period as 5 days, even if you store 8 days of data that is ingested and indexed, after 5 days you cannot access or perform any prediction for the data. but you can be queried from the cold storage.

Azure TSI Gen2 has well-partitioned and indexed data to optimize query performance. We know that if data is indexed, you can perform querying of your data from warm storage and cold storage.

We can configure alerts to be notifications when we process our data. The amount of data capturing, and processing speed might affect the data availability and number of partitions.

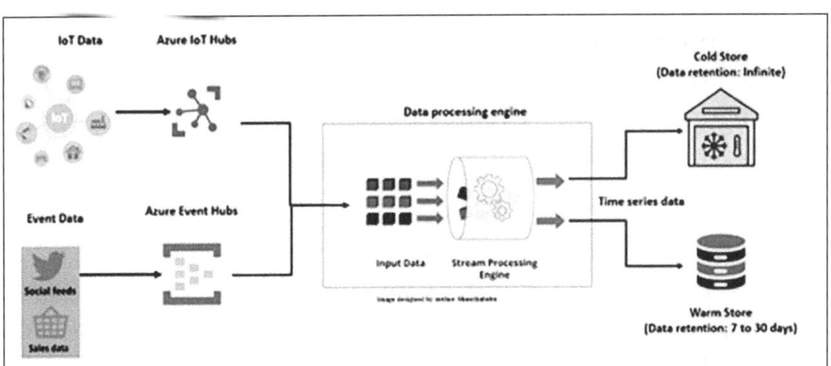

Figure 10.4: *Azure TSI data storage and process workflow*

Note: Azure TSI facilitates two different storage capabilities, such as **warm storage and cold storage.**

Cold storage: IoT and Event data will be sent to cold storage at regular intervals, and this will be kept as two copies each in the Azure storage account in chronological order and stored in the Azure storage account indefinitely and partitioned appropriately to optimize high-performance queries during operations.

Warm storage: This is optional storage so that it can be enabled or disabled based on the necessities. You can disable and utilize the data from cold storage. In this, the data retention time can be configured between 7 and 31 days.

High-level architecture of Azure TSI

Figure 10.5 shows the high-level architecture of Azure TSI implementation in a real-life state.

1. **Data Source**

   1a. Real-time data generated by manufacturing equipment, satellites, and medical devices are transmitted through IIoT devices along with time stamping for time series analysis.

   1b. Real-time data generated from various applications along with time stamping for time series analysis, the application would be social media, retail, and so on.

2. **Azure IoT Hub and Azure Event Hub**

   2a. Data transmitted from IIoT devices is such a way to be configured to fetch the Azure environment using Azure IoT Hub. It acts as a data integration pipeline to connect to the Azure TSI platform and devices. It fetches data from the source and delivers it to Azure TSI.

   2b. Data transfer from applications to specific events and such a way to be configured to fetch the Azure environment using Azure Event Hub. It acts as a data integration pipeline to connect to the Azure TSI platform and applications. It fetches data from the source and delivers it to Azure TSI.

3. **Azure Time Series Insights**

   Since Azure TSI has querying capability, the data in Azure TSI can be used to build various visualizations for analysis purposes. It provides line charts, sinusoidal charts, heat maps, and so on.

4. **Power BI**

   Additionally, the data can be utilized for high-quality and rich visualization development in a Power BI environment.

5. **Azure Databricks and Machine Learning**

   With Azure TSI as a serving layer, data can be further processed using Azure Databricks and Azure machine learning capabilities to build complex data analytics and models with real-time data as a part of stream analytics.

6. **Dashboard**

   Insights and intelligence –outcome from the overall architecture.

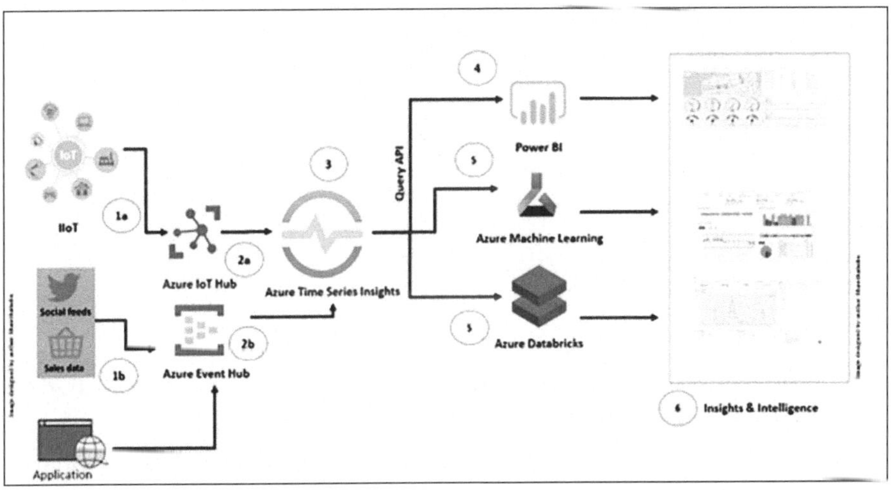

Figure 10.5: *High-level architecture of Azure TSI*

Benefits of Azure TSI Services:

- The major benefit is reducing the number of services, and architecture complexity and costs.
- It replaces Azure stream analytics services, Azure databases, and inbuilt storage Data Lake Storage Gen2.
- Data collection, preparation, and aggregation are simplified and support real-time analytics.
- Facilitating visualization features to build and preview the line graph and heat map.

- Provide a querying feature to access the data and expose the same via APIs.
- Avoiding costly downtime, which is the most expensive capability for Azure TSI.

Figure 10.6 shows the architectural modification – in near real-time streaming data analytics by introducing Azure Time Series Insights and replacing Azure Stream Analytics services with separate Azure SQL storage.

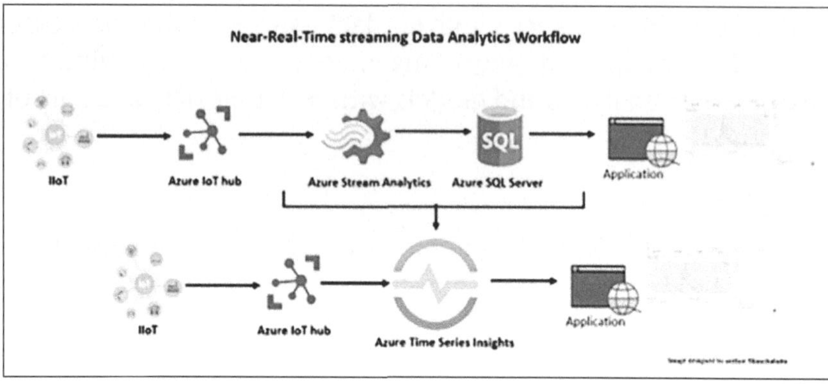

Figure 10.6: *Architectural modification using Azure Stream Analytics and Azure TSI (streaming data)*

Note:

- ✓ Benefits of Azure TSI Services:
- ✓ Reducing the number of services and architectural complexity and costs.
- ✓ It replaces Azure stream analytics services and Azure databases with inbuilt storage Data Lake Storage Gen2.
- ✓ Simplified data processing systems and support real-time analytics.
- ✓ Provide visualization, querying features to access the data via APIs.
- ✓ Avoid costly downtime which is an expensive capability for Azure TSI.

Creating Azure IoT hub instance

Follow these steps to create an Azure IoT hub:

1. Log into Azure Portal
2. You will land on the Azure portal, as shown in Figure 10.7:

***Figure 10.7**: Azure Environment*

3. You can search for your required Azure services/components in the search textbox or click from the available list.
4. Click **`Azure IoT Hub`** 

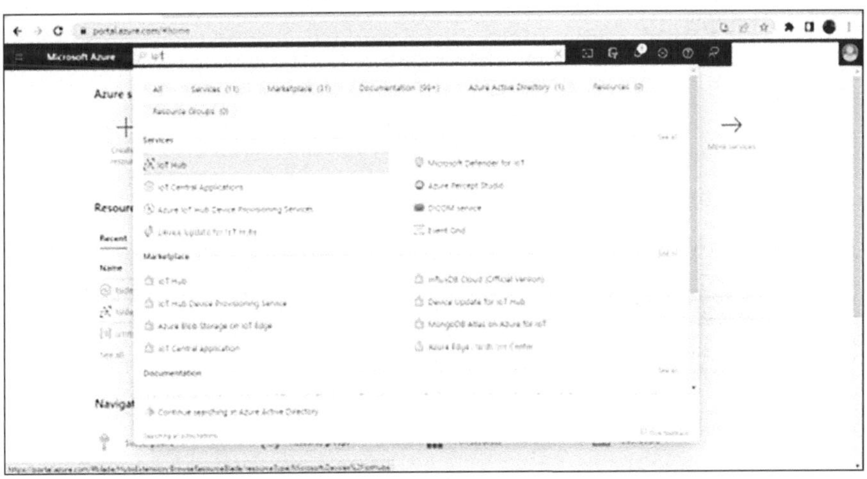

***Figure 10.8:** Azure IoT Hub Search in Azure portal*

5. Once you click the Azure IoT Hub icon from the previous screen, the portal will take you to the IoT Hub workspace, there you can see the list of existing IoT Hubs and provisioning to create new IoT Hubs also.
6. Click **`+ Create`** menu

Figure 10.9: *Azure IoT Hub Environment*

7. Once you click the create Azure IoT Hub menu, the portal will take you to the IoT Hub configuration screen, there you will have to provide the following details:

a. Resource Group

b. IoT hub name

c. Tire

d. Daily Message Limit

8. Resource group (Select the required resource group from the list)

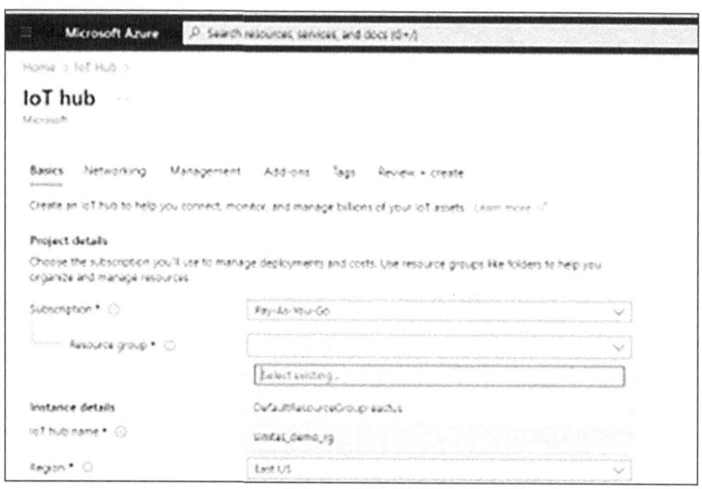

Figure 10.10: *Azure IoT Hub - Configuration – Resource group*

9. We need to provide a valid IoT hub name

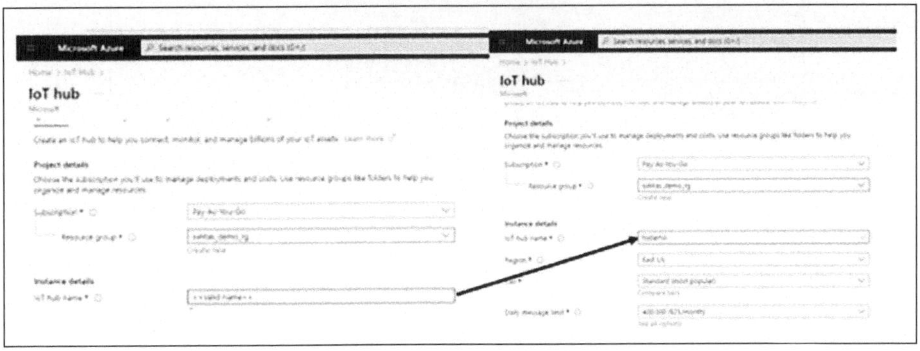

Figure 10.11: *Azure IoT Hub - Configuration – Instance name*

10. We have to select the appropriate `Tier` type from the list:

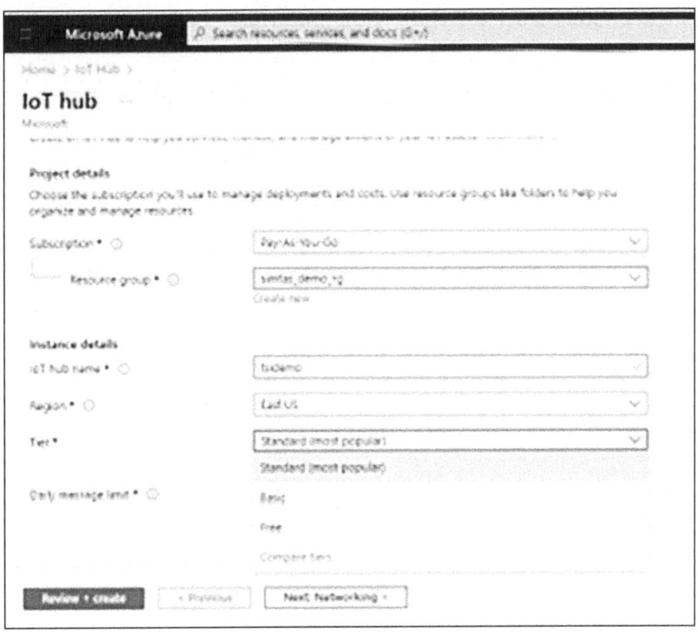

Figure 10.12: *Azure IoT Hub - Configuration – Tier selection*

11. We have to select the appropriate `Daily message limit:`

Figure 10.13: *Azure IoT Hub - Configuration – Daily message limit*

12. Once all configurations are completed, click the **`Create`** button.
13. Azure portal will validate all configurations and will take a few seconds to complete.

Figure 10.14: *Azure IoT Hub - Configuration completed and ready to create and deploy*

14. Once the validation is done successfully, click the **`Create`** button the Azure portal will be initializing the deployment process and validate all configurations, which will take a few seconds to complete.

Figure 10.15: *Azure IoT Hub - Configuration completed and deployment initializing*

15. **`Deployment`** in-process

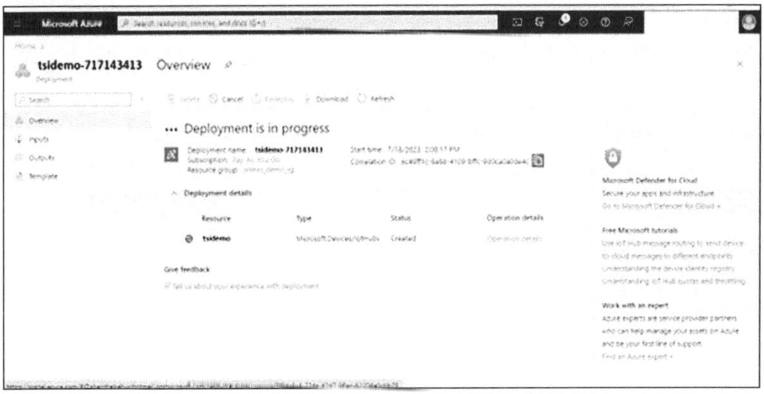

Figure 10.16: *Azure IoT Hub - Configuration completed and deployment in progress*

16. **`Deployment`** completed and ready to use

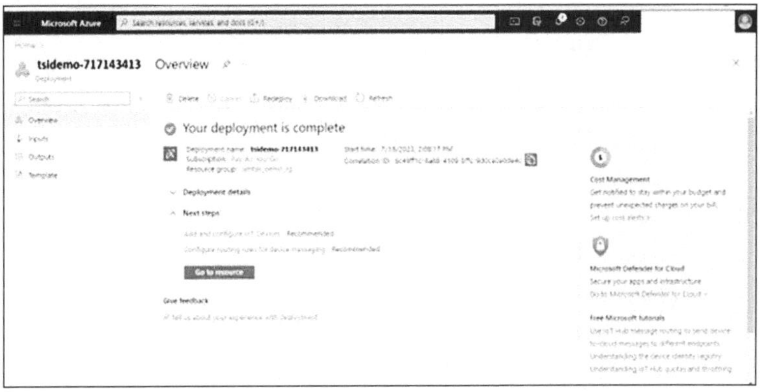

Figure 10.17: *Azure IoT Hub - Configuration completed and deployment completed*

17. Click **`Go to resource`**, which will take you to the newly created IoT Hub component.

Figure 10.18: *Azure IoT Hub - Go to resource and add IoT/Event devices*

18. Azure IoT Hub is ready to be configured with devices.

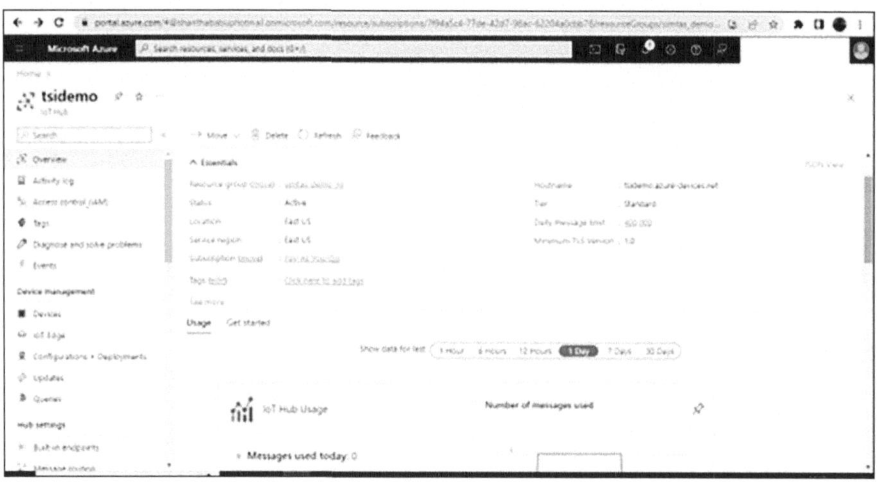

Figure 10.19: *Azure IoT Hub (tsidemo) – ready to add devices*

19. Click **`Devices`** in the left panel menu and the portal will take you to the devices list panel, either you can use any device or create a new device and configure it.

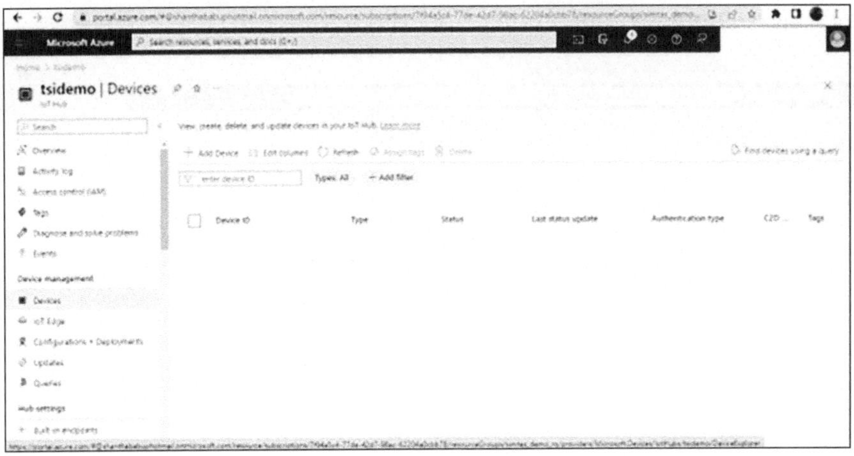

Figure 10.20: *Azure IoT Hub (tsidemo) –Devices addition environment*

20. Once you click the Add Device menu, the portal will take you to the device configuration screen. You have to configure the following details and click the **Save** button:
    a. Device ID (Device identity used for device authentication and access control)
    b. Authentication type (Symmetric keys must be in valid base-64 format with a key length of between 16 and 64 bytes.)
    c. Connect the device to an IoT hub (Enable or Disable the device's interaction with the IoT Hub)
    d. Parent devices (IoT Edge devices can be parents for child IoT devices. Child devices can communicate with an IoT hub through the parent device.)

Figure 10.21: *Azure IoT Hub (tsidemo) –Devices Configuration*

21. Device **AAAAA** is ready and connected with Azure IoT **`tsidemo`**

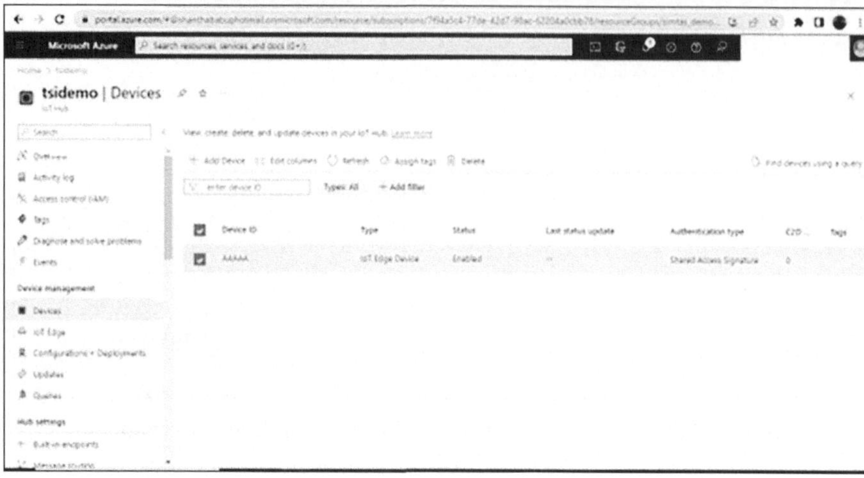

Figure 10.22: *Azure IoT Hub (tsidemo) –Devices (AAAAA) is ready*

22. Device **AAAAA** is ready and connected with Azure IoT **`tsidemo`**

Figure 10.23: *Device (**AAAAA**) is connected with Azure IoT Hub (**`tsidemo`**)*

Creating Azure TSI Gen2 environment

Let's follow the steps to create an Azure TSI environment:

1. Log into Azure Portal
2. You will land on the Azure portal as shown in *Figure* 10.24:

Figure 10.24: *Azure Environment*

3. You can search Azure TSI in the search text box, and you will get the TSI from the list as shown in Figure 10.25:

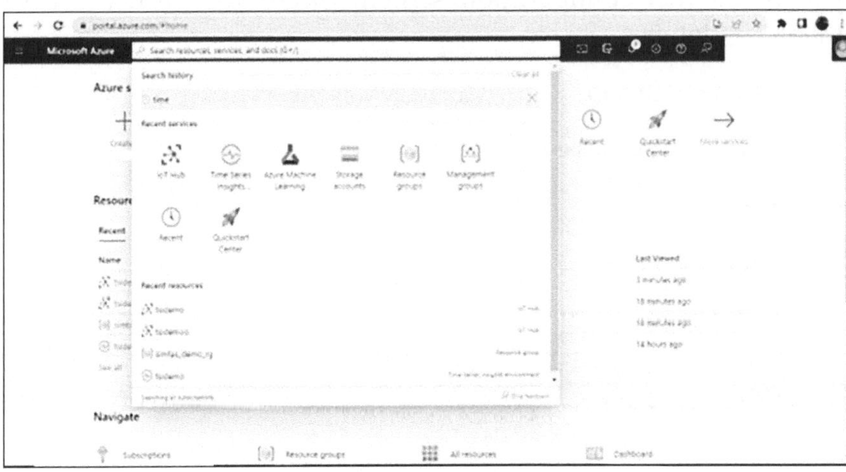

Figure 10.25: *Azure TSI Search in Azure portal*

4. Once you click the Azure TSI from the list on the previous screen, the portal will take you to the TSI environment, there you can see the list of existing TSI and provisioning to create new TSI.
5. Click **`+ Create`** menu

Figure 10.26: *Azure TSI Environment*

6. Once you click the create in Azure TSI environment, the portal will take you to the TSI configuration screen, where you have to provide the following details:
   a. **`Resource Group`**
   b. **`Environment name`**
   c. **`Tire`**
   d. **`Property name`**
   e. **`Cold store`**

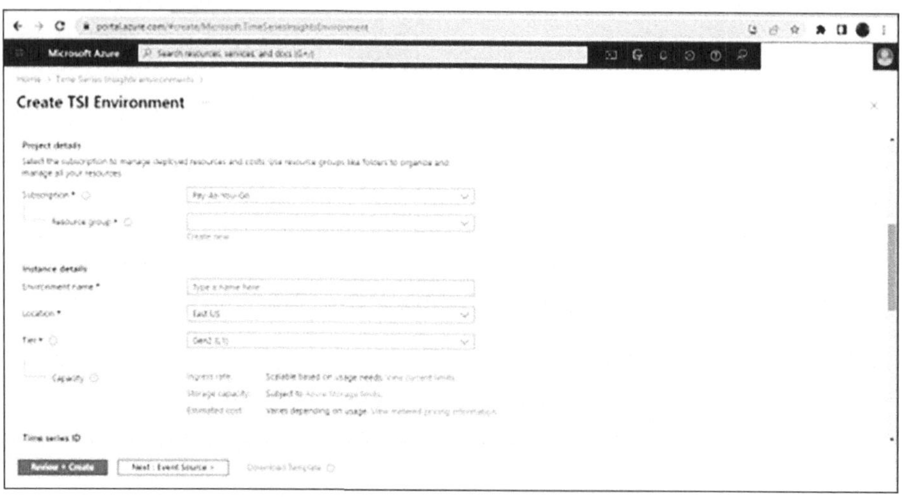

Figure 10.27: *Azure TSI Configuration*

7. **`Resource group`** (Select the required resource group from the list)

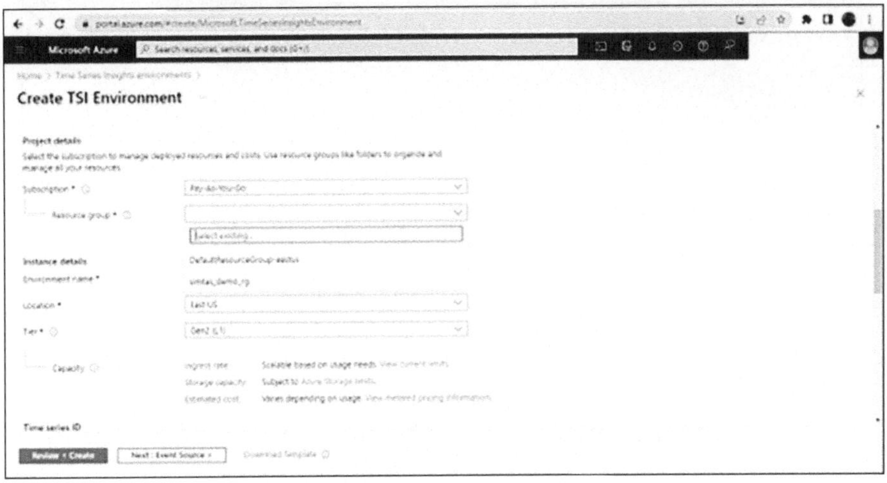

Figure 10.28: *Azure TSI Configuration – Resource group*

8. We need to provide a valid **`Environment name`** and **`Tier`** (Gen2)

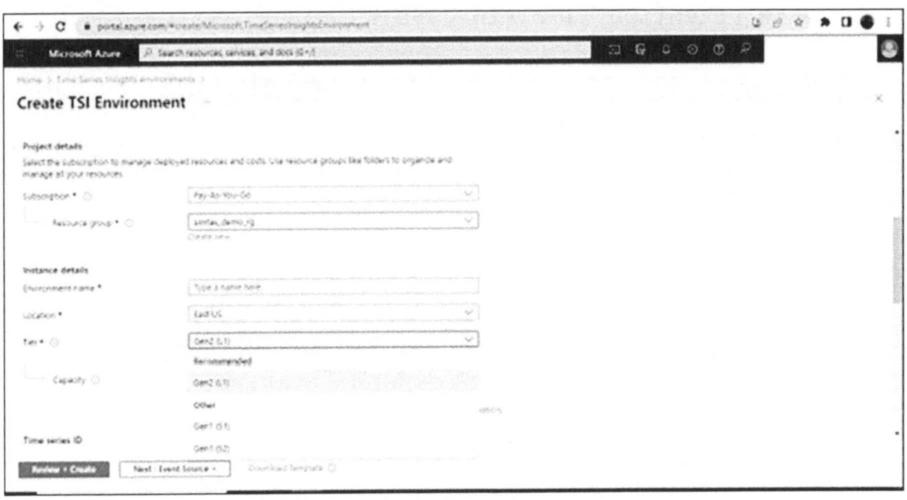

Figure 10.29: *Azure TSI Configuration – Tier*

9. We need to configure the cold storage appropriately:

    a. **`Storage account name`**

    b. **`Storage account kind`**

    c. **`Storage account replication`**

    d. **`Data Lake Storage Gen2`** **`(Enabled/Disabled)`**

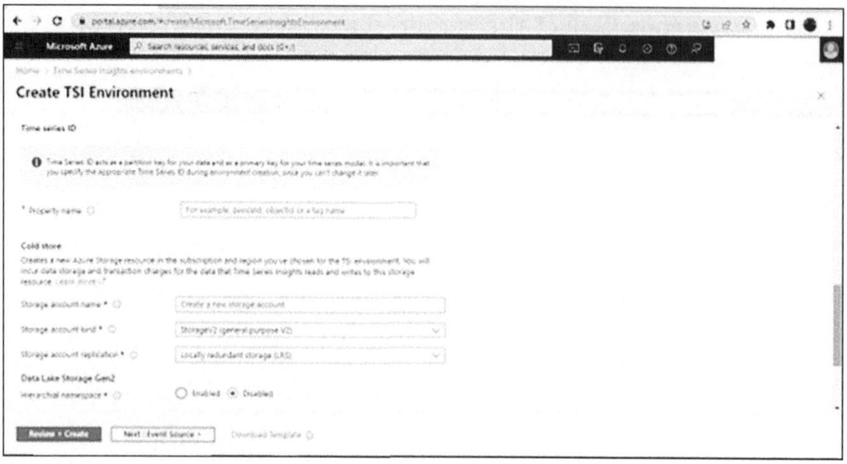

Figure 10.30: Azure TSI *Configuration – cold storage*

10. We need to configure the warm storage appropriately:
    a. **`Enable warm store`** (**Yes/No**)
    b. **`Data retention time (in days)`**

Figure 10.31: Azure TSI *Configuration – warm storage (default)*

11. Configured warm storage for 20 days

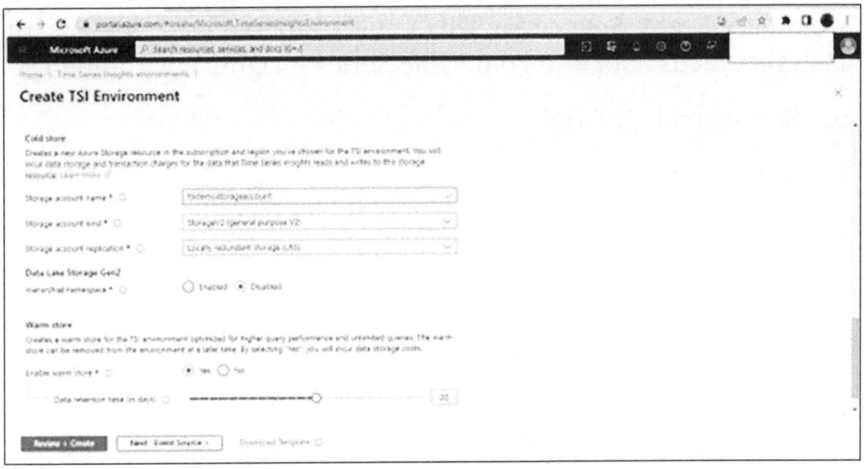

Figure 10.32: Azure TSI *Configuration – warm storage (for 20 days)*

12. Configure **Event Source** for TSI (An event source is the IoT Hub or Event Hub that feeds data into your Time Series Insights environment.)
    a. Source Type: IoT/Event
    b. Name
    c. IoT/Event Hub Name
    d. IoT/Event access policy name
    e. IoT/Event consumer group
    f. Start options and Timestamp

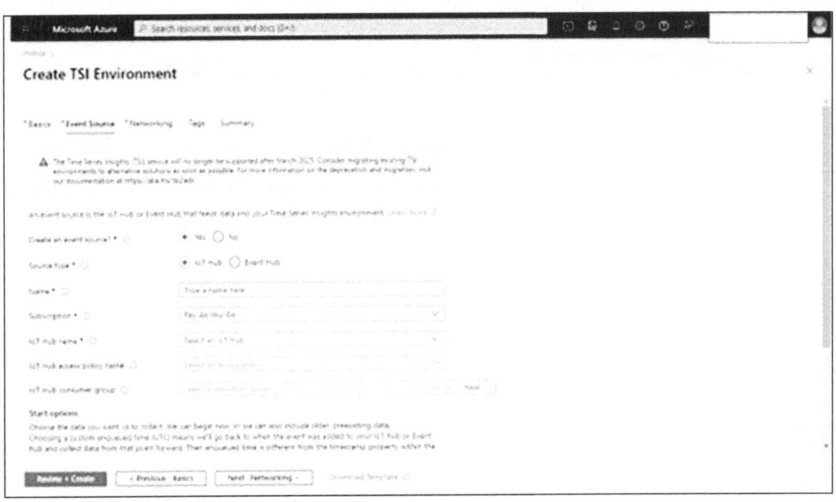

Figure 10.33: Azure TSI *Configuration – Event Source (default settings)*

13. Configure **Event Source** for TSI (An event source is the IoT Hub or Event Hub that feeds data into your Time Series Insights environment.)
    a. Source type: IoT Hub
    b. Name: **testtsidemo**
    c. IoT/Event Hub Name: **tsidemo**
    d. IoT/Event Access Policy Name: **Device**
    e. IoT/Event Consumer Group: **$Default**
    f. Start options and Timestamp: appropriately

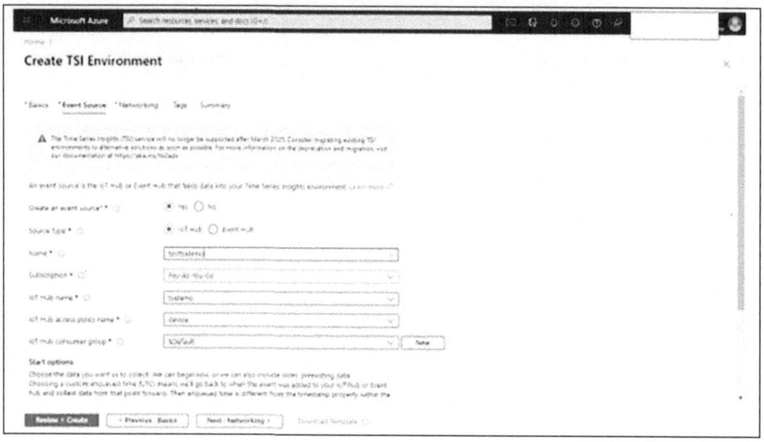

Figure 10.34: Azure TSI *Configuration – Event Source (name of IoT Hub and other details)*

14. Click **Review + Create** button.

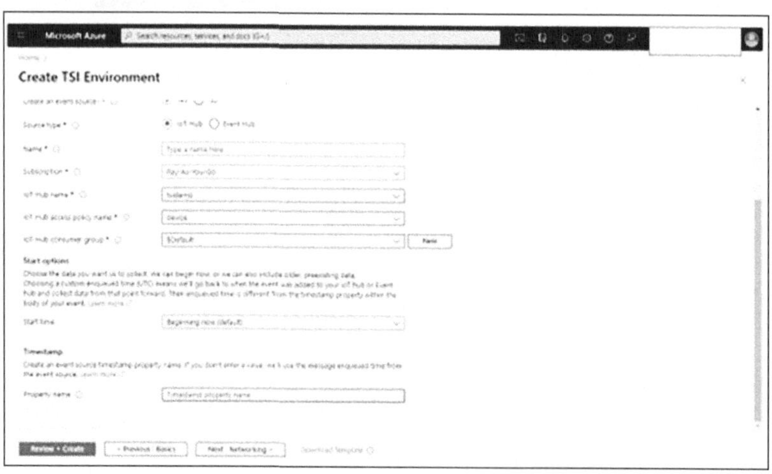

Figure 10.35: Azure TSI *Configuration –completed*

15. After clicking the **Review + Create** button, the portal will review the configuration and submit it for deployment.

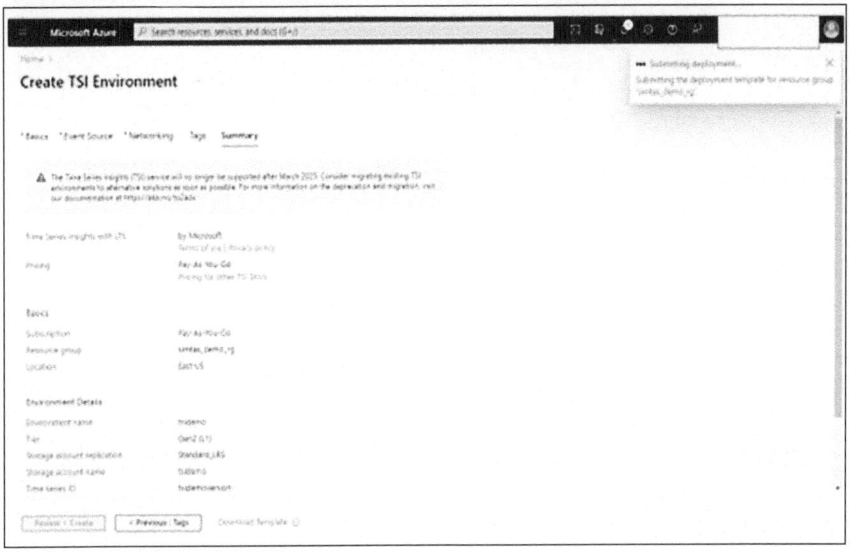

Figure 10.36: *Azure TSI Configuration –Review and Deployment Initialization*

16. **Deployment is in progress**

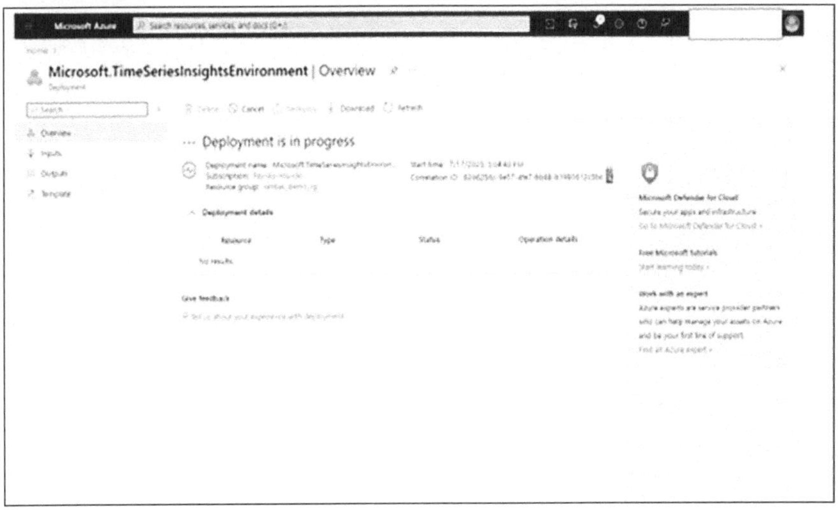

Figure 10.37: *Azure TSI Configuration –Review completed and Deployment in progress*

17. Deployment completed

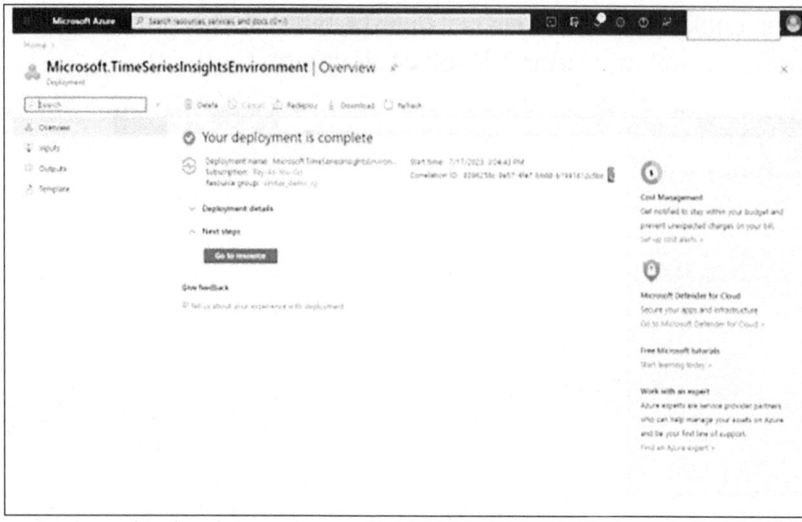

Figure 10.38: *Azure TSI Configuration –Review and Deployment completed*

18. Azure TSI Environment is ready

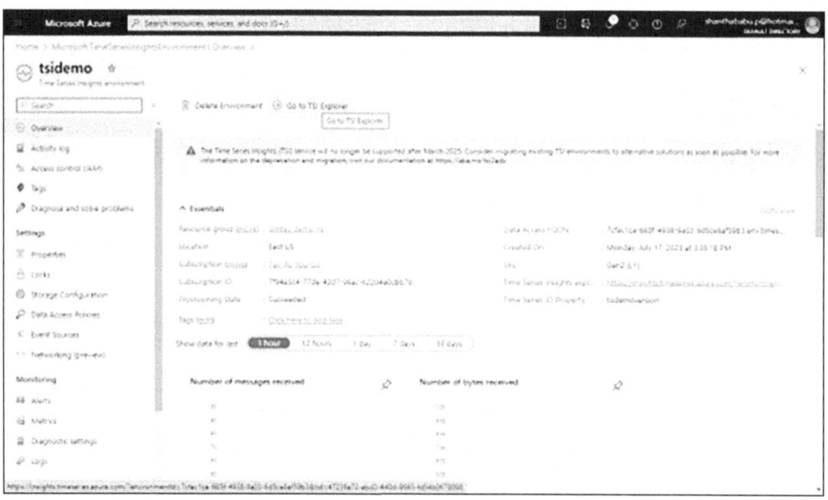

Figure 10.39: *Azure TSI (tsidemo) is ready to use*

19. Azure TSI Environment configuration check

Figure 10.40: *Azure TSI (tsidemo) configuration check*

Exploring Azure TSI Explorer

Azure TSI is a fully managed environment to explore and analyze billions of IoT and Events instantaneously.

Azure TSI Explorer consists of the following seven elements:

- **Environment Panel**: This is used to display all your Azure TSI environments.
- **Navigation Bar**: This will help us switch between the Model and Analyze pages.
- **Hierarchy Tree and Search Panel**: This helps us to select and search for specific data elements to be mapped.
- **Time Series Well**: This will show the currently selected data elements.
- **Chart Panel**: This will show the current working chart.
- **Timeline**: This will help us modify our working period for data elements and chart.
- **App Bar**: It provides user management options and permits us to change them and settings.

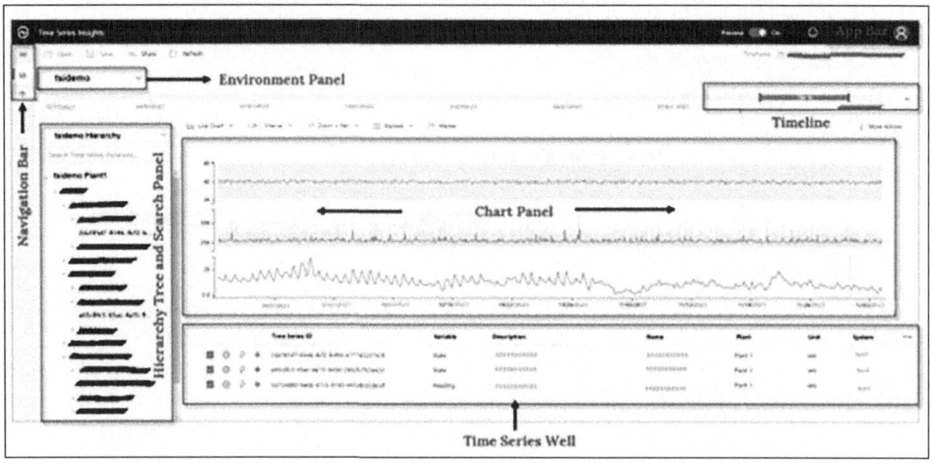

Figure 10.41: *Azure TSI Explorer*

Figure 10.42 shows the various visualization prepared in the Azure TSI Explorer environment.

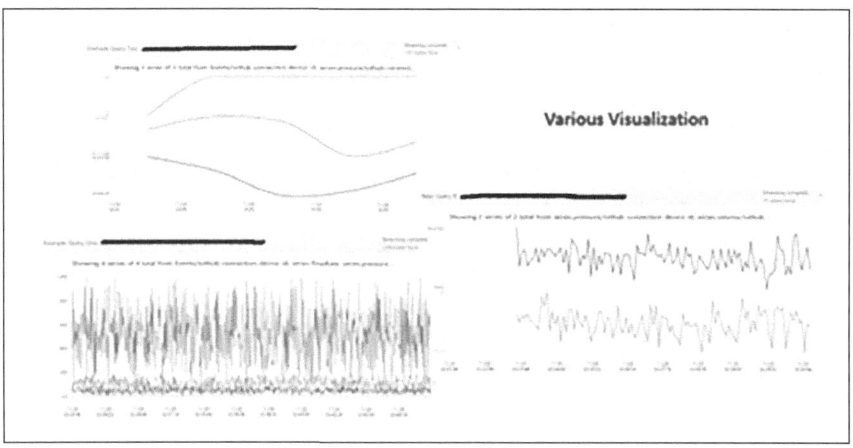

Figure 10.42: *Azure TSI Explorer – various visualization*

Azure TSI Gen2 provides the following panel needed to select the period to build the visualization.

Figure 10.43: *Azure TSI Explorer – panel*

With the help of Azure TSI Explorer, we were able to build various visualization charts from the data which is received from Azure IoT Hub and Azure Event Hub.

Querying on the data from the Azure TSI environment using C#, Please refer to the Microsoft link: https://learn.microsoft.com/en-us/azure/time-series-insights/time-series-insights-update-query-data-csharp

Conclusion

In this chapter, we have discussed the detailed studies of Azure Time Series Insights (TSI) and its significance in the industry, and how this is compact and handy to handle data from IoT and event-based applications. We explored how Azure TSI Gen2 is configured for analytics services for various data analytics functions, especially time series analysis.

We discussed components of Azure TSI and its major jobs separately in terms of integration, storage, data visualization, and query service explicitly.

We investigated Azure TSI's capabilities and benefited extensively with detail on each sub-topic as a quick start and play, near real-time insights analytics, innovative custom solutions, and scalability aspects.

We understood how Azure TSI data storage works and its categories with neat sketches and deep elaboration of cold storage and warm storage.

We discussed the high-level architecture of Azure TSI implementation from an industry point of view from end-to-end.

We walked through very detailed steps on how to create an Azure IoT hub instance and Azure TSI Gen2 environment, integrate them, and explore Azure TSI Explorer.

This chapter will provide a solid understanding of Azure TSI and its architectural benefits and capabilities from a time series analysis perspective.

In the next chapter, we will discuss **Amazon Forecast** services and their significance. We will explore the features and capabilities of the Amazon Forecast and how it helps in the time series forecasting space. We will also focus on Amazon Forecast best practices.

Points to remember

In this chapter, it is important to keep a few things in mind that will be handy throughout this book:

- Azure TSI Gen2 is an analytics service designed specifically for Industrial Internet of Things (IIoT) deployments.
- Azure TSI provides a set of powerful APIs for explicit industry manufacturing data from shop floor applications to integrate with the current workflow stream to demonstrate various data analytics functions, especially time series analysis.
- Azure TSI collects and stores the data and processes it, followed by querying and building various visualization of IoT data at different levels of scaling.
- The major components of Azure TSI are as follows:
    - Integration
    - Storage
    - Data Visualization
    - Query Service
- Azure TSI – Capabilities
    - Quick Start and Play
    - Near real-time insights analytics
    - Innovative Custom Solutions
    - Scalability
- In Azure TSI data is stored on the SSD storage model by default with Data Lake Storage Gen2 and has a faster data retrieval and efficient data retention policy of 400 days, which supports querying the data historically for up to 400 days.
    - Cold storage
    - Warm storage (7-31 days)
- Azure TSI - High-level architecture consists of the following blocks:
    - Data Source
    - Azure IoT Hub and Azure Event Hub
    - Azure Time Series Insights
    - Power BI

  - Azure Databricks and Machine Learning
  - Dashboard
- Benefits of Azure TSI Services:
  - Simplified architecture and cost reduced
  - Shortened the process of data collection, preparation, aggregation, and support for real-time analytics.
  - Facilitating visualization features
  - Data exposure via powerful APIs
  - Avoid costly downtime

Chapter 11
AWS Forecast

Introduction

In the previous chapter, we discussed detailed studies of the Microsoft Azure time series insights component and its significance. We learned how Azure TSI is functioning as a fully managed analytics, storage, and visualization service for near real-time data from IoT and how to scale them in the cloud environment for industry benefits. We further discussed Azure time series insights Gen2 for industrial IoT concerning various industries. The chapter also covered data exploration and visual anomaly detection using Azure Time Series Insights. At the end of the chapter, we learned best practices for planning and preparation for Azure time series insights Gen2 environment. We also made a comparison of Gen1 and Gen2 and explored a list of capabilities, key benefits, and key jobs.

This chapter will help readers to understand the Amazon Forecast and its significance. We will gain an understanding of how Amazon Forecast works and study the features of Amazon Forecast, exploring Time Series Forecasting principles using Amazon Forecast. We will learn to set up Permissions for Amazon Forecast. Wake through importing, building, evaluating, and cleaning processes in the Amazon Forecast. The chapter also entails a discussion on Amazon Forecast algorithms along with best practices of Amazon Forecast. Finally, we will prepare and clean data for the Amazon Forecast.

Structure

In this chapter, we will discuss the following topics:

- Understanding Amazon Forecast
- How the Amazon Forecast works
- Major features of Amazon Forecast
- Setup Amazon Forecast

- Amazon Forecast algorithms
- Best practices

Prerequisites

Concerning the chapter, we assume that the readers understand cloud environments such as Azure and AWS because *Chapter 10, Azure Time Series Insights* and *Chapter 11, AWS Forecast* focus on time series-based components. Let's discuss them in detail.

Understanding Amazon Forecast Service (AFS)

We discussed many forecasting techniques in all our previous chapters, accuracy is important when making any business decisions and eventually, it helps us to grow our business. Even if we have specific services to help us achieve minimal effort then that could be additional cost and time saving for us. This is one of the important strategies from AWS implementing Amazon Forecast specifically for time series analysis and forecasting.

At a high-level of understanding, Amazon Forecast uses a machine learning algorithm and set of processes internally to help us forecast future business outcomes such as buyers, sellers, resource plans, product demand in the market, and overall financial performance. Internally, it detects patterns and makes predictions for future forecasts for various aspects, including trending, seasonality, customer expansion, and capturing new customers in the market.

Amazon Forecast is a fully managed service that builds a way to use statistical and machine learning algorithms on historical and near real-time data to deliver substantially accurate time-series forecasts without any machine learning experience at hand.

As discussed, there are many use cases in *Chapter 4: Time Series Analysis and Forecasting Opportunities in various industries*, including banking, finance, logistics, retail, and healthcare. You can also use forecasts to predict domain-specific metrics.

Amazon Forecast services include multiple statistical algorithms, such as Exponential Smoothing, ARMA, ARIMA, and Non-Parametric Time Series (NPTS), and from the "Deep Learning" algorithm family, it includes DeepAR+ and CNN-QR (Quantile regression version of CNN).

Workflow for Amazon Forecast Service

Amazon Forecast workflow is typically similar to Machine Learning workflow and has various stages as shown in *Figure 11.1*:

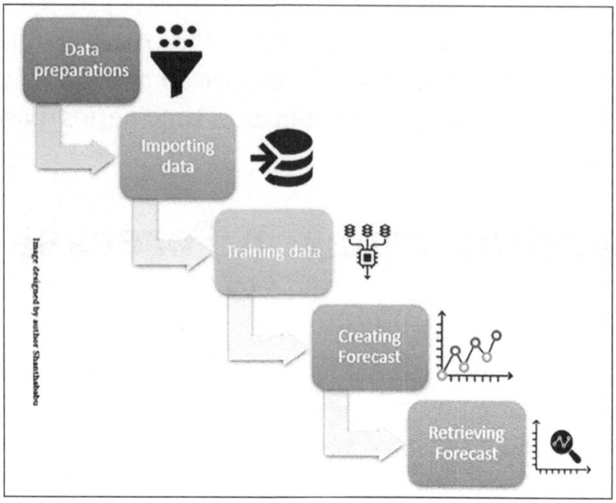

Figure 11.1: *Workflow of Amazon Forecast*

Figure 11.2 shows the high-level architecture for Amazon Forecasting using AWS components:

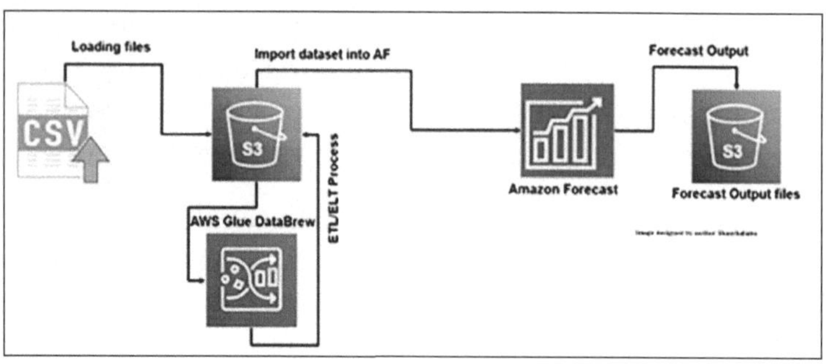

Figure 11.2: *High-level architecture for Amazon Forecasting using AWS components*

Data Preparations

All data analytics and machine learning data preparation are considered under stage -1. Even in the Amazon Forecast workflow, data preparation is a major task when you are preparing time series data sets. It is a time-consuming process because the quality time series is the critical representation of the forecasting to derive the accuracy.

In AFS, the input data collections are called **Dataset Groups**, this is a logical container to organize your input datasets, predictors, and forecasts. This container is used to train your forecasting model and is called **Predictors**.

Each **Dataset Group** can have a maximum of four or less than four datasets, which are as follows:

- Target Time Series Dataset
- Related Time Series Dataset (optional)
- Item Metadata Dataset (optional)
- Featurization Datasets (optional)

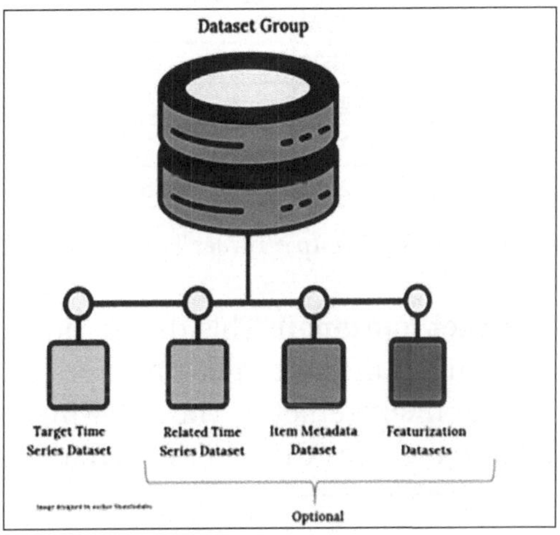

Figure 11.3: *Amazon Forecast – Dataset Group*

Target Time Series Dataset: This dataset is a historical time-series data input that includes target features, key observations, events, and timestamps. This dataset is mandatory as it indicates the target field that we need to forecast. *Figure* 11.4 shows the sample dataset for the target time series dataset for our purpose.

DATE	Diesel_price
16-04-2022	5
17-04-2022	6
18-04-2022	5.6
19-04-2022	5.12
20-04-2022	5.1
21-04-2022	5.34
22-04-2022	5.45
23-04-2022	4
24-04-2022	6.17
25-04-2022	4.6
26-04-2022	3.2
27-04-2022	5.13
28-04-2022	4.99
29-04-2022	5.2
30-04-2022	6.08

Figure 11.4: *Dataset Group - Target Time Series Dataset*

Related Time Series Dataset (optional): This dataset includes additional time-series data that is not included in the target time series dataset, which might enhance the accuracy of our final predictor. The following dataset has the related time series dataset and also includes the additional dimensions.

DATE	Diesel_price	Location
16-04-2022	5	NewYork
17-04-2022	6	NewYork
18-04-2022	5.6	Chicago
19-04-2022	5.12	Houston
20-04-2022	5.1	San Francisco
21-04-2022	5.34	Philadelphia
22-04-2022	5.45	San Diego
23-04-2022	4	NewYork
24-04-2022	6.17	Chicago
25-04-2022	4.6	Chicago
26-04-2022	3.2	San Francisco
27-04-2022	5.13	San Francisco
28-04-2022	4.99	Philadelphia
29-04-2022	5.2	Philadelphia
30-04-2022	6.08	Chicago
01-05-2022	5.95	Houston
02-05-2022	5.13	Houston
03-05-2022	4.8	San Diego

Figure 11.5: *Dataset Group - Related Time Series Dataset*

Item Metadata Dataset (optional): This type of dataset contains categorical features of either one or more of the data in the dataset that offers valuable background for the items in the target time-series dataset. The value of data has remained constant over the period. As we mentioned before, this type of dataset is optional, and value is added to dataset groups for detailed analysis. It includes metadata information about the target time or related time series datasets as dimension factors.

In our case, the Geographical Boundaries and Geographical Boundaries code act as metadata for the target column in diesel pricing.

DATE	Diesel_price	Geographical Boundarie	Geographical Boundary Cod
16-04-2022	5	NewYork	1
17-04-2022	6	NewYork	1
18-04-2022	5.6	Chicago	2
19-04-2022	5.12	Dallas	3
20-04-2022	5.1	San Francisco	4
21-04-2022	5.34	Philadelphia	5
22-04-2022	5.45	St. Louis	6
23-04-2022	4	NewYork	1
24-04-2022	6.17	Chicago	2
25-04-2022	4.6	Chicago	2
26-04-2022	3.2	San Francisco	4
27-04-2022	5.13	San Francisco	4
28-04-2022	4.99	Philadelphia	5
29-04-2022	5.2	Philadelphia	5
30-04-2022	6.08	Chicago	2

Figure 11.6: *Dataset Group - Item Metadata Dataset*

Featurization Datasets (optional): These datasets are built-in related time series for each item based on location or geographical boundaries mentioned in the preceding *Figure* 11.6.

Amazon Forecast offers the following types of featurization datasets:

- Holiday Featurization
    - List of holiday information based on location
- Weather Index
    - List of weather information based on location

Dataset Guidelines for Forecast

When preparing a dataset for Amazon Forecast, we must follow standards, best practices, and guidelines for a successful dataset import process, which includes following guidelines.

File Format

- It supports the following formats:
  - Comma-Separated Values (CSV) format (default)
  - Parquet format

File Name

File naming is the usual format.

- Must contain at least one alphabetic character in the file name.
- Names shouldn't contain numeric alone.

File Partitioned

- It doesn't support file partitioning for processing data, especially Parquet files.

Dataset Header

- Headers in CSV files are advisable to ignore during the process.
- Header is mandatory for Parquet files.
- Values shouldn't be separated using colons, tabs, spaces, or any other characters, only comma is allowed

Dataset Status

- Status of the dataset must be ACTIVE before importing and training operations.

Data Format and Timestamp

Amazon Forecast services supports the standard timestamp format "yyyy-MM-dd" along with the "HH:mm: ss" is optional. For example, 2023-01-02 20:10:00

Order of Attributes in the dataset

The order of the attributes indicated in the **Schema Definition** should match the order of the column in the input file that you are importing. Applicable for both CSV and Parquet files

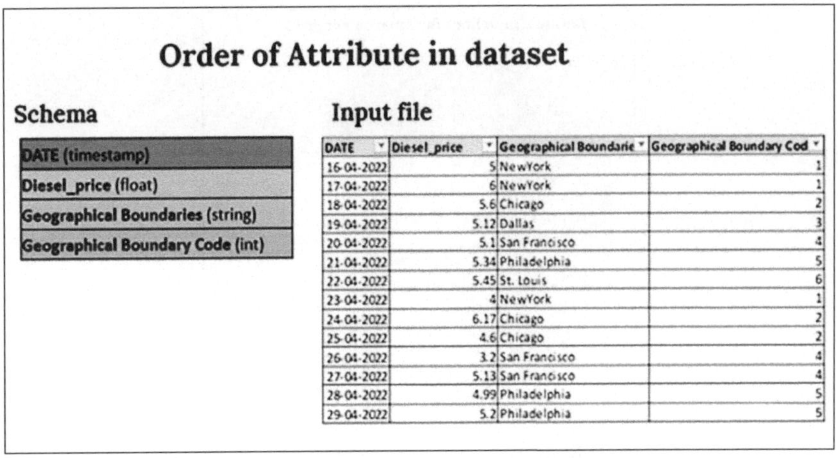

DATE	Diesel_price	Geographical Boundarie	Geographical Boundary Cod
16-04-2022	5	NewYork	1
17-04-2022	6	NewYork	1
18-04-2022	5.6	Chicago	2
19-04-2022	5.12	Dallas	3
20-04-2022	5.1	San Francisco	4
21-04-2022	5.34	Philadelphia	5
22-04-2022	5.45	St. Louis	6
23-04-2022	4	NewYork	1
24-04-2022	6.17	Chicago	2
25-04-2022	4.6	Chicago	2
26-04-2022	3.2	San Francisco	4
27-04-2022	5.13	San Francisco	4
28-04-2022	4.99	Philadelphia	5
29-04-2022	5.2	Philadelphia	5

Figure 11.7: *Order of Attributes in the dataset*

Dataset Updates: The dataset import task has to be taken care of based on the following scenarios in the Amazon Forecast "Full and Incremental" dataset updates:

- **Full Dataset Updates**
  - When importing a dataset into Amazon Forecast for the first time, that should always be a full import process, and the subsequent imports can either be a full or incremental dataset update process.
  - Once you perform the full update, the entire dataset will be replaced with the newly imported data.
- **Incremental Dataset Updates**
  - When you are doing the incremental process, the key information will be read from the currently active dataset, including columns such as timestamp, and geolocation. Do not include all this information with this incremental dataset update.
  - In both cases, we have to specify the import mode in "Forecast API".

Geolocation Information in the dataset

When you are using "Weather Index" in your dataset, you must include a geolocation attribute, and it is advisable to relate your time series datasets. This attribute should be defined with schemas in the geolocation attribute type. This geolocation will be in two different formats, as follows:

- Postal Code or Pin Code – Depends on the specific country
- Latitude and Longitude - Latitude and longitude in decimal format

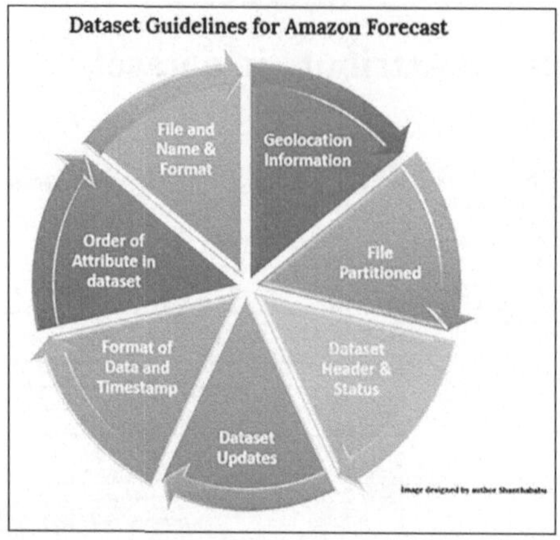

Figure 11.8: *Amazon Forecast – Dataset Guidelines*

Quality of Data

The quality of the data plays a vital role in data science and machine learning because it affects the outcome of the prediction and forecasting. Amazon Forecast can help us to deal with these challenges to some extent. This is a simple exercise using a histogram chart and evaluating the following specifically for time series datasets.

The density of the dataset: If the density of the data is higher, then the forecasting is more accurate, other forecasting will be a channeling task. Ultimately, this will help us identify the population of data points, missing values, and concentrations. We can identify this with a simple histogram chart, as shown in *Figure* 11.9.

Refer to *Chapter 2: Python for Time Series Data Analysis*, for more information about the data cleansing and preparation, and EDA process.

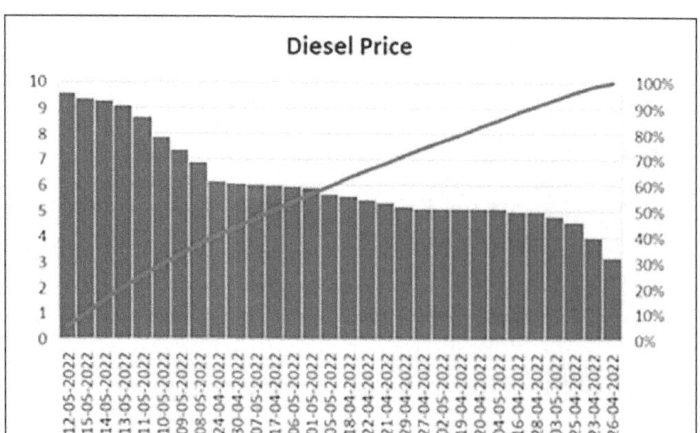

Figure 11.9: *Density of the dataset*

Importing data

Figure 11.10 shows the Amazon Forecast dataset group:

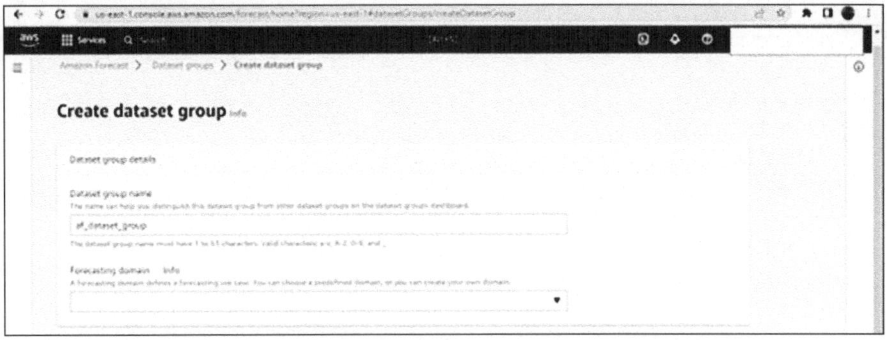

Figure 11.10: *Amazon Forecast dataset group*

Figure 11.11 shows the Amazon Forecast dataset group along with the available forecasting domains:

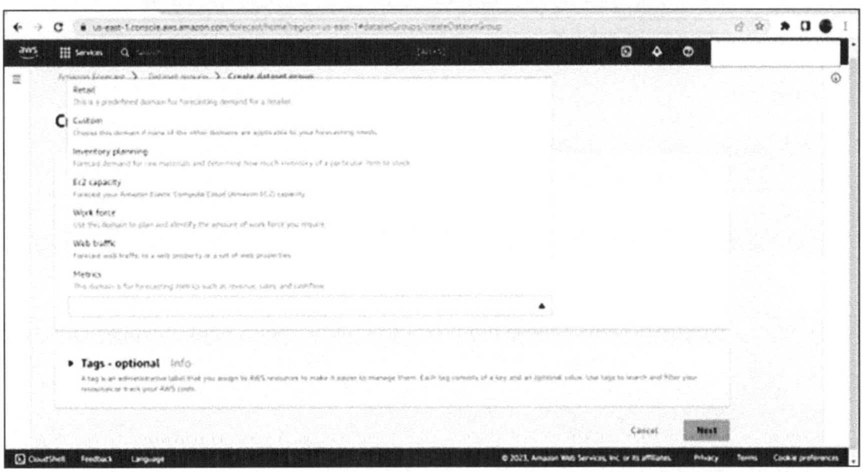

Figure 11.11: *Amazon Forecast dataset group – available forecasting domain*

Figure 11.12 shows the Amazon Forecast dataset group configuration:

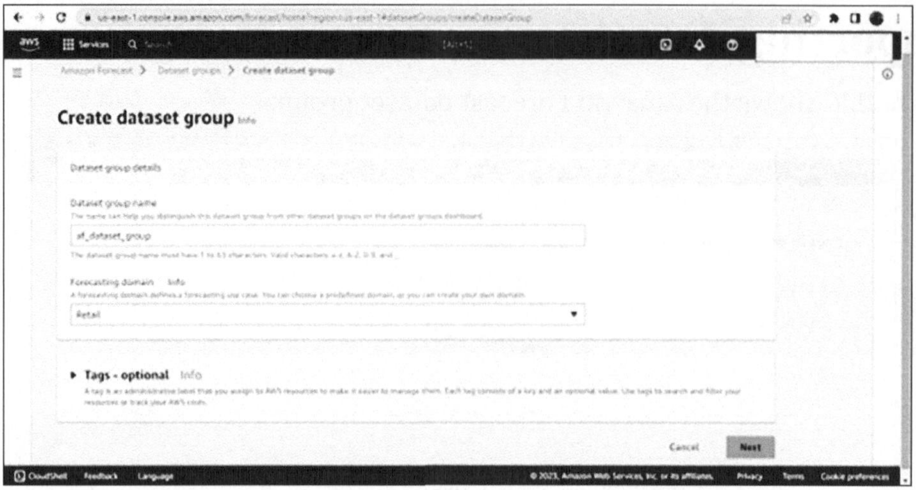

Figure 11.12: *Amazon Forecast dataset group – configuration*

Figure 11.13 shows the Amazon Forecast dataset details configuration:

Figure 11.13: *Amazon Forecast dataset details– configuration*

In the Amazon Forecast, we can create a dataset group using a console or API (CreateDataset) along with the following details:

- Frequency or interval
- Time zone information
- Domain or Custom domain
- (AF provides reasonable domains to make your job easier)

- Dataset types
- Geolocation
- Dataset Schema (Schema builder or JSON Schema)

Figure 11.14 shows the Amazon Forecast dataset import details: configuration:

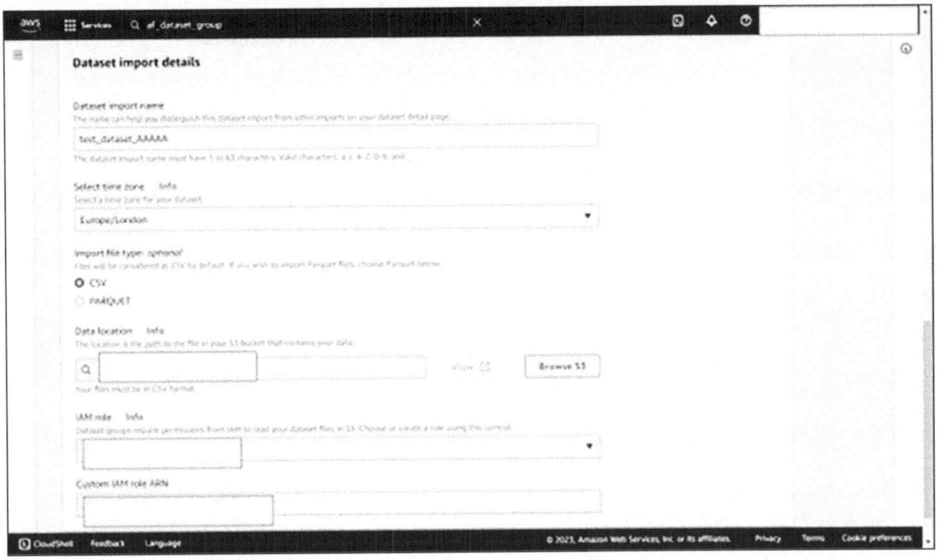

Figure 11.14: *Amazon Forecast dataset import details– configuration*

Figure 11.15 shows the Amazon Forecast Dataset Schema configuration:

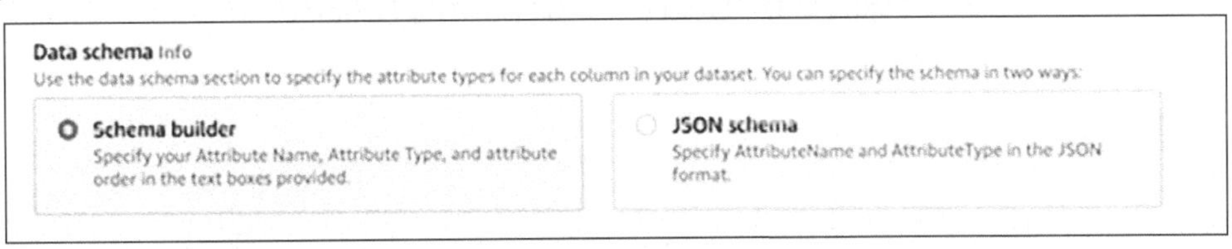

Figure 11.15: *Dataset Schema (Schema builder or JSON Schema)*

Figure 11.16 shows the Amazon Forecast Dataset Schema builder:

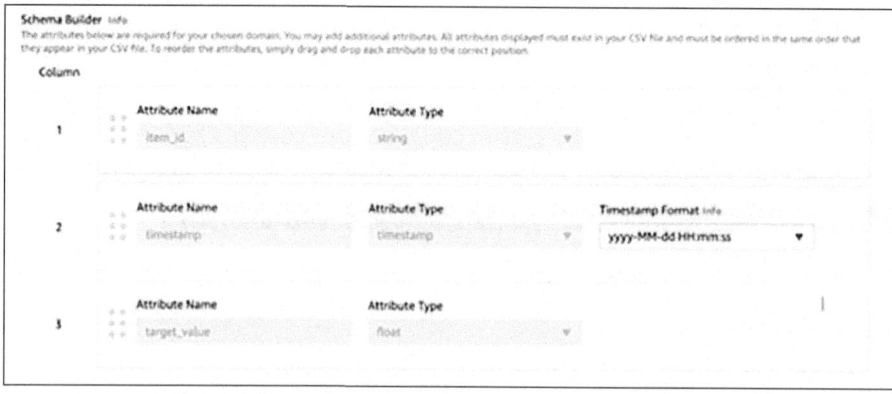

Figure 11.16: *Dataset Schema (Schema builder)*

Figure 11.17 shows the Amazon Forecast Dataset JSON Schema:

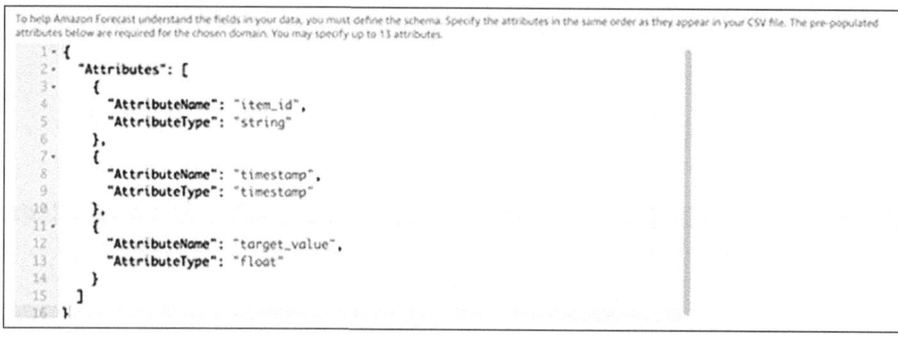

Figure 11.17: *Dataset Schema (JSON Schema)*

Training data

After importing time series data sets, the data will be trained in Amazon Forecast, training the data in the Amazon Forecast workflow process is called a "Predictor". This predictor is used to generate the forecasts. By default, Amazon Forecast can create predictors by applying a combination of the best algorithms to each time series dataset with the finest accuracy.

We need to configure the following values:

- Dataset group along with target time series dataset
- Forecast frequency with hourly, daily, weekly, and HH:mm:ss
- Forecast horizon is specifying the prediction length

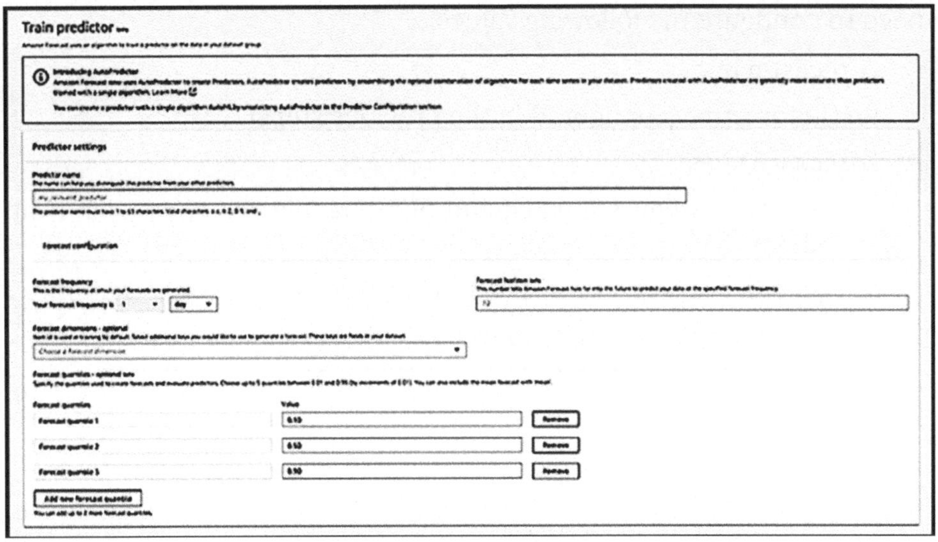

Figure 11.18: *Predictor configuration*

Auto Predictor and optional settings are shown in *Figure 11.19*:

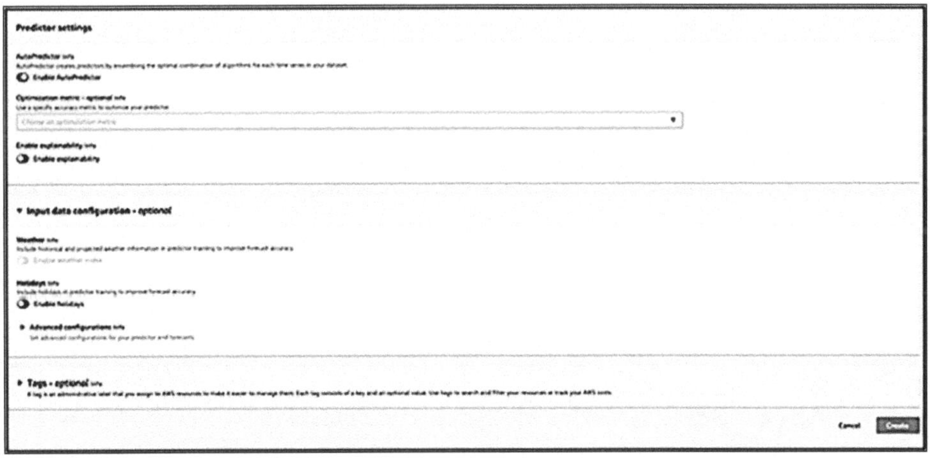

Figure 11.19: *Predictor configuration – Auto Predictor and optional settings*

Forecast creation and selection

Based on the number of target time series datasets in the data group, the equivalent of a number forecast of predictions will be created during this process under the forecast group.

We need to configure the following values:

- Forecast name
- Predictor name (configured in the previous steps)
- Forecast Types
    - We can configure a maximum of 5 quantile values ranging from .01 till .99
    - We can provide "mean" as a forecast type in the configuration
    - By default, the forecast values are .10, .50, and .90 quantiles

Figure 11.20: *Forecast configuration*

Figure 11.21 shows the Forecast output along with the range .10 to .95:

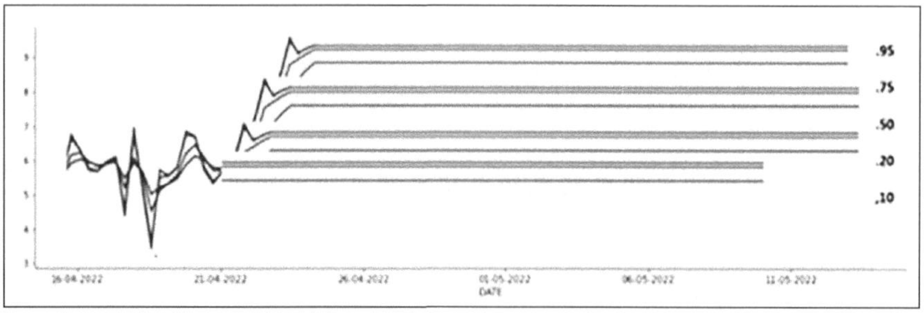

Figure 11.21: *Forecast output*

Retrieve the Forecast

Amazon Forecast helps us to view and analyze the generated forecasts in the preceding step with a simple configuration, as shown in *Figure* 11.21. By providing a target forecast, start date, end date, and for which column, clicking the button "Get Forecast" will get the forecast for the configured value as shown in *Figure* 11.22:

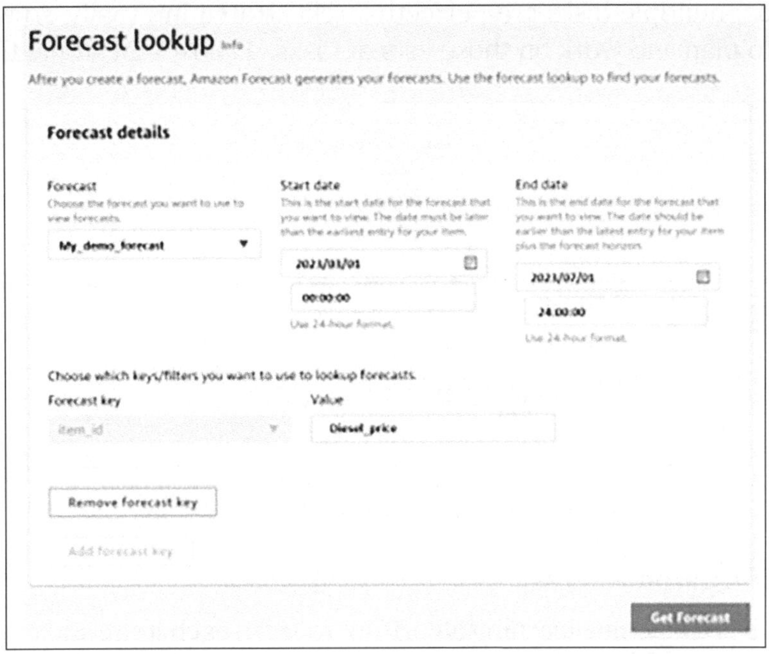

Figure 11.22: *Retrieve a Forecast – view and analyze the generated forecasts*

Figure 11.23 shows the retrieved forecast visualization:

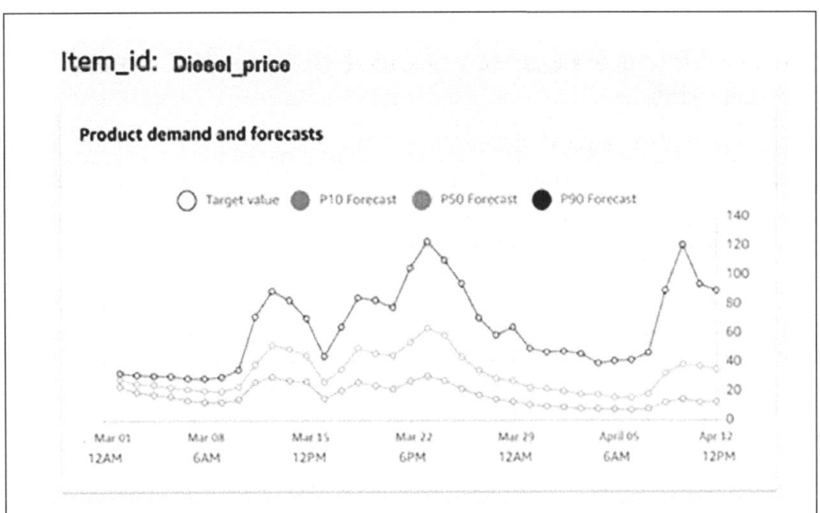

Figure 11.23: *Retrieve the Forecast - view and analyze the generated forecasts*

Orchestration of Amazon Forecast

We have discussed the end-to-end Amazon Forecast workflow. Concerning this service, multiple tasks are perfectly orchestrated internally, so we are not required to plan and work on those lists of tasks. *Figure* 11.24 shows the various stages:

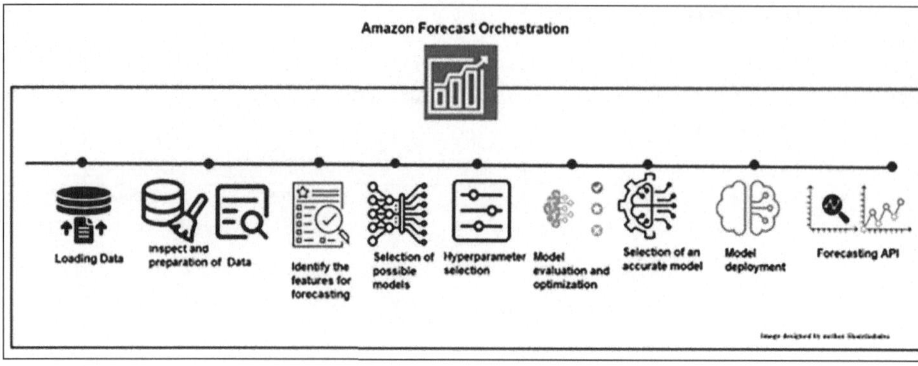

Figure 11.24: *Orchestration of Amazon Forecast*

Benefits of Amazon Forecast:

- It uses a machine learning algorithm to learn each item, and also uses the best ensemble of algorithms for each item considered for the analysis.
- This service automatically builds the optimal model for imported data.
- It supports explainability, and produces the report for the same, this will be an additional benefit to understand the affected ratings for forecasts.
- The workflow is accessible through either the AWS console or Amazon Forecast APIs
- It facilitates the **AutoPredictor** feature to create more accurate forecasts by applying the optimal techniques for each time series in each dataset.
- It manages infrastructure challenges are taken care of by Amazon, and this is a fully managed service.

Conclusion

In this chapter, we have discussed the detailed studies of Amazon Forecast workflow and its significant configuration details in the industry and how this is compact and handy to handle time series datasets.

We explored how Amazon Forecast workflow is configured for analytics services for various stages with neat sketches and detailed notes.

We discussed the data preparation process and best practices, along with the overview of how Amazon Forecast orchestrates internally with multiple stages.

We investigated the data group and Amazon Forecast's benefits precisely. We understand every detail about the dataset guidelines for Forecast.

We walked through very detailed steps on how to do data preparation, import data, train data, forecast creation, selection process, and retrieve the forecast.

Points to remember

In this chapter, it is important to keep a few things in mind that will be handy throughout this book:

- Amazon Forecast is a fully managed service, so managing infrastructure challenges are taken care of by Amazon itself.
- Amazon Forecast workflow is easily configurable and will take care of most of the tasks internally.
- Data preparation process and best practices to follow to predict accurate forecasting
- Each stage of the workflow is very important and easily achievable
    - Data preparation
    - Import data
    - Train data
    - Forecast creation and selection process
    - Retrieve the forecast
- Benefits of Amazon Forecast
    - Fully managed service
    - Easy access through
        - AWS console
        - Amazon Forecast APIs
    - It facilitates the **AutoPredictor** feature prediction

Index

B

C

D

G

H

I

J

K

L

M

N

Q

R

S

V

W

Z